W9-AFD-420

CONTENTS

AMERICAN COLLEGE TESTING PROGRAM
Third Edition

George Ehrenhaft
Former English Department Chairman
Mamaroneck High School
Mamaroneck, New York

Allan Mundsack
Professor of Mathematics
Los Angeles Pierce College
Los Angeles, California

Robert L. Lehrman
Former Science Department Supervisor
Roslyn High School
Roslyn, New York

Fred Obrecht
Professor of English
Los Angeles Pierce College
Los Angeles, California

Barron's Educational Series, Inc.

All inquiries should be addressed to:
Barron's Educational Series, Inc.
250 Wireless Boulevard
Hauppauge, New York 11788
http://www.barronseduc.com

Library of Congress Catalog No. 98-6242

International Standard Book No. 0-7641-0452-7

Library of Congress Cataloging-in-Publication Data

Barron's pass key to the ACT, American College Testing Program / by
George Ehrenhaft . . . [et al.]. — 3rd ed.
    p.   cm.
    ISBN 0-7641-0452-7
    1. ACT Assessment—Study guides. I. Ehrenhaft, George.
II. Barron's Educational Series, Inc.
LB2353.48.B38   1998
378.1'66'2—dc21   98-6242
                                              CIP

PRINTED IN THE UNITED STATES OF AMERICA
9 8 7 6 5 4 3

PREFACE

If you are planning to go to college, you may very well have to take the battery of tests making up the American College Testing program. This book was designed to help you understand the ACT battery and prepare for it.

Specifically, this book contains:
— a complete introduction to the ACT program
— a description of the different types of questions you will find on the ACT
— review and practice of the subject matter in each of the four test areas (English, mathematics, reading, and science reasoning)
— basic tips on how to cope with the different types of questions
— two complete simulated test batteries modeled exactly on the actual ACT (with answers carefully explained)

Because of the convenient size of this book, you can easily carry it with you and use it for impromptu study sessions—while waiting for an appointment, riding on a bus or train, or during study hall.

If, after studying the review sections and taking the two model tests, you believe that you are prepared to take the actual exam, you should approach the examination day with confidence. If you find you need more practice, you should work with the widely used *Barron's How to Prepare for the American College Testing Program (ACT)*, which has been helping students like yourself prepare for the ACT for nearly twenty years. It contains many practice exercises and additional model tests, with correct answers carefully explained.

ACKNOWLEDGMENTS

Pages 130–132, Passage: Theodore Gracyk, *Rhythm and Noise: An Aesthetics of Rock*, Duke University Press, Durham, NC, 1996, pp. 8–10.

Pages 137–139, Passage: "Stuttering: Hope Through Research," U.S. Department of Health and Human Services, National Institute of Health Publications 81-2250, GPO, Washington, D.C., May 1981.

Pages 145–148, Passage: "The Possibility of Intelligent Life in the Universe," U.S. House of Representatives, Report for the Committee on Science and Technology, GPO, Washington, DC, 1974.

Pages 156–157, Passage 1: Gerald Johnson, "Freedom of Inquiry is for Hopeful People," *This American People*, © 1951, renewed 1979 HarperCollins Publishers, Inc.

Pages 160–162, Passage 2: "Useful Information on Alzheimer's Disease," U.S. Department of Health and Human Services, National Institutes of Health, Rockville, Maryland.

Pages 164–167, Passage: Washington Irving, "Buckthorne," *Tales of a Traveller*, Library of America, 1991, pp. 500–502.

Pages 169–171, Passage 4: Wesley Barnes, *The Philosophy and Literature of Existentialism*, Barron's Educational Series, Inc., New York, 1968.

Pages 285–287, Passage: Emile Zola, *Germinal*, trans. by Stanley and Eleanor Hochman, New American Library, 1970, pp. 114–116.

Pages 290–291, Passage 2: Gabriele Sterner, *Art Nouveau: An Art of Transition from Individual to Mass Society*, Barron's Educational Series, 1982, pp. 87–90.

Pages 294–295, Passage 3: Rachel Carson, "The Sunless Sea," *The Sea Around Us*, Oxford University Press, 1989.

Pages 297–299, Passage 4: "Constitutional Rights of Children," Subcommittee on the Constitution of the Committee on the Judiciary of the United States Senate, Government Printing Office, Washington, D.C., 1978.

Pages 377–379, Passage 1: "Characteristics of the Abusive Situation," *Guide to Legal Relief*, Governor's Commission on Domestic Violence, New York, October, 1984.

Pages 381–383, Passage 2: "How Children Grow," General Clinical Research Centers Branch, Division of Research Resources, National Institute of Health, Bethesda, Maryland, June 1972.

Pages 385–388, Passage 3: From *The Awakening* by Kate Chopin. Copyright © 1964 by Capricorn Books Edition, New York.

Pages 390–392, Passage: Mario Pei, "Wanted: A World Language," Public Affairs Committee, New York, 1969.

TEST-TAKER'S CHECKLIST FOR THE ACT

Basic Strategies

Budget your time. Work swiftly: don't linger over difficult questions.

When you must, guess. There is no penalty for guessing, so answer every question.

Read each question carefully. Answer the question asked, not the one you may have expected.

Save the hardest questions for last.

Mark answers cleanly, accurately. Check the numbering of your answer sheet often. Erase cleanly; leave no stray marks.

Change answers if you have a reason for doing so. However, it's usually best not to change based on hunch or whim.

ACT National Test Dates

REGISTRATION CLOSING DATES	LATE REGISTRATION (PLUS $20 FEE)	TESTING DATES
September 21, 1998	October 2, 1998	**October 24, 1998**
November 9, 1998	November 20, 1998	**December 12, 1998**
January 4, 1999	January 15, 1999	**February 6, 1999**
March 8, 1999	March 19, 1999	**April 10, 1999**
May 10, 1999	May 21, 1999	**June 12, 1999**

(Registration dates may vary by a day or two; check with ACT at 319-337-1506 if there is a question.)

1

PREPARING FOR THE ACT

THE ACT ASSESSMENT

The ACT Assessment is a multiple-choice examination required for admission to many colleges. It takes 2 hours and 55 minutes to complete, and it contains four parts:

TEST	NUMBER OF QUESTIONS	LENGTH
English	75	45 minutes
Mathematics	60	60 minutes
Reading	40	35 minutes
Science Reasoning	40	35 minutes

Primary Focus of the ACT

Although the ACT is based on subjects studied in high school, the test emphasizes thinking skills. Rather than asking you to recall facts or to remember the content of courses, most of the questions require you to solve problems, draw conclusions, make inferences, and think analytically. Colleges like to know that prospective students have the depth of mind for figuring out answers rather than merely memorizing information.

The Four Parts of the ACT

1. The English Test assesses mastery of the understanding and skills needed to write well. In particular, it tests:

Usage and Mechanics: punctuation, basic grammar and usage, sentence structure	40 questions
Rhetorical Skills: writing strategy, organization, style	35 questions

Satisfactory performance on the English Test tells a college that you know the conventions of standard grammatical English and that you can punctuate and write complete, carefully structured sentences. The test further assesses your understanding of rhetoric, that is, whether you can tell when a piece of writing is unified, well organized, and consistent in style.

On the English Test you are given five prose passages, each about 325 words. Portions of the passage are underlined and numbered. Most of the questions ask you to decide whether the underlined sections are correct, and, if not, which of four alternative choices is the most appropriate substitute. An item may contain an error in punctuation, sentence structure, or some other aspect of grammar and usage. The remaining questions on the English Test, which ask you to judge the quality of expression, unity, clarity, or overall effectiveness of the writing, refer to passages in their entirety or to selected portions of the text.

2. The Mathematics Test measures knowledge and understanding of mathematics, in particular.

Pre-Algebra and Elementary Algebra	24 questions
Intermediate Algebra and Coordinate Geometry	18 questions
Plane Geometry	14 questions
Trigonometry	4 questions

Each of the 60 items presents a mathematical problem that you must solve by using algebra, geometry, or trigonometry. The problems are presented in the order of their difficulty.

For each problem, you must pick one of the five alternative solutions, one of which may be "None of the above." About half the items on the test are application items that require you to perform a sequence of operations. Another eight items require you to analyze the sequence of operations and conditions of the problem. The remaining problems test your basic mathematical proficiency.

3. The Reading Test measures your ability to understand materials similar to those read in college courses. The test consists of four passages, each about 750 words, drawn from four different areas of knowledge:

Prose Fiction: novels, short stories	10 questions
Humanities: art, music, dance, architecture, theater, philosophy	10 questions
Social Sciences: sociology, psychology, economics, political science, government, anthropology, history	10 questions
Natural Sciences: biology, chemistry, ecology, physical sciences	10 questions

Passages are given in the order of reading difficulty; the first is easiest, the last hardest. On a given ACT any of the four types of passages may be placed first, second, third, or fourth. The order is not announced ahead of time. Passages are taken from books, articles, periodicals, and other publications. Since each passage contains whatever information you need for answering the questions, no additional background or knowledge is required.

The 10 multiple-choice questions about each passage are arranged by level of difficulty, with the easiest first and the hardest last. Each question is followed by four choices. To answer the majority of the questions (26 out of 40) you need to draw inferences from the passage, perceive implications, distinguish the author's intent, and separate fact from opinion — show, in short, that you have more than a superficial grasp of the content of the passage. The remaining 14 questions ask about material explicitly stated in the passage.

4. The Science Reasoning Test assesses your ability to think like a scientist. On the test you must answer questions about seven sets of scientific information presented in three formats:

Data Representation: graphs, tables, other schematics	15 questions
Research Summaries: several related experiments	18 questions
Conflicting Viewpoints: alternative interpretations of scientific matters	7 questions

The sets of information come from biology, chemistry, physics, and the physical sciences, which include earth science, astronomy, and meteorology. Three of the seven sets of data are presented as graphs, charts, tables, or scientific drawings. Another three are summaries of research, and the seventh is a discussion of a controversial scientific issue.

The key word in this test is *reasoning*. Half the questions ask you to determine the accuracy and validity of conclusions and hypotheses based on the information presented. Another thirteen questions require you to generalize from given data by drawing conclusions or making predictions. The remaining seven questions check your understanding of the information itself. Simple arithmetic or algebra may be necessary to answer some of the questions.

The ACT reports no subscores on the Scientific Reasoning Test.

BEFORE TAKING THE ACT

Choosing a Test Date

Most college-bound students take the ACT during the spring of the junior year or at the beginning of the senior year. Which time you choose works neither for nor against you in the eyes of college admissions officials.

IF YOU TAKE THE ACT AS A:

JUNIOR	SENIOR
1. You will get a clearer picture of your prospects for admission to the colleges you may be considering. As a result, you can make more realistic college plans.	**1.** You are likely to earn higher scores, because you will have had more courses and more experience.
2. You will have more opportunities to retake the ACT. Hoping to improve scores, students often use the time between exams to prepare themselves more thoroughly.	**2.** You will have the opportunity to retake the ACT but with less preparation time between examination dates.
3. You can apply to a college for an early decision. Deadlines for most early decision applications fall between October 15 and November 15.	**3.** You will easily meet regular college application deadlines, which usually fall between January 1 and March 15 for September admissions.

Ultimately, the date you take the ACT may depend on your college application deadlines. Although most colleges leave the decision to the applicant, some require that you take the ACT at a particular time.

Registering for the ACT

The ACT is given several times a year. The exact dates, times, and testing sites are listed in a free booklet called *Registering for the ACT Assessment,* which is probably available in the guidance office of your school. Or you can contact:

ACT Registration Department
P.O. Box 414
Iowa City, Iowa 52243
Telephone: 319/337-1270

The booklet comes with a registration form and an explanation of the steps you must take to sign up. Pay particular attention to the registration deadlines. The regular registration deadline is approximately one month before the examination date. After that deadline, you may apply for late registration until about two weeks before the examination.

Ask also for *Preparing for the ACT,* a useful ACT publication containing general test-taking advice, a practice examination, and statistics to help you interpret your score.

TEST TAKING: A GUIDE TO SUCCESS

All the studying in the world won't mean a thing on test day unless you know how to take the test. Knowing the basics of test taking offers you the chance to succeed. Much of what you need to know is common sense. Anyone who has passed through high school knows, for example, that you should answer the question being asked, not a similar question or the one you think ought to be asked. Another common-sense tactic is to check regularly that the numbers on the answer sheet correspond with the numbers of the questions. If you put the answer to #9 in the space for #10, every subsequent answer will be in the wrong place.

As the ACT approaches, students sometimes feel apprehensive. Yes, it's normal to feel a bit uneasy about an approaching exam. In fact, some degree of tension can help your performance. With your adrenaline pumping, you can push harder toward the peak of your ability and perhaps turn in the performance of your life. If you're basically a fretter, you obviously have to prepare harder to take the ACT than someone who is blessed with a positive attitude. In the long run, however, some anxiety may work in your favor.

Fortunately, you can do many things to reach the most advantageous frame of mind for taking the ACT, the first of which is being well prepared.

Difficulty of Questions

Easy and hard questions are scattered throughout the English Test. On the Mathematics Test, however, problems are given in order of increasing difficulty from 1 to 60. Passages on the Reading Test are presented in order of difficulty, and the ten questions about each passage are also arranged from easiest to hardest. Similarly, the Science Reasoning Test presents sets of data in order of increasing difficulty, and questions about each set are arranged from the easiest to the hardest.

Answer every question on every test, even if you have to guess. You don't lose credit for a wrong answer, and you may make a lucky guess.

Before you resort to guessing, though, try to eliminate any outrageous choices. By discarding one choice that you know is way off the mark, the chances of hitting the jackpot are one in three. By eliminating two wrong answers, they jump to fifty-fifty, pretty decent odds in any circumstances.

Using Time Effectively

Each test on the ACT lasts a prescribed length of time. Once a test is over, you may not return to it. Nor are you permitted to work on a test that has not yet officially begun. After the first two tests, you'll have a 10- to 15-minute break.

To do your best on the ACT, it's useful to know approximately how much time you have to work on each problem or question. With practice, you will soon begin to sense whether you are working at a rate that will allow you to finish each test within its time limit. The following analysis indicates the time allowed for each test.

TEST	CONTENT	AVERAGE LENGTH OF TIME PER QUESTION	COMMENTS
English 75 questions	5 passages, 15 questions each.	30 seconds.	Easy questions should take only a few seconds.
Mathematics 60 questions	Questions increase in difficulty from beginning to end.	1 minute.	Spend as little time as possible on the early questions, to allow more time for the harder ones.
Reading 40 questions	4 passages, 10 questions each.	5 minutes per passage, 4 minutes for 10 questions or 25 seconds per question.	Some passages may take more or less time to completely master.
Science Reasoning 40 questions	7 sets of data with 5 to 7 questions per set; within each set, questions increase in difficulty.	5 minutes per set of data.	Try to spend less than 5 minutes on the early, easier questions, allowing more time for the harder ones.

The periods of time allowed for each test are sufficient for almost every student to finish. To answer all the questions, however, you must work deliberately. Avoid spending too much time on any one question. If you are puzzled by a question, leave it and move on to the next one. Later, if time permits, come back and try again. Work swiftly, but not at the expense of accuracy.

If you finish a test before the time is up, check your answers, especially those that you're unsure about. Make sure that you've blackened only one oval for each question. If time is about to be called and you haven't finished the test, fill in answers at random on your answer sheet. A lucky guess or two will raise your score.

ON ACT DAY

Getting Set

Let common sense be your guide on test day. After a good night's sleep, get up early, eat a good breakfast, and arrive at the test site by 8:15 A.M., 15 minutes before the test begins. Arrive 30 minutes ahead of time if you are not familiar with the location.

Take with you:
- Your ACT ticket of admission.
- Three or more sharpened #2 pencils with erasers.
- Identification.
- A dependable watch.
- A calculator with fresh batteries. (Take one you know how to use.)
- Candy or gum, if you feel the need. (Eating snacks or anything more substantial is not permitted during the examination.)

Leave at home:
- Books, notebooks, dictionaries, scrap paper.
- Radios, tape and CD players, beepers, cell phones.
- Noisy jewelry, including wristwatches that beep.

Throughout the exam, listen attentively to the proctors' announcements. Proctors will distribute test materials, instruct you in test procedures, show you how to fill out the answer sheet, and answer administrative questions. They will also keep order in the exam room, and tell you when to start and stop work. The proctors must also prevent cheating. *During the test, do nothing that might be construed as cheating.* If proctors suspect that you are giving or receiving help, they are obliged to dismiss you from the room and advise the ACT authorities not to score your answer sheet. In addition, you can be disqualified for continuing to work on a test on which time has been called, or for working on a test not yet officially begun.

If you need assistance during the exam, raise your hand to summon a proctor. Don't talk to anyone else, and don't leave your seat without a proctor's permission.

2

PREPARING FOR THE ENGLISH TEST

DESCRIPTION OF THE TEST

The English Test consists of 75 multiple-choice questions based on five prose passages with portions of their text underlined and numbered. Next to each numbered part are four responses corresponding to the test item. If the question is designed to measure your understanding of *usage and mechanics,* you must decide whether to leave the underlined portion as is or to substitute one of the alternatives. If the question is designed to measure your understanding of *rhetorical skills,* it may refer to a portion of the text, or it may ask about the passage as a whole. Questions measuring rhetorical skills may ask you to select how a general statement might be better supported or whether a different arrangement of the passage's parts might be appropriate. You have 45 minutes to complete the 75 items.

Here is a quick view of the test itself. Read this passage and answer the questions. Do not refer to the correct answers (given below each set of choices) until you have tried to answer the questions yourself.

All creatures in the animal kingdom have the instincts of curiosity and fear. Man alone was endowed with imagination, which
<u>1</u>

was bound to complicate matters for him. Whereas a fox, let us say, was able to shrug off the mysteries of the heavens and such whims of nature as lightning and earthquakes, man had demanded an explanation.
<u>2</u>

1. **A.** NO CHANGE
   B. imagination; which
   C. imagination, a fact which
   D. imagination, on which
   (CORRECT ANSWER: **C**)
2. **F.** NO CHANGE
   G. had been demanding
   H. demanded
   J. demands

And so began the myths, the ancient creeds, witchcraft, astrology, they

$\frac{\text{they}}{3}$

told fantastic tales of wanderings into

$\frac{\text{told fantastic tales}}{3}$

the unknown reaches of space and time, the distortions of the mental and physical capabilities of man himself. Evidently, these "explanations" were not enough: Man developed a thirst for something *beyond* the ever-growing knowledge brought to him by empirical scientific research. The French call this *le culte de merveilleux*. We call it science fiction. ☐4

(CORRECT ANSWER: **H**)
3. **A.** NO CHANGE
   B. fantastic tales
   C. They were told fantastic tales
   D. fireside stories

(CORRECT ANSWER: **B**)
4. If the writer wanted to include more information about the early history of science fiction, which of the following would be most effective for the passage as a whole?
   F. A listing of current science fiction writers
   G. A discussion of recent science fiction movies
   H. A discussion of the "fantastic tales" that made up the origins of science fiction
   J. A discussion of witchcraft.
(CORRECT ANSWER: **H**)

The *Usage/Mechanics* questions test your understanding of punctuation, grammar, and sentence structure.

1. *Punctuation* ✓	13%	These questions concern the use of punctuation marks (apostrophes, colons, commas, dashes, exclamation points, hyphens, parentheses, question marks, quotation marks, and semicolons) and, in particular, their function in clarifying the *meaning of the prose selection*.

2. *Basic Grammar and Usage* ✓	16%	Items in this category test your knowledge and understanding of verbs, adverbs, and adjectives; subject-verb agreement, and agreement of pronoun and antecedent; and the proper use of connectives.
3. *Sentence Structure* ✓	24%	These items deal with the makeup of the sentence, including the relationship of clauses, the correct use and placement of modifiers, parallelism, and consistency in point-of-view and tense.

The *Rhetorical Skills* questions are almost equally distributed among three categories: strategy, organization, and style.

1. *Strategy* ✓	16%	Questions on strategy involve examination of some of the options the author has decided upon. Chief among these is the author's choice of supporting material. Is it effective, appropriate, and sufficient in amount and quality? Another author option is the choice of writing vehicle—for example, the descriptive essay, the persuasive essay, the biography, or the comparison-contrast model. You will be asked to make some judgments concerning the writer's handling of these options.
2. *Organization* ✓	15%	Questions on organization will most often involve rearrangement of sentences in a paragraph or paragraphs within a passage. You may also be asked to spot extraneous material that has little or nothing to do with the main idea, and to indicate places

		where additional material might strengthen the paragraph.
3. *Style* ✓	16%	In these questions, you may be asked to choose an adjective that best describes the style of the prose passage, to select the best phrase of several that have the same words but in a different order, or to choose alternative words. You will be asked to select text that matches the style and tone of the passage, and to choose words or phrases that most concisely express an idea.

LONG-RANGE STRATEGY

As a student planning to take the ACT test, you are already engaged in what is probably the most important of the long-term strategies, that is, learning as much as you can about the test and about the questions you are expected to answer.

More suggestions:

- If you have enough time before you take the actual test, improve your prose "ear" by reading good, informative prose under relaxed conditions, perhaps even on a daily, limited basis. The Reading Review chapter contains a list of suggested prose reading materials.
- Be sure you understand the format of the English Test, the time limitations, the number and types of questions, and the form of the answer sheet.
- Discuss the test frankly with your English teacher. Ask about your strengths and weaknesses in the skills to be tested. Does your teacher see anything in your habits or work that suggests problems you may have with the test? If so, how can you deal with those problems?

- Search out all avenues of help. Perhaps your school counselor has practice tests or other materials on test taking. Also, if there are ACT study groups in your school or community, join one, by all means. The additional practice will give you confidence, and you will find that sharing problems with other prospective test-takers is another good way to build confidence.
- Talk with your friends and family about the test and any fears you might have. Keep in mind that the ACT is only one of several means by which you will be evaluated and your admission to a college or university determined. Do not magnify its importance to the degree that you cannot prepare or perform effectively.

Anxiety affects your perception and use of language. Before you take the ACT test, you should come to terms in your own mind that you will do your best and that nobody, including yourself, has a right to ask more of you than that.

TIPS

Concentrate. On the morning of the test, reduce as many of your distractions, obligations, and plans as possible. Have no social events planned—either before or after the test—so that your full attention is on your answers. Leave adequate time to arrive at the test center. It is better to be a little early.

Work carefully. Before you arrive, be familiar with the test directions. When the test begins, listen carefully to any directions read to you by a proctor or played on a tape. In marking the answer sheet, be sure to put each answer in the right space. If you skip a question because it is taking too much time, be careful to skip the corresponding space on the answer sheet. Focus only on the test; block out any distractions.

Pace yourself. You have 45 minutes to answer 75 questions, or roughly nine minutes for each passage and its questions.

Read with a purpose. Before you begin to answer the questions, quickly skim the passage. Then, answer each question in light of its context.

Carefully examine the underlined parts. Be sure that the answer you choose does not introduce another error while correcting the first!

Decide on the best answer. As you approach each question, it is probably best to think how the underlined portion would be expressed in standard written English.

When in doubt, try to **eliminate choices** by substituting each of the answers for the underlined portion of the text.

Have a **positive mental attitude!**

USAGE/MECHANICS

Punctuation

Comma	Among its many functions, the comma is used to set off independent clauses, items in a series, coordinate adjectives, parenthetical expressions, and nonrestrictive phrases or clauses.

Semicolon	The semicolon is generally used to separate coordinate elements in a sentence, that is, items of the same grammatical nature. Most often, it is used between related ideas that require punctuation weaker than a period, but stronger than a comma. In addition, the semicolon divides three or more items in a series when the items themselves contain commas.
Colon	The colon is a signal that something is to follow: a rephrased statement, a list or series, or a formal quotation. Use a colon in a sentence if you can logically insert *namely* after it.
Hyphen	The hyphen has two main uses: to divide syllables at the end of a line and to link words in certain combinations. It is also used in compound numbers from twenty-one to ninety-nine.
Apostrophe	In addition to indicating possession, the apostrophe is used to take the place of omitted numbers (class of '87) and omitted letters or words in contractions (wasn't [was not], o'clock [of the clock]), and to indicate plurals (A's, I.D.'s).
Dash	The main function of the dash, like parenthesis, is to enclose information within a sentence. Dashes are generally more forceful and therefore should be used sparingly, since they highlight the ideas and items they enclose.
Question Mark	A question mark indicates the end of a direct question. A question mark in parentheses signals doubt or uncertainty about a fact such as a date or a number.

Exclamation Point	An exclamation point is an indicator of strong *emotional* feelings, such as anger, joy, shock, surprise, or fear. It may also be used to express irony or emphasis. Like the dash, it should be used sparingly.
Quotation Marks	One of the main uses of quotation marks is to signal the exact words of a writer or speaker. Quotation marks are also used to enclose the titles of short literary or musical works (articles, short stories or poems, songs), as well as words used in a special way.
Parentheses	Parentheses, like dashes, are used to set off words of explanation and other secondary supporting details—figures, data, examples—that are not really part of the main sentence or paragraph. Parentheses are less emphatic than dashes and should be reserved for ideas that have no essential connection with the rest of the sentence.

FOCUS ON THE ACT

The following sample questions represent ways in which the above skills might be tested on your ACT Assessment.

What lies behind the creative genius of our greatest <u>authors</u> has been the subject of
      1

speculation over the past two centuries. There is little doubt that many of the <u>worlds</u> creative
      2

geniuses experienced miserable <u>lives</u> most often,
      3

1. **A.** NO CHANGE
   B. authors'
   C. authors,
   D. author's
2. **F.** NO CHANGE
   G. world's
   H. worlds'
   J. world's,
3. **A.** NO CHANGE
   B. lives:
   C. lives;
   D. lives,

they suffered a personal and extreme brand of deprivation that profoundly affected the quality of their daily lives. Almost always, the depth of their
___
4

misery is related to the greatness of their genius. One who reads both Emily Bronte's Wuthering
___
5

Heights and the best known critical discussions
___   ___
5   **6**

about her work cannot escape the conclusion,
___
7

that Emily was the product of a punitive and abusive environment, it is difficult to avoid the
___
8

further conclusion that the strength and authenticity of her novel the vulnerabilities and
___
9

palpable yearnings of its main characters—are related however, faintly to her personal affliction.
___
10

4. **F.** NO CHANGE
   G. always;
   H. always—
   J. always:
5. **A.** NO CHANGE
   B. "Wuthering Heights"
   C. Wuthering Heights
   D. Wuthering-Heights
6. **F.** NO CHANGE
   G. best, known
   H. best-known
   J. "best known"
7. **A.** NO CHANGE
   B. conclusion;
   C. conclusion—
   D. conclusion
8. **F.** NO CHANGE
   G. environment;
   H. environment—
   J. environment?
9. **A.** NO CHANGE
   B. novel;
   C. novel—
   D. novel:
10. **F.** NO CHANGE
    G. related; however faintly,
    H. related, however faintly,
    J. related (however faintly)

Answers and Explanations

1. A The noun *authors* is a simple object in this sentence and requires no punctuation.
2. G The plural *geniuses* are a possession of the world and require that it signal that possession with an apostrophe.
3. B The words occurring after *lives* form an independent clause and so must be set off with a stronger mark of punctuation. The colon is the best choice in this context because the

following statement gives specific focus to the general statement made in the sentence's introductory clause.

4. F   Set off introductory phrases with a comma.

5. A   Underline (set in italics) novels and other larger works of literature.

6. H   Hyphenate compound adjectives preceding the noun they modify.

7. D   The adjective clause following the noun *conclusion* is a restrictive modifier and so does not take separating punctuation.

8. G   The clause that follows necessitates a strong mark of punctuation. Since it is closely related in meaning to the previous independent clause, the most appropriate choice is the semicolon.

9. C   The dash at the end of this phrase requires a matching dash at the beginning. Dashes are appropriately used to give special emphasis to parenthetical phrases such as this one.

10. H   The phrase *however faintly* is parenthetical and must be set off by commas.

Basic Grammar and Usage

Subject-Verb Agreement	Nouns, verbs, and pronouns often have special forms or endings that indicate *number*—that is, whether the word is singular or plural. A verb must agree in number with the noun or pronoun that is its subject.
Principal Parts of Verbs	All verbs have four principal parts: *present* (NOW), *past* (YESTERDAY), *present participle* (the -ING form of the verb), and *past participle* (the form of the verb with HAVE). To find the principal parts of a verb, just remember the clues NOW, YESTERDAY, -ING, and HAVE.

The following list of principal parts features verbs that sometimes cause trouble in speaking and writing.

PRESENT	PAST	PAST PARTICIPLE
become	became	become
begin	began	begun
bid (offer)	bid	bid
bid (command)	bade	bidden
bite	bit	bit, bitten
blow	blew	blown
break	broke	broken
bring	brought	brought
burst	burst	burst
catch	caught	caught
choose	chose	chosen
come	came	come
dive	dived, dove	dived
do	did	done
drag	dragged	dragged
draw	drew	drawn
drink	drank	drunk
drive	drove	driven
eat	ate	eaten
fall	fell	fallen
fly	flew	flown
forget	forgot	forgot, forgotten
freeze	froze	frozen
get	got	got, gotten
give	gave	given
go	went	gone
grow	grew	grown
hang (suspend)	hung	hung
hang (execute)	hanged	hanged
know	knew	known
lay	laid	laid
lead	led	led
lend	lent	lent
lie (recline)	lay	lain
lie (speak falsely)	lied	lied

PRESENT	PAST	PAST PARTICIPLE
lose	lost	lost
pay	paid	paid
prove	proved	proved, proven
raise	raised	raised
ride	rode	ridden
ring	rang, rung	rung
rise	rose	risen
run	ran	run
see	saw	seen
shake	shook	shaken
shrink	shrank	shrunk
sing	sang, sung	sung
sink	sank, sunk	sunk
speak	spoke	spoken
spring	sprang	sprung
steal	stole	stolen
swim	swam	swum
swing	swung	swung
take	took	taken
tear	tore	torn
throw	threw	thrown
wear	wore	worn
weave	wove	woven
wring	wrung	wrung
write	wrote	written

Verb Forms and Verbals	A high percentage of verb-related errors occurs because the reader confuses *verb forms*—that is, the different forms that an action word can assume—with entirely different structures known as *verbals*—words formed from verbs but not used as verbs in a sentence. Known as *participles, gerunds,* and *infinitives,* verbals form important phrases within the sentence.

INFINITIVES	An infinitive is ordinarily preceded by *to* and is used as a noun, an adjective, or an adverb.
GERUNDS	A gerund always ends in *-ing* and functions as a noun.
PARTICIPLE	A participle acts as an adjective in the sentence.
Pronouns	Pronouns are most often employed as substitutes for nouns, but some can also be used as adjectives or conjunctions. To master pronouns and be able to spot errors in their use, you need to understand pronoun *case* (nominative, possessive, objective), pronoun *number* (singular or plural), and pronoun *class* (personal, demonstrative, interrogative, relative, indefinite).
PERSONAL PRONOUNS	A personal pronoun indicates by its form the person or thing it takes the place of: the person speaking (first person), the person spoken to (second person), or the person or thing spoken about (third person).
DEMONSTRA-TIVE PRONOUNS	Demonstrative pronouns (*this, that, these, those*) take the place of things being pointed out.
INTERROGATIVE PRONOUNS	Interrogative pronouns (*who, whom, whose, which,* and *what*) are used in questions. *Who, which,* and *what* are used as subjects and are in the nominative case. *Whose* is in the possessive case, *Whom* is in the objective case, and, like all objects, it is the receiver of action in the sentence. The most common error involving interrogative pronouns is the tendency to use *who* instead of *whom*.

RELATIVE PRONOUNS	Relative pronouns (*who, whom, whose, which, what,* and *that*) refer to people and things. When a relative pronoun is the subject of a subordinate clause, the clause becomes an adjective modifying a noun in the sentence.
INDEFINITE PRONOUNS	Indefinite pronouns (*all, another, any, both, each, either, everyone, many, neither, one, several, some,* and similar words) represent an indefinite number of persons or things. Many of these words also function as adjectives ("*several men*").

FOCUS ON THE ACT

The following sample questions represent ways in which the above skills might be tested on your ACT Assessment.

Operators and manufacturers of nuclear reactor power facilities are making increased use of robots to improve operations and maintenance, lower operating costs, increasing plant availability
1
————

1. A. NO CHANGE
B. increases
C. increase
D. increased

and equipment reliability, enhanced worker
2
————

2. F. NO CHANGE
G. enhancing
H. enhances
J. enhance

safety, and reduce worker exposure to radiation. There is no doubt in the field that advanced telerobotic systems can have made more effective
3
——————

3. A. NO CHANGE
B. can make
C. can be made
D. can be making

use of human operators, expert systems, and intelligent machines; in fact, few of the world's
4
———

4. F. NO CHANGE
G. some
H. one
J. none

leading nuclear plant designers believe that a
facility without modern robotic and telerobotic
systems <u>will have become</u> obsolete in a very few
5
years. The design of future nuclear plants and

supporting facilities—particularly <u>these</u> involving
6
fuel recycling—should incorporate considerations
for use of robotic systems.

   A committee of scientists critical of the move
toward robotics <u>believe</u> that existing methods for
7
controlling and preprogramming the typical robot
<u>is</u> appropriate for only a limited number of jobs in
8

nuclear facilities, mainly because <u>it simply require</u>
9
too much supervision. In addition, existing robots
are limited in their ability to sense their

surroundings and <u>interpreting</u> sensor data, a
10
prerequisite for handling unexpected problems
during the routine executions of tasks.

5. A. NO CHANGE
  B. would have
     become
  C. becomes
  D. will become
6. F. NO CHANGE
  G. they
  H. those
  J. that

7. A. NO CHANGE
  B. believes
  C. believed
  D. have believed
8. F. NO CHANGE
  G. were
  H. are
  J. will be
9. A. NO CHANGE
  B. it simply
     required
  C. they simply
     require
  D. it simply
     requires
10. F. NO CHANGE
  G. interpret
  H. interpreted
  J. has interpreted

Answers and Explanations

1. C The verb *increase* needs to be an infinitive to be parallel with
the series of infinitive phrases that comprise the end of the
sentence.
2. J The verb *enhance* needs to be an infinitive to be parallel with
the series of infinitive phrases that comprise the end of the
sentence.
3. B The passage is written in the present tense, and employs the
present tense in generally true statements.
4. G *Some* is the more logical choice of indefinite pronoun here;

the use of *few* in the text renders the sentence meaning-less.

5. D The future tense is made necessary by the trailing phrase ''in a very few years.''

6. H Demonstrative pronouns take the place of things *being pointed out*. In this case, the word *those* is more appropriate for the antecedent *facilities* because those facilities will be built in the future.

7. B The subject of the verb is the singular noun *committee*.

8. H The subject of the verb is the plural noun *methods*.

9. C The subject of the verb is the singular personal pronoun *it*, the antecedent of which is the noun *robot*.

10. G *Interpret* is one of a pair of parallel infinitives (*to sense* and *to interpret*) modifying the noun *ability*.

SENTENCE STRUCTURE

In addition to the NO CHANGE response, the questions on the ACT English Test that deal with sentence structure will offer three alternatives, each one a restructuring of the underlined part. Errors in sentence structure include such items as sentence fragments, run-on sentences, misplaced modifiers, and lack of parallelism. These topics are reviewed in this section.

Sentence Fragments	A sentence fragment is a part of a sentence that has been punctuated as if it were a complete sentence. It does not express a complete thought but depends upon a nearby independent clause for its full meaning. It should be made a part of that complete sentence.
Run-on Sentences	Probably the most common error in writing occurs when two sentences are run together as one. There are two types of run-on sentences: the *fused* sentence, which has no punctuation mark between its two independent clauses, and the *comma splice*, which substitutes a comma where either a period or a semicolon is needed.

Connec- tives	Connectives that join elements of equal rank are called coordinating conjunctions (*and, but, or, nor, for, yet*). Connectives that introduce a less important element are called subordinating conjunctions (*after, although, since, when*). *Coordinating conjunctions* link words, phrases, and clauses that are of equal importance.
Modifiers	
ADJECTIVES AND ADVERBS	The purpose of adjectives and adverbs is to describe, limit, color—in other words, to *modify* other words. Adjectives modify nouns or pronouns, and generally precede the words they modify. Adverbs describe verbs, adjectives or other adverbs. Some words can be used as either adjectives (He has an *early appointment*) or adverbs (He *arrived early*).
ADJECTIVES	Problems that students face with adjectives frequently relate to the use of degrees of comparison. There are three degrees: the *positive*—the original form of the word (*straight*); the *comparative*—used to compare two persons or things (*straighter*); and the *superlative*—used to compare more than two persons or things (*straightest*). If not understood, the spelling and form changes involved can sometimes confuse the unwary student.
ADVERBS	Adverbs (either as words, phrases, or clauses) describe the words they modify by indicating *when, how, where, why, in what order*, or *how often*. Probably the most persistent and frustrating errors in the English language involve either *incorrect modification* or else *inexact modification* that is difficult to pin down.

	In most cases, if you can keep your eye on the *word or phrase being modified*, it is easier to avoid the following pitfalls.
MISPLACED MODIFIERS	To avoid confusion or ambiguity, place the modifying words, phrases, or clauses near the words they modify.
DANGLING CONSTRUC-TIONS	A dangling modifier literally hangs in the air; there is no logical word in the sentence for it to modify. Frequently it is placed close to the wrong noun or verb, causing the sentence to sound ridiculous: *Driving through the park, several chipmunks could be seen.*

FOCUS ON THE ACT

The following sample questions represent ways in which the above skills might be tested on your ACT Assessment.

The life of famed watchmaker Abraham-Louis Breguet was, from beginning to end (1747– __1__

1823). A steady progression toward fame and __1__

fortune. Breguet soon revealed a lively interest that developed into a veritable passion for things mechanical in his stepfather's shop. He studied __2__

with the famed jeweler Abbot Marie for twelve years, his vocation was henceforth decided. __3__

1. **A.** NO CHANGE
   B. (1747–1823), a
   C. (1747–1823) a
   D. (1747–1823); a
2. **F.** NO CHANGE
   G. (Place at the beginning of sentence).
   H. (Place after the verb *revealed*).
   J. (Delete altogether; the phrase is not related).
3. **A.** NO CHANGE
   B. years his vocation
   C. years, then his vocation
   D. years, and his vocation

Living in the Swiss cantons on the French border,
_____
                        4

watch-making had already been developed on a
large scale by refugee French families, because it
                                    _____
                                         5

was limited almost exclusively to inexpensive
products. Young Breguet, on the contrary,
         _____
                        6

demonstrating very early a decided disgust for
_____
                        6

shoddy workmanship, as well as a genius for
_____
                        6

precision work, had an attitude he never lost.
_____
                        6

4. **F.** NO CHANGE
   G. (Place this phrase after *border*).
   H. (Place this phrase after *families*).
   J. (Delete altogether; the phrase is not related).

5. **A.** NO CHANGE
   B. but
   C. even though
   D. however

6. **F.** NO CHANGE
   G. Young Breguet, on the contrary, demonstrating very early a decided disgust for shoddy workmanship, as well as a genius for precision work, an attitude he never lost.
   H. Young Breguet, on the contrary, demonstrated very early a decided disgust for shoddy workmanship, as well as a genius for precision work, an attitude he never lost.
   J. Young Breguet, on the contrary, demonstrated very early a decided disgust for shoddy workmanship, as well as a genius for precision work, and had an attitude he never lost.

In 1802, Breguet, receiving the gold medal at
_____
                        7

an exhibition of industrial products, sat at the
_____
                        7

table of the first consul. Throughout his reign,
_____
        7

7. **A.** NO CHANGE
   B. In 1802, Breguet, receiving the gold medal at an

exhibition of industrial products, sitting at the table of the first consul.

C. In 1802, Breguet received the gold medal at an exhibition of industrial products, and sat at the table of the first consul.

D. In 1802, Breguet sat at the table of the first consul, receiving the gold medal at an exhibition of industrial products.

Napoleon's interest in the works of the watch master, principally those of high precision, never slackened.

The face studded with brilliant diamonds and
<u>   8   </u>

rubies, Napoleon acquired Breguet's most
<u>   8   </u>

ambitious creation the day after it was completed.
<u>   8   8   </u>

8. F. NO CHANGE

G. The face studded with brilliant diamonds and rubies, Breguet's most ambitious creation, the day after it was completed, was acquired by Napoleon.

H. The face studded with brilliant diamonds and rubies the day after it was completed, Napoleon acquired Breguet's most ambitious creation.

J. Napoleon acquired Breguet's most ambitious creation, the face studded with brilliant diamonds and rubies, the day after it was completed.

The fall of the empire did not affect either
<u>   9   </u>

his fortunes adversely or his renown, which had
<u>   9   </u>

spread throughout Europe. The exhibition of 1819
<u>   9   </u>

9. A. NO CHANGE

B. The fall of the empire did not adversely affect either his fortunes or his renown, which had spread throughout Europe.

C. Adversely, the fall of the empire did not affect either his fortunes or his renown, which had spread throughout Europe.

D. The fall of the empire did not affect either his fortunes or his renown adversely, which had spread throughout Europe.

in which Breguet presented a collection of his
most important works was a triumphant
compendium of his life, <u>by then more than</u>
10
<u>seventy years old.</u>
10

> **10. F.** NO CHANGE
> **G.** (Place this phrase at the beginning of the sentence).
> **H.** (Place this phrase, bracketed with commas, after the word *Breguet*).
> **J.** (Delete this phrase, it is not relevant).

Answers and Explanations

1. B This sentence contains the parenthetical interruption "from beginning to end (1747–1823)," which must be set off by commas. Any stronger mark of punctuation after the parentheses results in two fragmented sentences.

2. G The only logical position in this sentence for the prepositional phrase *in his stepfather's shop* is at the beginning of the sentence where it will correctly modify the noun *Breguet*.

3. D A compound sentence is the most appropriate vehicle for these two ideas of equal importance. A comma is used before the coordinating conjunction that joins coordinate clauses.

4. H The only logical position in this sentence for the participial phrase *Living in the Swiss cantons* is next to the noun it logically modifies, *families*.

5. B Only a connective signaling contrast like *but* makes sense in this context, especially in the light of the next sentence.

6. H This choice allows the main clause to emphasize the major characteristic of the subject, and correctly subordinates the parenthetical phrase, "an attitude he never lost."

7. C The act of receiving the gold medal is logically as important as sitting with the first consul, and should not be subordinated in a participial phrase.

8. J The phrase *The face studded with brilliant diamonds and rubies* modifies the noun *creation* and so must be placed next to it.

9. B The adverb *adversely* logically modifies only the verb *affect* and should be placed near it.

10. H The phrase *by then more than seventy years old* appropriately modifies the noun *Breguet* and should be placed next to it, set off by commas since it is a parenthetical addition.

Consistency and Tense	
VERB IN SUBORDINATE CLAUSES	Because *tense* indicates the time of the action and *voice* indicates whether the subject is the agent of the action (*active:* Tom *saw*) or the recipient of the action (*passive:* Tom *was seen*), both of these verb forms are central to the consistency of a sentence or passage.
THE PRESENT INFINITIVE	Always use the present infinitive (to run, to see), after a perfect tense (a tense that uses some form of the helping verb **have or had**).
THE SUBJUNCTIVE MOOD	Verbs may be expressed in one of three moods: the *indicative*, used to declare a fact or ask a question; the *imperative*, used to express a command; and the *subjunctive*, generally used to indicate doubt or to express a wish or request or a condition contrary to fact. The first two moods are fairly clear-cut.
IS WHEN, IS WHERE, IS BECAUSE	**The use of *is when, is where, is because* is always incorrect.** The reason is simple: *when, where,* and *because* introduce adverbial clauses; and a noun subject followed by a form of the verb *to be* must be equated with a noun structure, not with an adverb clause.
Parallelism	Parallel ideas in a sentence should be expressed in the same grammatical form. If they are not, the sentence will be unbalanced.

Transition-al Words and Phrases	Words of transition are clues that help the reader to follow the writer's flow of ideas. Confusion can result, however, when an illogical or incorrect connective is used. The following list includes more commonly used transitional words and phrases, and the concept they suggest.
CONCEPT	
Addition	also, furthermore, moreover, similarly, too
Cause and Effect	accordingly, as a result, consequently, hence, so, therefore, thus
Concession	granted that, it is true that, no doubt, to be sure
Conclusion	in short, that is, to conclude, to sum up
Contrast	although, but, however, nevertheless, on the contrary, on the other hand
Example	for example, for instance

FOCUS ON THE ACT

The following sample questions represent ways in which the above skills might be tested on your ACT Assessment.

Crime and Punishment by Fyodor Dostoevsky is a topical novel dealing with philosophical doctrines, political, and social issues
<u>1</u>

widely discussed in Russia just after the 1861 reforms. <u>By most critical essays,</u> treating
<u>2</u>

1. **A.** NO CHANGE
   B. politically
   C. politics
   D. that are political

2. **F.** NO CHANGE
   G. Because of most critical essays
   H. Most critical essays,
   J. Most critical essays

Dostoevsky's work <u>has employed</u> psychological
3
or biological points of view. Because *Crime and Punishment* is a passionate, masterly portrayal of internal psychological conflict, a general assumption has evolved in the general critical world that the author wrote, at least in part, from personal experience. <u>Nevertheless,</u> Dostoevsky's
4
biography has been endlessly probed, explored,

<u>and it was thoroughly analyzed.</u>
5

In 1849, Dostoevsky was convicted of

consorting with known radical <u>factions; however,</u>
6
he was <u>sentenced</u> to a four-year prison term.
6
Many critical commentaries on *Crime and Punishment* consider this experience formative and essential, certainly a major source of the creative impulses that eventually resulted in the execution of the novel. The epilogue of the novel <u>had been set</u> in Siberia, where he was
7
imprisoned. If, indeed, <u>he were talking</u> to his
8
fellow prisoners, then he must have focused on crime and guilt, and thought about the psychology of the criminal mind <u>granted that</u> he
9
lived among hardened convicts. One must ask, though, why he waited until 1865 to write *Crime and Punishment*. One possible answer <u>is because</u>
10
he wrote the novel in part to speak against foreign ideas adopted by the Russian radicals of the 1860s.

3. **A.** NO CHANGE
   B. have employed
   C. should employ
   D. employ

4. **F.** NO CHANGE
   G. Hence,
   H. On the contrary,
   J. Furthermore

5. **A.** NO CHANGE
   B. and being analyzed.
   C. and analyzed
   D. subject to analysis.

6. **F.** NO CHANGE
   G. factions, yet, he was sentenced
   H. factions and was sentenced
   J. factions; moreover, he was sentenced

7. **A.** NO CHANGE
   B. is set
   C. was set
   D. has been set

8. **F.** NO CHANGE
   G. he was talking
   H. he had talked
   J. he had been talking

9. **A.** NO CHANGE
   B. as he
   C. knowing that
   D. considering that

10. **F.** NO CHANGE
    G. is when
    H. is where
    J. is that

Answers and Explanations

1. C A noun is necessary in this position to be parallel with the other noun objects in this series, *doctrines* and *issues*.

2. J As it stands, this sentence contains an error in predication, beginning with one construction, *By most critical essays*, and continuing with a different one, *treating Dostoevsky's work has employed . . . points of view*. It is incorrect to separate a subject from its verb, as in choice H.

3. D The verb must agree with its plural subject *essays* and maintain the established present tense.

4. G The logic of the sentence requires a cause/effect transitional marker like *Hence*, not the contrast or addition markers suggested by the alternative choices.

5. C The parallel series of past participles in this sentence requires this option: *has been probed, explored, and analyzed*.

6. H The logic of this sentence requires a transitional word suggesting either *cause* or *addition*. Since the acts of *conviction* and *sentencing* seem to be of equal weight, the conjunction *and* is a sound choice.

7. B Use the historical present tense when relating events that occur in fiction.

8. F The subjunctive is the logical choice of mood in this *if* clause because it expresses a supposition.

9. B The use of the subordinating conjunction *as* is a sound choice in this position because it creates an adverb clause that modifies the verbs *focused* and *thought*. The other choices create modifiers of the subject to little effect.

10. J Only the use of the words *is that* in this spot forms a noun structure that equates with the noun *answer*. The other choices form adverb clauses that cannot equate with the noun.

RHETORICAL SKILLS

Kinds of Questions

Some questions on the English Test will ask you to choose the most effective introductions and conclusions, both of paragraphs and essays. Others will ask you to select the most logical transitions between sentences or between paragraphs. You will most likely be asked if a passage is appropriate for a particular audience or what kind of supporting details should be added to strengthen a paragraph. You may also be asked whether a particular sentence or paragraph is relevant to the selection.

Organization

The prose passages on the English Test will usually consist of the main idea and a body of supporting material that may include specific details, anecdotes, references, or reasons that relate to the central idea, along with transitional words and phrases. When you are asked to rearrange paragraphs in a passage, you must be able to identify the opening (which introduces the topic) and the closing (which summarizes the passage).

Style

The style of the writing within a passage should be consistent throughout. If it is not, you will surely be questioned about it. Writing styles range from formal for serious subjects to informal for light and colloquial topics. Popular writing falls someplace between the two, and is usually informative with longer sentences, and few colloquialisms. An elevated style is poetic in tone and is generally used for eulogies and other circumstances requiring ornate language. An esoteric style uses technical or specialized language that is characteristic of a particular profession, trade, or branch of learning.

Word Choice

Some of the questions on the English Test will require you to decide the appropriateness of a word in its context. A word is appropriate if it fits the reader, occasion, and purpose for which the writing is intended.

Wordiness

To avoid wordiness, eliminate language that either duplicates what has already been expressed or adds nothing to the sense of the statement.

Omissions

A common error in written English is the careless omission, especially the omission acceptable in speech but not in writing.

FOCUS ON THE ACT

The following sample questions represent ways in which the above skills might be tested on your ACT Assessment.

(1)

Modern literary criticism is a literary specialty composed of many varying and inharmonious parts. There are, however, five major trends in contemporary criticism that take into account almost every significant critical essay written in the twentieth century. It is the critics' differing opinions on the purpose of literature that create the divisions or schools of modern criticism. These schools or approaches to literature are the moral, the psychological, the sociological, the formalistic, and the archetypal. ☐1☐

1. This entire passage was probably written for readers who are:
   A. college or college-bound literature students.
   B. poor readers who require supplemental material.
   C. interested in the scientific method.
   D. foreign students preparing for an English proficiency test.

(2)

The oldest view, the moral approach, originated with Plato when he ordered Homer banished from his fictional utopian republic. Poetry, said Plato, by its very nature appeals to the emotions rather than to the intellect and is, therefore, potentially dangerous. Here is the first expression of concern over the effect of literature on life, and this concern becomes the primary concern of the moral critic, who gauges all literature by its ability to aid and comfort man, and convey a higher ideal of life. 2

2. Which of the following statements is best supported by the details supplied in paragraph number 2?

F. The moral view is the most important by far.

G. The moral approach is really a religious view.

H. The moral approach is the oldest and most noble of the critical modes.

J. The moral critical view requires rigid standards of behavior of its adherents.

(3)

As you can imagine, the psychologists got
<u>   3   </u>
into the act and started linking novels with
<u>   3   </u>
Freud and Jung and that crowd and their
<u>   3   </u>
theories that man is a victim of society and
<u>   3   </u>
his own biological drives. Psychological
<u>   3   </u>

3. Which of the suggested sentences below make the best introduction to paragraph 3 and the best transition from 2?

A. NO CHANGE

B. In contrast to this idea is the psychological approach to literature, a school that originated with Freud and his theory that man is a victim of both the repressive mores of society and his own biological compulsions.

C. The psychological approach to literature is our next mode of criticism.

D. Next, we have the psychological school of criticism, a hands-on way of looking at the nitty-gritty of an author's life.

critics argue that literature that advocates
chastity, gentility, and other virtues is frustrating
to the normal drives of man and is therefore
unhealthy. The psychological
————————————
4

school studies the author's life as a means
————————————————
4

of understanding his writings, the
——————————————
4

characters and their motivation in the
——————————————
4

literature itself, and the creative process as
——————————————————
4

a psychological evolution.
————————————
4

4. Suppose at this point in the passage the author wanted to
revise the third paragraph so that it is more appropriate for
younger students. Which of the following revisions of this sentence would accomplish that purpose most effectively?

F. NO CHANGE
G. The Freudian and post-Jungian school focuses upon
the subject's experiential past as a means of
explicating his creative output, personality projections,
and basic drives, as well as the genesis of the creative
process.
H. This way of talking about a book we have read lets us
think about the author's life to see if it is related to
the story, to think about the characters in the story
and decide whether or not they make sense, and to
ask why the author wrote the book.
J. Psychological criticism tells us to look at the authors
first, as if the author's life really always tells you that
much. Anyway, you study the author's life and
supposedly learn more about the book from an
analytical, what-makes-us-tick point of view.

Looking at what it is that makes folks tick
——————————————————————
5

when they get together in towns and the
————————————————————
5

like is what the sociological critic does. A
_____
                    5

     5. A. NO CHANGE
       B. As the boy's choir did in William Golding's novel *The Lord of the Flies,* man tends to organize his ruling bodies according to his inner drives.
       C. When people get together, whether they are savages or yuppies, they form social units. This process is what the sociological critic studies.
       D. The study of man's drives when he is organized into a state is the province of the sociological critic.

literary work is studied in order to discover the
degree to which it acts as a mirror of society
through contemporary social theory and practice.

   &boxed;6

     6. What kind of supporting details could strengthen this paragraph?
       F. A list of American states and major cities.
       G. A list of authors that have written "sociological novels."
       H. Examples of ways a novel can mirror contemporary society.
       J. A consistent way to gauge the quality of life.

          (5)
    Used as an isolated method, each approach to
literary commentary has serious drawbacks,
leading to narrow and restrictive readings. Used
collectively, however, the five approaches can
deal with every facet of a work, enabling a
balanced and complete interpretation of literature.

   &boxed;7

     7. This paragraph is organized according to which of the following schemes?
       A. A general statement followed by a number of specific examples.
       B. A narrative structure controlled by the events being described.
       C. A typical classification/division format where the topic is broken down into groups and labeled.
       D. A simple contrasting paragraph, with the point on the first sentence contrasting sharply with the next.

(6)

The most influential method of contemporary criticism, however, is the formalistic, or "new" criticism. Assuming that literature has intrinsic meaning, the school advocates the close study of texts themselves, rather than extrinsics such as society or the author's biography. The
<u>   </u>
8

<u>primary route by which a formalistic critic</u>
8

<u>reveals and expresses his views on a</u>
8

<u>classic work of literature is by means of</u>
8

<u>a very ambitious and comprehensive</u>
8

<u>examination and scrutiny of the text of the</u>
8

<u>novel itself.</u>
8

    8. F. NO CHANGE
       G. A close, in-depth examination of a work's structure and language is the primary characteristic of this highly analytical mode of commentary.
       H. A close, in-depth examination in which scholars scrutinize very minutely the actual text of a work of literature is the main primary characteristic of this highly analytical mode of commentary.
       J. The main way a critic reports on a book is really by looking very closely at the words and sentences.

(7)

The archetypal approach studies literature in its relation to all men, assuming a "collective unconscious" that binds all men from all time. The archetypal critic <u>eyeballs</u> a work in an
                  9

attempt to disclose its reliance on either a specific myth or a universal pattern of thought, both of which might reveal a man's subconscious

9. A. NO CHANGE
    B. peruses
    C. ponders
    D. studies

attempt to link himself with all humanity, past
and present. 〔10〕

10. Choose the sequence of paragraph numbers that makes the
structure of the passage most logical.
   F. 1, 3, 5, 6, 7, 4, 2.
   G. 1, 2, 4, 3, 7, 6, 5.
   H. 1, 2, 3, 4, 6, 7, 5.
   J. 1, 2, 7, 6, 5, 4, 3.

Answers and Explanations

1. A The subject and tone of the passage clearly addresses serious students of literature.

2. H The details supplied in paragraph 2 bear out solely this statement.

3. B This choice highlights the obvious contrast between the critical schools described in the two paragraphs, and effectively
introduces the topic that is supported in the paragraph. The
other choices fall short of introducing the paragraph topic or
depart markedly from the style and tone of the passage.

4. H This choice is written for a younger reading level, yet roughly
covers the main points of the original sentence. The other
choices (G and J) either do not communicate the main points
of the original sentence, or are not written for young readers.

5. D Only this choice concludes the paragraph clearly and effectively, while maintaining the style of the passage.

6. H The original paragraph *does* lack specific examples of literary works that mirror their contemporary society. The information conveyed in the other choices is off the topic of the
paragraph.

7. D The paragraph does, indeed, contain two sentences, one
contrasting sharply with the other.

8. G This choice is the only one that expresses the primary characteristics of the formalistic critic with economy of language and in a style consistent with that of the passage. The other choices are either wordy or lacking in content or compatible style.

9. D The word *studies* is consistent with the tone of the passage. The other choices suggest activities that are other than scholarly.

10. H The paragraphs in this passage are linked to each other by means of transitional statements, and by means of the controlling order established near the end of paragraph 1.

SAMPLE ENGLISH TEST

The ACT English Test consists of five prose passages and 75 questions, with a 45-minute time limit. The test is designed to measure your ability to discern and remedy errors and awkwardness in punctuation, grammar and usage, and sentence structure. You will also find questions about the prose—for whom the passage is intended, for example, or how the paragraph or sentence might be improved with reorganization or additional material.

The following two practice passages are intended to familiarize you with questions that approximate those on the ACT. Each passage is accompanied by 30 multiple-choice questions. These passages are approximately double the length of the ones on the actual test. If you wish to time yourself, allow 18 minutes to read each passage and answer the question.

DIRECTIONS: The following test consists of 60 items. Some concern underlined words and phrases in context; others ask general questions about the passages. Most of the underlined sections contain errors or inappropriate expressions. You are asked to compare each with the four alternatives in the answer column. If you consider the original version best, choose letter **A** or **F**: NO CHANGE. For each question, select the alternative you think best. Read each passage through before answering the questions based on it.

NOTE: Answers and explanations can be found at the end of each passage.

Passage 1

A peaceful oasis in the midst of the bustling San Fernando Valley, San Fernando Mission has been declared a historic cultural monument by the City of Los Angeles, according to a bronze plaque at the entrance to the mission. In addition to being an active religion center, many tourists
1　　　　　　2
come to the mission each year to stroll through
2

1. A. NO CHANGE
B. religions
C. religious
D. more religious
2. F. NO CHANGE
G. many tourists are invited to the Mission each year
H. it is a place where many tourists come each year
J. people come

the well-tended grounds and they admire the
3
unique architecture of the restored mission buildings.

3. A. NO CHANGE
B. they were admiring
C. admiring
D. admire

The entrance to the mission quadrangle opens onto the east garden, a large grass covered
4　　　　　　　　5

4. F. NO CHANGE
G. out into
H. wide into
J. for
5. A. NO CHANGE
B. grass-covered
C. grass covering
D. grass, covered

courtyard in the middle of which is a flower-shaped fountain modeled after one that stands in Cordova, Spain. Wind rustles through the branches of the trees, and water tinkles in the fountain, also the sounds of traffic outside the
6
walls only accentuate the tranquility of the setting. Strolling about the grounds, the smell of spring flowers scenting the air and the sunlight

6. F. NO CHANGE
G. while
H. moreover,
J. furthermore,

warm upon your back, <u>one can easily</u> imagine
                     7

being back two hundred years during the time of
the founding of the mission. The present-day
mission compound, however, with its air of
serenity and unhurried repose, is nothing like the
mission in its heyday, when it was the scene of
bustling activity and <u>the labor was diligent</u> by
                      8
hundreds of Indians under the direction of a few
Spanish Franciscan padres.

San Fernando Mission, founded in 1779 by
Padre Fermin Lasuen and named for a saintly
king of thirteenth-century Spain, <u>it was the</u>
                                   9
seventeenth of California's twenty-one missions
<u>stretching</u> in a chain from San Francisco to San
 10
Diego. The purpose of the mission chain was to

create centers of Christian civilization <u>who would</u>
                                         11
<u>want</u> to convert the California Indians and prepare
 11
them for Spanish citizenship.

Mission San Francisco was established
<u>centrally</u> between the missions of San
 12
Buenaventura and San Gabriel, at a distance of

one day's journey from each. The <u>site chosen</u> for
                                  13

the <u>mission—land</u> that had been used by Don
     14
Francisco Reyes, first mayor of the Pueblo de
Los Angeles, to graze cattle—was rich in water,

7. A. NO CHANGE
   B. you can easily
   C. it seems easy to
   D. one can easily

8. F. NO CHANGE
   G. diligent labor
   H. that labor was industrious
   J. labor that was diligent

9. A. NO CHANGE
   B. it had been
   C. it will be
   D. was

10. F. NO CHANGE
   G. and it stretched
   H. that was stretching
   J. widely stretched out

11. A. NO CHANGE
   B. which was hoping
   C. seeking
   D. needing

12. F. NO CHANGE
   G. in a great spot
   H. well within and
   J. OMIT the underlined phrase.

13. A. NO CHANGE
   B. cite chosen
   C. sight chose
   D. site choosed

14. F. NO CHANGE
   G. Mission: land
   H. Mission; land
   J. Mission. Land

in fertile, arable soil, and it had an Indian 15

population, all necessary elements for a 15

successful mission.

The chapel—an exact replica of the original, which was built between 1804 and 1806 and destroyed by the 1971 earthquake—is long and narrow, with adobe walls decorated by frescoes of native designs. The overall effect of the frescoes, the colorful Spanish altar hangings, and the stations of the Cross are, as one writer put it, 16

"a glorious, if barbaric spectacle!" Although there is a number of windows on the south wall 17

of the chapel, there is only one window on the north wall. It is not known whether this architectural detail was meant to keep out cold winds from the nearby mountains or as a defense 18

against a potential attack by hostile Indians. 18

Behind the chapel is a cemetery, where many of the natives and other early settlers attached to the mission were buried. Only a few wooden crosses and there is one large gravestone mark 19

the final resting places of approximately 2000 persons buried there. Beyond the burial grounds

is a fountain: fed by a small stream and 20

surrounded in foliage and a flower garden. 21

15. **A.** NO CHANGE
B. there also were Indians,
C. it had Indians,
D. in an Indian population,

16. **F.** NO CHANGE
G. was
H. is
J. will have been

17. **A.** NO CHANGE
B. were a number of
C. are a number of
D. should be a number of

18. **F.** NO CHANGE
G. hostile Indians.
H. defending against an Indian attack.
J. an attack against hostile Indians.

19. **A.** NO CHANGE
B. one large gravestone
C. there might have been a gravestone
D. there most likely is a gravestone

20. **F.** NO CHANGE
G. fountain. Fed
H. fountain; fed
J. fountain fed

21. **A.** NO CHANGE
B. overhead in the
C. about with
D. by

Across the compound, stands the
_____
22

"convento"—the largest original mission building
in California—with its famous corridor of

twenty-one Roman arches that today front San
_____
23

Fernando Mission Road. Two stories high, with
four-foot-thick adobe walls that keeps the inside
_____
24

cool on even the hottest summer day. It served
_____
25

as living quarters for the missionaries and visitors
in the early 1800's. Tourists taking pictures
_____
26
inside the mission should bring high-speed
_____
26
color film.
_____
26

22. F. NO CHANGE
G. Across the compound, stood
H. Across the compound stands
J. Across the compound, is standing

23. A. NO CHANGE
B. fronts
C. fronting
D. fronted

24. F. NO CHANGE
G. walls, that keep
H. , walls that keep
J. walls, that keeps

25. A. NO CHANGE
B. day, it
C. day—it
D. day: it

26. F. NO CHANGE
G. Retain the position of this sentence in the passage but place it in its own paragraph
H. Move this sentence to the beginning of the paragraph.
J. OMIT the underlined sentence.

Just inside the entrance hall an atmosphere is
_____
27
able to be felt of great age, perhaps due in part
_____
27
to the stillness that seems to echo within the
brick-floored rooms. Then again, this feeling
might be due to the odor, emanating from the
_____
28
nearby wine cellar, a musty smell that grows

27. A. NO CHANGE
B. may be feeling
C. one feels
D. an atmosphere can be felt

28. F. NO CHANGE
G. odor; emanating
H. odor. Emanating
J. odor emanating

stronger as one moves slowly down the whitewashed stairs—past a deep tub cut from

29

rock where grapes were once pressed underfoot.

30

29. A. NO CHANGE
B. stairs, passed
C. stairs; passed
D. stairs, past

30. Is the mention of the odor appropriate and effective at the end of this passage?

F. No, because it introduces a new element at the end of the passage.

G. Yes, because the musty odors of old buildings and old wine presses appropriately reflect the age of this historic mission.

H. Yes, because the description of the odor is somewhat suspenseful, and mentioning it gives a mysterious quality to the passage.

J. No, because an odor is generally perceived as offensive.

Answer Key

1. **C**	6. **G**	11. **C**	16. **H**	21. **D**	26. **J**
2. **H**	7. **B**	12. **J**	17. **C**	22. **H**	27. **C**
3. **D**	8. **G**	13. **A**	18. **G**	23. **B**	28. **J**
4. **F**	9. **D**	14. **F**	19. **B**	24. **H**	29. **D**
5. **B**	10. **F**	15. **D**	20. **J**	25. **B**	30. **G**

Answer Explanations

1. C The underlined word is intended to modify the noun *center* and so must be an adjective.

2. H The introductory phrase *In addition to being an active [religious] center* clearly refers to the mission, not the tourists. Therefore, the main clause must begin with the word *mission* or with the referent pronoun *it*.

3. D The infinitive *to admire* is parallel in construction with *to stroll*, with which it is paired: *to stroll . . . and to admire*.

4. F No other choice is idiomatically correct.

5. B Hyphenate a compound adjective that precedes the noun it modifies.

6. G Conjunctive adverbs (such as *also*, *moreover*, and *furthermore*) used to join clauses must be preceded by a semicolon. *While*, a subordinating conjunction used to introduce an adverb clause, is properly preceded by a comma.

7. B Avoid a shift in point of view, from the second person *your* to the third person *one*. Choice C incorrectly makes *it* the word modified by the introductory participial phrase.

8. G The prepositional phrase *of bustling activity* requires a parallel object, *diligent labor*. Choice J is wordy.

9. D The sentence has two subjects: *San Fernando/it. It* is unnecessary.

10. F The participial phrase *stretching in a chain . . .* correctly modifies the noun *missions*. Choice G incorrectly uses *it* to refer to the plural word *missions*. H also incorrectly uses a singular form, *was*, which does not agree with *missions*, the antecedent of *that*. J is wordy.

11. C The other options either carry meanings inappropriate to the sense of the passage or contain faulty grammar.

12. J *Centrally* repeats the idea of *at a distance of one day's journey from each. In a great spot* is too colloquial for this passage. Choice H is wordy.

13. A The correct word to use here is *site*, meaning location. The verb forms *chose* and *choosed* in choices C and D are incorrect.

14. F A pair of dashes precedes and follows an interrupting parenthetical element.

15. D Only this option is parallel with the other prepositional phrases: *in water, in . . . land, and in . . . population*.

16. H The singular subject *effect* requires the singular verb *is*. The predominant tense of the passage is the present.

17. C The phrase *a number of* is plural in meaning and takes the plural verb *are*. Choice B is wrong, since the predominant tense of the passage is the present. D changes the meaning of the clause.

18. G The infinitive phrase *to keep out* needs a parallel second object: *to keep out cold winds . . . or hostile Indians*.

19. B A simple noun is needed to form the other half of the compound subject: *crosses and . . . gravestone*.

20. J The participial phrase *fed by a small stream* is a restrictive

modifier and should not be separated from the noun it modifies, *fountain*, by a punctuation mark. Choice G introduces a
sentence fragment.

21. D The correct idiom is *surrounded by*.

22. H In an inverted sentence, do not use a comma to separate a
short adverb construction from the verb it modifies.

23. B The subject of the verb *front* is the relative pronoun *that*,
which refers to the singular noun *corridor*, not the plural
arches. Thus, the correct verb form is *fronts*. Choice C is a
participle, not a verb form. D shifts to the past tense.

24. H The subject of the verb *keep* is the relative pronoun *that*,
which refers to the plural noun *walls*. Do not use a comma to
separate a restrictive clause from the word it modifies (G and
J).

25. B A comma is used to separate the introductory phrase *two
stories high . . . day* from the main clause of the sentence.
Choice A creates a sentence fragment.

26. J This sentence has no bearing on the topic of the passage.

27. C As a rule, it is better to avoid the passive voice. The active
voice is more direct and forceful.

28. J The participial phrase *emanating from the nearby wine cellar*
is a restrictive modifier and cannot be set off by commas.
Choice H introduces a sentence fragment.

29. D A comma is called for at this point for clarity. A dash is too
great a mark of separation. Choices B and C incorrectly substitute the verb form *passed* for the preposition *past*.

30. G This descriptive paragraph adds a meaningful sense impres-
sion to the passage.

Passage 2

Each of the paragraphs in this passage is numbered, but may not
be in the most logical position. The last question asks you to select
the correct number.

(1)
Sometime around the middle of January, after
reading about standard organic gardening
techniques, prospective home gardeners should
make a list of the vegetables most enjoyed by

their families. Sitting down with a few seed catalogs, preferably those from local companies such as Santa Rosa Gardening Co. or Burbank Farms—whose catalogs contain detailing planting
1   2
instructions for Southern California, including the proper planting dates for each of the distinct climatic regions—they should review the directions for growing vegetables, narrowing the choices to crops easy to grow. And although January is an ideal time here to plant such winter vegetables such as beets, broccoli, peas, lettuce,
3
and Swiss chard, novice gardeners might do well to plan a spring garden as a first effort. For one thing, summer vegetables like tomatoes, zucchini, and beans are easy to grow, they
4
require little in the way of additional care once
4
they have been planted and are growing well. And for another, spring—traditionally a time of renewal—seems the right time of year to begin a gardening project.

(2)

These differences make it impossible that
5
gardeners in Southern California to follow in
5   6
an explicit way the advice given in nationally
6

circulated magazines and books on organic gardening. Instead, these methods must be
7
adopted to the particular climate in this area.
7

1. **A.** NO CHANGE
   B. farms—whose
   C. farms; whose
   D. farms. Whose
2. **F.** NO CHANGE
   G. details of
   H. detailed
   J. in detailed

3. **A.** NO CHANGE
   B. like
   C. such as;
   D. as

4. **F.** NO CHANGE
   G. grow. Since these vegetables require
   H. grow. Requiring
   J. grow, requiring

5. **A.** NO CHANGE
   B. to be a gardener
   C. to go on being a gardener
   D. for gardeners
6. **F.** NO CHANGE
   G. explicitly
   H. in a more explicit way
   J. explicitly and definitely
7. **A.** NO CHANGE
   B. should be adopted
   C. must be adapted
   D. must adopt

Some suggestions follow that may be helpful to fellow gardeners in the San Fernando Valley region.

(3)

Just as organic gardening differs from gardening with the help of a chemical company.
8

Gardening in Southern California differs
8

dramatically from gardening in almost every other part of the country. For one thing, crops will be
9

planted here almost any time during the year,
9

whereas spring gardens are the rule in most other parts of the country. Diversity of weather systems within the relatively small area that encompassing Southern California is another
10

distinction. For instance, coastal communities experience cool, damp weather for much of the year, while the San Fernando and San Gabriel valleys are blistering hot in summer and cold in winter—some inland valleys even encounter frost
11

and freezing temperatures! Thus, although these areas separate by fewer than fifty miles, the
12

climates are disparate, necessitating the use of distinct gardening techniques for each locale.

(4)

After deciding what vegetables to grow, a rough draft is made of the garden, which
13

8. F. NO CHANGE
  G. company;
    gardening
  H. company,
    gardening
  J. company:
    gardening

9. A. NO CHANGE
  B. can be planted
  C. have been
    planted
  D. ought to be
    planted

10. F. NO CHANGE
  G. encompassed
  H. has
    encompassed
  J. encompasses

11. A. NO CHANGE
  B. winter;—some
  C. winter—Some
  D. winter, some

12. F. NO CHANGE
  G. are separated
  H. must be
    separated
  J. were separated

13. A. NO CHANGE
  B. a rough draft
    should be made
  C. the gardener
    should make a
    rough draft
  D. it is necessary
    to make a
    rough draft

should be located in an area of flat well-drained
$\overline{14}$

ground that has gotten at least six full hours of
$\overline{15}$
sun daily. Taller-growing crops should be put on
the north side of the garden so that they do not
shade any low-growing vegetables; except those
$\overline{16}$
that cannot survive the intense summer sun. The
latter include lettuce and many other greens. The
rows, or beds, should be wide enough to

accommodate the particular kind of a crop to be
$\overline{17}$
grown. The wider the rows, of course, the more

crops the garden will have produced. This is
$\overline{18}$ $\overline{19}$
known as "intensive gardening" and is ideal for
small backyard gardens. One suggestion is to
make the beds three feet wide, with enough
space between them to allow easy access for

cultivating, weeding, and to harvest mature
$\overline{20}$

plants. However, two-foot beds are also okay.
$\overline{21}$

(5)

After the plan has been drawn up and the
seeds will be ordered, the next step is to prepare
$\overline{22}$

14. **F.** NO CHANGE
    G. flat,
    well-drained
    H. flat, well
    drained
    J. flat and well
    drained

15. **A.** NO CHANGE
    B. will have gotten
    C. got
    D. gets

16. **F.** NO CHANGE
    G. vegetables
    except
    H. vegetables:
    except
    J. vegetables.
    Except

17. **A.** NO CHANGE
    B. kind of a
    C. kinds of a
    D. OMIT the
    underlined
    words.

18. **F.** NO CHANGE
    G. would of
    produced.
    H. will produce.
    J. is producing.

19. **A.** NO CHANGE
    B. This close
    spacing
    C. Which
    D. This here

20. **F.** NO CHANGE
    G. harvesting
    H. to be
    harvesting
    J. so we can
    harvest the

21. **A.** NO CHANGE
    B. alright.
    C. all right.
    D. allright.

22. **F.** NO CHANGE
    G. should be
    ordered,
    H. were ordered,
    J. have been
    ordered.

the soil properly, one of the most important
23

procedures in insuring a successful harvest.

Testing the soil for deficiencies is a must;
24

soil-testing kits are available from most home
24

improvement stores and gardening centers. The
organic gardening books and magazines
mentioned earlier go into heavy detail regarding
25

soil composition, testing, and preparation.
Following their recommendations will contribute
for the success of the gardening project.
26

23. **A.** NO CHANGE
    B. properly. One
    C. properly; one
    D. properly; it is
      one
24. **F.** NO CHANGE
    G. must, as
      soil-testing
    H. must,
      soil-testing
    J. must because
      soil-testing
25. **A.** NO CHANGE
    B. much detail
    C. exquisite detail
    D. alot of detail

26. **F.** NO CHANGE
    G. in the success
    H. to the success
    J. for the
      successfulness

(6)

Once the condition of the soil is ascertained by
27

the person doing the gardening, deficient
27

elements (such as phosphorus, potassium,
27

magnesium, or sulphur) can be added. In
27

27. **A.** NO CHANGE
    B. Once the condition of the soil is ascertained by the
      gardener, elements that are lacking in sufficient
      quantity (such as phosphorus, potassium,
      magnesium, or sulphur) can be added by the
      gardener.
    C. Once the gardener ascertains the condition of the soil,
      he or she can add deficient elements (such as
      phosphorus, potassium, magnesium, or sulphur).
    D. Once, the gardener ascertains the condition of the
      soil, deficient elements (such as: phosphorus,
      potassium, magnesium, or sulphur) can be added.

addition to these <u>minerals; however,</u> enough
$$\overline{28}$$
fertilizer to get the seedlings off to a good start
should be incorporated into the soil. ☐ 29 ☐ 30

28. **F.** NO CHANGE
    G. minerals
        however,
    H. minerals,
        however—
    J. minerals,
        however,

29. This passage is most likely directed to readers who:
    A. are experts in gardening and need little advice.
    B. are residents of Southern California and have never had a garden.
    C. are residents of Freeport, Maine, and are just curious about gardening in a warmer state.
    D. have gardened so much that they hope never to see another bud.

30. Select the correct order of the numbered paragraphs so that the passage will read in logical sequence.
    F. NO CHANGE
    G. 3, 2, 1, 4, 5, 6
    H. 1, 2, 4, 5, 3, 6
    J. 4, 2, 3, 1, 5, 6

Answer Key

1. **B**	6. **G**	11. **A**	16. **G**	21. **C**	26. **H**
2. **H**	7. **C**	12. **G**	17. **D**	22. **J**	27. **C**
3. **D**	8. **H**	13. **C**	18. **H**	23. **A**	28. **J**
4. **J**	9. **B**	14. **G**	19. **B**	24. **F**	29. **B**
5. **D**	10. **J**	15. **D**	20. **G**	25. **B**	30. **G**

Answer Explanations

1. B A pair of dashes is used to separate a parenthetical element from the rest of the sentence; a comma is not used with the dash. Choice D introduces a sentence fragment.

2. H The correct choice is the past participle *detailed*, which acts as an adjective to modify the noun phrase *planting instructions*. The present participle *detailing* carries meaning that does not apply to this sentence. Choice J adds a word that does not make sense in the structure of the sentence.

3. D The sentence already contains the word *such (such winter vegetables as)*. Choice D offers an ungrammatical construction, *such . . . like*.

4. J This is the only correct option. The other choices produce sentence fragments or a comma splice.

5. D Idiomatic English requires the construction *impossible for gardeners . . . to follow*.

6. G The other choices are wordy or redundant.

7. C The correct word here is *adapted*, meaning modified to suit. *Adopted* means taken as is.

8. H Use a comma to separate an introductory adverb clause from the main clause.

9. B The verb phrase *can be planted* also means *are planted* in the context of this sentence. The other options do not carry this essential additional meaning.

10. J Use the present tense to express generally true statements.

11. A A dash is used for emphasis to separate a parenthetical comment from the rest of the sentence. It is not used together with a semicolon. Choice C incorrectly capitalizes the word *some*. D introduces a comma splice.

12. G The passive voice is required when the subject is acted upon. The present tense is consistent with the rest of the passage.

13. C Without a logical noun to modify (*gardener*, for example), the introductory phrase would dangle.

14. G Place a comma between coordinate adjectives. The compound adjective *well-drained* takes a hyphen when it precedes the noun it modifies.

15. D The predominant tense in this passage is the present.

16. G Do not use a punctuation mark to separate a restrictive phrase from the word it modifies. The phrase beginning *except those . . .* limits *low growing vegetables*. Choice J would create a sentence fragment.

17. D The other choices are unnecessarily wordy and also introduce an error (*Kind of a* is not idiomatic English.)

18. H The simple future tense, showing expectation, is appropriate here, because the passage is set in the present tense. *Would of* is incorrect grammatically.

19. B The pronoun *This* needs a specific antecedent for clear reference. Since there is none, the meaning of *this* has to be clarified. Choice C introduces a sentence fragment. D is redundant, and *here* repeats the meaning of *this*.

20. G The gerund *harvesting* is required, to be parallel with the other gerunds, *cultivating* and *weeding*.

21. C Choice A is colloquial. B and D are misspellings.

22. J The verb must agree in tense with *has been drawn*.

23. A Set off a nonrestrictive appositive phrase with a comma. Choice B introduces a sentence fragment; D, a comma splice.

24. F A semicolon is used to separate clauses that are closely related. The transitional words in Choices G and J change the meaning. H creates a comma-splice sentence.

25. B The other options are either inappropriate or incorrect.

26. H The correct idiom is *contribute to*.

27. C The passive voice (*is ascertained* and *can be added*) is less forceful and usually results in more wordy sentences than the active voice. Choice D incorrectly places a comma after the conjunction. *Once* and a colon after *such as*.

28. J The word *however* is used here as an adverb, not as a conjunctive adverb introducing a clause, and so should be set off by commas as a simple parenthetical word.

29. B The references to the southwestern climate, to aids for novice gardeners, and to gardening techniques indicate that this article is addressed primarily to first-time gardeners in Southern California.

30. G Paragraph (3) is clearly the introduction to this passage; it makes general statements about the topic that are supported by data in subsequent paragraphs. The phrase *These differences* that begins paragraph (2) directly relates to the ending of paragraph (3). The step-by-step process begins with paragraph (1) and continues in order with paragraphs (4), (5), and (6).

3

PREPARING FOR THE
MATHEMATICS TEST

DESCRIPTION OF THE TEST

The ACT test in mathematics is a 60-minute test designed to evaluate your mathematical achievement in courses commonly taught in high school. This test includes questions from the areas of pre-algebra, algebra, plane geometry, intermediate algebra, coordinate geometry, and trigonometry.

STRATEGY

The review in this chapter includes examples of problems with commentary on their solutions, as well as practice exercises with complete solutions and explanations. Work each practice problem on your own, and then check your solution with the one given in this book. If your answer is the same, you can be reasonably sure you did the problem correctly, even though your procedure may be different. The chapter is intended to be review, not a textbook on mathematics. No attempt is made to prove most statements; they are merely presented as facts. If you want more practice on a particular topic, consult a textbook that covers the material in a nonreview manner.

In summary:

Study	examples.
Work	Practice Exercises.
Check	your answers against solutions and explanations.
Consult	other sources for additional practice and review.

ARITHMETIC/PRE-ALGEBRA

Three meanings of the symbol "−"

1. When this symbol appears between two numbers, it always means "subtract." Thus 7 − 4 can be read either as "7 subtract 4" or "7 minus 4."

2. When the symbol appears to the left of a numeral, it is properly read as "negative." Thus, −8 is read as "negative 8." The word *negative* means that the number is located to the left of zero on the number line.

3. In any other position, however, the symbol "−" should be read as "opposite." In particular:

   −x means the opposite of x.

   −(−9) means the opposite of negative 9.

   −($a + b$) means the opposite of the sum of a and b.

   −[−(−8)] means the opposite of the opposite of negative 8.

   −5^2 means the opposite of 5 squared.

Order of Operation Rules

So that there is no ambiguity about an expression like

$$1 + 3 \cdot 4 \quad \text{or} \quad -2^2$$

the order in which operations are to be performed must be defined.

ORDER OF OPERATION RULES

1. Perform all operations inside grouping symbols first. Grouping symbols include parentheses: ( ), brackets: [ ], braces: { }, and a bar (vinculum): $\frac{2 + 3}{7}$.
2. Do all roots and exponents in order from left to right.
3. Do all multiplications and divisions in order from left to right. (This rule does NOT say, "Do all multiplications and then do all divisions.")

4. Do all additions and subtractions (and opposites) in order from left to right.

Operations with Signed Numbers

Absolute Value

The absolute value of any number is its distance from the origin on a number line. The symbol for this operation is $|x|$. An alternative (and more algebraic) definition of absolute value is

$$|x| = \begin{cases} x & \text{if } x \geq 0 \\ -x & \text{if } x < 0 \end{cases}$$

Addition

If the two numbers are either both positive or both negative, add the absolute values of the numbers and prefix the answer with the sign that is common to the original numbers.

$$(-2) + (-5) = -7 \qquad 5 + 3 = 8 \qquad -4 + (-6) = -10$$

If the two numbers have opposite signs, subtract the absolute values of the numbers (the smaller from the larger) and prefix the answer with the sign of the original number that has the larger absolute value.

$$-7 + 9 = 2 \qquad 4 + (-3) = 1 \qquad 5 + (-9) = -4$$

Subtraction

The definition of subtraction is

$$a - b = a + (-b)$$

This definition says, "a minus b equals a plus the opposite of b." In other words, to subtract, add the opposite of the second number.

$$2 - 5 = 2 + (-5) = -3 \qquad -7 - 8 = -7 + (-8) = -15$$
$$5 - (-3) = 5 + 3 = 8 \qquad -2 - (-4) = -2 + 4 = 2$$

Multiplication

To multiply two numbers, multiply their absolute values and prefix the answer with a sign determined by the following rule:

If the two numbers have the same sign, choose $+$. If the numbers have opposite signs, choose $-$.

$$(-3)(4) = -12 \qquad (-5)(-4) = 20 \qquad 3(-7) = -21$$

Division

The rule for division is similar to the rule for multiplication. Divide the absolute values of the numbers, and prefix the answer with a sign determined by the following rule:

If the two numbers have the same sign, choose $+$. If the numbers have opposite signs, choose $-$.

Exponentiation

The following equation defines exponentiation:

$$x^n = x \cdot x \cdot x \cdot \cdots \cdot x \qquad (n \text{ factors of } x)$$

It is important to remember that any exponent always refers only to the symbol immediately to its left. Thus:

$$-2^4 = -(2 \cdot 2 \cdot 2 \cdot 2) = -16 \; (-2^4 \text{ is read as "the opposite of 2 to the fourth power."})$$

and

$$(-2)^4 = (-2)(-2)(-2)(-2) = 16 \; (\text{The symbol immediately to the left of the exponent is the pair of parentheses.})$$

PRACTICE EXERCISES

Perform the indicated operations.

1. $3 - 5 \cdot 7$

2. $-2(3 - 4)^3 - 2$

3. $5\{2[3(4 + 1) - 3] - 2\} - 7$

4. $\dfrac{3(-4)}{2} + (-2)^2(3) - (-3)(-3)^2 + \dfrac{-5}{-1}$

SOLUTIONS

1. $3 - 5 \cdot 7 = 3 - 35 = 3 + (-35) = -32$

2. $-2(3 - 4)^3 - 2 = -2[3 + (-4)]^3 - 2$
$$= -2(-1)^3 - 2$$
$$= -2(-1) - 2 = 2 - 2$$
$$= 2 + (-2) = 0$$

3. $5\{2[3(4 + 1) - 3] - 2\} - 7$ (These steps show
$\quad = 5\{2[3(5) - 3] - 2\} - 7$ excruciating detail.
$\quad = 5\{2[15 - 3] - 2\} - 7$ Many steps may be
$\quad = 5\{2[15 + (-3)] - 2\} - 7$ omitted by
$\quad = 5\{2[12] - 2\} - 7$ experienced
$\quad = 5\{24 - 2\} - 7$ students.)
$\quad = 5\{24 + (-2)\} - 7$
$\quad = 5\{22\} - 7 = 110 - 7$
$\quad = 110 + (-7) = 103$

4. $\dfrac{3(-4)}{2} + (-2)^2(3) - (-3)(-3)^2 + \dfrac{-5}{-1}$

$\quad = \dfrac{3(-4)}{2} + 4(3) - (-3)(9) + \dfrac{-5}{-1}$

$\quad = \dfrac{-12}{2} + 12 - (-27) + 5$ (All multiplications
and divisions are
$\quad = -6 + 12 - (-27) + 5$ done before any
$\quad = -6 + 12 + 27 + 5$ additions or
$\quad = 6 + 27 + 5$ subtractions.)
$\quad = 33 + 5 = 38$

Divisibility

There are four relationships between a and b in the equation
$$a = bc,$$
where a, b, and c are whole numbers:

1. a is a *multiple* of b.
2. a is *divisible* by b.
3. b is a *factor* of a.
4. b is a *divisor* of a.

Prime and Composite Numbers

A whole number is *prime* if and only if it has exactly two factors.

A whole number greater than 1 is *composite* if and only if it is not prime.

Prime Factorization

It is important to be able to express a whole number as a product of prime factors. For example, $12 = 2 \cdot 2 \cdot 3 = 2^2 \cdot 3$.

Factor tree. Find the prime factorization of 72. First name any two factors of 72 (not necessarily prime), say 8 and 9. Each of these numbers can be factored. Continue this until all factors are prime. It is convenient to arrange these numbers in a tree.

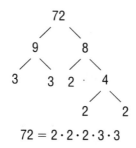

$$72 = 2 \cdot 2 \cdot 2 \cdot 3 \cdot 3$$

PRACTICE EXERCISES

Determine the prime factorization of each of the following numbers:

1. 50
2. 300
3. 73
4. 1617
5. 243

SOLUTIONS

1. $50 = 2 \cdot 5^2$
2. $300 = 2^2 \cdot 3 \cdot 5^2$
3. 73 is prime, so there is no prime factorization. The answer is not $1 \cdot 73$.
4. $1617 = 3 \cdot 7^2 \cdot 11$
5. $243 = 3^5$

Fractions

The Fundamental Principle of Fractions states that any fraction is equivalent to a fraction obtained by multiplying the numerator and denominator by the same nonzero number:

$$\frac{a}{b} = \frac{ak}{bk}, \quad b, k \neq 0$$

This property is used to reduce fractions to lowest terms:

$$\frac{12}{18} = \frac{2 \cdot 6}{3 \cdot 6} = \frac{2}{3}$$

$$\frac{90}{108} = \frac{45}{54} \quad (k = 2) \qquad \text{(This reduction can be done in stages.)}$$

$$= \frac{5}{6} \quad (k = 9)$$

This same property is used to rewrite a fraction so that it has a specific denominator:

$$\frac{5}{9} = \frac{?}{63} = \frac{35}{63} \quad (k = 7)$$

$$\frac{5}{8} = \frac{?}{120} = \frac{75}{120} \quad (k = 15)$$

Proper and Improper Fractions and Mixed Numbers

If the absolute value of the numerator is not smaller than the denominator, the fraction is improper, and it can be changed to a mixed number or a whole number. A mixed number is a special form that represents the sum of a whole number and a proper fraction:

$$\frac{7}{5} = 1 + \frac{2}{5} = 1\frac{2}{5}$$

The mixed number can be found by dividing the denominator into the numerator. The quotient becomes the whole number part of the mixed number, and the remainder becomes the numerator of the fraction part of the mixed number.

PRACTICE EXERCISES

Change each improper fraction to a corresponding mixed number.

1. $\frac{23}{5}$

2. $\frac{72}{16}$

Change each mixed number to a corresponding improper fraction.

3. $7\frac{3}{4}$

4. $5\frac{11}{12}$

SOLUTIONS

1. $4\frac{3}{5}$

2. $4\frac{1}{2}$ (Be sure to reduce the fraction to lowest terms.)

3. $7\frac{3}{4} = \frac{31}{4}$ (The numerator is $7(4) + 3 = 31$.)

4. $\frac{71}{12}$

Operations with Fractions

Addition and Subtraction

The rules for addition and subtraction of fractions are as follows:

$$\frac{a}{b} \pm \frac{c}{b} = \frac{a \pm c}{b}, \quad b \neq 0$$

These rules are very easy to apply; however, difficulty with these operations comes in four areas:

1. If the fractions do not have the same denominators, they must first be changed so that there is a common denominator. For example:

- $\frac{5}{12} + \frac{7}{16} = \frac{20}{48} + \frac{21}{48} = \frac{41}{48}$ The lowest common multiple (LCM) of 12 and 16 is 48.

2. If the numbers to be added or subtracted are given as mixed numbers, there are two methods of performing the operations. For example:

- $3\frac{2}{3} + 5\frac{1}{2} = 3\frac{4}{6} + 5\frac{3}{6}$ Add the fraction parts and whole number parts separately.

$ = 8\frac{7}{6}$ Since the fraction part is an improper fraction, the answer must be expressed in simplest form.

$ = 8 + 1\frac{1}{6} = 9\frac{1}{6}$

OR

- $3\frac{2}{3} + 5\frac{1}{2} = \frac{11}{3} + \frac{11}{2}$ Write each mixed number as an improper fraction and then add according to the rule.

$$= \frac{22}{6} + \frac{33}{6}$$

$$= \frac{55}{6} = 9\frac{1}{6}$$ Change the answer to a mixed number.

3. The answers must normally be expressed in simplest form.

$$\frac{1}{6} + \frac{1}{2} = \frac{1}{6} + \frac{3}{6} = \frac{4}{6} = \frac{2}{3}$$ The answer has been reduced.

4. In subtraction of mixed numbers, borrowing must be done carefully.

$$5\frac{2}{3} - 1\frac{3}{4} = 5\frac{8}{12} - 1\frac{9}{12}$$ Borrow 1 from the 5 and add it to the fraction part of the mixed number

$$= 4\frac{20}{12} - 1\frac{9}{12}$$

$$= 3\frac{11}{12}$$ $\left(1 + \frac{8}{12} = \frac{20}{12}\right).$

PRACTICE EXERCISES

Add or subtract as indicated, and express the answer in simplest form.

1. $\dfrac{3}{7} - \dfrac{1}{9}$

2. $\dfrac{7}{20} + \dfrac{3}{16}$

3. $4\dfrac{1}{2} - 2\dfrac{1}{3}$

4. $8 - 5\dfrac{5}{8}$

5. $3\dfrac{2}{5} - 1\dfrac{3}{4}$

6. $\left(-2\dfrac{3}{5}\right) + 1\dfrac{1}{2}$

SOLUTIONS

1. $\dfrac{3}{7} - \dfrac{1}{9} = \dfrac{27}{63} - \dfrac{7}{63} = \dfrac{20}{63}$

2. $\dfrac{7}{20} + \dfrac{3}{16} = \dfrac{28}{80} + \dfrac{15}{80}$ LCM of 20 and 16 is 80.

$\qquad\qquad = \dfrac{43}{80}$

3. $4\dfrac{1}{2} - 2\dfrac{1}{3} = 4\dfrac{3}{6} - 2\dfrac{2}{6} = 2\dfrac{1}{6}$

4. $8 - 5\dfrac{5}{8} = 7\dfrac{8}{8} - 5\dfrac{5}{8}$ Borrow 1 from 8.

$\qquad\qquad = 2\dfrac{3}{8}$

5. $3\dfrac{2}{5} - 1\dfrac{3}{4} = 3\dfrac{8}{20} - 1\dfrac{15}{20}$ Borrow 1 from 3 and add
to the fraction part.

$\qquad\qquad = 2\dfrac{28}{20} - 1\dfrac{15}{20}$

$\qquad\qquad = 1\dfrac{13}{20}$

6. $\left(-2\dfrac{3}{5}\right) + 1\dfrac{1}{2}$ All rules of sign that apply to
positive and negative integers
apply also to fractions.

$= \left(-2\dfrac{6}{10}\right) + 1\dfrac{5}{10}$

$= -1\dfrac{1}{10}$

Multiplication

The rule for multiplication of fractions is as follows:

$$\frac{a}{b} \cdot \frac{c}{d} = \frac{ac}{bd}, \quad b, d \neq 0$$

This rule states that, to multiply any two fractions, one must multiply the numerators and denominators separately.

Division

The rule for division is as follows:

$$\frac{a}{b} \div \frac{c}{d} = \frac{a}{b} \cdot \frac{d}{c}, \quad b, c, d \neq 0$$

This rule states that, to divide fractions, one must replace the divisor with its reciprocal and change the operation to multiplication.

- $2\dfrac{1}{2} \cdot 3\dfrac{5}{6} = \dfrac{5}{2} \cdot \dfrac{23}{6}$

    Mixed numbers must be changed to improper fractions before multiplying.

    $= \dfrac{115}{12} = 9\dfrac{7}{12}$

- $\left(-3\dfrac{4}{5}\right) \cdot \left(-6\dfrac{1}{3}\right) = \left(\dfrac{-19}{5}\right) \cdot \left(\dfrac{-19}{3}\right)$

    The same rules of signs apply.

    $= \dfrac{361}{15} = 24\dfrac{1}{15}$

PRACTICE EXERCISES

Perfom the indicated operations, and express the answers in simplest form.

1. $-2\dfrac{4}{9} \cdot 4\dfrac{1}{2}$

2. $3\dfrac{1}{3} \div 1\dfrac{3}{7}$

3. $12 \div 2\dfrac{2}{3}$

SOLUTIONS

1. $-2\dfrac{4}{9} \cdot 4\dfrac{1}{2} = \dfrac{-22}{9} \cdot \dfrac{9}{2}$

Cancel both 2 and 9.

$= \dfrac{-11}{1} \cdot \dfrac{1}{1} = -11$

2. $3\dfrac{1}{3} \div 1\dfrac{3}{7} = \dfrac{10}{3} \div \dfrac{10}{7}$

Change to improper fractions.
Replace divisor.

$= \dfrac{10}{3} \cdot \dfrac{7}{10}$

$= \dfrac{1}{3} \cdot \dfrac{7}{1}$

Cancel.

$= \dfrac{7}{3} = 2\dfrac{1}{3}$

3. $12 \div 2\frac{2}{3} = \frac{12}{1} \div \frac{8}{3}$

$= \frac{12}{1} \cdot \frac{3}{8}$

$= \frac{3}{1} \cdot \frac{3}{2}$

$= \frac{9}{2}$

$= 4\frac{1}{2}$

Percents

The word *percent* literally means hundredths, so 25% means $\frac{25}{100}$, which reduces to $\frac{1}{4}$. Since "hundredths" could also be interpreted as divided by 100, and dividing by 100 can most efficiently be accomplished by moving the decimal point two places to the left, 25% is also 0.25. Therefore we have two rules:

1. To change a percent to a fraction, omit the percent sign, divide by 100, and reduce the fraction.
2. To change a percent to a decimal, omit the percent sign and move the decimal point two places to the left.

To change either a fraction or a decimal to a percent, the rules above are reversed:

1. To change a fraction to a percent, multiply by 100 (do the division to get a decimal) and attach a percent sign.
2. To change a decimal to a percent, move the decimal point two places to the right and attach a percent sign.

Examples:
Change each percent to both a fraction and a decimal.

1. 78%   Fraction: $\frac{78}{100} = \frac{39}{50}$ Decimal: 0.78

2. 2.5%   Fraction: $\dfrac{2.5}{100} = \dfrac{25}{1000}$ (Multiply numerator and denominator

$= \dfrac{1}{40}$ by 10 and then reduce.)

Decimal: 0.025

3. $3\dfrac{1}{3}\%$ Fraction: $\left(3\dfrac{1}{3}\right) \div 100 = \dfrac{10}{3} \div 100 = \dfrac{10}{3} \cdot \dfrac{1}{100} =$

$\dfrac{1}{3} \cdot \dfrac{1}{10} = \dfrac{1}{30}$

Decimal: $3\dfrac{1}{3}\% = 3.333\ldots\% = 0.0\overline{3}$

Change each fraction or decimal to a percent.

4. $\dfrac{4}{5}$ $\dfrac{4}{5}(100\%) = \dfrac{400}{5}\% = 80\%$

5. 7 $7(100)\% = 700\%$

6. $\dfrac{3}{8}$ $\dfrac{3}{8}(100)\% = \dfrac{3}{8}\left(\dfrac{100}{1}\right)\%$

$= \dfrac{3}{2}\left(\dfrac{25}{1}\right)\% = \dfrac{75}{2}\% = 37\dfrac{1}{2}\% \text{ or } 37.5\%$

7. 0.34 $0.34 = 0.34(100)\% = 34\%$

PRACTICE EXERCISES

Change each percent to both a fraction and a decimal.
1. 53%
2. 129%
3. $12\dfrac{1}{2}\%$
4. 0.1%
5. 200%

Change each number to a percent.
6. 0.8

7. $\dfrac{1}{8}$

8. $\dfrac{3}{5}$

9. 0.003

10. $\dfrac{3}{11}$

SOLUTIONS

1. Fraction: $\dfrac{53}{100}$

Decimal: 0.53

2. Fraction: $\dfrac{129}{100} = 1\dfrac{29}{100}$

Decimal: 1.29

3. Fraction: $12\dfrac{1}{2} \div 100 = \dfrac{25}{2} \cdot \dfrac{1}{100}$

$$= \dfrac{1}{2} \cdot \dfrac{1}{4} = \dfrac{1}{8}$$

Decimal: $0.12\dfrac{1}{2} = 0.125$

4. Fraction: $\dfrac{0.1}{100} = \dfrac{1}{1000}$

Decimal: 0.001

5. Fraction: $\dfrac{200}{100} = 2$

Decimal: 2

6. $0.8 = 0.8(100)\% = 80\%$

7. $\dfrac{1}{8} = \dfrac{1}{8}(100)\% = 12\dfrac{1}{2}\%$ or 12.5%

8. $\dfrac{3}{5} = \dfrac{3}{5}(100)\% = \dfrac{300}{5}\% = 60\%$

9. $0.003 = 0.003(100)\% = 0.3\%$

10. $\dfrac{3}{11} = \dfrac{3}{11}(100)\% = \dfrac{300}{11}\% = 27.\overline{27}\% = 27\dfrac{3}{11}\%$

Applications of Percent

Most percent applications are variations of this sentence:

A is P percent of B.

In this sentence, A is the amount (or percentage), P is the percent (or rate), and B is the base. The key to solving a percent problem is to translate the problem into the form of the sentence above. Consider the following example:

The enrollment in an algebra class dropped from 30 students to 27. What percent of the class dropped out?

In this problem we are asked to find the percent, P.

The base is always the quantity before any change, **30**.

The number of students that dropped out is the amount (or percentage), 3. Hence the sentence is

3 is P percent of 30.

Once the problem has been written in the proper form a proportion may be written:

$$\frac{P}{100} = \frac{A}{B}$$

To solve any proportion, $\frac{x}{y} = \frac{z}{w}$, first cross-multiply, and then divide by the coefficient of the unknown.

In the problem above, $\frac{P}{100} = \frac{3}{30}$, $\begin{aligned} 30P &= 300 \\ P &= 10 \end{aligned}$ 10% of the students dropped.

Examples:

1. Find 12% of 350.

A is unknown, P = 12%, and B = 350. Substituting into the percent proportion gives

$$\frac{12}{100} = \frac{A}{350}$$
$$100A = 4200 \qquad \text{Cross-multiply.}$$
$$A = \underline{42} \qquad \text{Divide by 100.}$$

2. What percent of 75 is 90?

$A = 90$, P is unknown, and $B = 75$.

$$\frac{P}{100} = \frac{90}{75}$$

$$75P = 9000$$

$$P = 120 \qquad \text{The answer is } \underline{120\%}.$$

3. 35.1 is 78% of what number?

$A = 35.1$, $P = 78\%$, and B is unknown.

$$\frac{78}{100} = \frac{35.1}{B}$$

$$35.1 = (0.78)B \qquad \text{Divide by 0.78.}$$

$$B = \underline{45}$$

PRACTICE EXERCISES

Solve the following percent problems:

1. How much interest is earned in 1 year on an investment of $25,000 at 12% annual interest?

2. Last month Dale's paycheck was $840.00. If she is to receive a raise of 5% on this month's check, what should be the amount of this month's check?

SOLUTIONS

1. Interest is 12% of $25,000.

A is unknown, $P = 12\%$, and $B = 25,000$.

$$\frac{12}{100} = \frac{A}{25,000}$$

$$A = 0.12(25,000) = 3000$$

The interest is $3000.

2. This is a percent-increase type of problem.

Dale's new salary is 105% (100% + 5%) of her old salary.

The new salary is 105% of $840.

A is unknown, $P = 105\%$, $B = 840$.

$$\frac{105}{100} = \frac{A}{840}$$

$A = 1.05(840) = 882$

Dale's new salary is $882.

ALGEBRA AND COORDINATE GEOMETRY

Constants and Variables

If $a = b$, then b may be substituted for a in any expression with no change in meaning.

Examples:

Evaluate each expression if $a = 3$, $b = -2$, and $c = -5$. (The rules for order of operation given previously are important.)

1. $a + b - c$
$$3 + (-2) - (-5) = 3 + (-2) + 5$$
$$= 1 + 5 = 6$$

2. ab^2c
$$3(-2)^2(-5) = 3(4)(-5)$$
$$= 12(-5) = -60$$

3. $ab + ac - bc$
$$3(-2) + 3(-5) - (-2)(-5)$$
$$= -6 + (-15) - 10$$
$$= -6 + (-15) + (-10)$$
$$= -21 + (-10) = -31$$

PRACTICE EXERCISES

If $x = -2$, $y = 4$, and $z = -3$, evaluate the following expressions:

1. $x - yz$
2. $xy + yz$
3. xyz^2

SOLUTIONS

1. $x - yz = -2 - 4(-3)$
$$= -2 - (-12)$$
$$= -2 + 12 = 10$$

2. $xy + yz = -2(4) + 4(-3)$
$$= \quad -8 + (-12) = -20$$
3. $xyz^2 = -2(4)(-3)^2$
$$= -2(4)(9)$$
$$= -8(9) = -72$$

Similar Terms and Simplification

In an algebraic expression, *terms* are the parts separated by plus and minus signs. The numerical factor of any term is called its *coefficient*. Similar terms are terms that have exactly the same variable part (including exponents). Since multiplication is commutative, the order in which the variables appear is not important. Expressions with similar terms may be simplified by combining the coefficients and keeping the same variable factors. For example:

$$2x + 3y + 5x - 2y = 7x + y$$
$$-3xy^2 + 7x^2 - 5x^2 - 4xy^2 = -7xy^2 + 2x^2$$

Equations

The set of numbers that make an open equation true when substituted for the variable is called the *solution* set. The numbers themselves are called the *solution*. (The solution set of the equation $2x + 1 = 7$ is $\{3\}$.)

Equations that have the same solution set are called *equivalent* equations. There are two basic rules to use in order to solve equations. The application of either rule guarantees that an equivalent equation will result.

1. If $a = b$, then $a + c = b + c$ for any number c.

2. If $a = b$, then $ac = bc$ for any number $c \neq 0$.

The process of solving an equation is to produce a sequence of equivalent equations, the last one of which looks like

$$x = \text{constant}$$

from which the solution set can easily be found.

PRACTICE EXERCISES

Solve the following equations:

1. $5x - 6 = 2x + 9$

2. $3(m - 4) - (4m - 11) = -5$

3. $1.2(x + 5) = 3(2x - 8) + 23.28$

4. $\dfrac{2x + 1}{3} + \dfrac{1}{4} = \dfrac{2x - 1}{6}$

5. $\dfrac{3y - 1}{5} - \dfrac{2y + 1}{4} = 1$

SOLUTIONS

1. $\mathbf{5x - 6 = 2x + 9}$ Add $-2x$ to both sides.

$3x - 6 = 9$ Add 6 to both sides.

$3x = 15$ Divide by 3.

$x = 5$ Solution set is $\{5\}$.

2. $\mathbf{3(m - 4) - (4m - 11) = -5}$

$3m - 12 - 4m + 11 = -5$

$-m - 1 = -5$

$-m = -4$

$m = 4$ Solution set is $\{4\}$.

3. $\mathbf{1.2(x + 5) = 3(2x - 8) + 23.28}$ Multiply by 100.

$120(x + 5) = 300(2x - 8) + 2328$

$120x + 600 = 600x - 2400 + 2328$

$120x + 600 = 600x - 72$

$600 = 480x - 72$

$672 = 480x$

$x = \dfrac{672}{480} = 1.4$ Solution set is $\{1.4\}$.

4. $\dfrac{\mathbf{2x + 1}}{\mathbf{3}} + \dfrac{\mathbf{1}}{\mathbf{4}} = \dfrac{\mathbf{2x - 1}}{\mathbf{6}}$ Multiply by 12.

$4(2x + 1) + 3 = 2(2x - 1)$

$8x + 4 + 3 = 4x - 2$

$8x + 7 = 4x - 2$

$4x + 7 = -2$

$4x = -9$

$x = -\dfrac{9}{4}$ Solution set is $\left\{-\dfrac{9}{4}\right\}$.

5. $\dfrac{3y-1}{5} - \dfrac{2y+1}{4} = 1$ Multiply by 20.

$$4(3y-1) - 5(2y+1) = 20$$
$$12y - 4 - 10y - 5 = 20$$
$$2y - 9 = 20$$
$$2y = 29$$
$$y = \dfrac{29}{2}$$ Solution set is $\left\{\dfrac{29}{2}\right\}$.

Operations on Polynomials

Addition and Subtraction

To add or subtract polynomials, first use the distributive property as needed to get rid of parentheses and then combine similar terms. Usually the terms of a polynomial are arranged in the order of descending degree in a specified variable. For example:

$$(2x^2 - 6xy + 3y^2) - (x^2 - xy + 2y^2)$$
$$= 2x^2 - 6xy + 3y^2 - x^2 + xy - 2y^2$$
$$= x^2 - 5xy + y^2$$

Multiplication

Multiplication of a monomial by a polynomial of several terms is merely an extension of the distributive property.

$$-2a(3a^2 - 5a + 8) = -6a^3 + 10a^2 - 16a$$

Multiplication of two polynomials of more than one term each is also an extension of the distributive property. It is easier, however, to follow the rule "Multiply each term of one polynomial by each term of the other polynomial and then simplify."

$$(a + b - c)(2a - b + c)$$
$$= a(2a - b + c) + b(2a - b + c) - c(2a - b + c)$$
$$= 2a^2 - ab + ac + 2ab - b^2 + bc - 2ac + bc - c^2$$
$$= 2a^2 + ab - ac - b^2 + 2bc - c^2$$

Multiplication of two binomials is such a common operation that a special procedure has been devised to make it easy to do mentally.

Consider the product of two binomials:

$$(A + B)(C + D)$$

Call A and C the First terms of the binomials.
Call A and D the Outer terms.
Call B and C the Inner terms.
Call B and D the Last terms.
The product can be found by following the acronym FOIL.
For example, to multiply $(2x + 3)(x + 4)$:

> Multiply the First terms: $(2x)(x) = 2x^2$.
> Multiply the Outer terms: $(2x)(4) = 8x$.
> Multiply the Inner terms: $(3)(x) = 3x$.
> Multiply the Last terms: $(3)(4) = 12$.

Since the Outer product and the Inner product are similar terms, combine them and write the answer:

$$2x^2 + 11x + 12$$

Three products occur frequently and deserve special attention:

> Sum and difference binomials: $(A + B)(A - B) = A^2 - B^2$
> Binomial square: $(A \pm B)^2 = A^2 \pm 2AB + B^2$
> Binomial cube: $(A \pm B)^3 = A^3 \pm 3A^2B + 3AB^2 \pm B^3$

PRACTICE EXERCISES

Perform the indicated operations. Express each answer in the order of descending degree in some variable.

1. $(5x + 3xy - 8y) - (y - 6yx + 2x)$

2. $(2x - 3) - [(4x + 7) - (5x - 2)]$

3. $-3ab(4a^2 - 5ab + 2b^2)$

4. $(2x - 3)(4x^2 + 6x + 9)$

5. $(x + 3)(x - 5)$

6. $(3x + 1)(2x + 5)$

SOLUTIONS

1. $(5x + 3xy - 8y) - (y - 6yx + 2x)$
  $= 5x + 3xy - 8y - y + 6yx - 2x$
  $= 3x + 9xy - 9y$
2. $(2x - 3) - [(4x + 7) - (5x - 2)]$
  $= (2x - 3) - [4x + 7 - 5x + 2]$
  $= 2x - 3 - 4x - 7 + 5x - 2$
  $= 3x - 12$
3. $-3ab(4a^2 - 5ab + 2b^2)$
  $= -12a^3b + 15a^2b^2 - 6ab^3$
4. Multiply each term of the second polynomial first by $2x$ and then by -3:
  $(2x - 3)(4x^2 + 6x + 9)$
  $= 8x^3 + 12x^2 + 18x - 12x^2 - 18x - 27$
  $= 8x^3 - 27$
5. $(x + 3)(x - 5)$ Use FOIL.
  $= x^2 - 5x + 3x - 15$ Try not to write this line.
  $= x^2 - 2x - 15$
6. $(3x + 1)(2x + 5)$ Use FOIL. Do the
  $= 6x^2 + 17x + 5$ Outer and Inner mentally.

Factoring

The process of factoring is that of changing an expression from addition or subtraction to multiplication—creating factors. The property underlying all factoring rules is the distributive property:

$$ab + ac = a(b + c)$$

Notice that on the left there is the *sum* of terms, while on the right is the *product* of factors.

If an expression has a *common factor* other than 1 in all of its terms, application of the distributive property serves to factor it. Here are some examples:

- $4ab^2 + 2a^2b = 2ab(2b + a)$ The common factor chosen

- $39x^5y^3 - 26x^7y^2 + 52x^8y^5$
  $= 13x^5y^2(3y - 2x^2 + 4x^3y^3)$

  should be the greatest common factor of the terms. Choose the exponent on each variable to be the smallest exponent on that variable in the expression.

- $-25x^3y^2 - 20x^4y^3 + 15x^5y^4$
  $- 50x^5y^2$
  $= -5x^3y^2(5 + 4xy - 3x^2y^2 + 10x^3)$

  If the first term is negative, choose a negative common factor.

- $(x + 5)(x - 6) + (x + 5)(x - 1)$
  $= (x + 5)[(x - 6) + (x - 1)]$
  $= (x + 5)(2x - 7)$

  The common factor is the binomial $(x + 5)$.

- $pq + 3rq + pm + 3rm$
  $= (pq + pm) + (3rq + 3rm)$
  $= p(q + m) + 3r(q + m)$
  $= (q + m)(p + 3r)$

  The trick is to rearrange and group so that each group has a common factor.

- $8x^2 + 6xy - 12xy - 9y^2$
  $= (8x^2 + 6xy) - (12xy \boxplus 9y^2)$
  $= 2x(4x + 3y) - 3y(4x + 3y)$
  $= (4x + 3y)(2x - 3y)$

  Be very careful of signs.

PRACTICE EXERCISES

Factor completely.
1. $8x^3y^3 - 12x^2y^2$
2. $28a^2b - 14ab^2 + 7ab$
3. $-6a^5b^5 - 8a^4b^4 - 4a^3b^2$
4. $7m^3n^3 + 6$
5. $9x(3x + 2y) - 5y(3x + 2y)$

SOLUTIONS

1. $4x^2y^2(2xy - 3)$
2. $7ab(4a - 2b + 1)$ The 1 is easy to miss but very important.

3. $-2a^3b^2(3a^2b^3 + 4ab^2 + 2)$
4. The terms of the binomial have no common factor other than 1. It is not factorable. A nonfactorable polynomial is said to be prime.
5. $(3x + 2y)(9x - 5y)$

Difference of Squares, and Sum and Difference of Cubes

The following products are the bases for factoring special types of binomials:

$(a + b)(a - b) = a^2 - b^2$ Difference of squares.
$(a + b)(a^2 - ab + b^2) = a^3 + b^3$ Sum of cubes.
$(a - b)(a^2 + ab + b^2) = a^3 - b^3$ Difference of cubes.

Here is an example of each type:
- $25 - 49x^2 = (5 + 7x)(5 - 7x)$ Difference of squares.
- $x^3 + 8 = (x + 2)(x^2 - 2x + 4)$ Sum of cubes. Watch signs carefully.

- $125x^3 - 64y^3$
  $= (5x - 4y)(25x^2 + 20xy + 16y^2)$ Difference of cubes.

Factoring Trinomials of the Type $x^2 + Bx + C$

When two binomials of the type $(x + a)(x + b)$ are multiplied, a trinomial of the type $x^2 + Bx + C$ results, in which C is the product of a and b and B is the sum of a and b. To factor such a trinomial, look for two factors of C whose sum is B.

Examples:
Factor each of the following;

1. $x^2 + 7x + 12$ Search the factors of 12 to find a pair whose sum is 7. The factors of 12 in pairs are 1, 12; 2, 6; and 3, 4. The sum is 7. The factors are $(x + 3)$ $(x + 4)$.

2. $x^2 - 8x + 15$ The factors of 15 are 1 and 15 or 3 and 5. The factors are $(x - 3)(x - 5)$.

3. $x^2 - 3x - 40$ Since the sign of the third term is negative, the signs in the two binomials are different, and the middle term is the sum of two numbers with different signs. Search for a pair of factors so that the difference is 3, and adjust signs. The answer is $(x - 8)(x + 5)$.

4. $x^2 + 5x - 66$ Look for two factors of 66 whose difference is 5: 1, 66; 2, 33; 3, 22; 6, 11. The answer is $(x - 6)(x + 11)$.

Factoring Trinomials of the Type $Ax^2 + Bx + C$

Factoring trinomials of this type frequently involves trial and error, and it is important to be able to multiply binomials quickly by the FOIL method to find the correct combination for the factors.

Examples:

Factor each of the following:

1. $6x^2 + 19x + 10$ There are two possibilities for the first
   $(2x \quad)(3x \quad)$ terms of the binomials. Guessing that
      2   5   the correct choice is $2x$ and $3x$, list the
      5   2   ← factors of 10 and check them, adding
      1   10   the outer and inner products in the
    10   1   hope of getting $19x$. The answer is
                   $(2x + 5)(3x + 2)$.

2. $8x^2 - 2x - 3$ There are two possibilities for the first
   $(\quad 1)(\quad 3)$ terms of the binomials and only one for
    2x   4x   ← the second terms, so begin there, and
    4x   2x   list the factors of $8x$. Since the sign of
     x   8x   the third term is negative, subtract the
    8x   x   outer and inner products in the hope of
                   getting $2x$. Then adjust the signs to make the middle term negative. The answer is $(2x + 1)(4x - 3)$.

An alternative procedure is to multiply the coefficients of the first and third terms and look for a pair of factors of that number whose sum or difference is the second coefficient. Then rewrite the second term using those numbers, group, and factor.

Example 1:
$2x^2 + 5x - 12$

Multiply 2 times 12. Look for factors of 24 whose difference (because the third term is negative) is 5. $24 = 3 \cdot 8$.

$2x^2 + 8x - 3x - 12$
$(2x^2 + 8x) - (3x - 12)$
$2x(x + 4) - 3(x + 4)$

Rewrite $5x$ using 3 and 8.
Group.
Factor out the common factor in each group.

$(x + 4)(2x - 3)$

$(x + 4)$ is a common factor.

Example 2:
$24x^2 - 34x + 5$
$24x^2 - 4x - 30x + 5$
$(24x^2 - 4x) - (30x - 5)$
$4x(6x - 1) - 5(6x - 1)$
$(6x - 1)(4x - 5)$

Multiply 24 times 5. $120 = 4 \cdot 30$.
Rewrite $\sim 34x$ using 4 and 30.
Group.

Perfect Square Trinomials

If the first and last terms of a trinomial are squares, it is worth considering the special form of a perfect square trinomial:

$$a^2 + 2ab + b^2 = (a + b)^2$$

For example, $x^2 + 10x + 25$ is a perfect square trinomial. The correct factorization is $(x + 5)^2$. [The factorization $(x + 5)(x + 5)$ is also correct.]

General Strategy for Factoring a Polynomial
1. If a polynomial has a common factor, *always* factor that first.
2. If there is no common factor (or if the common factor has already been factored out):
   a. factor a binomial according to the rule for the difference of squares or the sum or difference of cubes;
   b. factor a trinomial according to the appropriate rule;
   c. consider factoring by grouping if there are more than three terms.
3. Look for tricks.

Here are some examples:

- $250x^3 + 54y^3$
  $= 2(125x^3 + 27y^3)$
  $= 2(5x + 3y)(25x^2 - 15xy + 9y^2)$

  There is a common factor of 2. A sum of cubes is in the parentheses. Be sure the common factor appears in the answer.

- $-288x^2 + 8y^4$
  $= -8(36x^2 - y^4)$
  $= -8(6x - y^2)(6x + y^2)$

  The common factor is -8. In the parentheses is the difference of squares. By reversing the terms, a correct answer would also be obtained: $8(y^2 - 6x)$ $(y^2 + 6x)$.

- $4x^4 - 5x^2 + 1$
  $= (4x^2 - 1)(x^2 - 1)$
  $= (2x - 1)(2x + 1)(x - 1)(x + 1)$

  There is no common factor. Factor the trinomial. Now each binomial is the difference of squares.

- $9x^2y^2 - 6xy + 1 = (3xy - 1)^2$

  This is a perfect square trinomial.

PRACTICE EXERCISES

Factor completely.

1. $5x^2y^2 - 10xy$

2. $2x^2 - x - 10$

3. $-5x^2 - 15xy + 50y^2$

4. $8a^3 - b^3$

5. $9x^2 + 30xy + 25y^2$

6. $16u^4 - v^4$

SOLUTIONS

1. $5x^2y^2 - 10xy = 5xy(xy - 2)$

2. $2x^2 - x - 10 = (2x \quad)(x \quad)$

	2	5
	5	2←
	10	1
	1	10

The difference of the outer and inner products is x. The answer is $(2x - 5)(x + 2)$.

3. $-5x^2 - 15xy + 50y^2$
   $= -5(x^2 + 3xy - 10y^2)$
   $= -5(x + 5y)(x - 2y)$

   -5 is the common factor.

4. $8a^3 - b^3$
   $= (2a - b)(4a^2 + 2ab + b^2)$ Difference of cubes.

5. $9x^2 + 30xy + 25y^2$
   $= (3x + 5y)^2$ A perfect square trinomial.

6. $16u^4 - v^4$
   $= (4u^2 + v^2)(4u^2 - v^2)$
   $= (4u^2 + v^2)(2u + v)(2u - v)$

   Two layers of difference of squares.

Quadratic Equations

An equation is called *quadratic* if it is equivalent to

$$ax^2 + bx + c = 0, \quad a \neq 0$$

An equation in this form is said to be in *standard* form.

An important rule used in the solution of quadratic equations is sometimes called the Zero Product Principle (ZPP):

If $AB = 0$, then $A = 0$ or $B = 0$.

Example:

$$3x^2 + 5 = 2x$$
$$3x^2 - 2x + 5 = 0 \qquad \text{Standard form.}$$
$$(3x - 5)(x + 1) = 0 \qquad \text{Factor.}$$
$$3x - 5 = 0 \quad \text{or} \quad x + 1 = 0 \qquad \text{ZPP}$$
$$x = \frac{5}{3} \quad \text{or} \qquad x = -1 \quad \text{Solve each linear equation.}$$

The solution set is $\left\{\dfrac{5}{3}, -1\right\}$.

If the coefficient of the linear term in the standard form of the quadratic equation is zero ($b = 0$), it is easier to solve the equation by isolating x^2 and taking the square root of both sides, remembering that there are two solutions to such an equation — one positive and the other negative.

$$2x^2 - 10 = 0$$
$$2x^2 = 10$$
$$x^2 = 5$$
$$x = \pm\sqrt{5}.$$

The solution set is $\{\sqrt{5}, -\sqrt{5}\}$.

The Quadratic Formula

A quadratic equation that cannot be solved by factoring can always be solved by using the quadratic formula:

$$x = \frac{-b \pm \sqrt{b^2 - 4ac}}{2a}$$

Fractions

Algebraic fractions can be reduced by using the Fundamental Principle of Fractions:

$$\frac{a}{b} = \frac{ak}{bk}, \; b, k \neq 0$$

Multiplication and Division

Multiplication and division of fractions are merely extensions of the same procedure. It is important to factor all expressions first and to cancel only common *factors* from any numerator and any denominator. Most errors are made by attempting to cancel *terms*, not factors.

Examples:

1. Reduce: $\dfrac{15x + 7x^2 - 2x^3}{x^2 - 8x + 15}$

$\dfrac{x(5 - x)(3 + 2x)}{(x - 3)(x - 5)}$ Factor.

$\dfrac{-x(3 + 2x)}{(x - 3)}$

The factors $(x - 5)$ and $(5 - x)$ are not equal, but they are opposites. Therefore, when canceled, these factors yield -1.

2. Multiply: $\dfrac{a^3 + a^2b}{5a} \cdot \dfrac{25}{3a + 3b}$

$\dfrac{a^2(a + b)}{5a} \cdot \dfrac{25}{3(a + b)}$ Cancel a, $(a + b)$, and 5.

$\dfrac{a}{1} \cdot \dfrac{5}{3}$

$\dfrac{5a}{3}$

Addition and Subtraction

The same rules for addition and subtraction that are used in arithmetic apply to the addition and subtraction of algebraic fractions.

$$\frac{a}{b} \pm \frac{c}{b} = \frac{a \pm c}{b}, \ b \neq 0$$

Example:

Subtract: $\dfrac{3}{x^2 - 5x + 6} - \dfrac{2}{x^2 - x - 2}$

Factor each denominator: $(x - 2)(x - 3)$
$(x - 2)(x + 1)$

Therefore the LCD is $(x - 2)(x - 3)(x + 1)$. The numerator and denominator of the first fraction must be multiplied by the factor $(x + 1)$, and those in the second fraction by $(x - 3)$,

$$\frac{3(x + 1)}{(x - 2)(x - 3)(x + 1)} - \frac{2(x - 3)}{(x - 2)(x - 3)(x + 1)}$$

$$= \frac{3(x + 1) - 2(x - 3)}{(x - 2)(x - 3)(x + 1)}$$

$$= \frac{3x + 3 - 2x + 6}{(x - 2)(x - 3)(x + 1)}$$

$$= \frac{x + 9}{(x - 2)(x - 3)(x + 1)}$$

PRACTICE EXERCISES

Perform the indicated operations and simplify.

1. $\dfrac{z^2 - z - 6}{z - 6} \cdot \dfrac{z^2 - 6z}{z^2 + 2z - 15}$

2. $\dfrac{a^3 - b^3}{a^2 - b^2} \div \dfrac{a^2 + ab + b^2}{a^2 + ab}$

3. $\dfrac{2}{x + 1} + \dfrac{6}{x - 1}$

4. $\dfrac{2x}{2x^2 - x - 1} - \dfrac{3x}{3x^2 - 5x + 2}$

SOLUTIONS

1. $\dfrac{(z - 3)(z + 2)}{z - 6} \cdot \dfrac{z(z - 6)}{(z + 5)(z - 3)}$

$$= \frac{z + 2}{1} \cdot \frac{z}{z + 5}$$

$$= \frac{z(z + 2)}{z + 5}$$

2. $\dfrac{(a - b)(a^2 + ab + b^2)}{(a - b)(a + b)} \cdot \dfrac{a(a + b)}{a^2 + ab + b^2}$

$$= \frac{1}{1} \cdot \frac{a}{1} = a$$

3. The LCD is $(x + 1)(x - 1)$.

$$\frac{2(x - 1)}{(x + 1)(x - 1)} + \frac{6(x + 1)}{(x + 1)(x - 1)}$$

$$= \frac{2x - 2 + 6x + 6}{(x + 1)(x - 1)}$$

$$= \frac{8x + 4}{(x + 1)(x - 1)}$$

4. Factor each denominator:

$$(2x + 1)(x - 1)$$
$$(3x - 2)(x - 1)$$

The LCD is $(2x + 1)(3x - 2)(x - 1)$.

$$\frac{2x(3x - 2)}{(2x + 1)(3x - 2)(x - 1)} - \frac{3x(2x + 1)}{(2x + 1)(3x - 2)(x - 1)}$$

$$= \frac{2x(3x - 2) - 3x(2x + 1)}{(2x + 1)(3x - 2)(x - 1)}$$

$$= \frac{6x^2 - 4x - 6x^2 - 3x}{(2x + 1)(3x - 2)(x - 1)}$$

$$= \frac{-7x}{(2x + 1)(3x - 2)(x - 1)}$$

Exponents and Radicals

The following laws of exponents apply to all real-number exponents:

1. $x^m \cdot x^n = x^{m+n}$

2. $(x^m)^n = x^{mn}$

3. $(xy)^m = x^m \cdot y^m$

4. $\dfrac{x^m}{x^n} = x^{m-n}$, $x \neq 0$

5. $\left(\dfrac{x}{y}\right)^m = \dfrac{x^m}{y^m}$, $y \neq 0$

6. $x^0 = 1$, $x \neq 0$

7. $x^{-m} = \dfrac{1}{x^m}$, $x \neq 0$

    a. $\left(\dfrac{x}{y}\right)^{-m} = \left(\dfrac{y}{x}\right)^m$, $x, y \neq 0$

    b. $\dfrac{1}{x^{-m}} = x^m$, $x \neq 0$

Here are some examples:

- $x^{5/3} \cdot x^{-2/3} = x^{3/3} = x^1 = x$
- $(x^{3/2})^4 = x^6$
- $(x^3 y)^3 = (x^3)^3 y^3 = x^9 y^3$
- $\dfrac{x^5}{x^6} = x^{-1} = \dfrac{1}{x^1} = \dfrac{1}{x}$
- $\dfrac{a^3 b}{a^{-2} b^2} = a^{3-(-2)} b^{1-2} = a^5 b^{-1} = \dfrac{a^5}{b}$
- $\left(\dfrac{x^2}{y^4}\right)^{-3} = \left(\dfrac{y^4}{x^2}\right)^3 = \dfrac{y^{12}}{x^6}$
- $\dfrac{3^{-2}}{3^{-3}} = 3^{-2-(-3)} = 3^1 = 3$

PRACTICE EXERCISES

Simplify and write without negative exponents.

1. $\dfrac{x^{10}}{x^4}$

2. $\left(\dfrac{4x^3}{y^2}\right)^3$

3. $\left(\dfrac{a^2 b^3}{2a^{-2} b}\right)^{-2}$

4. $\dfrac{2}{a^{-7}}$

SOLUTIONS

1. $\dfrac{x^{10}}{x^4} = x^{10-4} = x^6$

2. $\left(\dfrac{4x^3}{y^2}\right)^3 = \dfrac{4^3 x^9}{y^6} = \dfrac{64x^9}{y^6}$

3. $\left(\dfrac{a^2b^3}{2a^{-2}b}\right)^{-2} = \left(\dfrac{2a^{-2}b}{a^2b^3}\right)^2 = \dfrac{2^2a^{-4}b^2}{a^4b^6}$

$$= 4a^{-4-4}b^{2-6} = 4a^{-8}b^{-4} = \dfrac{4}{a^8b^4}$$

4. $\dfrac{2}{a^{-7}} = 2a^7$

*n*th Root

The definition of an *n*th root is as follows:

a is an *n*th root of *b*   if and only if $a^n = b$.

The symbol for the *n*th root of *b* is $\sqrt[n]{b}$. According to the definition, this is the number that, when raised to the *n*th power, yields *b*. If *n* is even and *b* is negative, the *n*th root of *b* is not a real number. $\sqrt[n]{b} = b^{1/n}$.

Also $b^{m/n} = \sqrt[n]{b^m} = (\sqrt[n]{b})^m$ if all the radicals are defined.

Simplest Radical Form

A radical expression is said to be in simplest radical form (SRF) if the following conditions are met:

1. The radicand has no perfect *n*th-power factors.
2. There are no fractions in the radicand.
3. There are no radicals in a denominator.

Here are some examples of these rules:

- $\sqrt{12}$ is not in simplest radical form because the radicand has $4 = 2^2$ as a factor. To put $\sqrt{12}$ in SRF, factor the radicand so that one factor is the largest square factor of the radicand. Then use the rule of radicals.

$$\sqrt[n]{xy} = (\sqrt[n]{x})(\sqrt[n]{y})   \text{for all defined radicals.}$$

The square factor can be extracted from the radical.

$$\sqrt{12} = \sqrt{4 \cdot 3} = \sqrt{4} \cdot \sqrt{3} = 2\sqrt{3}$$

- $\sqrt[3]{32x^3y^8} = \sqrt[3]{(8x^3y^6)(4y^2)}$ Separate the radicand into
  $$= \sqrt[3]{8x^3y^6} \cdot \sqrt[3]{4y^2}$$ cube and noncube parts.
  $$= 2xy^2\sqrt[3]{4y^2}$$

- $\sqrt{\dfrac{5}{8}}$ is not in SRF because of rule 2 above. To simplify,

  multiply the numerator and denominator by some number in order to make the denominator a perfect square. Then use the rule of radicals

  $$\sqrt[n]{\frac{x}{y}} = \frac{\sqrt[n]{x}}{\sqrt[n]{y}}$$

  for all defined radicals.

  $$\sqrt{\frac{5}{8}} = \sqrt{\frac{10}{16}} = \frac{\sqrt{10}}{\sqrt{16}} = \frac{\sqrt{10}}{4}$$

- $\dfrac{7}{\sqrt[3]{12}}$ is not in SRF because of rule 3 above. To simplify,

  multiply the numerator and denominator by an appropriate radical to make the bottom radicand a perfect nth power.

  $$\frac{7}{\sqrt[3]{12}} = \frac{7\sqrt[3]{18}}{\sqrt[3]{216}} = \frac{7\sqrt[3]{18}}{6}$$ Since $12 = 2 \cdot 2 \cdot 3$, one more 2 and
  two 3's are needed to make a perfect cube. Multiply by $2 \cdot 3 \cdot 3 = 18$ in the radical.

- $\dfrac{2}{3 - \sqrt{2}}$ is not in SRF because of rule 3 above. To simplify, multiply by an appropriate radical expression, sometimes called the *conjugate* of the denominator. In this case, multiply the numerator and denominator by $3 + \sqrt{2}$.

  $$\frac{2(3 + \sqrt{2})}{(3 - \sqrt{2})(3 + \sqrt{2})} = \frac{2(3 + \sqrt{2})}{9 - 2} = \frac{2(3 + \sqrt{2})}{7}$$

PRACTICE EXERCISES

Simplify. Assume all variables are nonnegative.

1. $2^{1/3} \cdot 2^{1/4}$

2. $\dfrac{1}{8^{-4/3}}$

3. $\sqrt{500}$

4. $\sqrt{20x^6}$

5. $\sqrt[4]{x^5 y^7}$

SOLUTIONS

1. $2^{1/3} \cdot 2^{1/4} = 2^{1/3\ +\ 1/4} = 2^{7/12}$

2. $\dfrac{1}{8^{-4/3}} = 8^{4/3} = (\sqrt[3]{8})^4 = 2^4 = 16$

3. $\sqrt{500} = \sqrt{(100 \cdot 5)} = \sqrt{100} \cdot \sqrt{5} = 10\sqrt{5}$

4. $\sqrt{20x^6} = \sqrt{(4x^6)(5)} = \sqrt{4x^6}\sqrt{5} = 2x^3\sqrt{5}$

5. $\sqrt[4]{x^5 y^7} = \sqrt[4]{(x^4 y^4)(xy^3)}$
   $= \sqrt[4]{x^4 y^4} \cdot \sqrt[4]{xy^3} = xy\sqrt[4]{xy^3}$

Operations with Radicals

All of the following discussion assumes that the radicals represent real numbers, that is, there are no even roots of negative numbers.

Any radicals with the same index may be multiplied or divided according to the following rules:

$$\sqrt[n]{x}\ \sqrt[n]{y} = \sqrt[n]{xy} \quad \text{and} \quad \frac{\sqrt[n]{x}}{\sqrt[n]{y}} = \sqrt[n]{\frac{x}{y}}$$

Radicals may be added and subtracted only if both the indices and the radicands are the same.

$$a\sqrt[n]{x} \pm b\sqrt[n]{x} = (a \pm b)\sqrt[n]{x}$$

PRACTICE EXERCISES

Perform the indicated operations and simplify. Assume all variables are nonnegative.

1. $5\sqrt{8} - 3\sqrt{72} + 3\sqrt{50}$

2. $6\sqrt[3]{128m} - 3\sqrt[3]{16m}$

3. $\sqrt{2}(\sqrt{32} - \sqrt{9})$

4. $(\sqrt{7} + \sqrt{3})(\sqrt{7} - \sqrt{3})$

5. $(4\sqrt{5})^2$

SOLUTIONS

1. $5\sqrt{8} - 3\sqrt{72} + 3\sqrt{50}$

Simplify each radical term first.

$5\sqrt{8} = 5\sqrt{4 \cdot 2} \quad 5 \cdot 2\sqrt{2} = 10\sqrt{2}$

$3\sqrt{72} = 3\sqrt{36 \cdot 2} \quad 3 \cdot 6\sqrt{2} = 18\sqrt{2}$

$3\sqrt{50} = 3\sqrt{25 \cdot 2} \quad 3 \cdot 5\sqrt{2} = 15\sqrt{2}$

$10\sqrt{2} - 18\sqrt{2} + 15\sqrt{2} = 7\sqrt{2}$

2. $6\sqrt[3]{128m} - 3\sqrt[3]{16m}$

$6\sqrt[3]{128m} = 6\sqrt[3]{(64)(2m)}$

$\qquad = 6 \cdot 4\sqrt[3]{2m} = 24\sqrt[3]{2m}$

$3\sqrt[3]{16m} = 3\sqrt[3]{(8)(2m)}$

$\qquad = 3 \cdot 2\sqrt[3]{2m} = 6\sqrt[3]{2m}$

$24\sqrt[3]{2m} - 6\sqrt[3]{2m} = 18\sqrt[3]{2m}$

3. $\sqrt{2}(\sqrt{32} - \sqrt{9})$ \qquad Apply the distributive property.

$= \sqrt{64} - \sqrt{18}$

$= 8 - \sqrt{9 \cdot 2} = 8 - 3\sqrt{2}$

4. $(\sqrt{7} + \sqrt{3})(\sqrt{7} - \sqrt{3})$

   $= \sqrt{49} - \sqrt{9}$ This is the same FOIL for binomials.

   $= 7 - 3 = 4$

5. $(4\sqrt{5})^2 = 16\sqrt{25}$ Square each factor.

   $= 16 \cdot 5 = 80$

Graphing

The distance formula and the midpoint formula.

The distance between two points in the plane (x_1, y_1) and (x_2, y_2) can be found by the formula:

$$d = \sqrt{(x_2 - x_1)^2 + (y_2 - y_1)^2}.$$

The coordinates of the midpoint of the segment between these points is:

$$\left(\frac{x_1 + x_2}{2}, \frac{y_1 + y_2}{2} \right).$$

Linear Equations

The graph of every linear equation is a line in the rectangular coordinate system. A linear equation is one that is equivalent to $Ax + By = C$ in which not both A and B are zero. A linear equation written in the form $Ax + By = C$ is in *standard form*.

The two ordered pairs obtained by choosing each variable in turn to be 0 are the coordinates of the intercepts of the graph of a linear equation, that is, by choosing $x = 0$, one obtains the ordered pair $(0, b)$, which identifies the *y*-intercept. The ordered pair $(a, 0)$ identifies the *x*-intercept.

For any two ordered pairs (x_1, y_1) and (x_2, y_2) on the graph of a linear equation, the following is called the *slope formula:*

$$m = \frac{y_2 - y_1}{x_2 - x_1} \quad \text{if } x_1 \neq x_2$$

If $x_1 = x_2$, then the line is vertical, and it has no slope. If $y_1 = y_2$, then the line is horizontal, and it has slope 0. Zero slope is very different from no slope.

A linear equation written in the form

$$y = mx + b$$

is said to be in *slope-intercept* form because the coefficient of x (m) is the slope of the line and b is the y-intercept. This form is most useful for determining the slope of a line, given its equation.

From the slope formula comes the *point-slope* form of the equation of the line:

$$y - y_1 = m(x - x_1)$$

in which m is the slope and (x_1, y_1) is a given fixed point on the line. This form is most useful for determining the equation of a line with certain given characteristics.

PRACTICE EXERCISES

Find the slope of the line:

1. through (2, 3) and (−1, 5)
2. with equation $2x - 3y = 5$

Find the standard form of the equation of the line:

3. through (−8, 1) and (3, 5)

SOLUTIONS

1. $\dfrac{y_2 - y_1}{x_2 - x_1} = \dfrac{5 - 3}{-1 - 2} = \dfrac{2}{-3} = \dfrac{-2}{3}$

2. Solve the equation for y: $y = \dfrac{2}{3}x - \dfrac{5}{3}$.

The slope is the coefficient of x: $\dfrac{2}{3}$.

3. First find the slope: $m = \dfrac{5 - 1}{3 - (-8)} = \dfrac{4}{11}$.

Choose either ordered pair, and plug into the point-slope form:

$$y - 5 = \frac{4}{11}(x - 3)$$
$$11y - 55 = 4(x - 3)$$
$$11y - 55 = 4x - 12$$
$$-4x + 11y = 43$$

or

$$4x - 11y = -43$$

Conic Sections

If an equation of the type

$$Ax^2 + Bxy + Cy^2 + Dx + Ey + F = 0$$

has a graph, the graph is a conic section (or one of its degenerate forms). A *conic section* is either a circle, an ellipse, a parabola, or a hyperbola.

Circle

The equation of the circle in the plane comes from the distance formula:

$$(x - h)^2 + (y - k)^2 = r^2$$

Ellipse

An ellipse is determined by an equation of the type

$$\frac{x^2}{a^2} + \frac{y^2}{b^2} = 1 \quad \text{or} \quad \frac{x^2}{b^2} + \frac{y^2}{a^2} = 1 \qquad$$ Center at the origin. The larger denominator is always a^2.

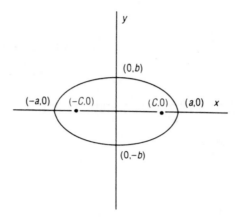

$$c = \sqrt{a^2 - b^2}$$

The points $(c, 0)$ and $(-c, 0)$ are the foci of the ellipse. The points $(a, 0)$ and $(-a, 0)$ are the vertices. The segment between the vertices is the major axis.

If the center is not at the origin, the equation of an ellipse with major axis oriented horizontally is

$$\frac{(x - h)^2}{a^2} + \frac{(y - k)^2}{b^2} = 1$$

If the larger denominator is under the variable y, then the major axis is vertical, and the foci are located c units from the center in a vertical direction.

Parabola
The equation of a parabola is either

$$y - k = a(x - h)^2 \qquad \text{or} \qquad x - h = a(y - k)^2$$

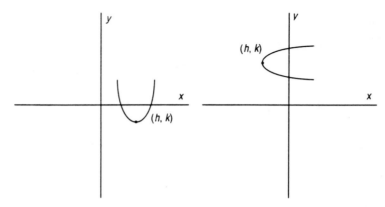

In both cases the vertex is at the point (h, k). In the first case the parabola is oriented vertically, so that there is a maximum or a minimum point, depending on whether a is negative or positive, respectively. In the second case the parabola is oriented horizontally, and there is a point farthest to the left or farthest to the right depending on whether a is positive or negative.

Hyperbola

A hyperbola is defined by an equation of the type

$$\frac{x^2}{a^2} - \frac{y^2}{b^2} = 1 \quad \text{or} \quad \frac{y^2}{a^2} - \frac{x^2}{b^2} = 1$$ Center at the origin. The positive term identifies a^2, not the larger value as with an ellipse.

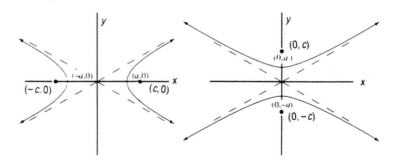

$$c = \sqrt{a^2 + b^2}$$

The points $(c, 0)$ and $(-c, 0)$ are the foci of the hyperbola. The points $(a, 0)$ and $(-a, 0)$ are the vertices. The segment between the vertices is the transverse axis.

If the center is not at the origin [at some point (h, k)], then the equation of a hyperbola with a horizontal transverse axis is

$$\frac{(x-h)^2}{a^2} - \frac{(y-k)^2}{b^2} = 1$$

PRACTICE EXERCISES

Discuss the graph of each equation.

1. $x^2 + y^2 - 10x - 4y - 7 = 0$
2. $x - 2 = (y - 1)^2$
3. $\dfrac{(x-3)^2}{25} + \dfrac{(y+4)^2}{16} = 1$

SOLUTIONS

1. $x^2 + y^2 - 10x - 4y - 7 = 0$ Complete the square in each variable:

$$x^2 - 10x \qquad + y^2 - 4y \qquad = 7$$

Take half of the coefficient of each linear term, square it, and add the result to both sides of the equation.

$$x^2 - 10x + 25 + y^2 - 4y + 4 = 7 + 25 + 4$$

$$(x - 5)^2 + (y - 2)^2 = 36 \quad \text{Standard form.}$$

The graph is a circle with center at (5, 2) and radius 6.

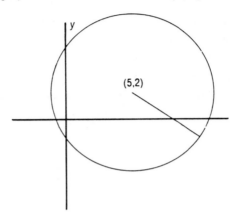

2. Written as $x - 2 = (y - 1)^2$, this equation is the standard form of the equation for a parabola oriented

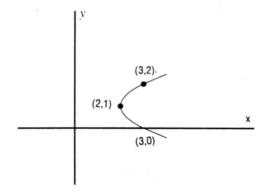

horizontally with a vertex at (2, 1), which happens to be the point farthest to the left. Locating a couple of other points gives the graph.

3. $\dfrac{(x - 3)^2}{25} + \dfrac{(y + 4)^2}{16} = 1$ This is the standard form of an ellipse with major axis horizontal, of length $2a = 10$, minor axis of length $2b = 8$, and center at point $(3, -4)$.

The foci are located $c = \sqrt{5^2 - 4^2} = \sqrt{9} = 3$ units horizontally from the center, $(3 + 3, -4)$ and $(3 - 3, -4)$.

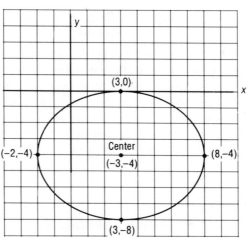

Functions

A function is a set of ordered pairs of real numbers in which no two ordered pairs have the same first component.

An example of a function according to this definition is

$$f = \{(1, 1), (2, 4), (3, 9), (4, 16), (5, 25)\}$$

The equation $f(x) = y$, read as "f of x equals y," is special notation for functions to indicate that the ordered pair, $(x, y,)$ is in the function. In the example, $f(4) = 16$ conveys the same information as $(4, 16) \in f$.

The *domain* of a function is the set of all first components of the ordered pairs in the function. The *range* is the set of all second components of the ordered pairs. In the example:

$$\text{Domain} = \{1, 2, 3, 4, 5\}$$
$$\text{Range} = \{1, 4, 9, 16, 25\}$$

Many times a function is given by the rule that generates the ordered pairs, rather than by the ordered pairs themselves. For example, $g(x) = x^2$. The domain in this case should always be chosen to be the largest set of real numbers for which the defining rule makes sense—no division by 0 or square roots of negative numbers. The range is usually a more difficult question; it can be determined by examining the rule itself or by observing the graph of the function.

PRACTICE EXERCISES

Find the domain and range of each function.

1. $f(x) = x^2 + 1$

2. $g(x) = \dfrac{1}{x}$

3. $h(x) = \sqrt{x - 1}$

SOLUTIONS

1. Domain: R
Range: $\{y \mid y \in R \text{ and } y \geq 1\}$

2. Domain: $\{x \mid x \in R \text{ and } x \neq 0\}$
Range: $\{y \mid y \in R \text{ and } y \neq 0\}$

3. Domain: $\{x \mid x \in R \text{ and } x \geq 1\}$
Range: $\{y \mid y \in R \text{ and } y \geq 0\}$

Systems of Equations

The graphs of two linear equations may intersect at one point, be parallel, or coincide. The solution set of a system of two linear equations in two variables will therefore be either:

1. $\{(a, b)\}$ if the graphs intersect at a single point, (a, b).
2. $\{\ \ \}$ if the graphs are parallel lines.
3. $\{(x, y)|(x, y)$ is any point on the line} if the lines are coincident.

There are several methods of solving systems of two linear equations with two variables.

The elimination or addition method will work for all 2 by 2 systems. In this method, after suitably manipulating the coefficients of one or both of the equations, the equations are added—left side to left side and right side to right side—so that one of the variables is eliminated. The resulting equation is then solved, and the solution is substituted into one of the original equations to find the value of the other variable.

Example:
   Solve:

$$2x + 3y = -1$$
$$3x + y = 2$$

Multiply both sides of the second equation by -3.

$$\begin{aligned} 2x + 3y &= -1 \\ -9x - 3y &= -6 \\ \hline -7x &= -7 \\ x &= 1 \end{aligned}$$ Add both sides of the equations.

Substitute 1 into either equation, and solve.

$$3(1) + y = 2$$
$$3 + y = 2$$
$$y = -1$$

The solution set is $\{(1, -1)\}$.

The substitution method is useful when one of the equations is easy to solve for one of its variables.

Example:
   Solve:

$$5x - 4y = 9$$
$$3 + x = 2y$$

Solve the second equation for x and substitute into the first equation.

$$x = 2y - 3$$
$$5(2y - 3) - 4y = 9$$
$$10y - 15 - 4y = 9$$
$$6y - 15 = 9$$
$$6y = 24$$
$$y = 4 \qquad \text{Substitute 4 into either equation.}$$
$$3 + x = 2(4)$$
$$3 + x = 8$$
$$x = 5$$

The solution set is $\{(5, 4)\}$.

PRACTICE EXERCISES

Solve by any method.
1. $2x + 3y = 10$
     $-3x + 2y = 11$
2. $2x = y + 6$
    $y = 5x$

SOLUTIONS

1. Multiply both sides of the first equation by 3 and the second by 2.

$$3(2x + 3y) = (10)3$$
$$2(-3x + 2y) = (11)2$$
$$6x + 9y = 30$$
$$\underline{-6x + 4y = 22} \quad \text{Add.}$$
$$13y = 52$$
$$y = 4 \qquad \text{Substitute 4 into one of the original equations.}$$

$$2x + 3(4) = 10$$
$$2x + 12 = 10$$
$$2x = -2$$
$$x = -1$$

The solution set is $\{(-1, 4)\}$.

2. Use the substitution method. Replace y in the first equation by $5x$ from the second.

$$2x = y + 6$$
$$y = 5x$$
$$2x = 5x + 6$$
$$-3x = 6$$
$$x = -2 \qquad \text{Substitute } -2 \text{ into the equation}$$
$$y = 5(-2) \qquad \text{used to substitute.}$$
$$y = -10$$

The solution set is $\{(-2, -10)\}$.

Exponential and Logarithmic Functions

An *exponential function* is any function of the type

$$f(x) = a^x \quad \text{for any positive number } a, \quad a \neq 1.$$

The following is a definition of a *logarithmic function:*

$$y = \log_a x \quad \text{if and only if} \quad x = a^y.$$

Four fundamental properties of logarithms are easily derived from the definition given above:

1. $\log_a(xy) = \log_a x + \log_a y$ The logarithm of a product is the sum of the logarithms.

2. $\log_a\left(\dfrac{x}{y}\right) = \log_a x - \log_a y$ The logarithm of a quotient is the difference of the logarithms.

3. $\log_a x^n = n \log_a x$ The logarithm of a power is that power multiplied by the logarithm.

4. $\log_a a^x = x$ and $a^{\log_a x} = x$.

When no base is indicated, the base is understood to be 10. Base 10 logarithms are called common logs.

PRACTICE EXERCISES

1. Write as a logarithmic equation:

$$8^{-(1/3)} = \frac{1}{2}$$

2. Write as an exponential equation:

$$\log_{1/4} 16 = -2$$

Evaluate.

3. $\log_3 \dfrac{1}{9}$

4. $\log_3 \sqrt{3^5}$

5. $\log_3 27^{1/2}$

Solve.

6. $\log_x 125 = -3$

7. $\log_x 4 = 1$

8. $\log_5 x = 0$

SOLUTIONS

1. $\log_8 \dfrac{1}{2} = -\dfrac{1}{3}$

2. $\left(\dfrac{1}{4}\right)^{-2} = 16$

3. $\log_3 \dfrac{1}{9} = x$

$3^x = \dfrac{1}{9} = 9^{-1} = (3^2)^{-1} = 3^{-2}$ So $x = -2$.

4. $\log_3 \sqrt{3^5} = x$

$3^x = \sqrt{3^5} = (3^5)^{1/2} = 3^{5/2}$ So $x = \dfrac{5}{2}$.

5. $\log_3 27^{1/2} = x$

$3^x = 27^{1/2} = (3^3)^{1/2} = 3^{3/2}$ So $x = \dfrac{3}{2}$.

6. $\log_x 125 = -3$ Write the equation in exponential form.

$x^{-3} = 125$ Raise both sides to the $-\frac{1}{3}$ power.

$x = 125^{-(1/3)}$

$= \sqrt[3]{\dfrac{1}{125}} = \dfrac{1}{5}$

7. $\log_x 4 = 1$ $x^1 = 4$ A rule is $\log_b b = 1$. The
$\qquad\qquad\quad\; x = 4$ logarithm of the base is always 1.

8. $\log_5 x = 0$ $5^0 = x$ A rule is $\log_b 1 = 0$. The
$\qquad\qquad\quad\; x = 1$ logarithm of 1 in any base is 0.

The Binomial Theorem

The expression $n!$ (read as "n factorial") is defined as follows:

$$n! = n(n - 1)(n - 2)(n - 3) \cdot \cdots \cdot 2 \cdot 1$$
$$1! = 1$$
$$0! = 1$$

Factorials allow easy counting of combinations.
The number of combinations of n things taken r at a time is

$$_nC_r = \frac{n!}{r!(n - r)!}$$

$$\left(_nC_r = C_{n,r} = \binom{n}{r} \right)$$

For example, the number of different combinations of 20 books on a shelf that will hold 8 books is

$$_{20}C_8 = \frac{20!}{8!12!}$$
$$= 125{,}970$$

The combination numbers turn out to be useful in the formula to raise a binomial to a power. This formula is known as the Binomial Theorem.

$$(a + b)^n = {_nC_0}a^n + {_nC_1}a^{n-1}b^1 + {_nC_2}a^{n-2}b^2 + \cdots$$
$$+ {_nC_r}a^{n-r}b^r + \cdots + {_nC_n}b^n$$

The coefficients of the terms in the Binomial Theorem are found in the nth row of Pascal's triangle, an array of numbers in which each entry other than the 1 at the end of each row is found by adding the two numbers immediately above it.

1	Row 0
1 1	Row 1
PASCAL'S 1 2 1	Row 2
TRIANGLE 1 3 3 1	
1 4 6 4 1	
1 5 10 10 5 1	
1 6 15 20 15 6 1	

Using Pascal's triangle, we can easily write the expansion of

$$(x + y)^6$$

as follows:

$$(x + y)^6 = 1x^6 + 6x^5y + 15x^4y^2 + 20x^3y^3 + 15x^2y^4 + 6xy^5 + 1y^6$$

PRACTICE EXERCISES

Evaluate.

1. $7!$

2. $_{10}C_4$

SOLUTIONS

1. $7! = 7 \cdot 6 \cdot 5 \cdot 4 \cdot 3 \cdot 2 \cdot 1 = 5040$

2. $_{10}C_4 = \dfrac{10!}{4!(10 - 4)!}$

$\qquad = \dfrac{10!}{4!6!}$ 　　　　Cancel 6!.

$\qquad = \dfrac{10 \cdot 9 \cdot 8 \cdot 7}{4 \cdot 3 \cdot 2 \cdot 1}$ 　　　Cancel common factors.

$\qquad = 10 \cdot 3 \cdot 1 \cdot 7 = 210$

Complex Numbers

A complex number is any number in the form $a + bi$, in which a and b are real numbers and $i = \sqrt{-1}$.

$$a + bi = c + di \quad \text{if and only if} \quad a = c \text{ and } b = d$$

The following are the definitions of the operations on complex numbers:

- *Absolute value:* $|a + bi| = \sqrt{a^2 + b^2}$ (Note that i is not used in the radicand.) The absolute value of a complex number is called its modulus.
- *Conjugate:* The conjugate of $a + bi$ is $a - bi$. (Change the sign of the imaginary part.)
- *Addition:* $(a + bi) + (c + di) = (a + c) + (b + d)i$ (Add the real parts and add the imaginary parts separately.)
- *Subtraction:* $(a + bi) - (c + di) = (a - c) + (b - d)i$ (Subtract the real parts and subtract the imaginary parts.)
- *Multiplication:* $(a + bi)(c + di) = (ac - bd) + (ad + bc)i$ (Rather than use the definition, it is common to treat the complex numbers like binomials and multiply by the FOIL method.)
- *Division:* $\dfrac{a + bi}{c + di} = \dfrac{(a + bi)(c - di)}{(c + di)(c - di)}$ (Multiply the numerator and denominator by the conjugate of the denominator.)

PRACTICE EXERCISES

Perform the indicated operations. Express answers in the standard form, $a + bi$.

1. $\sqrt{-125}$
2. $\sqrt{-9} \cdot \sqrt{-36}$
3. $(-3 + 2i) + (4 + 5i)$
4. $(-3 - 4i) - (-1 - i)$
5. $2i(4 - 3i)$
6. $\dfrac{1 + i}{2 - i}$

SOLUTIONS

1. $\sqrt{-125} = \sqrt{(-1)(25)(5)} = \sqrt{-1} \cdot \sqrt{25} \cdot \sqrt{5}$
   $= i \cdot 5 \cdot \sqrt{5} = 5i \sqrt{5}$
2. $\sqrt{-9} \cdot \sqrt{-36} = (3i)(6i) = 18i^2 = 18(-1) = -18$
   (The rule from algebra, $\sqrt{ab} = \sqrt{a} \sqrt{b}$, does not apply to this problem because the factors are not real numbers.)
3. $(-3 + 2i) + (4 + 5i) = 1 + 7i$

4. $(-3 - 4i) - (-1 - i) = -2 - 3i$

5. $2i(4 - 3i) = 8i - 6i^2 = 8i - 6(-1)$
$\qquad\qquad\quad = 8i + 6 = 6 + 8i$

6. $\dfrac{1+i}{2-i} = \dfrac{(1+i)(2+i)}{(2-i)(2+i)} = \dfrac{2+i+2i+i^2}{4-i^2} =$

$\dfrac{1+3i}{4-(-1)} = \dfrac{1+3i}{5}$

GEOMETRY
Angles

An *angle* is the union of two rays with a common endpoint.

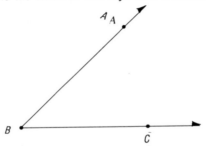

The angle shown above consists of ray *BA* and ray *BC*. The common endpoint *B* is called the *vertex*.

Two angles that have the same measure are called *congruent*.

Angles can be classified according to their measure.

- The measure of an *acute angle* is between 0° and 90°.
- A *right angle* measures 90°.
- The measure of an *obtuse angle* is between 90° and 180°.
- A *straight angle* measures 180°.

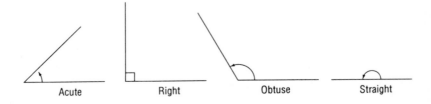

Acute   Right   Obtuse   Straight

Two angles are called *adjacent* if they have a common side and the interiors of the angles do not intersect.

A segment, a ray, or a line that contains the vertex of an angle such that it forms two congruent adjacent angles with the sides of the angle is called an *angle bisector.*

There are always two pairs of *vertical angles* formed by the intersection of two lines. In the figure shown below, angles *AEB* and *DEC* are vertical angles, and angles *AED* and *BEC* are also vertical angles.

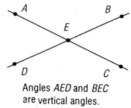

Angles *AED* and *BEC*
are vertical angles.

Two angles are *complementary* if their sum is 90°. Two angles are *supplementary* if their sum is 180°. Notice that both definitions specify two angles. These definitions do not apply to three or more angles.

Complementary   Supplementary

Perpendicular lines are two lines that intersect to form a right angle. Of course, if there is one right angle, then there must be four of them.

If two parallel lines are intersected by a third line (called the *transversal*), then the following angles are congruent:

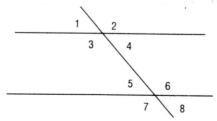

Corresponding angles: 1 and 5, 2 and 6, 3 and 7, 4 and 8
Alternate interior angles: 3 and 6, 4 and 5
Alternate exterior angles: 1 and 8, 2 and 7
Vertical angles: 1 and 4, 2 and 3, 5 and 8, 6 and 7
Interior angles on the same side of the transversal are supplementary. Angles 4 and 6 are supplementary, and 3 and 5 are supplementary. Exterior angles on the same side of the transversal are also supplementary: 2 and 8, 1 and 7.

Polygons

Triangles

A *triangle* is a polygon with three sides. Triangles may be classified according to the lengths of their sides.

- An *equilateral triangle* has three congruent sides.
- An *isosceles triangle* has at least two congruent sides.
- A *scalene triangle* has no two congruent sides.

A triangle may also be classified according to the measure of its angles.

- An *equiangular triangle* has three congruent angles.
- An *acute triangle* has all acute angles.
- A *right triangle* has one right angle.
- An *obtuse triangle* has one obtuse angle.

An *altitude* of a triangle is a segment from a vertex perpendicular to the opposite side (the base). Each triangle has three altitudes, and the lines that contain all three intersect at a point. The area of any triangle is $\frac{1}{2}$ of the product of the length of an altitude and the length of the base to that altitude:

$$A = \frac{1}{2}bh$$

The following are important properties of triangles:

1. Base angles of an isosceles triangle are congruent. (If two sides are the same length, then the angles opposite those sides are congruent.)

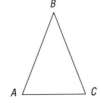

If $AB = BC$, then $m\angle A = m\angle C$.

2. The sum of the measures of the angles of any triangle is 180°. Therefore the sum of the measures of the angles of an *n*-sided polygon is $(n - 2)(180°)$.
3. The angles of an equilateral triangle are congruent. They each have measure 60°.
4. The sum of the exterior angles of a triangle (taking one at each vertex) is 360°. An exterior angle is formed by extending one side of a triangle through the vertex.
5. If the sides of a right triangle have lengths a, b, and c (c is the length of the hypotenuse), then these numbers satisfy the Pythagorean Theorem:

$$a^2 + b^2 = c^2$$

Quadrilaterals

A *quadrilateral* is a polygon with four sides. The following are definitions of certain quadrilaterals with special characteristics:

- A *trapezoid* has one pair of opposite sides parallel.

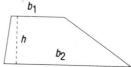

- A *parallelogram* has both pairs of opposite sides parallel.

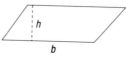

- A *rectangle* is a parallelogram with a right angle (and, hence, four right angles).

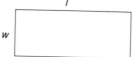

- A *square* is an equilateral rectangle or a regular quadrilateral.

- A *rhombus* is an equilateral parallelogram.

Areas of Quadrilaterals

The following are area formulas for the quadrilaterals defined above:

Trapezoid: $A = \dfrac{1}{2}h(b_1 + b_2)$

Parallelogram: $A = hb$

Rectangle: $A = lw$

Square: $A = s^2$

Rhombus: $A = hb = \dfrac{1}{2}$ times (product of diagonals)

Circles

A *circle* is the set of points in a plane that are a given fixed distance from a given point. The given distance is called the *radius* and the fixed point is the *center*. A segment whose endpoints are on the circle is called a *chord*. A chord that also contains the center is a *diameter* (the longest chord). A line that contains a chord of a circle is a *secant line*. A line that contains only one point of a circle is a *tangent line*.

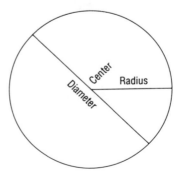

The length around a circle is called its *circumference*. The formula for the circumference is

$C = \pi d$ (π times diameter)   or $C = 2\pi r$ (2π times radius)

The area formula for a circle is

$$A = \pi r^2$$

A *central angle* is an angle with its vertex at the center of a circle. The measure of a central angle is the same as the measure of its intercepted arc. Thus there are 360° of arc in a circle.

An *inscribed angle* is an angle formed by two chords of a circle; its vertex is on the circle. The measure of an inscribed angle is one-half the measure of its intercepted arc.

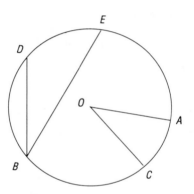

Angle *AOC* is a central angle.
Angle *DBE* is inscribed.

TRIGONOMETRY
Angles

An angle is in standard position if its initial side is the positive *x*-axis and the vertex is at the origin. If the terminal side of the angle then lies in quadrant I, the angle is called a quadrant I angle; if it lies in quadrant II, it is called a quadrant II angle; etc. A positive angle is measured counterclockwise, and a negative angle is measured clockwise from the positive *x*-axis.

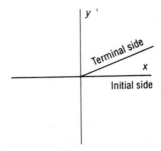

Standard Position

There are several measurement systems for angles. Two of them will be reviewed here.

1. Degree-minute-second: 1 degree $= 1° = \dfrac{1}{360}$ of a revolution

$$1 \text{ minute} = 1' = \dfrac{1}{60}°$$

$$1 \text{ second} = 1'' = \dfrac{1}{60}'$$

2. Radians: 1 radian is the central angle subtended by an arc equal in length to the radius of the circle.

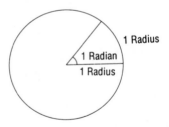

2π radians $= 360°$ (The equal sign is used here to mean that the two numbers measure the same angle.)

Therefore:

$$\pi \text{ radians} = 180°$$
$$\dfrac{\pi}{2} \text{ radians} = 90°$$
$$\dfrac{\pi}{3} \text{ radians} = 60°$$

Most angles of interest are multiples of these five, so these should be memorized.

$$\frac{\pi}{4} \text{ radians} = 45°$$

$$\frac{\pi}{6} \text{ radians} = 30°$$

Generally, to convert an angle measurement from degrees to radians, multiply the number of degrees by $\frac{\pi}{180}$. The measurement of an angle in radians is commonly expressed in terms of π. ($1° = \frac{\pi}{180}$ radians.)

To convert an angle measurement from radians to degrees, multiply the number of radians by $\frac{180}{\pi}$. The π normally cancels. (1 radian $= \frac{180}{\pi}$.)

If two different angles in standard position have the same terminal side, the angles are called *coterminal*. Coterminal angles can be found by adding or subtracting multiples of 360° or 2π to or from the original angle.

The acute angle formed by the terminal side of the angle and the nearer portion of the *x*-axis is called the *reference* angle.

PRACTICE EXERCISES

Convert from degree measure to radian measure.

1. 210°

2. −540°

Convert from radian measure to degree measure.

3. $\dfrac{5\pi}{4}$

4. $\dfrac{7\pi}{9}$

Find: a. The smallest positive angle that is coterminal with the given angle
     b. The reference angle

5. 478°

6. −815°

SOLUTIONS

1. $210\left(\dfrac{\pi}{180}\right) = \dfrac{7\pi}{6}$

2. $-540\left(\dfrac{\pi}{180}\right) = -3\pi$

3. $\dfrac{5\pi}{4}\left(\dfrac{180}{\pi}\right) = 225$

4. $\dfrac{7\pi}{9}\left(\dfrac{180}{\pi}\right) = 140$

5. a. $478 - 360 = 118$
   $118°$ is in quad. II.
   b. $180 - 118 = 62$

6. a. $-815 + 3(360) = -815 + 1080 = 265$
   $265°$ is in quad. III.
   b. $265 - 180 = 85$

Definitions of Trigonometric Functions

Choose a point, (x, y), on the terminal side of an angle, θ, in standard position. The distance from the origin is $r = \sqrt{x^2 + y^2}$

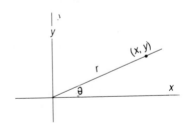

$\sin \theta = \dfrac{y}{r}$ $\qquad\qquad\qquad\qquad\qquad$ Sine

$\cos \theta = \dfrac{x}{r}$ $\qquad\qquad\qquad\qquad\qquad$ Cosine

$\tan \theta = \dfrac{y}{x},\quad x \neq 0,\ \theta \neq 90° \pm 180n°$ $\qquad$ Tangent

$\csc \theta = \dfrac{r}{y},\quad y \neq 0,\ \theta \neq \pm 180n°$ $\qquad$ Cosecant

$$\sec \theta = \frac{r}{x}, \quad x \neq 0, \ \theta \neq 90° \pm 180n° \qquad \text{Secant}$$

$$\cot \theta = \frac{x}{y}, \quad y \neq 0, \ \theta \neq \pm 180n° \qquad \text{Cotangent}$$

In each case above, $n = 0, 1, 2, \ldots$

This information should be memorized for the four quadrants:

I: All positive.
II: Sine and cosecant positive, others are negative.
III: Tangent and cotangent positive, others negative.
IV: Cosine and secant positive, others negative.

(ASTC is a helpful mnemonic aid.)

A function of any angle is equal to $\pm$ the same function of the reference angle. The sign of the function value is determined by ASTC.

PRACTICE EXERCISES

Name the quadrant in which the angle θ must lie for the following to be true:
1. $\sin \theta > 0$ and $\tan \theta < 0$
2. $\cos \theta < 0$ and $\csc > 0$
3. $\cot \theta > 0$ and $\sec \theta < 0$
4. $\sec \theta > 0$ and $\sin \theta < 0$

SOLUTIONS

1. ASTC indicates that the sine is positive in quads. I and II, while the tangent is negative in quads. II and IV. Both are true only in quad. II.
2. $\cos \theta < 0$ in II and III
   $\csc \theta >$ in I and II
   Both are true only in quad. II.
3. $\cot \theta > 0$ in I and III
   $\sec \theta < 0$ in II and III
   Both are true only in quad. III.
4. $\sec \theta > 0$ in I and IV
   $\sin \theta < 0$ in III and IV
   Both are true only in quad. IV.

Identities

An *identity* is an equation that is true for all cases for which the functions involved are defined. There are many identities in trigonometry, and the following list should be memorized:

- *Reciprocal identities*

$$\sin x = \frac{1}{\csc x} \qquad \csc x = \frac{1}{\sin x}$$

$$\cos x = \frac{1}{\sec x} \qquad \sec x = \frac{1}{\cos x}$$

$$\tan x = \frac{1}{\cot x} \qquad \cot x = \frac{1}{\tan x}$$

- *Quotient identities*

$$\tan x = \frac{\sin x}{\cos x} \qquad \cot x = \frac{\cos y}{\sin x}$$

- *Pythagorean identities*

$$\sin^2 x + \cos^2 x = 1 \qquad \text{Note that } \sin^2 x = (\sin x)^2.$$
$$\tan^2 x + 1 = \sec^2 x$$
$$1 + \cot^2 x = \csc^2 x$$

- *Sum and difference identities*

$$\cos (A \pm B) = \cos A \cos B \mp \sin A \sin B$$
$$\sin (A \pm B) = \sin A \cos B \pm \sin B \cos A$$
$$\tan (A \pm B) = \frac{\tan A \pm \tan B}{1 \mp \tan A \tan B}$$

- *Double-angle identities*

$$\sin 2A = 2 \sin A \cos A$$
$$\cos 2A = \cos^2 A - \sin^2 A = 2 \cos^2 A - 1 = 1 - 2 \sin^2 A$$
$$\tan 2A = \frac{2 \tan A}{1 - \tan^2 A}$$

- *Half-angle identities*

$$\sin \frac{A}{2} = \pm \sqrt{\frac{1 - \cos A}{2}}$$

$$\cos \frac{A}{2} = \pm \sqrt{\frac{1 + \cos A}{2}}$$

$$\tan \frac{A}{2} = \pm \sqrt{\frac{1 - \cos A}{1 + \cos A}} = \frac{\sin A}{1 + \cos A} = \frac{1 - \cos A}{\sin A}$$

PRACTICE EXERCISES

Use the identities above to find each function value.

1. $\cos 15°$

2. $\tan 75°$

3. $\sin 195°$

4. $\cos \frac{\pi}{8}$

SOLUTIONS

1. Find two angles whose difference is 15° (45° and 30° will do).

$$\begin{aligned}
\textbf{cos 15°} &= \cos (45 - 30)° \\
&= \cos 45 \cos 30 + \sin 45 \sin 30 \\
&= \left(\frac{\sqrt{2}}{2}\right)\left(\frac{\sqrt{3}}{2}\right) + \left(\frac{\sqrt{2}}{2}\right)\left(\frac{1}{2}\right) \\
&= \frac{\sqrt{6}}{4} + \frac{\sqrt{2}}{4} \\
&= \frac{\sqrt{6} + \sqrt{2}}{4}
\end{aligned}$$

2. Several choices are possible. Choose the half-angle tangent formula.

$$\mathbf{tan\ 75°} = \tan \frac{1}{2}(150°) = \frac{\sin 150°}{1 + \cos 150°}$$

$$= \frac{\dfrac{1}{2}}{1 + \dfrac{-\sqrt{3}}{2}}$$

$$= \frac{1}{2 - \sqrt{3}} = 2 + \sqrt{3}$$

3. $\mathbf{sin\ 195°} = \sin (150 + 45)°$

$\qquad\qquad = \sin 150 \cos 45 + \sin 45 \cos 150$

$$= \left(\frac{1}{2}\right)\left(\frac{\sqrt{2}}{2}\right) + \left(\frac{\sqrt{2}}{2}\right)\left(\frac{-\sqrt{3}}{2}\right)$$

$$= \frac{\sqrt{2}}{4} + \frac{-\sqrt{6}}{4} = \frac{\sqrt{2} - \sqrt{6}}{4}$$

4. $\mathbf{cos\ \dfrac{\pi}{8}} = \cos \dfrac{\left(\dfrac{\pi}{4}\right)}{2} = \sqrt{\dfrac{1 + \cos\left(\dfrac{\pi}{4}\right)}{2}}$

$$= \pm\sqrt{\dfrac{1 + \dfrac{\sqrt{2}}{2}}{2}}$$

$$= \pm\sqrt{\dfrac{2 + \sqrt{2}}{4}} \qquad \text{Choose the}$$

positive sign because

$\dfrac{\pi}{8}$ is in quad. I.

$$= \frac{\sqrt{2 + \sqrt{2}}}{2}$$

4

PREPARING FOR THE READING TEST

DESCRIPTION OF THE TEST

The ACT Reading Test contains four kinds of reading:

1. *Prose Fiction*—a passage drawn from a novel or short story.
2. *Humanities*—a selection from a work on art, music, architecture, theater, or dance.
3. *Social Sciences*—an excerpt from a work on sociology, psychology, economics, anthropology, history, government, political science, or another related field.
4. *Natural Sciences*—a sample of writing drawn from biology, chemistry, physics, ecology, astronomy, meteorology, or other scientific fields.

Each passage is about 750 words, or roughly two pages of a typical book. The passages are arranged by level of reading difficulty, with the easiest passage first and the hardest, last. On a given ACT, the prose fiction passage may be first, second, third, or fourth. The same holds true for the other passages. The order is not announced ahead of time.

Each passage is followed by ten multiple-choice questions—40 questions in all. Some of the questions test what the passages say explicitly.

Many more of the questions, however, ask what the passage implies or suggests.

The ten questions about each passage are arranged according to level of difficulty, the easiest question being first, and the hardest last. The focus of the questions is objective—on what the author of the passage thinks and says—not on what readers believe the author ought to think or say.

TIPS

You've probably observed that people cope with tests in a variety of ways. In fact, the manner in which you take a test is as personal and individual as your fingerprints.

Considering the variety of test-taking styles, it would take a very long list to describe every tactic that has helped other students taking the ACT Reading Test. What works for them may not work for you and vice versa. Nevertheless, some tactics help everyone, regardless of ability or test-taking style. Many of the following tactics can improve your score. Give them an honest chance to work for you.

1. **Pace yourself.** You have less than nine minutes per passage. If you spend five minutes reading a passage, you still have four minutes left to answer ten questions, or almost 25 seconds per question.

2. **Understand the test directions.** Know what the directions say before you walk into the exam room. They will be similar to the following:

   DIRECTIONS: There are four passages in this test. Each passage is followed by several questions. After reading a passage, choose the best answer to each question and blacken the corresponding oval on your answer sheet. You may refer to the passages as often as necessary.

3. **Decide on a reading technique.** On the ACT, different approaches to a reading passage carry different advantages and disadvantages.

Option A. *Read the passage carefully from start to finish.* Don't try to remember every detail, however, because you could get bogged down in material that's irrelevant to the questions.

Option B. *Skim the passage for its general idea.* Read faster than you normally would and once you've caught the drift of the passage, go right to the questions. Refer to the passage as you answer the questions.

Option C. *Skim the passage to get its general meaning; then go back and read it more thoroughly.* Two readings enable you to grasp the passage better than if you read it only once. Then proceed to the questions.

Which option is best—A, B, or C? Only you can decide:

Option A takes longer at the start, but allows you to make up the time later.

Option B saves time and keeps your mind free of needless details.

Option C requires the most time but offers you the firmest grip on the passage.

4. **Concentrate on paragraph openings and closings.** When reading quickly for the gist of a passage, focus on the openings and closings. Skip the material in between until you need the details to answer specific questions.

5. **Use paragraphs as clues to help you understand the passage.** Paragraphs are used to build the main idea of a passage, and each paragraph in some way reinforces the author's point.

6. **Decide whether to use an underlining technique.**

Option A. *Underline key ideas and phrases.* Highlight the important points of a reading passage or put a checkmark next to them in the margin.

Option B. *Don't underline anything.* You don't know what's important and the time you spend underlining might be better spent rereading the passage or studying the questions.

Option C. *Underline answers only.* After you have read the questions and returned to the passage, identify tentative answers to the questions.

7. **Decide when to read the questions.**

Option A. *Study the questions before you read the passage.* When you know the questions beforehand, you can read a passage more purposefully. You can look for the main idea of the passage, seek out specific details, and locate the meaning of a phrase or idea.

Option B. *Study the questions after you read the passage.* With the passage fresh in your mind, you can probably answer two or three questions immediately. Direct your second reading of the passage to the remaining questions.

Option C. *Read the questions one by one, not as a group.* After reading the passage, start with the first question and answer it by referring to the passage. Then go on to the next question. Whatever you do, don't even think of answering a question before reading the passage from start to finish.

8. **Suspend your prior knowledge.** Occasionally, a reading passage may deal with a subject you know about. Read both passage and questions with an open mind.
9. **Identify each question by type.** Usually the wording of a question will tell you whether you can find the answer by *referring* directly to the passage or by using your *reasoning* powers. You alone know which question types you customarily handle with ease and which give you trouble and will require more time.
10. **Answer general questions before detail questions.** A reader with a good understanding of the whole passage can often answer general questions without rereading a word. Get the easier questions out of the way before tackling the more time-consuming ones.
11. **Do the easy passages first.** The passages on the ACT are supposed to be arranged according to difficulty, but you may be more knowledgeable about specific subjects. If you're equally good in everything, then stick with the order of the test.
12. **Stay alert for "switchbacks."** These are the words and phrases frequently used to alert you to shifts in thought. The most common switchback word is *but.* Others include *although, however, nevertheless, on the other hand, even though, while, in spite of, despite, regardless of.*

PROSE FICTION
Passages

One passage of prose fiction appears on the ACT. Before you read a word, you'll probably recognize its distinctive look: quotation marks, several short lines of text, frequently indented sentences. Even without dialogue, though, you'll know that it's fiction before you've read more than a few lines. It will be a piece of a story, perhaps describing a place, portraying a person, or showing characters in action.

A typical prose fiction passage consists of both dialogue and narration. Besides questions about *setting, character, mood,* and *use of language,* you may also be asked to *specify the main point* of the passage, *make comparisons, draw inferences,* and *arrange events in the order in which they occurred.*

HUMANITIES
Passages

The humanities passage on the ACT relates to such creative and cultural disciplines as history, art, music, architecture, theater, and dance. The passage may discuss Impressionist painting or the origins of jazz. It could be a portrait of Sir Laurence Olivier, an analysis of current British literature, or a critique of modern dance—almost any sort of passage on a multitude of topics.

A passage about a cultural matter will sometimes consist only of *facts,* but a passage that after a quick reading may seem factual and objective may actually be full of opinions. Frequently on the ACT you are asked to distinguish between fact and opinion.

The ACT humanities passage may be about fine or performing arts or it may be about architecture. You may get a sample of cultural history, the history of theater, for example. Or you might find a piece of literary history.

Ten sample questions and answer explanations follow this approximately 750-word humanities passage about the difficulties of clearly defining musical styles like rock, pop, and rock 'n' roll.

The distinction between rock and rock 'n' roll was firmly established among rock fans, musicians, and critics by 1967 and was taken for granted in early issues of *Rolling Stone*. Rock is generally understood as popular
5   music closest to, but superseding, rock and roll; it is sometimes contrasted with "pop," which is regarded as more commercial in its aims. Jon Landau reflects common wisdom when he says that "The Beatles, the Stones and Dylan were the first inductees to rock's (as opposed
10   to rock and roll's) pantheon."

Yet critical efforts to delineate rock as a distinct musical genre have been few and have tended to emphasize its cultural impact. Just as Duke Ellington disdained the label "jazz" (he preferred the more inclusive phrase
15   "Negro music"), critic Robert Christgau proposes "semi-popular music" as a better phrase than "rock." It acknowledges that genuine mass popularity, as measured by record sales, often eludes influential and critically acclaimed musicians. In 1973, Christgau proposed
20   that rock was "all music derived primarily from the energy and influence of the Beatles—and maybe Bob Dylan, and maybe you should stick pretensions in there someplace." But "influence" covers a multitude of sins. It may seem that their status as songwriters is foremost, but
25   their position as *recording* artists has equal relevance to their status as founders of rock.

Bob Dylan's supposedly commercial sellout of 1965, when he began recording and then playing concerts with an amplified band, is a key event in the break from rock
30   and roll. His self-titled debut album (recorded in 1961) features only two original compositions; the other eleven are blues and traditional folk tunes. Dylan was marketed as a "folk" musician, and subsequently as a protest singer. Critics and fans recognized that the folk and
35   blues traditions predated rock and roll and so regarded them as purer and less commercial than rock and roll. (Muddy Waters, master of the electrified Chicago blues, was also marketed as a folk musician at this time; witness albums with such titles as *Folk Singer* and *The Real*

40   *Folk Blues.*) The audience for this music typically dis-
     dained rock and roll and regarded Dylan's decision to
     electrify as an abandonment of "genuine" music. So they
     seem at a loss to comprehend the *aesthetic* motivation
     for his change of direction. At his second electric con-
45   cert, at Forest Hills, one fan taunted him with the shout-
     ed question, "Where's Ringo?" In the same vein, a
     reviewer remarked that fans who came for "protest
     songs. . . got the Beatles, instead." The Beatles still rep-
     resented rock and roll, although not for very much
50   longer. Dylan represented something else, supposedly
     more artistic even if *musically* simpler. "Folk records"
     were not perceived as commercial and mass-marketed
     popular music. The irony here is that Dylan was aggres-
     sively marketed by Columbia Records, and "Blowin' in
55   the Wind" had been a major hit for Peter, Paul and Mary
     in 1963.

          It is difficult, today, to grasp the anger that was direct-
     ed against Dylan. His concerts throughout 1965 and
     1966 were a nightly repeat of the turmoil that had greet-
60   ed Stravinsky's *Le Sacre du Printemps* in 1913. Many
     critics began talking about a "new" and "old" Dylan, as
     though discussing two different people. One letter to
     Sing Out! took the form of an obituary: "His last illness,
     which may be termed an acute case of avarice, severely
65   affected Mr. Dylan's sense of values, ultimately causing
     his untimely death." And there is that sublime moment,
     preserved on the so-called Royal Albert Hall bootleg,
     when someone screams "Judas!" and Dylan drawls "I
     don't believe you. You're a liar!" before launching a
70   majestic version of his current hit, "Like a Rolling
     Stone." In retrospect, it seems that popular-music audi-
     ences were not yet prepared for the possibility of artists
     who were stylistically adept and willing to abandon gen-
     res as frequently as a snake sheds its skin. In short,
75   while Dylan's songs were acknowledged to be lyrically
     complex and challenging, the audience was not prepared
     for any *musical* challenge or surprise. Hence, their sense
     of betrayal and ensuing anger.

          Theodore Gracyk, *Rhythm and Noise: An Aesthetics of Rock*

1. The author alludes to "Blowin' in the Wind" (lines 54–55) as an example of:

   A. a folk song that became popular.
   B. a protest song.
   C. one of Dylan's greatest hits.
   D. a song that Dylan wrote.

   In order to answer this question, you need to understand the context in which the example is given—a paragraph that discusses, among other things, the relative popularity of various styles of music. Folk music is least likely to be commercially successful, but the author cites "Blowin' in the Wind" as an exception to the rule. Therefore **A** is the correct answer. **B** may be enticing as an answer because folk songs are said to be synonymous with protest songs, but the context in which the example appears does not support this choice. **C** is incorrect because the passage says that "Blowin' in the Wind" was a hit for Peter, Paul and Mary, not for Bob Dylan. **D** is not mentioned in the passage.

2. According to the passage, Bob Dylan disappointed many of his fans and followers by:

   F. performing music written by people other than himself.
   G. spending more time making records than playing in live concerts.
   H. turning his back on rock music.
   J. switching from folk guitar to electric guitar.

   The answer to this question is found in the discussion of Dylan's relationship with his fans, a discussion that dominates the second half of the passage. Lines 41–42 says that Dylan's "decision to electrify" upset his audience. Therefore, **J** is correct. **F** may be historically accurate, but in this passage the fans' discontent grew from other sources. **G** is not discussed, and **H** is contrary to fact. Dylan, his fans thought, turned his back on folk music.

3. The author of the passage attributes Bob Dylan's "sellout" (line 27) to Dylan's

   A. boredom with the same old music year after year.

B. desire to be different from other recording stars.

C. wish to make more money in record sales.

D. attempt to make a comeback after a long time out of the limelight.

The answer hinges on the understanding of the adjective *commercial.* By using that word to describe the sellout, the author suggests that Dylan's change was not an artistic, but a financial, decision. **C**, therefore, is the answer. Choices **A**, **B**, and **D** are not related to Dylan's so-called "sellout."

4. The term *genuine* music (line 42) refers to:

F. Duke Ellington's style of music.

G. music in the folk and blues traditions.

H. the kind of music played by Muddy Waters.

J. early Beatles' music.

The meaning of *genuine* must be inferred from the context in which it appears. According to lines 37–40, fans accused Dylan of abandoning the music they preferred. Since they "disdained rock and roll" (lines 40–41), the reference must be to the "purer," more genuine music of the folk and blues tradition (lines 35–36) that predated rock and roll. Therefore, **G** is the correct answer. **F** is not a reasonable choice because Duke Ellington's music—jazz—is discussed only in regard to its name and popularity, not its character. Discard **H** because Muddy Waters, like Dylan, was a folk musician. **J** is incorrect, too, because in the passage the Beatles are labeled rock musicians.

5. The author refers to Stravinsky's *Le Sacre du Printemps* (line 60) in order to illustrate that:

A. Bob Dylan often spoke insultingly to his audience.

B. Stravinsky was a musical rebel.

C. the piece marked a turning point away from traditional music.

D. the audience was upset.

Note the context in which Stravinsky's name is mentioned. The author is discussing the concertgoer's reaction to new music. In 1913 the audience hooted and booed Stravinsky, just as in 1965 and 1966 audiences hooted and booed Dylan. **D** is correct. **A** is accurate, but Stravinsky is not compared to Dylan in that regard. Choices **B** and **C** earmark Dylan and Stravinsky as musical rebels, but the author is comparing the reactions of audiences rather than comparing the two composers' music.

6. Duke Ellington said that he played "Negro music" rather than "jazz" (lines 14–15) because:

   F. jazz was too narrow a term.
   G. he knew that white people played jazz, but they wouldn't play "Negro music."
   H. Ellington, a Harlem musician, did not want to be associated with New Orleans jazz.
   J. jazz reminded Ellington of the time his people were slaves.

   The key to unlocking the answer lies in line 14, where you see the word *inclusive*. By using that word the author tells you that Ellington thought the name jazz was too narrow to apply to all the different styles of music he performed. The phrase "Negro music," however, was broad enough to encompass many kinds of jazz. Therefore, **F** is the best answer. None of the other choices applies in any reasonable way.

7. The passage says that the Beatles and Bob Dylan are esteemed figures in the rock music world for all of the following reasons EXCEPT:

   A. they were the first to be installed in rock music's Hall of Fame.
   B. they composed and performed songs that they had written themselves.
   C. they made a huge number of recordings.
   D. they are considered to be among the founders of the entire rock movement.

   Because the Beatles' reputation is discussed only in the first half of the passage, concentrate your search for the answer there. In your search, look for all of the choices. The one you don't find is the correct answer. Eliminate **B**. In line 24, both the Beatles and Dylan are referred to as "songwriters." **C** is implied by the phase, "their position as *recording* artists" (line 25). **D** is not a good choice, considering the quotation by music critic Robert Christgau (lines 19–22.) Only membership in the Hall of Fame is not mentioned, making **A** the correct answer.

8. Based on information in the passage, the historical relation between rock music and rock 'n' roll is:

   F. rock music grew out of the rock 'n' roll tradition.
   G. rock and roll developed from rock music.
   H. the two types of music grew up independent of each other.
   J. rock music and rock 'n' roll were considered identical until 1967.

   Concentrate on the first paragraph, in which the relation of rock and rock 'n' roll is discussed. **F** makes an inaccurate statement, exactly the opposite of the truth: Rock supersedes rock 'n' roll (lines 4–5); that is, rock is the larger musical form from which rock 'n' roll emerged. **G**, therefore, is the answer. **H** is contradicted by information in the passage. **J** is incorrect because of the word *by* in line 3, which indicates that the distinction between rock and rock 'n' roll had been made *before* 1967.

9. According to the passage, the term *rock* music is hard to define because:

   A. rock music keeps changing over time.
   B. rock music in its purest form is no longer being written or recorded.
   C. critics and musicians have never agreed on its meaning.
   D. rock music is too diverse.

   Much of the first half of the passage is devoted to describing the various guises of rock music. The discussion implies that rock music, although generally regarded as "popular" music, consists of many different forms. Therefore, **D** is correct. **A** and **B** are not mentioned in the passage. **C** describes an effect of the difficulty rather than a cause.

10. Robert Christgau proposes that a better name for rock music is "semi-popular music" (lines 15–16) because:

   F. not all of the best rock music becomes popular with the public.

   G. rock music is usually not as popular as rock and roll.

   H. rock is mostly second-rate music that tries to imitate the Beatles and Bob Dylan.

   J. today's rock music is rarely as popular as the Beatles and Bob Dylan in their prime.

   To answer this question, you must interpret material in the passage. Choice **F** corresponds in meaning to the idea that "genuine mass popularity, as measured by record sales, often eludes influential and critically acclaimed musicians" (lines 17–19). Choice **G** is not discussed in the passage. Nor does any material in the passage support **H** or **J**.

SOCIAL SCIENCES
Passages

   The ACT reading comprehension test includes a passage from the social sciences. By definition, *social* sciences focus on people, usually people in groups. A social scientist may be interested in *anthropology*, the study of society's customs and values and the relationships of people to each other and their environment. *Economics*, or how people earn and spend money, is also a social science, as are *sociology*, the study of society's functions and institutions, and *political science*, the study of people's laws and governments. *Psychology* is also considered a social science, even though psychologists study individual behavior as well as the behavior of groups.

   You can answer all the questions related to the ACT passage if you understand the main principles of writing followed by social scientists. More often than not, social scientists write to inform others about their observations, to report on their research, and to expound their theories. Their domain is reality, not the world of imagination.

   Social scientists are concerned about problems ranging from drug addiction to depression, from child abuse to abortion. Social science literature is filled with books and articles about such crucial issues. The passage on the ACT may be an argument for or against a policy or issue. Yet, you can expect it to be relatively free of inflammatory language and controversial opinion. A passage about an issue that usually evokes strong feelings will be written objectively. Yet, some issues really don't have two sides. No one, for instance, favors AIDS or child abuse. ACT questions often try to determine whether you understand the author's ideas, not whether you agree with them. Keep in mind that authors have feelings about their subjects. Total objectivity is an ideal rarely achieved. A passage may appear to present just the facts, but readers should stay alert for

Here is a Social Science passage about stuttering, followed by ten sample questions for you to answer. Compare your approach to the analysis following each question.

Stuttering is a disorder in which the rhythmic flow, or fluency, of speech is disrupted by rapid-fire repetitions of sounds, prolonged vowels, and complete stops—verbal blocks. A stutterer's speech is often uncontrollable—
5   sometimes faster, but usually slower than the average speaking rate. Sometimes, too, the voice changes in pitch, loudness, and inflection.

Observations of young children during the early stages of stuttering have led to a list of warning signs that can
10   help identify a child who is developing a speech problem. Most children use "um's" and "ah's," and will repeat words or syllables as they learn to speak. It is not a serious concern if a child says, "I like to go and and and and play games," unless such repetitions occur
15   often, more than once every 20 words or so.

Repeating whole words is not necessarily a sign of stuttering; however, repeating speech sounds or syllables such as in the song "K-K-K-Katy" is.

Sometimes a stutterer will exhibit tension while pro-
20   longing a sound. For example, the 8-year-old who says, "Annnnnnnd-and-thththen I I drank it" with lips trembling at the same time. Children who experience such a

stuttering tremor usually become frightened, angry, and frustrated at their inability to speak. A further danger
25 sign is a rise in pitch as the child draws out the syllable.

The appearance of a child or adult experiencing the most severe signs of stuttering is dramatic: As they struggle to get a word out, their whole face may contort, the jaw may jerk, the mouth open, tongue protrude, and
30 eyes roll. Tension can spread through the whole body. A moment of overwhelming struggle occurs during the speech block.

While the symptoms of stuttering are easy to recognize, the underlying cause remains a mystery.
35 Hippocrates thought that stuttering was due to dryness of the tongue, and he prescribed blistering substances to drain away the black bile responsible. A Roman physician recommended gargling and massages to strengthen a weak tongue. Seventeenth century scientist Francis
40 Bacon suggested hot wine to thaw a "refrigerated" tongue. Too large a tongue was the fault, according to a 19th-century Prussian physician, so he snipped pieces off stutterers' tongues. Alexander Melville Bell, father of the telephone inventor, insisted stuttering was simply a
45 bad habit that could be overcome by reeducation.

Some theories today attribute stuttering to problems in the control of the muscles of speech. As recently as the 50s and 60s, however, stuttering was thought to arise from deep-rooted personality problems, and psy-
50 chotherapy was recommended.

Stutterers represent the whole range of personality types, levels of emotional adjustment, and intelligence. Winston Churchill was a stutterer (or stammerer, as the English prefer to say). So were Sir Isaac Newton, King
55 George VI of England, and writer Somerset Maugham.

There are more than 15 million stutterers in the world today and approximately 1 million in the United States alone.

Most stuttering begins after a child has mastered the
60 basics of speech and is starting to talk automatically. One out of 30 children will then undergo a brief period

of stuttering, lasting 6 months or so. Boys are four times as likely as girls to be stutterers.

65 Occasionally stuttering arises in an older child or even in an adult. It may follow an illness or an emotionally shattering event, such as a death in the family. Stuttering may also occur following brain injury, either due to head injury or after a stroke. No matter how the problem begins, stutterers generally experience their

70 worst moments under conditions of stress or emotional tension: ordering in a crowded restaurant, talking over the telephone, speaking in public, asking the boss for a raise.

Stuttering does not develop in a predictable pattern. In

75 children, speech difficulties can disappear for weeks or months only to return in full force. About 80 percent of children with a stuttering problem are able to speak normally by the time they are adults—whether they've had therapy or not. Adult stutterers have also been known to

80 stop stuttering for no apparent reason.

Indeed, all stutterers can speak fluently some of the time. Most can also whisper smoothly, speak in unison, and sing with no hesitations. Country and western singer Mel Tillis is an example of a stutterer with a successful

85 singing career.

Most stutterers also speak easily when they are prevented from hearing their own voices, when talking to pets or small children, or when addressing themselves in the mirror. All these instances of fluency demonstrate

90 that nothing is basically wrong with the stutterer's speech machinery.

Stuttering: Hope Through Research,
U.S. Department of Health and Human Services

1. According to the passage, stuttering will be a lifelong problem for:

A. males who stuttered in childhood.

B. males and females who began stuttering in childhood.

C. only a small percentage of childhood stutterers.

D. anyone who fails to get help.

A question that begins with "According to the passage . . ." indicates that you'll find the answer in the text itself. No interpretation is necessary.

Because the question pertains to lifelong stuttering, the answer will be found later in the passage rather than sooner because the first half defines and explains stuttering, especially as it applies to children. In lines 64–65, focus turns to stuttering in older children and adults. That's where your search for the answer should begin. Choice **A** is precisely the opposite of what is stated in lines 76–78 (i.e., 80 percent of childhood stutterers speak normally by the time they reach adulthood). **B** is far too broad. Choice **D** may be true for some stutterers, but the passage does not discuss help for stutterers. Because only 20 percent of childhood stutterers continue to stutter in adulthood, choice **C** is correct.

2. The passage indicates that during moments of speech blockage, a stutterer may experience all of the following symptoms EXCEPT:

F. facial distortion.

G. severe frustration.

H. body tension.

J. trembling head and hands.

Find the paragraphs that discuss the symptoms of stuttering. They appear early in the passage. Examine those paragraphs for allusions to each of the four choices. The choice that you don't find is the correct answer. Choice **F** is eliminated by lines 27–29. Choice **G** is eliminated by lines 22–24, and **H** by line 30. Therefore, the passage alludes to all the choices except "trembling head and hands." **J**, therefore, is correct.

3. Based on information in the passage, which of the following is LEAST likely to occur?

A. A man begins to stutter after a traumatic divorce.

B. A schoolgirl temporarily stops stuttering during summer vacation.

C. An actress stutters off stage but not during performances.

D. A boy stutters mostly when telling bedtime stories to his baby sister.

As you did in the previous question, seek the choice that is not alluded to in the passage. In contrast to the previous question, however, the choices do not echo precisely the words in the passage. Rather, you must interpret information. For example, Choice **A** can be interpreted from "emotionally shattering event" (lines 65–66.) **B** is implied by the statement (68–70) that stuttering occurs generally during moments of stress. (Presumably, the schoolgirl's relief from stress allowed her to stop stuttering during summer vacation.) **C** may be interpreted from the fact that a performer like Mel Tillis stutters off stage but not on. Therefore, the event least likely to occur is described in Choice **D**. In fact the passage says that, while talking to small children, people rarely stutter (lines 86–88).

4. One can infer from the passage that a parent whose young child repeats the same word over and over while learning to speak would be advised to:

F. take the child to see a speech therapist.

G. help the child relax when speaking.

H. accept the fact that the child will be a stutterer.

J. keep track of the frequency of repetitions.

This question should draw your attention to the section of the passage that discusses young children, approximately lines 8–25. The word *infer* in the question indicates that you'll need to interpret material in the passage to find the answer. Choice **F** is not a good choice because the passage says that repeating whole words is not a cause for concern (lines 16–17). Choice **G** is an issue only to the extent that relaxation provides temporary relief to most stutterers. **H** suggests that parents can do nothing, which is not the case, and **J**, the best answer, is implied by lines 14–15, which say that a high frequency of word repetition—"once every 20 words or so"—should alert parents to a stuttering problem.

5. According to the passage, young children usually begin to stutter:

   A. after learning to speak fluently.
   B. after a severe emotional shock.
   C. during prolonged periods of stress or tension.
   D. when they lack the vocabulary to express themselves.

   The answer to this question comes from one of two places in the passage—lines 8–25 or lines 59–60. Both sections pertain to children and stuttering. The second section is a more fruitful place to look, however, because the material pertains more directly to the origins, rather than the symptoms, of stuttering. Choice **A** is the correct answer. It paraphrases lines 59–60. **B** and **C** refer to unusual circumstances. (Note that the question says *usually*.) Choice **D** is not discussed in the passage.

6. Until the 19th century, authorities apparently regarded stuttering as:

   F. a sign of low intelligence.
   G. an emotional problem.
   H. a physical ailment.
   J. a lack of self-discipline.

   A historical perspective on stuttering (through the 17th century) appears in lines 35–42. None of the theories include **F**, **G**, or **J**. Choice **J** is drawn from a theory by Alexander Melville Bell (lines 44–45), who lived in the 19th century. Because the question says *until* the 19th century—meaning *before* the 19th century—Bell's theory does not apply. All the old antidotes for stuttering involve forms of physical therapy. Therefore, **H** is the correct answer.

7. One can infer from the passage that stutterers may find relief by:

   A. avoiding situations that typically cause stuttering.
   B. practicing speech in front of a mirror.
   C. preparing what they have to say ahead of time.
   D. speaking more slowly.

   To answer this question, read lines 74–91, in which the author lists occasions when stutterers find relief. Option **B** may appear to be the answer until you compare it to lines 88–89 of the passage, which say "addressing themselves in the mirror," a phrase rather different from "practicing speech in front of a mirror." Because the meanings differ from each other, **B** cannot be the answer. Neither **C** nor **D** is mentioned in the passage, leaving **A** as the correct choice.

8. One may assume that stuttering is NOT caused by a physical disorder of a person's speech apparatus because:

F. all stutterers speak fluently from time to time.
G. stuttering sometimes appears and disappears for no apparent reason.
H. famous people, including athletes, have been stutterers.
J. highly intelligent people have been known to stutter.

If stuttering were a physical disorder, stutterers would probably never enjoy moments of speaking freely. **F** is correct. This idea is expressed in the passage in lines 81–83 in slightly different form. Choices **G**, **H**, and **J** have no apparent relation to physical disorders.

9. The author's main purpose in this passage is to point out that:

A. treatment is available for stutterers identified early enough in life.
B. the effects of stuttering are widely known, but uncertainty surrounds its causes.
C. stutterers should not be held responsible for their speech disorder.
D. the symptoms of stuttering are confusing and often misunderstood.

A "main idea" question such as this requires you to stand back from the passage and consider what it's all about. What do all the details add up to? Much of the passage raises questions about the causes of stuttering. A large segment also describes its effects. All things considered, then, **B** is the best answer. **A** is alluded to so briefly that it could not describe the main idea. **C** is a valid interpretation that may be drawn from material in the passage, but it does not describe the main intent of the author. The idea in **D** does not coincide with the passage, which describes symptoms of stuttering but makes no effort to interpret them.

10. By pointing out that famous and successful people have been stutterers, the author means to imply all of the following EXCEPT:

   F. stuttering is not a serious handicap in life.
   G. stuttering is unrelated to I.Q.
   H. the public is generally tolerant of stutterers.
   J. stuttering is not a personality disorder.

   This question, like earlier ones, asks you to find the item that isn't implied by the passage. **F** is implied by the fact that many successful people have been stutterers. **G** is stated outright in lines 51–52. **J**, according to lines 46–48, is false; stuttering has been thought to arise from personality problems. The passage never discusses attitudes towards people who stutter. Therefore, choice **H** is the correct answer.

NATURAL SCIENCES
Passages

Out of a flood of publications by biologists, ecologists, chemists, physicists, geologists, and other natural scientists, the ACT questioners pick one passage. It comes from a textbook or an article, a research or lab report—from almost any scientific writing. The only certainty is that it pertains to the natural world.

A passage of scientific writing can be a wide-ranging story about the world's endangered species. Or it can be an excerpt from a report on hypothermia, or the greenhouse effect, or volcanoes, or brain waves. Whatever the topic, the passage will probably contain many factual statements, along with statistics and other data, all intended to give an accurate account of reality. There is no science fiction on this part of the ACT.

One type of writing from the natural sciences, however, is meant to alert readers to a problem. Few published works about the environment, for example, are strictly informative. Lethal air and filthy water are not subjects to be unemotional about. Therefore, a passage on that subject, while informative, might also hold a warning about contaminating one of the earth's major sources of clean water.

Don't presume that what you studied in high school gives you easy access to a passage. You may know that one of the choices provided as a possible answer to a question may be a valid statement. If the passage doesn't support that choice, however, don't pick it. You're being tested only on the contents of the passage, not on what you may know about the subject.

Required reading in most school science courses is often far more exacting than the science passage on the ACT, which is accessible to the general reader. But you must also be ready for more difficult reading, a passage taken from the literature of scientific research, for example. Researchers often fill their reports with the technical terms of their disciplines. Don't get stuck on these specialized words and phrases. Your aim is to discover the general message of the passage. No passage on the ACT will be beyond reach. With the main point of the passage in mind, you should be able to answer every question the ACT asks about the passage.

Here is a Natural Science passage about hibernation. After you have read it, answer the ten sample questions. Compare your approach to the analysis following each question.

Have you ever wondered what it is that tells groundhogs when to begin hibernating in winter and when to awaken in spring? Biologists have, for if they could tap that enzyme, chemical, gene, or whatever, they might be able to apply it
5 to other species, including man.

Hibernation, unlike sleep, is a process in which all unnecessary bodily functions are discontinued, for example, growth. The animal's body temperature remains about 1° above the temperature of its environment. During
10 this period, animals appear to be immune to disease and if subjected to a lethal dose of radiation, the animal will not die until the hibernation period is over. (As a point of interest, bears do not hibernate, they only sleep more deeply in winter.)
15   Early in this century, Dr. Max Rubner proposed that aging was a result of the amount of energy expended in tissues. "Rubner found that the total lifetime energy

expenditure per gram of tissue during the adult stage is
roughly constant for several species of domestic animals.
20 'The higher the metabolism, the shorter the life span and
vice versa.' ''

In this vein, scientists found that the storage of body fat
was vital to a hibernating animal's survival: it loses 20–40
percent of its body weight while dormant. The body fat
25 involved here is called ''brown fat'' and differs structurally
from normal, white fat cells, which gives it a greater heat
producing potential. A low temperature signals the brown
fat to increase in temperature, which warms the animal's
blood and spreads the warmth to other parts of the body.
30 Newborn human babies have an unusually high percentage
of brown fat, which diminishes as they grow older. Adults
do have some brown fat, and those with underproductive
thyroid glands have more than normal:

Rats subjected to cold temperatures show an increased
35 ratio of brown fat to white fat. It seems reasonable to
expect that cold acclimation in man, through a carefully
controlled program of cyclic hypothermia . . ., will
increase brown fat deposits. After these deposits reach a
certain body level, they might perform the same regulatory
40 functions in human hibernation that brown fat performs in
natural hibernators.

About ten years after Rubner's experiments, Drs.
Jacques Loeb and John Northrop discovered that reduced
temperatures extended the life span of fruit flies. In
45 applying this to animals, however, those that were not
natural hibernators who had not been prepared for
hibernation, developed ventricular fibrillations (where the
heart muscle quivers and stops pumping blood). When a
person ''freezes to death'' this is the cause, not ice
50 crystals forming in the veins.

The process involved in artificially cooling an animal's
body temperature is called induced hypothermia. Research
in this field led space biologist Dale L. Carpenter
(McDonnell Douglas—Long Beach) to determine that both
55 hibernating and non-hibernating animals have the same
basic temperature control and he believes that ''were a

non-hibernating mammal to be artificially biochemically prepared with proper enzymes and energy producing chemicals, it could hibernate." He found that if an animal
60 was cooled just until its heart began quivering and then rewarmed, it could survive. If cooled a second time, a slightly lower temperature could be achieved before ventricular fibrillations occurred, and so on. Each exposure to the cold seemed to condition the heart to accept lower
65 temperatures. This is cyclic hypothermia.

Even with this kind of progress, however, the search goes on for the chemical or enzyme that triggers the hibernation process, that tells the animals it is winter or spring. Scientists hope to gain some insight into this
70 mystery from human infants, who besides having more brown fat than adults, seem less susceptible to ventricular fibrillations. They have different forms of hemoglobin and myoglobin in their tissues that are more efficent in attracting and releasing oxygen. This may hold the clue.
75 If hibernation could be induced in humans, this could solve the problem of interstellar travel. One would not have to worry about traveling near the speed of light, for the crew would not age as fast and would have more time to reach their destination. Maxwell Hunter suggests that
80 this "biological time dilation" be applied not only to the crews, but to those that remain on Earth.

We are thus faced with the prospect of a whole society dilated in time. This would form the basis for a Galactic Club that was based on travel rather
85 than communication . . .

We are not talking about timefaring in the classic science fiction sense where people are able to go both backward and forward in time at will . . . We are postulating, rather, dilating the time experienced by people
90 in one direction in the future . . . which would permit a society to expand throughout the galaxy. If, when one went to bed at night, he actually went into hibernation during which many months passed, it would not seem any different to him than a standard eight-hour sleep . . .
95 When a ship returned home, its crew would be greeted by

friends, business colleagues, etc., who had aged no more than the crew.

Report of the Committee on Science and Technology, "The Possibility of Intelligent Life in the Universe"

1. By pointing out that freezing to death is not caused by ice crystals in the veins (lines 49–50), the author of the passage implies that:

   A. the research findings of Drs. Loeb and Northrop are questionable.
   B. death by freezing results from several complex causes.
   C. readers should not believe the old wives' tale about ice crystals in the veins.
   D. freezing is different from ordinary frostbite.

   To infer what the author had in mind, look to the passage for clues. The author used quotation marks for the phrase "freezes to death," an indication that it shouldn't be taken literally. In effect, the author is saying that the phrase is imprecise, that death is not caused by the actual freezing of blood or by the freezing of any other part of the body.

   Choice **A** is irrelevant. **B** may sound right, but notice the ambiguous word "several." The passage states the death is caused by ventricular fibrillation, which is a single cause, not "several" causes. **C** implies that many people believe that "freezing to death" occurs when ice crystals form in the veins. Here, the author is setting the record straight. **C** is correct. **D** is a poor choice. The passage does not mention frostbite.

2. A conclusion that may be drawn from research described in the passage is that:

   F. in severe cold a human infant is likely to survive longer than an adult.
   G. a person with many brown fat cells will live longer than someone with many white fat cells.
   H. animals living in cold places live longer than animals in warm places.

J. metabolic rates in animals remain constant throughout life.

To answer a question using inductive reasoning, you need to think logically and to find the evidence in the passage for drawing a valid conclusion. Guard against overgeneralization. A conclusion may sound right, but it you can't find material in the passage to back it up, consider it wrong! Similarly, on its face a conclusion may seem invalid, but if it can be supported with facts in the passage, you have to consider it correct.

Question writers take great pains to avoid arguments over answers to test questions. In their phrasing of questions and answers they often include such hedging words as *may, often, almost, mostly, usually, generally, rarely, sometimes*—words that forestall controversy.

In answering ACT questions, be wary of conclusions stated as absolutes. They are *often* invalid precisely because they leave no room for exceptions. However, correct answers *often* contain a hedging word that renders the statement valid.

Choice **F** seems to correspond with the statement that newborn babies have an "unusually high percentage of brown fat, which diminishes as they grow older" (lines 30 and 31). Since brown fat, according to the passage, serves as a warming agent, it stands to reason that a baby can tolerate severe cold longer than an adult. Notice also that this choice contains the hedging phrase "is likely." **F** is correct. **G** implies that the focus of the passage is longevity rather than hibernation. Since longevity is not the real issue in the passage, however, this is not a good choice. **H** is wrong, because the passage does not discuss animals living in warm places. Notice also that this choice is stated as an absolute, which makes it immediately suspect. **J** is wrong. Since the passage alludes to metabolism in "the adult stage" of life, you may assume that older stages are characterized by different rates of metabolism.

3. Based on information in the passage, all of the following are valid conclusions EXCEPT:

    A. human beings may some day have the ability to hibernate.

B. long-term space exploration will be given a big boost when the process of hibernation is fully understood.

C. it remains unclear why certain creatures have the capacity to hibernate.

D. by means of hibernation the life span of human beings can be extended indefinitely.

To find the answer, identify the one conclusion that *cannot* legitimately be drawn from the facts in the passage. The discussion after question 2 may give you some hints on how to think out the answer.

Choice **A** is valid. It is the premise in the passage on which the discussion of interstellar travel is based. **B** is valid. The last part of the passage points out that long-term space travel depends on learning the secrets of hibernation. **C** is valid. Much of the passage is about past and present efforts to understand hibernation. **D** is *not* valid. Although aging slows down during hibernation, it doesn't stop altogether. Hibernation may lengthen life but not extend it indefinitely. **D** is correct.

4. As used in the passage, the meaning of *metabolism* is the:

F. rate at which food is digested.

G. speed at which an organism uses up energy.

H. rate at which blood replenishes its supply of oxygen.

J. rate at which the bodily functions of a hibernating animal slow down.

Even if you know the word, don't depend on your prior knowledge of what it means. Because "metabolism" is a common word, it's likely that the question is asking for an uncommon definition. Don't be fooled into choosing the most popular definition. Determine the meaning of the word only from the way it is used in the passage.

Choice **F** corresponds to the everyday definition of metabolism. The passage, however, does not link metabolism to the digestion of food. **G** resembles the explanation of metabolism given in the passage: "energy expenditure per gram of tissue." **G** is correct. **H** is discussed in the passage but not in connection with metabolism. **J** has nothing to do with metabolism.

5. As used in the passage, the word *dilated* (line 83) means all of the following EXCEPT:

A. causing years to seem like no more than a moment.
B. programming space travelers to hibernate during stellar voyages.
C. having the earth's people hibernate for the same span as stellar travelers.
D. assuring that people remain young by means of hibernation.

The word *dilated* is not unusual, but the idea of a "dilated society" (line 83) is. The word may be defined right in the text or implied by the general meaning of the passage. You'll see the consequences of dilating a society by rereading lines 75 through 97.

Choice **A** is a consequence of a dilated society. **B** is a feature of a dilated society. **C** describes what happens in a dilated society. Space travelers return to friends, business colleagues, etc., who had aged no more than they had during flights to the stars. **D** is *not* a consequence of a dilated society. Therefore, **D** is correct.

6. Based on information in the passage, in which of the following ways are animals in deep sleep similar to animals in hibernation?

F. Body temperature.
G. Resistance to disease
H. Slowing down of bodily functions
J. Rate of growth

To answer this comparison question, draw your inference out of the parts of the passage where you find references to hibernation and sleep.

Choice **F** is wrong. Only hibernating animals experience changes in body temperature as the environment warms and cools (lines 6–9). **G** is wrong. Line 10 says that hibernating animals appear to have a natural immunity to disease. Sleep, however, is no defense against disease. **H** is supported by lines 6–12. The bodily functions of all animals, whether in hibernation (like the groundhog) or in a deep sleep (like the bear), slow down during extended periods of rest. **H** is correct. **J** is wrong. Growth continues during sleep, but during hibernation, according to lines 7–8, it stops.

7. Hibernating animals differ from nonhibernating animals in all of the following ways EXCEPT in the:

   A. number of brown cells.
   B. presence of a certain enzyme in the body.
   C. tolerance to extremely cold temperatures.
   D. metabolic rate.
   Because characteristics of hibernating animals are discussed throughout the passage, deal with the choices one at a time.
   Choice **A** is wrong. Lines 22–27 indicated that hibernating animals have a higher percentage of brown fat cells than other animals. **B** is wrong. Lines 3 and 67 refer to scientists' quest to find the enzyme that sets off hibernation. Presumably, nonhibernating animals lack such an enzyme. **C** is wrong. Experiments described in lines 42–48 found that natural hibernators withstand cold temperatures more readily than nonhibernators. **D** is the correct choice, because the passage discusses metabolism as a function of the life span of *all* animals, hibernators and nonhibernators alike.

8. Based on the passage, which of the following procedures holds the greatest promise for inducing human hibernation?

   F. Promoting the growth of brown fat cells in the body.
   G. Changing the activity of the thyroid gland.
   H. Conditioning the heart to adapt to lower temperatures.
   J. Increasing the amount of oxygen in body tissue
   Solving a problem from facts is not far different from drawing a conclusion, but, to answer this question, use deductive, instead of inductive, reasoning—that is, consider a number of pieces of information to determine the only reasonable solution to the problem. For example:
   FACT 1: Arthur lies dead on the floor with a bullet in his chest.
   FACT 2: Harold stands over Arthur with a smoking gun in his hand.

PROBLEM: Figure out who killed Arthur.

You can assume that the ACT will present problems somewhat harder to solve than Arthur's murder. The point is to use every available scrap of evidence to solve the problem.

Choice **F** is discussed in lines 22–41. At one time, brown fat cells seemed like a key to human hibernation, but years of research have been unsuccessful. **G** is discussed in lines 32–33. People with underproductive thyroids have a more than normal amount of brown fat cells. To induce the formation of more brown fat cells by slowing the thyroid, however, is hazardous to health. **H** is fully discussed in the passage, but in spite of some progress, the search for a better answer goes on. **J** is discussed in lines 72–74, which says this procedure "may hold the clue." **J** is correct.

9. Based on information in the passage, scientists can predict which of two kittens from the same litter is likely to live longer by:

A. studying the brown fat cell/white fat cell ratio in each kitten.

B. analyzing the kittens' enzyme secretions.

C. measuring the kittens' metabolic rates.

D. comparing the amounts of hemoglobin and myoglobin in each kitten's blood.

To answer this question, search the passage for references to longevity. Since life span is discussed in the second paragraph, focus your attention there.

Choice **A** is wrong, because the passage discusses brown and white fat cells with regard to heat production in the body, not to life span. **B** is wrong. According to the passage, enzymes are thought to bring about hibernation and have nothing to do with length of life. **C** coincides with Rubner's finding that the "higher the metabolism, the shorter the life span and vice versa" (lines 20 and 21). **C** is correct. **D** is wrong, because the composition of blood, while important to hibernation, has nothing to do with longevity.

10. In which of the following sequences (from earliest to latest) were the discoveries made?

   I. In extreme cold, nonhibernating animals develop ventricular fibrillations.
   II. The heart can be conditioned to adapt to low temperatures.
   III. An organism's energy expenditure is related to its life span.
   IV. Fruit flies live longer when their body temperature is lowered.

   F. I, III, IV, II
   G. III, II, IV, I
   H. III, IV, I, II
   J. IV, I, III, II

   Sequence questions such as this consume a good deal of time on the ACT. Consider saving them for last. By then you'll know how much test time remains, and you won't neglect other, less time-consuming questions.

   First skim the passage to locate the four sequenced items. Mark them I, II, III, and IV. Begin by finding either the first or the last item in the sequence. Nonfiction passages often cue the reader with such words and phrases as *first, to begin, initially, in the first place, to start, early on, finally, in conclusion, last, in the end, most recently.* Intermediate steps are often cued with *then, next, also, soon after, in the meantime, secondly, in addition,* and many other similar transitional words.

   Once you've identified either the first or last item, go directly to the question choices and start eliminating those that can't be right. If you know the first item in a sequence, start looking for the last item, and vice versa. Once you've located both the first and the last items, you may have the answer. If you haven't, of course, you'll also need to identify either the second or third item.

   Choice **F** is wrong. The paragraph in which ventricular fibrillations (line 47) are discussed, begins with the phrase "About ten years after Rubner's experiments, . . ." Discovery number I, therefore, could not have occurred first. **G** seems like a possibility. According to lines 15–18, discovery number III was made by Rubner early in this century. Therefore, the proper sequence must begin with III. The last number in this choice refers to a discovery made ten years after Rubner's. Since more recent discoveries are discussed later in the passage, discovery I cannot be the last in the sequence. **H** is a possibility. Aside from choice **G**, it is the only one that starts with discovery number III. Indeed, this sequence corresponds with the order of discoveries described in the passage. **H** is correct. **J** is wrong, because it begins with discovery number IV, which took place after Rubner's work.

SAMPLE READING TEST

Now that you are acquainted with the various types of reading passages and questions on the ACT, see whether you can apply what you have learned. This exercise consists of four passages, each accompanied by ten questions. Because the passages in this Sample Test vary in length from those on the ACT Reading Test, you may wish to allow yourself about 45 minutes, rather than the 35 minutes allotted on the ACT, to complete the exercise. Don't let yourself be distracted by the time limit, however. For the moment, devote yourself to recalling and using the test-taking tactics suggested throughout this chapter.

DIRECTIONS: This test consists of four passages, each followed by ten multiple-choice questions. Read each passage and then pick the best answer for each question. Refer to the passage as often as you wish while answering the questions.

Passage 1

SOCIAL SCIENCE: This passage is adapted from an article titled "Freedom of Inquiry Is for Hopeful People" by Gerald W. Johnson. The passage discusses the relationship between a government and its people.

When Jefferson listed "the pursuit of happiness" as one
of the rights that government cannot justly take from any
man, except as punishment for crime, he stepped into a
dark and mysterious corner of the realm of ideas. Nobody
5 denies the truth of what he said; but the reason for that is
that nobody knows exactly what it means.

The word "happiness" cannot be defined precisely
because it means different things to different people, or to
the same people at different times or in different
10 circumstances. The word "pursuit" is almost as vague.
Together, they express an idea that a man cannot always
comprehend as it applies to himself, and that he can
rarely, if ever, comprehend as it applies to anyone else.

The only interpretation of the phrase that is not open to
15 some fatal objection seems to be this: the right to the
pursuit of happiness is the right to be let alone.

Instantly, this raises the question, how is government
going to govern if it lets people alone? The function of
government is not to let people alone, but to interfere with
20 them. Government is instituted to protect certain
inalienable rights, among them life, liberty, and the pursuit
of happiness: therefore its business, its reason for being,
is to interfere with those who would infringe these rights,
and not merely to interfere, but to prevent their doing what
25 they would like to do. These people may be wrong, but
they are nevertheless people, and they do not like it when
government stops them from doing as they please.

There is no logical answer to this. The only answer is
an illogical one—consider what would happen if
30 government were abolished altogether. In that case, the
right to the pursuit of happiness would not be respected at
all. The strongest would impose his will on all others, and
there would be no liberty except the liberty of the
strongest. This is anarchy; and it was the secret fear of
35 some founders of the republic that democracy must
inevitably degenerate into anarchy.

Furthermore, there are some men—never a majority,
but a definite number, and important out of all proportion
to their number—for whom the pursuit of happiness

40 consists in finding out what is true. They are critics of
everything; and among other things they are critics of
government, which lays upon the American government
the duty of protecting those who attack it. This is the basis
of the maxim beloved of early liberals, "That government

45 is best that governs least." It means that government
should interfere with the individual only as far as is
absolutely necessary to protect the general welfare.

Two factors work constantly against this ideal—one is
human nature, the other is the passage of time. Any group

50 of men given a chance to wield power—and a government
is just that—will try to extend that power. This is the first
factor. As more people are crowded together in the same
area, more activity by government is required to maintain
order. This is the second factor. Neither can be eliminated.

55 Each is capable of becoming a threat to all liberty. Since
some extension of governmental power is necessary as the
population grows, it is easy for governors to convince
themselves that any extension of their power is justifiable.
This tendency must be held within bounds by steady

60 counterpressure from people who know their rights and
mean to maintain them.

1. According to the passage, the phrase "pursuit of happiness" is
difficult to define because:

   A. no one knows exactly what Jefferson had in mind.
   B. each generation views happiness differently.
   C. the words have different meanings to different people.
   D. the meaning of the phrase has changed since Jefferson
   wrote it.

2. The author believes that a widely acceptable definition of "pursuit of happiness" is the right of the people:

   F. to do whatever they please provided they don't interfere
   with the rights of others.
   G. to be free of interference by the government.
   H. to be free of all laws that restrict their pleasure.
   J. to seek happiness in whatever way they want.

3. During the early days of the country, liberals believed that government:

   A. should base its decisions on what is best for the greatest number of people.
   B. should be as inconspicuous as possible in people's lives.
   C. is the servant of the people.
   D. has the right to protect itself from criticism.

4. The last paragraph in the passage implies that governments must be carefully monitored because:

   F. they tend to expand their power as time goes on.
   G. over time, an entrenched bureaucracy is certain to develop.
   H. as government grows, it inevitably starts to limit the people's freedoms.
   J. big organizations are susceptible to corruption.

5. The main purpose of the passage is to:

   A. define the term "pursuit of happiness."
   B. alert readers to the dangers of big government.
   C. argue that democracy is a difficult form of government to maintain.
   D. clarify the relationship between the government and the people.

6. Based on information in lines 29–34, which of the following is NOT likely to occur if government were to be abolished?

   F. Anarchy would spread.
   G. The weak would fall prey to the strong.
   H. The right to pursue happiness would no longer be respected.
   J. Society would become more alert to the dangers of dictatorship.

7. Some of America's founding fathers feared the emergence of anarchy in the United States because:

   A. too much influence was given to the people.
   B. the government didn't claim enough power to prevent it.

C. many colonists were almost fanatic in their desire for basic liberties.

D. Jefferson's ideals were too abstract and lofty to be used as a solid defense against it.

8. According to the passage, some citizens have interpreted "the pursuit of happiness" to mean:

F. the right to state their opinions in a free press.

G. being confident that the government will always tell the truth.

H. the freedom to express their views about anything at all.

J. having a government help people who need it most.

9. Which of the following does the author of the passage believe to be the basic purpose of government?

A. To protect the rights of the individual

B. To provide for the general welfare of the population.

C. To allow people to express themselves freely

D. To permit people to pursue happiness in whatever manner they choose

10. The passage suggests that an educated citizenry is important because:

F. intelligent and well-educated people are needed to run the country.

G. people need to know their rights in order to maintain them.

H. educated people will put up with less interference by the government.

J. it takes a well-informed people to choose a government's leaders wisely.

Passage 2

NATURAL SCIENCE: This passage is from a government publication titled *Useful Information on Alzheimer's Disease.* It discusses what science has discovered about the causes and cures of this dread disease.

Microscopic brain tissue changes have been described in Alzheimer's disease since Aloise Alzheimer first reported them in 1906. These are the plaques and tangles—senile or neuritic plaques (degenerating nerve cells combined
5   with a form of protein called amyloid) and neurofibrillary tangles (nerve cell malformations). The brains of Alzheimer's disease patients of all ages reveal these findings in autopsy examination.

Computer-Assisted Tomography (CAT scan) changes
10   become more evident as the disease progresses—not necessarily early on. Thus a CAT scan performed in the first stages of the disease cannot in itself be used to make a definitive diagnosis of Alzheimer's disease; its value is in helping to establish whether certain disorders
15   (some reversible) that mimic Alzheimer's disease are present. Later on, CAT scans often reveal changes characteristic of Alzheimer's disease, namely an atrophied (shrunken) brain with widened sulci (tissue indentations) and enlarged cerebral ventricles (fluid chambers). . .
20   As research on Alzheimer's disease progresses, scientists are describing other abnormal anatomical and chemical changes associated with the disease. These include nerve cell degeneration in the brain's nucleus basalis of Meynert and reduced levels of the
25   neurotransmitter acetylcholine in the brains of Alzheimer's disease victims. But from a practical standpoint, the "classical" plaque and tangle changes seen at autopsy typically suffice for a diagnosis of Alzheimer's disease based on brain tissue changes. In fact, it is only through
30   the study of brain tissue from a person who was thought to have Alzheimer's disease that definitive diagnosis of the disorder can be made.

The "clinical" features of Alzheimer's disease, as opposed to the "tissue" changes, are threefold:
35   1. Dementia—significant loss of intellectual abilities such as memory capacity, severe enough to interfere with social or occupational functioning;

2. Insidious onset of symptoms—subtly progressive and irreversible course with documented deterioration over
40   time;

3. Exclusion of all other specific causes of dementia by history, physical examination, laboratory tests, psychometric, and other studies.

Based on these criteria, the clinical diagnosis of
45 Alzheimer's disease has been referred to as "Alzheimer's diagnosis by exclusion," and one that can only be made in the face of clinical deterioration over time. There is no specific clinical test or finding that is unique to Alzheimer's disease. Hence, all disorders that can bring on similar
50 symptoms must be systematically excluded or "ruled out." This explains why diagnostic workups of individuals where the question of Alzheimer's disease has been raised can be so frustrating to patient and family alike; they are not told that Alzheimer's disease has been specifically diagnosed,
55 but that other possible diagnoses have been dismissed, leaving Alzheimer's disease as the likely diagnosis by the process of elimination.

Scientists hope to develop one day a specific test for Alzheimer's disease, based on a specific laboratory or
60 genetic finding ("marker"). Some think that the results from genetic research may lead to a diagnostic marker for certain persons evaluated for Alzheimer's disease. For example, recent research has discovered a protein, called "Alzheimer's disease-associated protein," in the autopsied
65 brains of Alzheimer's patients. The protein is mainly concentrated in the cortex covering the front and side sections of the brain, regions involved in memory function. If researchers can perfect a test to detect the protein in the cerebrospinal fluid, it may be possible to
70 use this method of diagnosis on living patients. Many scientists are working at developing other tests or procedures that may someday identify living persons with the disorder, perhaps even early in its course before behavioral changes become evident. Still, a specific
75 diagnostic marker for Alzheimer's disease is not yet available.

Meanwhile, Alzheimer's disease is the most over-diagnosed and misdiagnosed disorder of mental functioning in older adults. Part of the problem, already

80 alluded to, is that many other disorders show symptoms that resemble those of Alzheimer's disease. The crucial difference, though, is that many of these disorders—unlike Alzheimer's disease—may be stopped, reversed, or cured with appropriate treatment. But first they must be
85 identified, not dismissed as Alzheimer's disease or senility.

11. According to the passage, Alzheimer's disease:
    A. strikes at any time during old age.
    B. was unknown before 1906.
    C. is hereditary.
    D. is more common in women than in men.

12. Which of the following is NOT a symptom of Alzheimer's disease?
    F. Loss of memory
    G. Gradual deterioration of social skills
    H. Increasingly severe headaches
    J. Declining ability to figure out solutions to everyday problems

13. The passage says that the most telling indication of Alzheimer's disease is:
    A. a shrunken brain.
    B. fluid in the brain.
    C. degeneration of nerve cells.
    D. discoloration of brain tissue.

14. The passage implies that the key to accurate diagnosis of Alzheimer's disease lies in:
    F. more advanced technology.
    G. greater understanding of other diseases similar to Alzheimer's.

     H. more thorough study of the chemistry of the brain.
     J. genetic research.

15. A scientist preparing to work with Alzheimer's disease would probably be well-advised to study:

     A. anatomy.
     B. organic chemistry.
     C. psychology.
     D. nutrition.

16. The passage suggests that Alzheimer's disease is "over-diagnosed and misdiagnosed" (lines 77–78) because:

     F. medical research on Alzheimer's disease is still in its infancy.
     G. its symptoms are like those of several other diseases.
     H. inflated statistics will increase funds allocated to Alzheimer's research.
     J. the symptoms of Alzheimer's disease vary from person to person.

17. The passage suggests that one important reason for diagnosing Alzheimer's disease in living people is:

     A. that physicians will then know how to handle Alzheimer's patients.
     B. to improve the treatment of victims of similar, but reversible, diseases.
     C. to reduce the death rate of Alzheimer's patients.
     D. to emotionally prepare patients and their families for the onset of the disease.

18. The author of the passage apparently believes that the most frustrating aspect of Alzheimer's disease for patients and their families is:

     F. not knowing for sure that the patient has been properly diagnosed.

    G. that Alzheimer's symptoms differ according to the individual.

    H. that no one can predict how long before a patient is totally disabled by the disease.

    J. that few Alzheimer's patients recover from the disease.

19. According to the passage, computers:

    A. have limited value in diagnosing Alzheimer's disease.

    B. are essential to physicians working with Alzheimer's patients.

    C. help doctors make definitive diagnoses of Alzheimer's disease.

    D. are crucial in tracing the progress of Alzheimer's disease in individual patients.

20. Based on the passage, it is safe to assume that:

    F. Alzheimer's disease will never be cured.

    G. a vaccine may one day prevent Alzheimer's disease.

    H. current research is focusing on diagnosis of Alzheimer's disease.

    J. Alzheimer's disease is becoming more prevalent in our society.

Passage 3

PROSE FICTION: This passage is an excerpt from a short story, "Buckthorne," by the 19th-century American author Washington Irving. The narrator of the passage recalls his boyhood years in a boarding school.

    I was sent at an early age to a public school sorely against my mother's wishes; but my father insisted that it was the only way to make boys hardy. The school was kept by a conscientious prig of the ancient system who

5   did his duty by the boys entrusted to his care; that is to say we were flogged soundly when we did not get our lessons. We were put into classes and thus flogged on in droves along the highways of knowledge, in much the

same manner as cattle are driven to market, where those
10 that are heavy in gait or short in leg have to suffer for the
superior alertness of longer limbs of their companions.

For my part, I confess it with shame, I was an incorri-
gible laggard. I have always had the poetical feeling, that
is to say I have always been an idle fellow and prone to
15 play the vagabond. I used to get away from my books
and school whenever I could and ramble about the
fields. I was surrounded by seductions for such a temperament. The school house was an old fashioned whitewashed mansion of wood and plaister, standing on the
20 skirts of a beautiful village. Close by it was the venerable
church with a tall Gothic spire. Before it spread a lovely
green valley, with a little stream glistening along through
willow groves; while a line of blue hills bounding the
landscape gave rise to many a summer day dream as to
25 the fairy land that lay beyond.

In spite of all the scourgings I suffered at that school
to make me love my book I cannot but look back upon
the place with fondness. Indeed I considered this fre-
quent flagellation as the common lot of humanity and
30 the regular mode in which scholars were made. My kind
mother used to lament over the details of the sore trials I
underwent in the cause of learning; but my father turned
a deaf ear to her expostulations. He had been flogged
through school himself and swore there was no other
35 way of making a man of parts; though, let me speak it
with true reverence, my father was but an indifferent
illustration of his theory, for he was considered a griev-
ous blockhead.

My poetical temperament evinced itself at a very early
40 period. The village church was attended every Sunday by
a neighbouring squire; the lord of the manor, whose
park stretched quite to the village and whose spacious
country seat seemed to take the church under its protection. Indeed you would have thought the church had
45 been consecrated to him instead of to the Deity. The
parish clerk bowed low before him and the vergers hum-
bled themselves unto the dust in his presence. He

always entered a little late and with some stir, striking
his cane emphatically on the ground; swaying his hat in
50   his hand, and looking loftily to the right and left as he
walked slowly up the aisle, and the parson, who always
ate his Sunday dinner with him, never commenced service until he appeared. He sat with his family in a large
pew gorgeously lined, humbling himself devoutly on vel-
55   vet cushions and reading lessons of meekness and lowli-
ness of spirit out of splendid gold and morocco prayer
books. Whenever the parson spoke of the difficulty of a
rich man's entering the kingdom of heaven, the eyes of
the congregation would turn towards the "grand pew,"
60   and I thought the squire seemed pleased with the application.

    The pomp of this pew and the aristocratical air of the
family struck my imagination wonderfully and I fell des-
perately in love with a little daughter of the squire's,
65   about twelve years of age. This freak of fancy made me
more truant from my studies than ever. I used to stroll
about the squire's park, and lurk near the house: to catch
glimpses of this little damsel at the windows, or playing
about the lawns; or walking out with her governess.
70   I had not enterprize, nor impudence enough to venture
from my concealment; indeed I felt like an arrant poach-
er, until I read one or two of Ovid's *Metamorphoses,*
when I pictured myself as some sylvan deity and she a
coy wood nymph of whom I was in pursuit. There is
75   something extremely delicious in these early awakenings
of the tender passion. I can feel, even at this moment,
the thrilling of my boyish bosom, whenever by chance I
caught a glimpse of her white frock fluttering among the
shrubbery. I carried about in my bosom a volume of
80   Waller, which I had purloined from my mother's library;
and I applied to my little fair one all the compliments
lavished upon Sacharissa.

    At length I danced with her at a school ball. I was so
awkward a booby that I dared scarcely speak to her; I
85   was filled with awe and embarrassment in her presence;
but I was so inspired that my poetical temperament for

the first time broke out in verse and I fabricated some glowing lines, in which I berhymed the little lady under the favourite name of Sacharissa. I slipped the verses,
90   trembling and blushing, into her hand the next Sunday as she came out of church. The little prude handed them to her mamma; the mamma handed them to the squire; the squire, who had no soul for poetry, sent them in dudgeon to the schoolmaster; and the schoolmaster,
95   with a barbarity worthy of the dark ages, gave me a sound and peculiarly humiliating flogging for thus trespassing upon Parnassus.

Washington Irving, "Buckthorne," Tales of a Traveller

21. The narrator's father sent his son to a public school mainly:

   A. to toughen him up.
   B. to meet people from the upper class.
   C. because of its excellent curriculum.
   D. because the boy was a trouble maker.

22. The term "poetical feeling" (line 13), as used by the speaker, means that he:

   F. enjoyed writing poetry.
   G. views himself as a budding poet.
   H. was a romantic dreamer.
   J. loved reading poetry more than anything.

23. The speaker attributes his poor record in school to:

   A. too many distractions.
   B. a learning disability.
   C. friends who led him astray.
   D. being unhappy in a boarding school.

24. The narrator compares his schooling to a cattle drive (lines 7–9) in order to make the point that:

   F. students were grouped according to ability.
   G. the students were treated inhumanely.

    H. weak students were punished for their deficiencies.

    J. individuality was discouraged.

25. As a youth, the narrator believed that in order to learn in school you:

    A. should have small classes.

    B. had to be punished.

    C. should study hard.

    D. needed enthusiastic teachers.

26. The boy's attitude toward the country squire was shaped in part by:

    F. the influence of the schoolmaster.

    G. the squire's daughter.

    H. the teachings of the church.

    J. his observation of how others behaved.

27. The narrator introduces the squire into the passage for all of the following reasons EXCEPT:

    A. to explain who the man's daughter was.

    B. to add humor to the passage.

    C. to point out the man's hypocrisy.

    D. to illustrate the evils of England's class structure.

28. The name Sacharissa is:

    F. the first name of the girl with whom the narrator falls in love

    G. a name invented by the narrator because he didn't know the girl's real name.

    H. the woman to whom the poet Waller wrote love poems.

    J. the name of a wood nymph in Ovid's *Metamorphoses*.

29. Which of the following best describes the narrator's feelings about the situations described in the passage?

    A. amused by the trials of growing up.

    B. Bitter about the way he was treated by adults.

C. Nostalgic about the days of his boyhood.

D. Glad that those years are over and done with.

30. At the end of the passage the boy is flogged by the school-master because he:

F. embarrassed the girl

G. fell in love with someone above him

H. had illicit thoughts about the girl

J. wrote poetry

Passage 4

HUMANITIES: This passage, from Wesley Barnes' *The Philosophy and Literature of Existentialism,* describes the thought of the French philosopher and writer Andre Gide.

In considering André Gide, novelist (1869–1951), we have a French Protestant in conflict with his desire to taste the more lively aspects of life. His revolt took the course of freedom from parental and other social ties, sexual
5 unconventionality, a frank and nonhypocritical way of meeting experience, and a private and bizarre morality. Gide, mellowing somewhat, would never accept orthodox religion. He had much of the Renaissance spirit within him. With a will as strong as Luther's, with an influence
10 on him from the Bible as strong as any early Puritan's, Gide also brought a pagan spirit worthy of a Herrick or Donne in their earlier days. However, Gide went well beyond their pagan spirit to out-devil the devil. Compared to the indictments which sent Socrates to his death as a
15 corrupter of youth, Socrates' alleged offenses must be considered tepid indeed when put next to the incitements and corruptions Gide offered to youth in his long life.

Gide encouraged the revolt against rational and literary
values. Not only did he encourage the revolt against, but
20 also urged the negation of that traditional world of values
prior to 1916. He supported Dada. (Dadaism was a revolt
in poetry and painting formulated during World War I. Its
theses were that all social conventions must go; the
individual could do no wrong if he did not write
25 traditionally; one must behave outrageously in public.
Complete anarchy must reign. The movement finally
collapsed from its own excesses in 1926. The existential
qualities come from an overturning of all traditionals in the
name of the freedom of the individual spirit.) Gide's
30 article—"Dada"—encouraged the movement's supporters
to refuse to be confined and to abolish every tie to the
past.

Gide's support of Dadaism, his theories, and his own
personal life, aided the existential trend through breaking
35 down conventions and traditions in the myths. One
effective way to break down absolutes is to give their
original meanings a new twist. The French dramatists
(Cocteau, Anouilh, and Giraudoux), with Gide a leader,
sneered at old meanings, but gave the myths more
40 humanity, if more profanity. In an excellent account in *The
Classical Tradition,* Gilbert Highet traces the
reinterpretation of the myths. Gide's *Oedipus* indicates one
coming from nowhere, one with no traditions, one with no
past history, one with no outside support, and therefore,
45 one in a magnificent position. We are close to the
existentialist here. In the epic and traditional sense, the
hero stood with the basic essentials of his society.

Gide was as effective as Ibsen in striking at the Victorian
inhibitions: in those Victorian prohibitions were supports
50 for traditional conduct, particularly in the social life of the
family. There is vitality in Gide, as opposed to the more
philosophic nature of Nietzsche. Part of the violent
irresponsibility of Gide came from his problem with love.
The existentialist is not eager and not able to find a way to
55 involve himself in love with someone else. The relationship
must be one he can enter, but one he can leave with no

possibility that he will start out a subject and end as
object. Gide, religious in nature, and equally irreligious,
did much to aid Sartre in abolishing God. His use of the
60 myth was such as to take away dignity and any touch of
the sacred. However, Gide's work with the myth was not
as disastrous as his view of Christianity in literature. He
stated, and with undeniable force, that for a Christian to
be a tragic figure is nearly impossible. If a person repents
65 with any degree of sincerity, the soul is saved. In theory,
if a person can escape the temporal law, he could commit
any number of serious offenses and have his soul saved if
he repented.

Wesley Barnes, *The Philosophy and Literature of Existentialism*

31. According to the passage, the Dada movement faded away
because:

A. it was too outrageous.
B. it was corrupt.
C. Gide and others became disillusioned with it.
D. World War I began.

32. According to the passage, Gide was deeply influenced by:

F. Socrates.   **H.** the thinkers of the Renaissance.
G. the Bible.   **J.** Henrik Ibsen.

33. Based on information in the passage, Gide had the LEAST in
common with:

A. Donne.   **C.** Nietzsche.
B. Cocteau.   **D.** Sartre.

34. The use of the word *disastrous* in line 62 suggests that, in the
author's view, Gide:

F. ruined the stories of classical mythology.
G. was an atheist.
H. didn't understand Christianity.
J. distorted Christian doctrine.

35. According to the passage (lines 11 and 13), Gide went well beyond Herrick and Donne to "out-devil the devil." This means that, compared to Herrick and Donne, Gide:

    A. had more radical religious views.
    B. had a more intense fear of the devil.
    C. had a more evil influence on his readers.
    D. was more fascinated by devil worship.

36. Based on information in the passage, which of the following statements is most clearly an opinion rather than a fact about Gide?

    F. Gide influenced the beliefs of others.
    G. Gide lived an unconventional life.
    H. Gide rejected orthodox Christianity.
    J. Gide was a leader among French writers of his time.

37. The main purpose of the passage is to explain Gide's:

    A. values and philosophy.   **C.** literary output.
    B. lifestyle.   **D.** place in cultural history.

38. Based on the material in lines 21–29, Dadaists probably believe all of the following EXCEPT:

    F. it is acceptable for a man to wear lipstick.
    G. the family is an obsolete institution.
    H. war is the natural condition of humankind.
    J. originality is what gives art its value.

39. Based on ideas in lines 54–58, one might infer that existentialists:

    A. have the ability to control their emotions.
    B. love only themselves and other existentialists.
    C. do not care about earthly matters.
    D. do not value enduring relationships with other people.

40. *Oedipus* is cited in the passage (line 42) to illustrate Gide's:

 F. religious background.
 G. concern for humanity.
 H. spiritualism.
 J. rejection of classical literature.

Answer Key

1. **C**	8. **H**	15. **B**	22. **H**	29. **A**	36. **G**
2. **G**	9. **A**	16. **G**	23. **A**	30. **J**	37. **A**
3. **B**	10. **G**	17. **B**	24. **H**	31. **A**	38. **H**
4. **F**	11. **A**	18. **F**	25. **B**	32. **G**	39. **D**
5. **D**	12. **H**	19. **A**	26. **J**	33. **C**	40. **G**
6. **J**	13. **C**	20. **H**	27. **D**	34. **J**	
7. **A**	14. **J**	21. **A**	28. **H**	35. **A**	

Answer Explanations

1. C This answer is found in lines 7–10, which state that the meaning of "happiness" varies from person to person. Choice A is incorrect because Jefferson's intent is not critical to defining the term. B and D are wrong because neither is mentioned in the passage.

2. G A paraphrase of this answer is found in lines 15–16. None of the other answers is mentioned in the passage.

3. B The answer corresponds to material in lines 44–45, which alludes to one of the beloved maxims of early liberals: "That government is best which governs least." Choices A, C, and D express beliefs that may be liberal, but the passage does not discuss them.

4. F Lines 49–51 imply this answer in the discussion of human nature and time—two factors that cause government to change. G may be true but it's irrelevant, H is a questionable assertion, and J may be true but not germane to the passage.

5. D This is the best choice because most of the passage directly or indirectly pertains to the rights of the people and their government. The passage discusses choices A, B, and C, but only as ancillary matters.

6. J This is the only event that is not mentioned in lines 30–36. Therefore, J is the correct answer.

7. A Lines 32–34 argue that when excessive power is granted to the people, the strong could impose their will on the weak, resulting in anarchy. B is a reasonable answer but not as clearly related to the text of the passage. C is not discussed in the passage. D, although mentioned in the passage, is not related to anarchy.

8. H In lines 40–43, the author refers (somewhat humorously) to people who derive happiness from criticizing everything, including government. G is discussed in the passage, but only as a goal of a free society, not as a practice that creates happiness. F and J are not mentioned in the passage.

9. A Lines 22–25 state that the government's main business is to prevent infringement on the people's rights. B, C, and D certainly are worthly goals, but are not the government's primary concern.

10. G This idea is strongly suggested in the last sentence of the passage. Citizens must know their rights in order to maintain them. F, H, and J, although valid observations, are not discussed in the passage.

11. A Line 79 of the passage indicates that Alzheimer's strikes older adults, and line 7 says that the patients may be "of all ages." Therefore, Alzheimer's could strike any time during old age. B is wrong because 1906 is the date of the first report of changes in brain tissues, not the date of the discovery of the disease. C and D are not discussed in the passage.

12. H Headaches are not mentioned in the passage as a symptom of Alzheimer's disease. Lines 35–37 mention the other choices: loss of memory, deterioration of social skills, and the overall decrease of mental functioning.

13. C Lines 4–6 discuss the changes in nerve cells that are a clearcut indication of Alzheimer's disease. Both A and B are symptoms characteristic of Alzheimer's disease but cannot be used for positive diagnoses. D is not mentioned in the passage.

14. J According to lines 58–60, scientists are hopeful that genetic research will lead to foolproof diagnosis of Alzheimer's disease. F seems possible but technology without the knowledge of how to use it is not the key to unlocking the Alzheimer's puzzle. G describes an approach that is too indirect. H sounds like a sensible approach, but it is not as useful as genetic research.

15. B Based on the account of current research on Alzheimer's (lines 63–68), scientists are studying proteins and other organic compounds found in the human body. Therefore, researchers must know all about organic chemistry. Choices A, C, and D are basic subjects for all physicians but not particulary helpful in finding cures for Alzheimer's disease.

16. G As explained in lines 80–81, "many other disorders show symptoms that resemble those of Alzheimer's disease." F is incorrect because the passage suggests that research has been going on for quite some time and has made considerable progress. H and J may be valid observations but neither is discussed in the passage.

17. B Because Alzheimer's is incurable, a means to identify it would allow physicians to provide proper treatment to patients with similar, but curable, diseases. A is not an issue in the passage. C may be desirable but not the impetus behind research into Alzheimer's disease. D describes a relatively minor reason for Alzheimer's research.

18. F Alzheimer's disease is diagnosed by the process of elimination (lines 49–50), but a positive identification of the disease cannot be made except by autopsy after the patient has died. G and H are true but are not the cause of family frustration. J is an incorrect statement.

19. A Based on the second paragraph of the passage, computers are somewhat useful in diagnosing Alzheimer's disease but cannot provide definitive diagnoses. B, C, and D attribute greater value to computers that anything suggested by the passage.

20. H The whole passage discusses the current state of research on diagnosing Alzheimer's disease. F, G, and H are not discussed in the passage.

21. A The narrator says his father sent him to public school to make him "hardy" (line 3). Later he mentions that flogging was the way to make "a man of parts" (line 35), an expression that means a solid, well-rounded individual. No mention is made in the passage to support either B or C. Choice D, however, may seem accurate only if you interpret chronic laziness as a form of trouble making.

22. H The narrator defines the phrase in lines 14–15: "I have always been an idle fellow and prone to play the vagabond," that is, a lazy fellow who likes to wander about dreamily. Had the term not been so specifically defined in the passage, choices F, G, and J might have had some merit. But since you're told exactly what the phrase means, they must be dismissed.

23. A The boy is distracted by "seductions" (line 17) such as the lovely green valley, the little stream and the blue hills. B is not a good answer unless you consider excessive dreaminess a learning disability. C is not relevant because the narrator does not discuss friends. D would not stand up as a reasonable choice either because the boy is not really unhappy about being in a boarding school; he's only unhappily in love.

24. H Lines 8–11 say that inferior cattle, i.e., those that are slow or have short legs, suffer as a result. F is contrary to fact; the boys are in mixed groups, an arrangement that emphasizes differences in ability among them. G makes a valid point, but is too inclusive. The narrator's concern, after all, is the weaker students like himself, not all the students in the school. J may accurately describe conditions at the school, but it doesn't explain the narrator's comparison of school and a cattle drive.

25. B In lines 28–30, the narrator says that as a youth he thought flogging was a standard practice in education. A is never mentioned. C sounds reasonable, but the narrator fails to attribute success in school with hard studying. D is of no interest to the narrator.

26. J Many details in the paragraph about the squire (lines 39–61) refer to people who humble themselves in his presence. F is not accurate because it would be out of character for the narrator to portray the squire as an object of humor or derision. G is wrong; the girl is never shown being anything but loyal to her father. H has no bearing on the boy's attitude toward the squire.

27. D The passage was not written as a social or political commentary on England. It's more personal and light-hearted, although somewhat bittersweet. A is accurate and is necessary in order for the reader to appreciate the girl's character. B seems obvious, because the portrait of the squire is intended to be funny. C is also a key reason why the squire appears in the passage.

28. H Line 82 implies that Waller's poems were "lavished upon Sacharissa." F is incorrect; the narrator does not know the girl's name. G cannot be right because the name Sacharissa is not the narrator's invention; he got the name from a book of love poems. J is a poor choice. Ovid's work does not relate to the choice of names for the young girl the narrator has fallen in love with.

29. A The narrator's point of view throughout the passage is somewhat ironic, as though he is poking fun at the situations and people in his youth. He also makes fun of himself. B describes a feeling that some young people may have, but not the narrator of the passage. C pretty well misses the point; nostalgia suggests a sense of longing. If anything, the narrator does not miss the days of his youth. D identifies what the narrator may feel, but the passage does not suggest any sense of regret or bitterness about the way the boy was treated during those years.

30. J He is flogged for "trespassing on Parnassus" (line 97), the mythical place where only gods dwell. By writing poetry, he overstepped the acceptable boundaries of behavior for schoolboys. F is wrong because it remains unclear whether the girl was embarrassed, or whether she showed her mother the poem because she was an obedient and prissy little child. G is inaccurate because no mention is made of any distinctions in social class. H is not mentioned in the passage.

31. A This choice is supported by line 27, which says that Dadaism "collapsed from its own excesses in 1926." B is an opinion held by many critics, but it does not explain Dada's demise. C contradicts information in the passage. D is irrelevant to the decline of Dada.

32. G The correct answer, G, is supported by lines 9–10, which state that the Bible strongly influenced Gide. F is compared to Gide in line 10, but it is not considered an influence on him. H is not mentioned in the passage. J is compared to Gide in line 48, but is not considered an influence on him.

33. C Nietzsche was more philosophical than Gide, according to the fourth paragraph. A has a "pagan spirit" similar to Gide's, according to lines 11–12. B is a dramatist who shared Gide's views, according to line 38. D has religious views similar to Gide's, according to line 59.

34. J This answer is implied by the explanation of Gide's deviant views on traditional Christian doctrine. F and G are not mentioned in the passage. H is probably not valid. Gide merely disregarded traditional Christian doctrine.

35. A This choice correctly suggests that Gide's views on religion were more extreme than Herrick's and Donne's. B is not supported by the passage. C may be the author's opinion but is irrelevant to the question. D is not mentioned in the passage.

36. G This statement expresses an opinion about Gide's lifestyle, which may have been conventional for an artist at the time but unconventional from a traditionalist's point of view. F is a fact supported by evidence throughout the passage. H is a fact supported by statements in lines 7–8 and 58–59. J is a fact supported by line 38.

37. A This correct answer captures the essence of the passage, which focuses on the beliefs and attitudes reflected in Gide's writing. B is implied by the passage but is not its main point.

C is mentioned in the passage but not sufficiently enough to be the main purpose. D is too broad.

38. H This answer is correct, because it is *not* mentioned in the passage. F and G can be inferred from the Dadaists' rejection of all social conventions. J is implied throughout lines 18–32.

39. D The correct choice, D, supports the idea that existentialists need to enter and leave relationships without emotional attachments. Choice A contradicts Gide's views on Victorian inhibitions. B and C are not supported by the passage.

40. G This answer describes Gide's reinterpretation of *Oedipus*, which presents the hero as a more down-to-earth character, one who "stood with the basic essentials of his society." F is unrelated to Gide's *Oedipus*. H contradicts Gide's basically materialistic value structure. J is not supported by the passage.

5

PREPARING FOR THE SCIENCE REASONING TEST

DESCRIPTION OF THE TEST

Be prepared for a science test that is probably different from any you have ever taken. It will draw on your general background in science, but will not ask you to make use of your knowledge of scientific facts. Everything you need to know in order to answer the questions will be given to you. This is a test of science reasoning, not knowledge of subject matter.

All questions are multiple choice. Your choice of answer will be in the form of key letters, either A-B-C-D or F-G-H-J, in alternate questions. There are 40 questions altogether, and you have 35 minutes in which to answer them. You answer by filling in the appropriate space on the answer sheet.

The questions are in seven groups, each group containing five or six questions. Each group starts with a "passage," consisting of information given to you in the form of graphs, diagrams, paragraphs, or tables. The questions in each group can be answered from the information in the passage.

Testing Reasoning Skills

In the Science Reasoning Test, there are three distinctly different kinds of passages, each testing a different kind of reasoning skill.

- **Data Representation.** Two or three of the seven passages will present you with some sort of graph or chart. The questions that follow will ask you to interpret the information given, and to draw conclusions from it.

- **Research Summaries.** Three or four passages will each present you with a description of a scientific experiment and the results of the investigation. You will be asked to evaluate the experimental method, to interpret the results, and to appreciate some of the implications of the experimental findings.

180

• **Conflicting Viewpoints.** One passage will give you two paragraphs to read. The paragraphs will deal with some controversial scientific question. The scientists who wrote the paragraphs disagree with each other. You will be asked to evaluate the arguments of each, identify the points of disagreement, and recognize the evidence that each scientist cites in favor of his viewpoint. You will not be asked to decide who is right.

Cognitive Levels

Within each group of questions, the level of difficulty is graded. The first questions in the group are the easiest; as you go further into the group, the questions will call for deeper levels of understanding. Three cognitive levels are tested in each group:

• **Understanding.** These questions, about two in each group, test only your ability to know what the passage is saying. If it is a graph, do you know what the variables are and what values of them are presented? If it is an experiment, can you identify the nature of the experimental problem and the kind of data that were taken? If it is a controversy, do you know what points are at issue?

• **Analysis.** About three questions will ask you to find the deeper meanings in the passage. If it is a graph, can you tell how the variables relate to each other and what is implied by the relationship? If it is an experiment, were controls adequate, and what conclusions logically flow from the data? If it is a controversy, how well do the arguments flow from the facts presented by each scientist?

• **Generalization.** What further study might be suggested by the graph, experiment, or controversy? How do the results impact society at large? What does the study imply for systems that were not part of the study itself?

Improving Your Prospects

It would be folly to try to prepare for this test by reviewing what you learned in your science courses, because you will not be asked to recall specific items of information. Nevertheless, it is probably true that experience in studying science enhances your chances of doing well on this test, particularly if you have had advanced courses and done any investigative laboratory work. More important, it is your scientific attitude that will tell. If you are accustomed to evaluating information skeptically, demanding firm and reliable data before accepting claims of new knowledge or special pleading, you have an advantage.

There is something you can do to promote this attitude. Read about science—not textbooks, but newspaper and magazine articles about new developments. Magazines such as *Science Digest* and *Discover* are excellent sources. Some newspapers have superb science coverage; when you read the daily paper, pay particular attention to articles about new developments in science. The *Los Angeles Times* and *The New York Times* (Tuesday's edition) have extensive specialty coverage of science. For detailed study, select articles that deal with advances in fundamental science, rather than material about new kinds of technology.

In reading such articles, use the same kind of technique that is recommended in taking the ACT. First, read the whole article as quickly as you can, without stopping to understand all the details. Then look at it again and highlight the information that is most crucial to understanding of the whole article. In particular, look for the kind of information that is relevant to the three kinds of questions in the Science Reasoning Test:

Data Presentation: If there are diagrams or graphs, study them to make sure you know exactly what variables are represented, what values of the variables are given, how these values were obtained, and how they relate to each other.

Research Summaries: If experimental results are quoted, see what experiments were done and what was found. How were measurements made? Were there adequate controls? How does the conclusion follow from the results of the experiment?

Conflicting Viewpoints: A good journalist always tries to present all sides of an issue, and many new discoveries contradict canonical ideas. If scientists disagree with the conclusions reached in the article, what is the nature of the disagreement and what is the evidence that each side brings to uphold its viewpoint?

And always look for suggestions in the article of questions left unanswered, additional data needed, the impact of the new discovery on the future progress in science, and the impact of the discovery on society at large.

TIPS

There is a special skill to taking a multiple-choice test. In some cases, there is even a danger of getting the "wrong" answer by knowing too much. This is because it may be possible to read into the question some subtle idea that did not occur to the person who wrote the question. Good item-writers try to avoid this pitfall, but they do make mistakes. In this test, the candidate who gets the right answer is not necessarily the one who knows most about the subject. It is the one who understands the passage thoroughly and *bases the choice of answer strictly on the contents of the passage.* Extraneous information can lead you to confusion and misinterpretation of the question.

A multiple-choice test is highly structured and formalized. To do well in such a test, you must be thoroughly familiar with the mechanics of the test. There is always some anxiety in a testing situation, but you can reduce it by being familiar with the forms of the test in advance. If the test looks familiar, you will not waste time figuring out how to go about answering questions. When you go into the testing room, for example, you should expect to find that in some questions the choices are labeled **A, B, C,** and **D**, while in others your choices will be **F, G, H,** and **J**. You should know what the answer sheet will look like, and that you must mark it with a soft lead pencil. And you must expect to find a group of five to seven questions relating to each passage. With all these mechanical details out of the way, you can go into the testing room ready to work. You should also know that there are certain tactics that will enable you to demonstrate your ability to the best advantage.

Start by scanning the passage. Read the passage or look at the data presentation quickly, just to get a rough idea of what it is all about. This should take no more than 20 seconds. Do not stop to study in detail any part that you do not understand. With this background, you are ready to move into a more careful study of the passage.

Read the passage again. Now you can take as much as a minute or even more to understand the passage thoroughly. Feel free to mark up the test booklet with notes. Underline key words.

Answer the first question in the group. In most tests, it is a good policy to skip questions you cannot answer immediately, but there is an exception in this test. The first question in each group will probably be a simple test of understanding. If you cannot answer it, you may well get the others wrong as well. If necessary, go back to the passage to find the answer. If you cannot answer the first question, skip the whole passage and come back to it later.

Skip the hard questions. After you have answered the first question, do not initially spend more than 30 seconds or so on any question. If you have time at the end, you can come back and reread the questions you could not get the first time around.

Read all the choices. If you think you have found the right answer at once, do not stop reading. You may discover that there is some idea that has not appeared in the one you think is right. Think of the process as one of eliminating the incorrect answers, rather than selecting the right one. You may find that you can throw out three of the four choices quite easily.

If the answers are numerical, estimate. Calculation takes time, and you should avoid it whenever possible. You can usually eliminate three obviously wrong choices quite easily. For example, suppose a graph shows that an object has traveled 32 meters in seven seconds, and you are asked to find its speed. You are given these choices:

    A. 220 m/s
    B. 40 m/s
    C. 4.6 m/s
    D. 1.4 m/s

You know that 32 divided by 7 will be a little over 4, so you can pick out **C** as the answer without doing the calculation.

Pace yourself. With 35 minutes to answer the questions for seven passages, you have just five minutes for each passage. If you find yourself spending more than that on one passage, skip it and come back to it later. On average, you should spend about two minutes reading each passage and 30 seconds answering each question.

Answer every question. When you have finished doing the easy questions, go back and try again on some that you skipped. If you have only 30 seconds left at the end, turn to the answer sheet, find those questions you have not answered, and mark them at random. However, be careful not to give more than one answer to any question. There is no penalty for guessing, but an item will be marked wrong if you have given two answers.

DATA REPRESENTATION QUESTIONS

Many kinds of scientific investigations result in a collection of data, and the authors often try to find a clear and simple way to display their data. It may be a data table, some kind of graph, or a diagram. The Data Representation questions require you to interpret these displays.

Here is a sample Data Representation passage that illustrates the kind of question that might be asked at each of the three cognitive levels:

Passage 1

Two species of the microorganism *Paramecium* are grown in cultures, and the population density is measured daily. The upper graph shows the results if the two species are raised in separate cultures. The lower graph shows the results if the two species are grown together in a single culture.

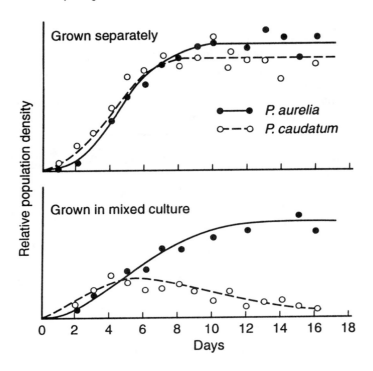

Increase in populations of two species of *Paramecium* when grown in separate cultures (above) and when grown together (below). Although both species thrive when grown separately, *P. caudatum* cannot survive when grown with *P. aurelia*.

From *The Economy of Nature* by Robert E. Ricklefs. ©1976 by Chiron Press. Reprinted with permission.

1. When the two species are grown together,
    A. both species reach maximum population density in 18 days.
    B. both species stop reproducing after 12 days.
    C. populations of both species grow fastest after 6 days.
    D. both species reproduce fastest after two days.

This question is at the *understanding* level of cognition. Both **B** and **D** are wrong because the graphs do not indicate rate of reproduction; the population density depends on other factors in addition to reproduction rate. **A** is wrong because the graph levels off at a maximum at 10 days, not 18. The slope of the graph indicates the rate of increase of the population density, and is greatest at 6 days; the answer is **C**.

2. When the two species are cultured together,

   F. *P. aurelia* is unaffected, but it inhibits the population of *P. caudatum*.
   G. *P. aurelia* reproduces more rapidly than *P. caudatum*.
   H. it takes about a week for the populations to begin to interfere with each other.
   J. each species inhibits the population growth of the other.

   This is an *analysis* question. **G** is wrong because factors other than reproduction rate may affect the population size. **F** is wrong because the population of *P. aurelia* grows more slowly in the presence of *P. caudatum* than without it. **H** is wrong because the growth of the *P. caudatum* population starts to diminish in less than 5 days. The answer is **J**.

3. Comparison of the two graphs seems to imply that

   A. the two species of *Paramecium* are competing for the same resources.
   B. no two microorganisms can live successfully in the same culture.
   C. *P. caudatum* could not survive in the wild.
   D. *P. aurelia* is a more common species than *P. caudatum*.

   This question calls on you to decide what general conclusion can reasonably be reached from the information given. **B** is wrong because the experiment deals with only two organisms, and says nothing about any other combinations. **C** and **D** are both wrong because conditions in the wild are nothing at all like those in a culture dish. It seems reasonable that *P. caudatum* is losing out in competition with *P. aurelia;* the answer is **A.**

Tactics

Most of the Data Representation passages will give you numerical data. There are certain techniques to follow in answering questions based on this kind of passage. Start by asking yourself certain questions about the chart, graph, or table.

What are the variables? In a data chart, the names of the variables will usually appear at the tops of the columns. If there are more than two columns, there might be more than two variables. In a graph, the names of the variables will be given at the side and bottom of the graph. A line graph may contain more than one curve, representing different experiments or different experimental conditions that are additional variables. In this case, the separate curves may be labeled, or the curves may be distinguished from each other in some way and a key supplied. In any case, be sure you understand just what variable distinguishes one curve from another.

What are the units of measure? These will usually be given along with the name of the variable. In a data chart, they will be at the top of the column. In a graph, they will be stated at the bottom and sides of the graph, along with the name of the variable.

What are the values of the variables? In a data chart, the values are entries in the table. In a graph, the values are read off the scales at the bottom and sides of the graph.

Are there any trends? Check to see whether there is an obvious consistent increase or decrease of any values as you move through the chart or graph.

Are there any correlations? If there are trends in any of the variables, how do they relate to trends in other variables? As one variable increases, does another increase or decrease?

These questions are not always applicable, but if they are, it will help you try to find answers to them.

Kinds of Data Representation

While scientists can invent methods of data representation to suit their particular needs, certain kinds are in common use. Here are some examples of forms of numerical data representation that might be encountered.

Data tables. This is the most direct way of presenting data. It is nothing more than a list of the values of the variables. Example: The table below gives the elemental composition of the earth's crust, in two forms:

Composition of the Earth's Surface: Atoms of Each Element
in a Sample of 10,000 Atoms, and Percent by Weight

Element	Symbol	No. of Atoms	Percent by Weight
Oxygen	O	5330	49.5
Silicon	Si	1590	25.7
Hydrogen	H	1510	0.9
Aluminum	Al	480	7.5
Sodium	Na	180	2.6
Iron	Fe	150	4.7
Calcium	Ca	150	3.4
Magnesium	Mg	140	1.9
Potassium	K	100	2.4
All others	—	370	1.4
Total		10,000	100.0

From **Chemistry for Changing Times** by John W. Hill. © 1984 by Burgess Publishing Company.

Variables? There are three: the name of the element and two numerical variables (the number of atoms of each kind and the relative weight of each). The second column is not an additional variable; it is simply another way of specifying the variables in Column 1.

Units? This question does not apply to Columns 1 and 2, since the entries in these columns are not measurements. In this table, the units are named in the title of the chart and in the head of each column. In Column 3 the unit is the number of atoms in a sample of 10,000. In Column 4 it is percent by weight, and it does not involve the number of atoms of each element in the sample.

Values? These are the numbers in the column. In Column 3, for example, we learn that out of every 10,000 atoms, 5,330 are oxygen. Column 4 tells us that these oxygen atoms constitute 49.5 percent of the weight of the sample.

Trends? There are none. Do not be misled by the fact that the numbers in Column 3 are decreasing. This is only because the person who made the chart elected to list the elements in order of decreasing frequency. There can be no trends because the entries in Column 1 are not numerical.

Correlations? Columns 3 and 4 both show decreasing values going down the column. This only indicates that the element with fewer atoms contributes less to the weight of the sample. The interesting fact here is that there are deviations from the strict order. Hydrogen, for example, is the third most common element, but its weight is less than any of the others. This should tell you that each hydrogen atom weighs far less than any other atom in the group.

Line Graphs. This is the most usual way of representing a function of two variables. In pure mathematics, the variables are *x* and *y*, but in scientific applications, they are usually measured quantities of some sort. If there are more than two variables, the graph may contain several curves. This example represents the rate at which gases are exchanged in the lungs and skin of a frog, per unit of body weight, as a function of temperature.

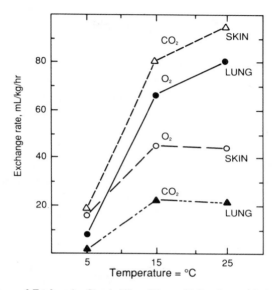

From **General Zoology** by Claude Vilee, Warren Walker Jr., and Robert D. Barnes. © 1978 by W. B. Saunders. Reprinted by permission of the publisher.

Variables? There are no less than four in this graph: kind of gas, body organ, and two numerical variables—temperature and exchange rate. Exchange rate and temperature are measured quantities and form the axes of the graph. The other variables are distinguished by labels on the curves.

Units? This question applies only to the numerical variables that form the function. Temperature is in degrees Celsius and exchange rate is in milliliters of gas per kilogram of body weight per hour.

Values? These are represented by the coordinates of points on the graph. Looking at the curve for "CO_2 lung," for example, the point at 15°C is at the level of about 21 mL/kg/hr on the ordinate. On this graph, it is interesting to note that each curve has been drawn from only 3 data points.

Trends? Surely, all values of the exchange rate increase with temperature, except that two of them drop off slightly at temperatures above 15°C.

Correlations? At all levels, "O_2 skin" and "CO_2 lung" move the same way, as do "CO_2 skin" and "O_2 lung."

Bar Graphs. A bar graph is used to show the distribution of some single variable. If several variables are involved, more than one graph is needed. In the bar graphs shown below, a comparison is made between the skull lengths of European moles before and after the severe winter of 1946–47.

Variables? In each graph, there are two numerical variables: along the abscissa, skull length (within 0.25 mm); on the ordinate, percent of the total number of moles that fall in each range. The four graphs give data for four groups: males and females before and after

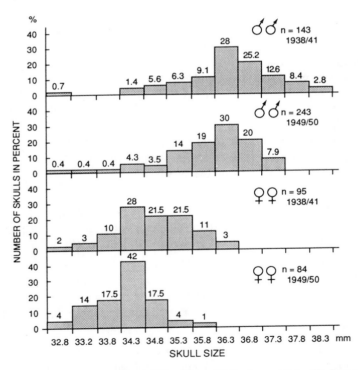

From **General Zoology** by Claude Vilee, Warren Walker Jr., and Robert D. Barnes. © 1978 by W. B. Saunders. Reprinted by permission of the publisher.

the hard winter. The additional information given is the actual number of moles in each of the four groups.

Units? For skull size, millimeters; for the length of each bar, percent of the total.

Values? These are read from the ordinate scale, for each size category. In this example, the value of the ordinate is also written in, so that it is unnecessary to read it off the scale. In the top graph (1938—41 males) the bar for the skull length 35.8 mm extends to just under 10% on the ordinate scale; the actual value is given as 9.1%.

Trends? In each of these graphs there is a typical normal distribution, with the largest number of individuals falling near the middle of the distribution and successively smaller numbers on both sides of the center. It is also clear that in both groups, females have smaller skulls than males. The most obvious feature is that the skull lengths were considerably smaller after the hard winter.

Correlations? Only that at all times, the females' skulls are smaller.

Qualitative Data Representation

The examples above give the most widely used methods of representing measurement data. Many others are in use, and any scientist can invent one as he feels the need for it. In addition to these, there are many kinds of diagrammatic representations that may not involve measurement at all. These will be used to show the relationships between phenomena or parts of a system. Some kinds of diagrams in wide use are family trees, evolutionary trees, geologic cross-sections, flow charts, and so on.

Try These

On the next pages, you will find a couple of sample data representation passages. Read each one carefully and answer the questions. You must commit yourself to your answers; write them down before you check with the explanations.

Passage 1

In the diagram below, Curve I shows how the theoretical activity of an enzyme varies with temperature. Curve II shows the theoretical rate at which the enzyme is destroyed as the temperature rises. Curve III is the net reaction rate of the enzyme, Curve I minus Curve II. The dotted lines represent measured reaction rates for two different enzymes.

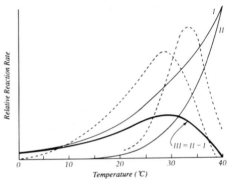

From **Botany: An Ecological Approach** by William A. Jensen and Frank B. Salisbury. © 1972 by Wadsworth Publishing Company, Inc. Reprinted by permission of the publisher.

1. As the temperature increases,
   A. activity of an enzyme increases and destruction decreases.
   B. activity increases to about 30°C and decreases above that temperature.
   C. both activity and destruction increase with temperature.
   D. both activity and destruction decrease above 30°C.

2. For the enzyme in the study, the temperature of 30°C is a point at which:
   F. the enzyme has been completely destroyed.
   G. the rates of theoretical activity and destruction are equal.
   H. the balance between theoretical activity and destruction results in maximum reaction rate.
   J. there is negligible destruction of the enzyme.

3. If the enzyme-controlled preparation were heated to 45°C and then gradually cooled,

   A. the reaction rate would increase and peak at 30°C.
   B. there would be no reaction at all.
   C. the reaction rate would start out high and gradually drop off as the temperature drops.
   D. the reaction rate would start out low and steadily increase as the temperature drops.

4. What is the relationship between the theoretical model and the actual measured values for real enzymes?

   F. Real enzymes agree exactly with the theoretical model.
   G. The information given does not provide an answer to the question.
   H. Real enzymes incorporate the same processes as the theoretical model, but with different constants.
   J. Real enzymes do not follow the theoretical model at all.

5. What step should be taken to determine the optimum temperature of an industrial process that uses an enzyme-controlled reaction?

   A. Control the temperature at 30°C.
   B. Experimentally determine the temperature at which the reaction rate is greatest.
   C. Experimentally determine the temperature at which the enzyme activity is greatest.
   D. Find the best compromise between high reaction rate and minimum destruction of the enzyme.

Answers and Explanations

The independent variable in this graph is temperature, and the dependent variables are different for each curve. For Curve I, it is the theoretical enzyme activity; for Curve II it is the rate of destruction of the enzyme; for the others, it is the net reaction rate. Temperature is in °C, but no units are given for the dependent variables; only relative rates are indicated. The value of temperature is read off the scale. The trends in both Curve I and Curve II show a definite increase with temperature, but in Curve II the increase starts out slow and then rises steeply. Curve III and the dotted curves show a rough correlation. Now let's look at the answers.

1. C This is an *understanding* question, requiring you just to read the graph. Curve I is activity and Curve II is destruction, and both increase with temperature.

2. H In this *analysis* question, you have to go beyond the mere reading of the graph and figure out what is happening. The reaction rate curve is III. At first, it increases as the enzyme activity goes up. At higher temperatures, the destruction of the enzyme increases rapidly, until it slows down the reaction rate and eventually reverses it at 30°C.

3. B Again, you must *analyze* the meaning of the graphs. Curve II shows complete destruction of the enzyme at 40°C, and cooling the reaction mixture down will not bring the enzyme back to life.

4. H *Analysis* again. The curves for the real enzymes show precisely the same pattern as the theoretical curve, so J is wrong. F is wrong because the peaks of activity are not at the same temperature as in the theoretical model. Since the pattern is the same, it is reasonable to assure that the same processes are at work, but with different constants.

5. D Now you have to *generalize* the meaning of the curves to a broader context. Choice A is wrong because every enzyme has different constants. It might seem that B is right, but at the maximum reaction rate temperature, the enzyme is being destroyed at a considerable rate, and would have to be replaced in the reaction vessel. The engineer in charge would have to make a compromise between a good reaction rate and the need to replace the enzyme.

Passage 2

Female lizards of a certain species can exhibit either male-like or female-like behavior. The chart shows kind of behavior, hormone levels, and size of a developing ovum.

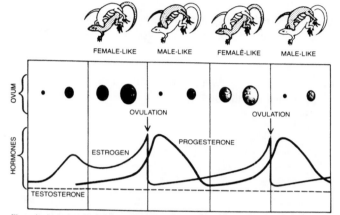

1. What event marks the change from female-like to male-like behavior?

A. Minimum progesterone level
B. Sudden increase in testosterone level
C. Ovulation
D. Growth of the ovum

2. Which of the following would explain the pattern of hormone production by the ovary?

F. As the ovum grows, the ovary produces more progesterone.
G. Progesterone and estrogen production both decrease as the ovum grows.
H. Progesterone production is stimulated by the concentration of estrogen in the blood.
J. At the time of ovulation, hormone production by the ovary switches from estrogen to progesterone.

3. Which of the following statements best accounts for the development of either male-like or female-like behavior?

   A. High estrogen levels produce male-like behavior.
   B. High progesterone levels produce male-like behavior.
   C. Low estrogen levels produce female-like behavior.
   D. High progesterone levels produce female-like behavior.

4. Which of the following changes might be a cause of the growth of the ovum?

   F. Increase in estrogen level
   G. Male-like behavior
   H. Increase in progesterone level
   J. Female-like behavior

5. There are no males in this species, and all eggs develop without fertilization. What might be a reasonable hypothesis to explain the existence of male-like behavior?

   A. The species has evolved from one in which male courtship behavior stimulates females to ovulate.
   B. At certain stages, the production of the male hormone testosterone induces male-like behavior.
   C. In all male lizards, high progesterone levels induce courtship behavior.
   D. Female-like behavior in male lizards or other species induces females to ovulate.

Answers and Explanations

1. C   The behavior is female-like in the second phase, and male-like in the third. Therefore, the transformation occurs at the end of the second phase, where the word OVULATION appears on the chart. Choice A is wrong because at the time of transformation, progesterone level is increasing. B is wrong because testosterone level, shown by the dotted line, is steady throughout. D is wrong because the

ovum is growing steadily long before the transformation.

2. J Ovulation is marked by a sudden drop in estrogen level and a rapid increase in progesterone, so it seems as though the ovary is switching from one to the other. F is wrong because progesterone actually drops almost to zero during the middle phase of ovum growth. G is wrong because progesterone level first drops and then rises during ovum growth. H is wrong because progesterone level decreases drastically while estrogen level is increasing.

3. B The conversion to male-like behavior coincides with a rapid increase in progesterone level. Choice A is wrong because estrogen level drops suddenly when the change to male-like behavior occurs. C is wrong because the change to female-like behavior occurs while the estrogen level is increasing. D is wrong because the change to female-like behavior occurs when progesterone level is very low.

4. F Estrogen level is increasing all the while the ovum is growing. G is wrong because the ovum grows rapidly while the behavior is female-like. H is wrong because the ovum starts its growth when there is no progesterone. J is wrong because there is substantial ovum growth during the male-like phase.

5. A It is clear that the female-like lizard ovulates when stimulated by a male-like partner, at the end of phase 2. B is wrong because the chart shows that testosterone level is always low and does not change. C is wrong because there is no evidence that male lizards have any progesterone at all. D is wrong because there is no evidence that any male lizards exhibit female-like behavior.

RESEARCH SUMMARIES QUESTIONS

The passage for a Research Summaries question is a description of an experiment. You will be asked the purpose of the experiment, to interpret the results, and perhaps to detect flaws in the experimental design. Here is a sample of a typical Research Summaries passage, along with a typical question at each of the three cognitive levels:

Passage 3

A series of experiments were done to test the hypothesis that air pollution affects fertility.

Experiment 1. Four groups of female mice, with 40 mice in each group, were mated and then exposed to different diets and concentrations of carbon monoxide in the air. The two diets tested were high protein (16%) and low protein (8%). Air was either free of carbon monoxide or contaminated with 65 parts per million of carbon monoxide. This is a pollution level that can be found in cities with heavy traffic. The number of females who became pregnant was then recorded:

> High protein, clean air: 38
> High protein, polluted air: 36
> Low protein, clean air: 19
> Low protein, polluted air: 9

Experiment 2. The experiment was repeated, this time using ozone instead of carbon monoxide as the pollutant:

> High protein, clean air: 35
> High protein, polluted air: 22
> Low protein, clean air: 20
> Low protein, polluted air: 21

1. Since the problem deals with the effects of polluted air, why were groups of mice exposed to clean air?

   F. to keep a healthy strain of mice going

G. so that they could be compared with mice exposed to polluted air

H. so that the effects of protein in the diet could be evaluated

J. to compare the effects of ozone and carbon monoxide

This is an *understanding* level question. It asks you to apply your knowledge of the meaning of a control. Unless there was a group given clean air, there is no way of telling whether the pollutants really make a difference in the fertility of the mice. The answer is G.

2. Which of the following conclusions is justified by the data?

A. Carbon monoxide pollution by itself reduces the fertility of mice.

B. A high protein diet promotes good health in mice.

C. Proteins protect the fertility of mice against the damage caused by carbon monoxide.

D. Air pollutants reduce the fertility of mice fed on a low protein diet.

This is an *analysis* question. You must study the data and find in it an implication that supports one of the offered answers. A is probably not a good answer because there is very little difference between the mice in good air and air polluted with carbon monoxide. (You must be prepared to make judgment calls in deciding between two answers.) B is wrong because nothing in the experiment deals with the general health of the mice. D is wrong because there is no justification for extending the results from the carbon monoxide experiment to pollutants in general; indeed, ozone seems to make very little difference if the protein level is low. The answer is C; fertility is little affected by carbon monoxide if there is plenty of protein, but mice produce very few offspring in air polluted with carbon monoxide if the protein level in the diet is low.

3. Which of the following would be an appropriate response to the results of this experiment?

F. Start a program to inform women who want to become pregnant that they should move to regions with lower air pollution.

G. Do a similar experiment on women, to see if their ability to become pregnant is affected by air pollutants.

H. Start a massive campaign to reduce air pollution, particularly in cities.

J. Start a research program to find out more about how air pollutants affect the fertility rate in animals.

This *generalization* question requires you to apply the results of the experiment in a broader area. F is wrong because mice are not women; there is no evidence that women would react the same way. G is wrong; it is good theoretical science, but where would you find women who would volunteer for the experiment? H is wrong; while reducing air pollution would probably be a good idea, this experiment does not provide enough evidence to justify such a massive program. J is a good idea; with more data in hand, it might be possible to get a better idea of how women might be affected.

Tactics

It is worthwhile to approach the Research Summaries questions in a systematic way. Every experiment has certain features in common, and you should look for them.

Purpose. What was the experiment designed to find out? (In the experiment above, the purpose was to find out whether air pollutants affect fertility.)

Design. How was the experiment set up? (Groups of female mice were exposed to various conditions and mated.)

Variables. What measurements and observations were made? The independent variables are those made by the experimenter (ozone and carbon monoxide content of the air, protein content of diet); the dependent variable is the outcome of the experiment (number of mice in each group that became pregnant.)

Controls. What precautions were taken to make sure that the results that were found were not due to something other than the independent variables? (One group was exposed to high protein diet and clean air, for comparison with the other groups.)

Results. What conclusions could properly be deduced from the data? (In mice, a low protein diet reduces fertility and carbon monoxide reduces it still further; ozone reduces fertility to about the same extent as a low protein diet, but does not reduce it further if the diet is low in protein.)

Try These

Here are a couple of sample Research Summaries passages, with questions. Remember to write down your answers to each question as you go along, before you read the explanations.

Passage 1

A horticulturist investigated the effects of using a high-nitrogen fertilizer on the growth of privet plants.

Fifty 1-year-old privet plants were divided into 10 lots of 5 plants each. All were watered every third day with equal amounts of water. In 9 of the lots, different amounts of high-nitrogen fertilizer were added to the water once every 2 weeks for a year. The heights of the plants were measured at the end of the year.

These were the results:

Fertilizer concentration (g/L)	Average height of plant/(cm)
0	22.2
5	26.3
10	29.0
15	28.7
20	27.9
25	29.0
30	28.6
35	20.9
40	16.3
45	13.0

1. For a commercial grower, what is the most efficient concentration at which to apply the fertilizer?

   A. 5 g/L
   B. 10 g/L
   C. 20 g/L
   D. 40 g/L

2. What was the purpose of applying water without fertilizer to one group of plants?

   F. To keep a healthy stock of plants for future experiments
   G. To find out whether the minimum amount of fertilizer has any effect
   H. To find out how much water is needed to promote healthy growth
   J. To find out whether there is any nitrate in the tap water

3. In order for the results of this experiment to be meaningful, which of the following would NOT have to be the same for all the experimental samples?

   A. The soil in which the specimens were planted
   B. The amount of time it took for the plants to flower

C. The particular variety of privet used

D. The number of hours of daylight to which the plants were exposed

4. In growing chrysanthemums to produce flowers, how would a grower determine what concentration of fertilizer should be used?

F. Find out by doing a similar experiment with chrysanthemums

G. Use a concentration of 10 g/L

H. Do a similar experiment, but use a different dependent variable

J. Grow the plants in sunlight, because it is known that sunlight makes plants bloom

5. Which of the following circumstances would NOT invalidate the results of the experiment?

A. Accidental destruction of the sample that was given a concentration of 20 g/L

B. The discovery that half the plants had been potted in a different soil

C. The discovery that the water used already contained substantial amounts of nitrogen

D. The discovery that some of the plants were of a different variety of privet

6. Which of the following hypotheses is suggested by the data?

F. Privet plants cannot grow unless there is nitrogen in the soil

G. If other conditions are equal, the amount of fertilizer does not affect plant growth

H. High concentrations of fertilizer damage the roots of plants

J. Any addition of fertilizer to the soil slows photosynthesis

Answers and Explanations

The purpose of this experiment is to discover the best concentration of nitrate fertilizer to apply to privets. The independent variable in this experiment is the amount of fertilizer applied; the dependent variable is the height of the plants after a year. For valid results, many controls are needed: all samples must match in kind of soil, genetic composition of the plants, and so on. Here are the correct answers:

1. B Administration of 10 g/L produces as much growth as higher concentrations; using more would be a waste of money. Choice D, 40 g/L, actually impedes growth.

2. G This is the control group. Unless plants were grown without any fertilizer, it would not be possible to know whether only 5 g/L had any effect at all. There is no test being made of the amount of water needed, and a chemical test would be the only valid way of finding out if there is nitrate in the tap water.

3. B The time of flowering is not any part of the experiment. Surely any variation in the soil, the genetics of the samples, or the amount of light would introduce uncontrolled variables into the experiment.

4. H F would be the right answer if the grower were looking for the best possible growth, but with chrysanthemums, the dependent variable is not growth, but the number and quality of the flowers. A concentration that promotes growth might not improve flowering.

5. A Since the results show little difference in the range 10 g/L through 30 g/L, the 20 g/L sample is not really necessary to reach the proper conclusion. Unless the other variables are controlled, however, it would not be possible to know why there is a difference in the growth.

6. H While there may be other reasons why concentrations above 30 g/L reduce the amount of growth, damage to the roots is surely one possibility, and can be accepted as a hypothesis for further testing. No tests were made of a complete absence of nitrogen, or of the effect on photosynthesis, but the experiment clearly shows that moderate concentrations of nitrogen promote growth.

Passage 2

A physicist is investigating the effect that different conditions have on the force of friction. The material used is an ordinary brick, with a mass of 1.8 kg. It is pulled across the surface of a wooden table. Friction is measured by pulling the brick with a string attached to a spring scale, calibrated in newtons (N). When the brick is pulled at constant speed, the reading on the scale is equal to the force of friction between the brick and the table top.

Experiment 1

The brick is placed on the table in three different positions. First, it is allowed to rest on its broad face (area = 180 cm^2), then on its side (area = 130 cm^2), and finally on its end (area = 56 cm^2).

Table 1

Area (cm^2)	Friction (N)
180	7.1
130	7.3
56	7.2

Experiment 2

A wooden block of mass 0.6 kg is made to the same dimensions as the brick, and the experiment is repeated.

Table 2

Area (cm^2)	Friction (N)
180	1.2
130	1.1
56	1.2

Experiment 3

This time, the wooden block is loaded by adding 1.2 kg of extra mass on top of it, to give it the same weight as the brick.

Table 3

Area (cm^2)	Friction (N)
180	3.5
130	3.6
56	3.7

1. From Experiment 1, it would be reasonable to hypothesize that:

   A. the surface area of contact does not affect the amount of friction.
   B. friction is large in a brick-to-wood contact.
   C. the amount of friction depends on the way the weight of the object is distributed.
   D. heavy objects have more friction than light ones.

2. Which combination of experiments shows that the amount of friction depends on the weight of the object?

   F. Experiment 1 and Experiment 2
   G. Experiment 1 and Experiment 3
   H. Experiment 2 and Experiment 3
   J. Experiment 1, Experiment 2, and Experiment 3

3. In doing Experiment 3, what was the purpose of adding enough weight to the wooden block to make its weight equal to that of the brick?

   A. To test the hypothesis that adding weight increases friction
   B. To find the relationship between surface area of contact and friction
   C. To find out whether the density of the material influences the amount of friction
   D. To control other factors and test the effect of the nature of the materials in contact

4. The experimenter repeated the experiment with the un-loaded wooden block mounted on three tiny wooden points, which were the only contact with the table top. If the results of all these experiments hold good for extreme values of the experimental variables, about how much would the friction be?

F. About 0.4 N
G. Substantially less than 1.2 N
H. About 1.2 N
J. Substantially more than 1.2 N

5. Common experience indicates that it is much harder to slide some boxes across a floor than others. Which of the following reasons why this is true is demonstrated in these experiments?

A. Friction is greater if there is more surface in contact.
B. A heavy box will have more friction against the floor than a light one.
C. Objects of irregular shape have more friction because they dig into the floor.
D. The amount of friction depends on how the weight of the object is distributed.

6. The results of these experiments suggest that, if three bricks were piled up and pulled along as before, the amount of friction would be about:
F. 3.6 N.
G. 7.2 N.
H. 14.4 N.
J. 22.6 N.

Answers and Explanations

In all these experiments, the dependent variable is the measured amount of friction. Independent variables are surface area in Experiment 1, type of material in Experiment 2, and weight in Experiments 2 and 3. An important control would be to use the same table top in all experiments, and to be sure that it is level.

1. A In spite of the fact that one surface is almost three times as great as another, there is no substantial difference in the amount of friction. The small differences are surely due to experimental variation. This is obvious when it is noted that the value obtained for the 130-cm^2 surface is a little larger than that for the 180-cm^2 surface. B is wrong because there is no comparison with other readings to decide what constitutes large friction. C is wrong because the experiment did not vary weight distribution. D is wrong because the same object was used throughout.

2. H In these two experiments, both the surface area of contact and the kind of materials in contact are the same, and the only difference is in the weight. The other three choices all include Experiment 1, in which a different kind of material is in contact with the surface, and this might be the reason for the difference in results.

3. D With the weight added, all other variables are controlled and the only difference between the brick and the wooden block, as far as contact with the table top is concerned, is in the nature of the material. The other choices are wrong because the experiment makes no comparison of different weights, surface areas, or densities.

4. H The data indicate that friction does not depend on surface area of contact. This is tested to extreme limits by repeating the experiment with a very small surface area. If the relationships hold up for extreme values, the friction should be the same for a very small area as for a large one.

5. B Comparing Experiment 2 with Experiment 3 shows that, even if the materials and the surface area in contact are the same, friction is greater when the weight of the object is greater. There is no evidence in these experiments that shape or weight distribution affects friction. Choice A is wrong because the experiments do not show any difference due to surface area.

6. J Experiments 2 and 3 show that, when the effective weight of the wooden block is increased by raising the mass from 0.6 kg to 1.8 kg, the friction triples. This suggests that friction is proportional to the weight of the object. Since three bricks weigh three times as much as one, the friction with three bricks ought to be three times as great as with a single brick.

Passage 3

A geologist is trying to find out what factors affect the speed of flow of the water in a river. On two occasions, the scientist measures the speed of flow at various points in the river:
—in summer, when the river is 1.2 m deep at the center;
—in spring, when it is 4.1 m deep at the center.
These are the results:

Location in river	Speed, m/s summer, 1.2 m deep	Speed, m/s spring, 4.1 m deep
Middle, near surface	4.2	11.9
Middle, near bottom	1.6	1.8
Surface, edge of straight part	2.8	6.0
Surface, outer edge of curve	5.0	13.5
Surface, inner edge of curve	0.7	1.4

1. In what part of the river does the amount of water in the river have the LEAST effect on the speed of the water?

   A. The edge of a straight section
   B. The bottom
   C. The surface
   D. The outer edge of a curved section

2. What significant question CANNOT be answered from the data taken in this research program?

   F. At what time of the year is erosion at the outer edge of a curved section greatest?
   G. In what part of the river is the largest amount of water carried in spring?

H. Is the speed of the water in the middle of the river greater on a straight section or a curved section?

J. Does the amount of water in the river affect the speed of flow of the water?

3. Which of the following hypotheses, implied by the data, could account for the surface speed at the inner edge of a curved section?

A. The water is very shallow at that location.

B. Larger sedimentary particles are carried where water flows faster.

C. Dense growth of water plants slows the water at that location.

D. The water is unusually deep at that location.

4. Which of the following environmental hazards would a plant have to tolerate in order to thrive in the outer edge of a curved section?

F. Periods of near-stagnant water

G. Seasonal changes in water depth and speed

H. Spurts of deep water following storms

J. Fast-flowing water near the bottom, where the plants are rooted

5. In traveling on a river, which tactic is likely to be most efficient?

A. In curved sections, travel upstream in the middle and downstream at the edges

B. In straight sections, keep as close to the edge as possible

C. In curved sections, use the outer parts of the curve downstream and the inner parts upstream

D. In straight sections, always use the middle of the river

6. One difference between a straight river and one with many curves is that in a straight river,

F. the speed of the water would not vary much throughout the year.

G. the amount of water flowing would be greater.

H. the water would be flowing more slowly at the bottom than at the top.

J. the surface speeds would not be much different in different parts of the river.

Answers and Explanations

This study is not strictly an experiment, since the geologist does not control the independent variables; he merely selects them. There are basically two: depth of water (controlled by selecting the time of year) and location in river. The dependent variable is speed of flow.

1. B At the bottom, there is very little difference between the speed in spring and in summer. In all other locations, the speed in spring, when there is a lot of water, is at least twice as great as in summer.

2. H No measurements were made to compare the speed in the middle in a straight and a curved section. Where water is flowing faster, there must be more of it going by, and it therefore erodes the banks more effectively.

3. A Comparing the spring and summer rates shows that water flows faster where it is deeper. The extremely slow rate at the inner edge of a curve might well be due to shallowness. There is no information in the study about particle size or plant growth.

4. G While the flow is always substantial, it is considerably faster in spring. It is slower in summer but never really stagnant, and there is nothing to show that there are spurts of rapid flow. The outer edge is a deep region.

5. C This tactic puts the boat in the fastest part of the river while going downstream, and the slowest part while going against the current upstream. The data do not give any information about the difference between the middle and edges of a straight section.

6. J   In a curved river, the water swings wildly from side to side as it goes around a curve. This does not happen in a straight river. The water flows faster in spring, and everywhere flows faster on top than on the bottom. We have no information about the total amount of water in the river.

CONFLICTING VIEWPOINTS QUESTIONS

Scientists may lack sufficient evidence to reach a definite conclusion, and often disagree with each other. Here is a sample Conflicting Viewpoints passage with questions at each of the three cognitive levels.

Passage 3

Two scientists disagree on the causes of the long-term trend of a warmer earth.

Scientist A

There has been a steady increase in the average temperature of the earth for the last 150 years. Since 1861, the average temperature, all over the world, has gone up one degree Fahrenheit. This may not seem like much, but if the trend continues, the result will be disastrous. The polar ice caps would melt, flooding all coastal areas and reducing the total land area of the earth by 30 percent. All climatic zones would change; farmland would turn to desert and forest would turn into prairie. This change in global climate is caused by the accumulation of certain gases in the atmosphere. Due to our massive burning of coal, oil, and gas, the carbon dioxide level in the atmosphere has more than doubled since 1861. Carbon dioxide is like a blanket around the earth, preventing the radiation of heat out into space. Unless drastic steps are taken to reduce the buildup of carbon dioxide, the world as we know it will disappear. Industry must learn to function without releasing this and other greenhouse gases into the air.

Scientist B

Before placing an enormously expensive burden on industry, we must be sure of our ground. While the greenhouse effect may well be a part of the reason for the warming of the earth, it cannot be the whole story. Most of the temperature increase occurred before 1940, but most of the carbon dioxide increase has happened since then. Something else is contributing to the warming of the earth. The temperature of the earth depends strongly on the level of sunspot activity on the sun. The sun heats up during high sunspot years. The "little ice age" of 1640 to 1720, when the average temperature was two degrees low, was a period of low sunspot activity. Solar activity goes through cycles. When activity is high, increased levels of ultraviolet radiation deplete the ozone layer of the upper atmosphere and the increased flow of charged particles from the sun affects the formation of clouds. All of these effects have complex and poorly understood effects on the earth's climate, and could easily result in long-range and cyclic climate changes.

1. The two scientists agree that

    F. sunspot activity affects the climate of the earth.
    G. there is a trend to a warmer earth.
    H. the major cause of warming is carbon dioxide.
    J. something must be done to avert a catastrophe.

    This is an *understanding* question. F is wrong because Scientist A does not address the question of sunspot activity at all. H is wrong because Scientist B thinks that sunspot activity may play the major role. J is wrong because Scientist B does not suggest any action. The answer is G; both agree that the earth has gotten warmer.

2. In responding to Scientist B, Scientist A might reply that

   A. the measured value of the increase in sunspot activity is far too small to account for the observed warming.
   B. it is widely known that it is the carbon dioxide in the atmosphere that produces the warming.
   C. the flow of charged particles from the sun actually decreases during periods of high sunspot activity.
   D. it is possible to cut down on the atmospheric carbon dioxide by promoting the growth of plants.

   To answer this analysis question, you have to eliminate proffered answers that do not deal with issues discussed by either scientist, such as D. Appeals to authority, like B, are not acceptable scientific debate. C is an insult to Scientist A, who surely knows the properties of an easily measurable phenomenon. The answer is A, because there is a strong element of judgment in making this decision, and it can be questioned.

3. What course of action might be suggested by Scientist B and opposed by Scientist A?

   F. Convene a committee of industry and government leaders to determine what steps can be taken to reduce carbon dioxide emission.
   G. Start a long-range research project to explore the possibility of neutralizing the flow of charged particles from the sun.
   H. Investigate the possibility that other greenhouse gases such as methane have an important effect on warming.
   J. Start a long-range research project to evaluate the relative importance of carbon dioxide and sunspot activity.

   Now you must look for an appropriate *generalization.* F is wrong because Scientist B does not believe that carbon dioxide is at the heart of the problem. G is wrong; Scientist B has not committed himself to the idea that charged particles are the major culprit. H is wrong; neither scientist has suggested that other gases are involved. J is right; Scientist B feels that more information is needed, but Scientist A might object to a long-range project on the ground that the problem of carbon dioxide is too urgent.

Tactics

There will be one Conflicting Viewpoints passage on the test. If possible, you should allow a little more time for this question than for the others.

Start by reading both statements quickly, without trying to remember everything in them. On the second reading, look for several specific kinds of information; underline the pertinent parts of the passage. This is what you should look for:

What is the basic point at issue? You probably know the answer to this from your first, quick reading. In the passage above, the issue is whether sunspot cycles contribute to global warming.

What is the position of each of the scientists on the question? Scientist A believes that greenhouse gases are adequate to account for global warming; Scientist B thinks sunspot activity also contributes.

What is the evidence that Scientist A brings to the issue? The temperature increase coincides with a massive increase in the amount of carbon dioxide in the atmosphere.

What is the evidence that Scientist B brings? The temperature increase began long before most of the carbon dioxide was added to the air. Global temperature changes have occurred in the past, correlated with sunspot cycles.

What flaws did Scientist A find in the argument of Scientist B? In this case, Scientist A did not address the question of sunspots at all.

What flaws did Scientist B find in the arguments of Scientist A? Scientist A neglected to take into account the known effects of sunspot activity on the earth's climate.

As you read the questions, the first thing you should do is eliminate the obviously wrong answers. In many cases, this will be enough to determine the correct choice.

Try These

Using this approach, find the answers to the questions about the following passages. Write them down.

Passage 1

From the standpoint of environmental damage, is it wise to build more nuclear power plants? Two scientists present opposing views.

Scientist 1

The whole nuclear power industry is a blueprint for disaster. It produces radioactive gases that can escape into the atmosphere in case of an accident, like the one that happened at Chernobyl. A nuclear plant produces low-level waste that must be stored in isolation, and we do not have any place to put it. The multibillion-dollar salt-dome storage facility in New Mexico is an expensive mistake; water is already leaking into it. A nuclear plant has a life of only about 40 years, and it must then be kept carefully isolated for thousands of years. It is much better to meet our energy needs by burning oil and natural gas, with a gradual shift to coal as the liquid and gas fuels are exhausted. Further, we have hardly begun to explore the potential of other fuels, such as oil shale, garbage, and biomass. And we have yet to make any substantial use of nonfuel energy sources, such as solar, geothermal, and wind power. Most important, we can learn to use energy more efficiently so that we do not have to produce so much of it.

Scientist 2

Like it or not, we must continue to develop nuclear energy. The burning of fuels increases the amount of carbon dioxide and other gases in the air. In the last hundred years, there has already been a substantial increase. It produces the greenhouse effect, in which the heat received from the sun is more effectively trapped by the atmosphere. The resulting increase in temperature will melt the polar ice caps and change the climates all over the world. Within the next century we will find coastal cities flooded, fertile farm belts turned to desert, and massive displacement of populations. Nuclear energy can be made safely. The Chernobyl accident was a disaster only because the reactor core was not enclosed in a concrete containment. Nuclear technology is constantly improving. It is already clear that safe, smaller nuclear generating stations can be built cheaply. Energy conservation and nonfuel energy sources are very important, but they will probably not adequately increase our energy supply. To preserve our atmosphere, we must replace fuel burning with nuclear reactors.

1. The most important objection that Scientist 1 has to the expansion of the nuclear energy industry is that it would result in:

   A. exposure of people to damaging radiation.
   B. drastic changes in the earth's climate.
   C. exhaustion of the supply of fossil fuels.
   D. decrease in the efficiency of our use of energy.

2. Both Scientist 1 and Scientist 2 base their arguments on the need to:

   F. conserve scarce energy resources.
   G. produce energy cheaply and efficiently.

H. protect the human environment.

J. make the best use of fossil fuels.

3. What is a point on which both Scientist 1 and Scientist 2 agree?

A. Nuclear energy poses inescapable risks to the environment.

B. The major current environmental problem is the accumulation of carbon dioxide in the atmosphere.

C. We must learn to use available energy resources more efficiently.

D. Solar energy will make little contribution to our energy problem.

4. Which of the following developments would greatly strengthen the case presented by Scientist 2?

F. An unquestionably safe and adequate facility for the storage of radioactive wastes

G. Statistical evidence that the earth's climate has not changed in the last century

H. Evidence that the standard concrete containment for a nuclear reactor could not stand up against a possible explosion

J. Development of a highly efficient process for producing usable energy from sunshine

5. Which point in the statement by Scientist 1 was not rebutted by Scientist 2?

A. The site of a used-up nuclear power plant is forever unusable.

B. A nuclear plant might release radioactive materials into the environment.

C. Burning of fuels poses no threat to the environment.

D. We can safely obtain much more energy from coal, oil shale, garbage, and biomass.

6. What evidence did Scientist 2 present to support his basic argument?

F. The disaster at the nuclear plant in Chernobyl
G. The availability of energy from wind-driven generators
H. The possibility of small, safe nuclear reactors
J. The recorded increase in the amount of carbon dioxide in the atmosphere

7. Which of the following developments would tend to weaken the position of Scientist 2?

A. The depletion and increasing scarcity of fossil fuels
B. Improvement in the safety of nuclear reactors
C. The invention of a cheap and effective way to remove carbon dioxide from smoke stacks
D. Reduction in energy need as a result of higher efficiency of usage

Answers and Explanations

1. A Scientist 1 sees potential danger of three kinds: escape of radioactive material from a reactor, and from radioactive waste, and persistence of radioactivity in a used-up plant. B is wrong because that concern belongs to Scientist 2. C and D have no bearing on Scientist 1's concerns.

2. H Scientist 1's concern is the damage to the environment by release of radioactivity; Scientist 2 is concerned with the accumulation of carbon dioxide. None of the other issues is raised by either scientist.

3. C Both scientists mention this. Choice A is wrong because Scientist 2 thinks the risks can be handled. B is wrong because Scientist 1 does not mention this problem at all. D is wrong because neither scientist evaluated the degree of contribution that solar energy could make.

4. F A safe and adequate storage facility for radioactive waste would eliminate one of Scientist 1's most important reasons for opposing the development of nuclear energy. G is wrong; it would weaken the case of Scientist 2, not strengthen it. H is wrong because one of Scientist 2's main points is that nuclear energy can be made safe. J is irrelevant.

5. A Scientist 2 did not deal with the problem of the used-up nuclear plant. B is wrong because Scientist 2 claims that a nuclear generating plant can be made safe. C is wrong because Scientist 1 made no such claim. Since Scientist 2 claims that burning alternative fuels would pollute the atmosphere, D is wrong.

6. J This is evidence that there is a real danger from the greenhouse effect. F is wrong because it is not a support for his argument, but a weakness that must be explained away. G and H are plausible arguments, not real evidence.

7. C This would drastically reduce the atmospheric pollution, and make it more believable that fuels could be burned with safety. Choice A is wrong because the loss of fossil fuels would increase the importance of other sources of energy, such as nuclear. B would strengthen Scientist 2's argument, not weaken it. D is irrelevant; both scientists might agree to this.

Passage 2

What is causing the loss of trees in the Appalachians? Two differing opinions are presented below.

Scientist 1

The forests of the high Appalachian Mountains are being destroyed. Millions of dead spruce and fir trees cover the peaks of the mountains, from Maine to Georgia. The new growth is low shrubbery, like blackberries, instead of trees.

These forests are dying because of a combination of air pollution and unusual weather patterns. Recent years have shown a substantial increase in the concentration of ozone and of nitrogen and sulfur oxides in the air. The oxides come from the burning of fossil fuels. Rain, snow, and fog in the mountains pick up these oxides and turn acid. Ozone is produced by the action of ultraviolet light on the hydrocarbons in the air, which are found in automobile exhaust and wastes from certain industrial processes. This pollution has been going on for decades, and the effect is cumulative. The last straw was added by the unusually high temperatures and drought of recent years. Unless serious steps are taken to reduce air pollution, there is a distinct danger that we will lose all our forests.

Scientist 2

There is no substantial evidence that air pollution is the culprit in the Appalachians. Trees in the high mountains are living precariously at best and are easily destroyed. The hot, dry summers and cold winters of recent years could easily account for the damage. Also, the spruce budworm and other insect pests are now unusually abundant and have done a great deal of damage to the trees. There have been other instances of massive die-off of trees at high elevations in years past, when the air was purer. If the chief source of damage were air pollution, we would expect that the damage would be worse at lower elevations, where the factories and automobiles that produce pollution are concentrated. Yet there is little evidence of damage to the commercial forests at lower elevations. This does not mean that we should ignore air pollution; it is clearly a threat, and we must learn more about it and develop ways to control it.

1. According to Scientist 2, what would be expected to happen to the forest in future years?

    A. Return of a permanent, self-sustaining forest in the high Appalachians

B. Permanent conversion of the high mountains to low-growing shrubbery instead of trees

C. Development of timber-producing commercial forest in the high mountains

D. Regeneration of the forest, which will again be killed off from time to time

2. Without challenging any facts, what might Scientist 1 say to counter Scientist 2's argument about the effect of insect pests?

   F. Insects do not really do much damage.
   G. The insects have been able to proliferate so well because pollution has weakened the trees.
   H. Insect populations are being well controlled by birds.
   J. Insects are actually helpful because they cross-pollinate the trees.

3. What further development would weaken the case made by Scientist 2?

   A. Destruction of the blackberry bushes that are replacing the forests
   B. Evidence of damage to commercial forests at lower elevations
   C. Insect infestations of low-level forests
   D. Evidence that the mountain-top forests are showing signs of healthy regeneration

4. What is the opinion of Scientist 2 with respect to the problem of the effect of polluted air on the high forests?

   F. Polluted air does not damage forests, and no action is needed.
   G. The evidence is inadequate to prove that the damage in the high Appalachians is due to polluted air, but the problem needs to be studied further.
   H. Polluted air damages trees and may soon present a problem to commercial forests at lower levels.

J. There is no substantial pollution in the air at high elevations, so it is not damaging the trees.

5. Suppose there were to appear a healthy new crop of spruce and fir trees on the mountain tops. Which of the following studies would NOT contribute to a resolution of the difference of opinion between the two scientists?

   A. A study to determine whether there has been any change in the ozone levels in the air
   B. A study of weather patterns over the preceding few years
   C. A study of changes in automobile exhausts due to new antipollution devices in cars
   D. A study of the conditions under which spruce seeds survive in the soil

6. What is a point on which both scientists agree?

   F. The air is being polluted by waste products of industry and transportation.
   G. The spruce budworm is a major cause of the destruction of forests.
   H. Stressful weather conditions alone can account for the destruction of the Appalachian forests.
   J. Low-elevation commercial forests are in imminent danger of destruction by polluted air.

7. To refute Scientist 2's opinion, Scientist 1 might:

   A. show that there is extensive damage to trees wherever in the world the air pollution levels are high.
   B. show that healthy spruce forests recover easily from damage by the spruce budworm.
   C. claim that spruce trees thrive at lower elevations, but are poorly adapted to the extremes of mountaintop weather.
   D. show that, because of atmospheric circulation patterns, the air at high elevations is not heavily polluted.

Answers and Explanations

1. **D** Scientist 2 believes that from time to time unusual weather conditions kill off the high forest, even if there is no air pollution. Choice A is wrong because Scientist 2 does not believe that the forest can ever be permanent. B is wrong because he thinks that the forest can regenerate itself after it has been destroyed. C is wrong because he has never made any such suggestion.

2. **G** Scientist 1 believes that pollution has damaged the trees, and might well suggest that this damage makes them subject to attack by insects. The other answers are wrong because they ignore the observable facts that the insects are rife and harmful.

3. **B** One of the points that Scientist 2 makes is that pollution at low levels does not seem to be damaging the forests there. Choice A and C are irrelevant. D is wrong because regeneration of the high forest would support Scientist 2's contention that forest destruction occurs naturally from time to time.

4. **G** Scientist 2 makes no claim that polluted air is innocent; but only that the evidence for its guilt is not conclusive. That is why F and H are wrong. He makes no claim that mountain air is unpolluted, so J is wrong.

5. **D** Choice A and C are wrong because, if such studies showed a substantial decrease in pollution, Scientist 1's claim that pollution destroys the forest would be upheld. B is wrong because a correlation of weather patterns with forest regeneration would tend to support Scientist 2.

6. **F** Both scientists recognize the existence of pollution, and both see that it is a problem. G is wrong because Scientist 1 might well think that the insects can damage only unhealthy trees. H is wrong because Scientist 1 thinks that the main cause of damage is pollution, and the weather is just a contributing factor. J is wrong because Scientist 2 has not found any damage to low-

elevation trees, although he might agree that this could be a long-range problem.

7. A This would strongly reinforce Scientist 1's opinion that the major cause of damage to trees is air pollution. B is wrong because Scientist 2 believes that forest destruction and recovery are common events. C is wrong because Scientist 2 thinks that mountaintop trees may be destroyed by extremes of weather alone. D is wrong because any such demonstration would undermine Scientist 1's claim that air pollution is the chief culprit.

SAMPLE SCIENCE REASONING TEST

Now that you have had practice on all three kinds of questions, here is a complete test, much like the one you will have to take. In trying it out, it is important that you time yourself. Allow only 35 minutes to complete the whole test. Remember these rules:

For each passage, study it carefully and answer the first question.

For the other questions, skip any that you cannot answer within a half minute or so.

When you have finished all those questions, go back and work on the ones you skipped. If you are not sure of an answer, make your best guess.

If you still have any unanswered questions and there is only a minute left, enter answers at random.

Look at your clock and start NOW. Good luck!

DIRECTIONS: This test consists of several distinct passages. Each passage is followed by a number of multiple-choice questions based on the passage. Study the passage, and then select the best answer to each question. You are allowed to reread the passage.

Passage 1

The table below lists some of the properties of the noble gases.

Gas	Atomic number	Atomic mass (daltons)	Density at 0°C (g/L)	Boiling point (°C)	Specific heat (J/g · K)
Helium	2	4.0	0.18	−269	5.19
Neon	10	20.2	0.90	−246	1.029
Argon	18	39.9	1.78	−186	0.519
Krypton	36	83.8	3.74	−152	0.247
Xenon	54	131.3	5.86	−107	0.158
Radon	86	222	9.91	−62	0.093

1. Which of the listed properties does not increase as the atomic number increases?

   A. Density
   B. Boiling point
   C. Atomic mass
   D. Specific heat

2. Plotted as a graph, which pair of variables would yield a straight line passing through the origin?

   F. Atomic mass and density
   G. Specific heat and boiling point
   H. Atomic number and boiling point
   J. Specific heat and density

3. If a mixture of all these gases were cooled down, starting at room temperature, which one would liquefy first?

   A. Argon
   B. Helium
   C. Xenon
   D. Radon

4. What is a reasonable hypothesis to account for the close proportionality between density and atomic mass?

   F. One gram of any of these gases contains the same number of atoms as 1 gram of any other.
   G. The larger the mass of the atoms, the larger their size.
   H. The larger the mass of the atoms, the smaller their size.
   J. One liter of any of these gases contains the same number of atoms as 1 liter of any other.

5. Which of the following combinations of properties would produce a nearly constant value for all of the gases?

   A. Atomic mass times boiling point
   B. Density times atomic number
   C. Boiling point times specific heat
   D. Specific heat times atomic mass

Passage 2

Three experiments are done to test the competitive survivability of different mutant strains of fruit fly (*Drosophila*).

Experiment 1

Three pure-bred strains of *Drosophila* are used: wild type, white-eye, and yellow-body. Fifty fertilized eggs of each strain are placed, separately, into standard culture bottles. They go through larval stages, and then form pupae. The adults that hatch out of the pupa cases are counted:
   wild type: 42   white-eye: 36   yellow-body: 25

Experiment 2

Pairs of strains are grown together, with their larvae in the same culture bottle. Fifty eggs of each strain are placed in the bottle, and the number of adults of each kind that hatch out of the pupa cases are counted:
   Trial 1: wild type, 43   white-eye, 16
   Trial 2: wild type, 38   yellow-body, 22
   Trial 3: white-eye, 18   yellow-body, 27

Experiment 3

Fifty eggs of each of the three strains are placed in the same culture bottle, with the following numbers of adults produced:

wild type: 33   white-eye: 8   yellow-body: 20

6. In Experiment 2 what was the purpose of growing two different strains of larvae in the same bottle?

   F. To find out how competition between strains affects survivability
   G. To test the effect of crowding larvae in the culture bottles
   H. To determine the results of crossing two different strains
   J. To see whether the white-eye or yellow-body character can be transferred from one larva to another

7. What important variable was controlled by Experiment 1?

   A. Availability of food supply
   B. Survivability of each strain in the absence of competition
   C. Number of eggs to be used in the experiment
   D. Transformation of larvae to the pupa stage

8. Comparison of the results shows that competition:

   F. increases the survivability of the wild type.
   G. is most detrimental to the yellow-body.
   H. is most favorable to the yellow-body.
   J. is most detrimental to the white-eye.

9. What design factor in the experiments was crucial in establishing the existence of competition between strains?

   A. Keeping all culture bottles under the same conditions.
   B. Supplying only enough food for about 60 larvae
   C. Testing strains in advance to be sure they were purebred
   D. Using no more than 3 different strains

10. What do these results imply about the structure of natural populations?

   F. About one fourth of all flies in nature are expected to be yellow-bodied.

G. One reason why the wild type is most common in nature is that its larvae survive best in competition.

H. There will be no white-eyed flies in natural populations.

J. In the course of time, white-eyed and yellow-bodied flies will completely disappear in nature.

11. The evidence seems to show that yellow-bodied flies do not suffer in competition with the wild type. Why, then, are there so few yellow-bodied flies in nature?

A. The evidence is misleading because the total number of flies in the experiment is so small.

B. White-eyed flies promote the survivability of the yellow-bodied, and they are rare in nature.

C. Under natural conditions, many factors other than competition determine survivability.

D. When yellow-bodied flies mate with wild type, their offspring are wild type.

Passage 3

Experiments were done to find out how long it takes for the immune system to come into operation.

Experiment 1

Non-virulent bacteria were injected into a non-immune rabbit, and the numbers of bacteria were assayed for 3 days, at 10 hour intervals.

Experiment 2

Virulent bacteria were injected into a rabbit, and bacteria levels were assayed.

Experiment 3

Another rabbit was immunized against the bacteria, and then injected with virulent bacteria. The same assay was done.

The graph below shows the result of these experiments.

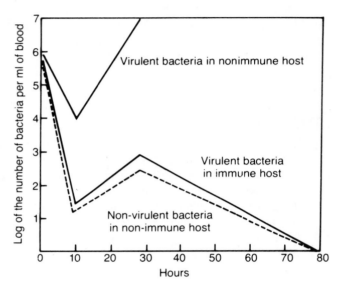

From Stanier/Doudoroff/Adelberg. *The Microbial World*, 2e © 1963, p. 601.
Reprinted by permission of Prentice Hall, Inc. Englewood Cliffs, New Jersey.

12. In what way was the change of concentration of virulent bacteria in a nonimmune host different from the others?

F. It increased after the first 10 hours.
G. It did not decrease after the period of increase.
H. It increased steadily throughout the entire period.
J. It decreased more rapidly at first.

13. What inference can be drawn from the graphs?

A. Virulent bacteria always cause death of any host.
B. Nonvirulent bacteria can be as dangerous as virulent bacteria.
C. The immune system offers no protection against virulent bacteria.
D. An immune host reacts to virulent bacteria as though the bacteria were not virulent.

14. What inference can be drawn from the data for the first 10 hours?

   F. The body of the nonimmune host is able to promote an attack against all bacteria.

   G. In that period, the immune system cannot distinguish virulent from nonvirulent bacteria.

   H. In that period, immunity offers no protection against virulent bacteria.

   J. Virulent bacteria will kill a nonimmune host.

15. During what period does the immune system provide protection?

   A. The first 10 hours only

   B. 10 hours to 30 hours

   C. 10 hours to 80 hours

   D. Throughout the whole 80 hours

16. Which of the following hypotheses might emerge from the graphs?

   F. Nonimmune animals have no protection against invading bacteria.

   G. There are two different mechanisms of immunity, one of which is lacking in nonimmune animals.

   H. The immune system of an immune host cannot control the concentration of nonvirulent bacteria.

   J. Virulent bacteria cause the host animal to develop immunity.

Passage 4

To find out how the electric current through various materials is controlled, a physicist applies various potential differences to three different objects and measures the current produced in each case.

Experiment 1: 10 meters of #30 copper wire

Potential difference (volts)	Current (milliamperes)
0	0
0.2	60
0.4	120
0.6	180
0.8	240
1.0	300

Experiment 2: 10 meters of #30 aluminum wire

Potential difference (volts)	Current (milliamperes)
0	0
0.2	40
0.4	80
0.6	120
0.8	160
1.0	200

Experiment 3: OC26 transistor

Potential difference (volts)	Current (milliamperes)
0	0
0.2	5
0.4	15
0.6	60
0.8	115
1.0	190

17. What scales on the voltmeter and ammeter would be most appropriate in making these measurements?

A. 0–20 V, 0–20 A
B. 0–5 V, 0–5 A
C. 0–1 V, 0–10 A
D. 0–1 V, 0–0.5 A

18. Why were the wires of identical dimensions used in Experiments 1 and 2?

F. To increase the variety of readings of the current
G. To determine how the material of which the wire is made affects the current
H. To determine how the dimensions of the wire affect the current
J. To compare the properties of a wire with those of a transistor

19. Which readings serve as controls on the proper adjustment of the meters?

A. The readings on the transistor
B. All the zero readings
C. All the readings at 1.0 volt
D. The readings on the copper wire

20. When a 10-volt potential difference is applied to the aluminum wire, the ammeter records 1100 milliamperes. This indicates that:

F. the proportionality between potential difference and current does not hold for large values.
G. there is no usable rule relating potential difference to current.
H. large potential differences reduce the current in the wire.
J. aluminum wire reacts differently from copper wire.

21. Resistance is defined as the ratio of potential difference to current. Which of the following statements holds true over the range of values in the experiments?

   A. All three objects have the same resistance.
   B. The objects have different resistances, but the resistance is constant for each.
   C. None of the objects has constant resistance.
   D. Each wire, but not the transistor, has constant resistance.

22. On the basis of these experiments, what hypothesis might be proposed?

   F. Transistors respond to applied potential differences in the same way as metal wires.
   G. In any circuit, a transistor will have more current than a wire.
   H. Transistors are too unreliable to be used in most electronic circuits.
   J. Transistors and wires can be used for different purposes in electronic circuits.

Passage 5

The graph below represents the number of boys born per thousand girls in the United States for a period of years. (♂♂= males; ♀♀ = females):

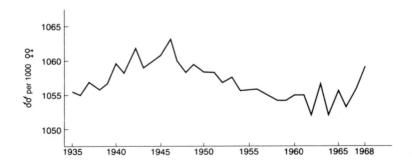

Human Genetics by Edward Novitski. © 1977 by Macmillan Publishing Company, New York.

The following graph represents the sex ratio at birth as a function of the ages of the parents. (Sex ratio is the fraction of all newborn babies that are male.)

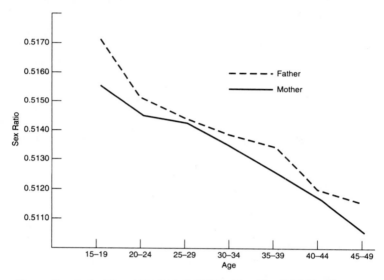

Human Genetics by Edward Novitski. © 1977 by Macmillan Publishing Company, New York.

23. The sex ratio in 1946 was:

   A. 1063/2063
   B. 1063/2000
   C. 1063/2
   D. 1063/1052

24. Which general statement is true?

   F. There has been a steady decline in the proportion of male births.
   G. At all times, more boys than girls are born.
   H. The total number of male births decreases with the age of the parents.
   J. Younger parents have more children than older ones.

25. A couple in their early twenties decide that they would like to have a girl. Would it be a good idea for them to wait 5 years?

    A. No; the probability of having a boy goes up substantially in those years.
    B. Yes; the probability of having a girl goes up substantially during those years.
    C. No; the increased probability of having a girl is too small to make much difference.
    D. Yes; the probability of having a boy goes down substantially during those years.

26. The sex ratio increased during the war years 1940 to 1946, and started to rise again during the Vietnam war in 1967. This increase has been noticed during war years in other countries and during other wars. A possible explanation is that:

    F. many men are killed in wars, so the number of male babies increases to compensate.
    G. as younger men die in the war, more babies are fathered by older men.
    H. prolonged periods of sexual abstinence favor the production of the kind of sperm that produce male babies.
    J. this may be merely a statistical accident with no real significance.

27. Is it the age of the mother or of the father that is most significant in determining the sex ratio?

    A. The father, since the line for the father lies always above the line for the mother
    B. The mother, since the line for the mother always lies below that for the father
    C. They affect the result equally, since both follow the same pattern of decrease with age.
    D. It is impossible to tell from the graphs because people generally tend to marry spouses of about their own age.

Passage 6

A chemist performs a series of experiments to determine the relative chemical activities of three metals. Metal *A* is considered more active than metal *B* if metal *A* will replace metal *B* in a solution.

Experiment 1

A piece of steel wool is placed into a solution of copper sulfate. Copper sulfate is blue because of the copper ions in it. The result of the experiment is that metallic copper forms on the steel wool and the blue solution turns colorless.

Experiment 2

A bundle of fine copper wire is placed into a solution of iron(II) sulfate, which is colorless. No change is observed.

Experiment 3

A fine spray of metallic mercury is inserted into a solution of copper sulfate. No change is observed.

Experiment 4

A bundle of fine copper wire is inserted into a solution of mercuric sulfate, which is colorless. The wire acquires a coating of the silvery color of mercury, and the solution acquires a bluish tint.

28. The results of Experiments 1 and 2 indicate that:

    F. copper is more active than iron.
    G. relative activity depends on how the experiment is done.
    H. iron is more active than copper.
    J. the two metals are probably equally active.

29. In Experiment 4, why did the solution become bluish?

    A. Some of the copper of the wire went into solution.
    B. Removal of the mercury revealed the true color of the solution.

    C. The silvery color of the deposited mercury reflects light and has a bluish cast.

    D. Some of the mercury in the solution changes to copper, which gives the solution a bluish color.

30. Why was there no reaction in Experiment 2?

    F. Copper is not soluble in water.

    G. The metal in the solution is the more active of the two.

    H. Metallic iron and metallic copper cannot mix.

    J. The iron sulfate solution was already saturated.

31. What would probably happen if steel wool were placed into a solution of mercuric sulfate?

    A. It is impossible to predict the result without experiment.

    B. Mercury would plate out on the steel wool.

    C. Nothing would happen.

    D. The solution would turn bluish.

32. Suppose fibers of metal X were placed into separate solutions of mercuric, copper, and iron sulfates. Copper and mercury deposit on the metal, but iron does not. Which of the following represents the order of activity of the four metals, from highest to lowest?

    F. Metal X, mercury, copper, iron

    G. Mercury, copper, metal X, iron

    H. Copper, mercury, iron, metal X

    J. Iron, metal X, copper, mercury

33. An investigator hypothesizes that the relative activity of any metal depends only on the structure of its own atoms. Which of the following observations would support this view?

    A. In their reactions with sulfates, all the metals can be arranged in a linear sequence according to their activities.

    B. In any kind of reaction, there will always be some metals that are more active than others.

    C. If one metal is more active than another, it will be more active in any chemical reaction, not just with sulfates.

D. In any reaction, it is always possible to compare two metals and find out which is more active.

Passage 7

Will future human evolution increase the number of twins in the population? Two scientists present opposing views.

Scientist 1

It is an established principle, the rule of Darwinian fitness, that natural selection favors the individuals who leave the largest number of viable and fertile offspring. It is also known that there is a genetic tendency that causes some women to produce more than one ovum at a time. These women will bear twins more often than other women. Since they have more offspring than other women, selection will favor them and the frequency of twin births will increase in time. This did not happen in the past because the conditions of life were so different. A woman in a hunter-gatherer society had to spend much of her time collecting plant food, while carrying her baby with her. She also had to be ready to run or otherwise protect herself from wild animals. Her chance of survival, avoiding both starvation and predation, was much worse if she was carrying two babies instead of only one. Thus, the genes that promote twinning carried an enormous liability, which more than offset the selective advantage of having twins. Under modern conditions, however, these negative features disappear and a woman who bears twins is likely to leave more offspring than one who does not. The frequency of the gene that promotes the release of more than one ovum at a time will increase in the population.

Scientist 2

You cannot think of evolutionary change in terms of a single feature. When many factors affect an outcome, it is necessary to consider how they interact to produce an optimum condition. Twins are often born prematurely, and their average birth weight is only 5.5 pounds. Single babies, on the average, come into the world weighing 7.5 pounds. Premature birth and low birth weight result in many kinds of medical problems. Twins' prospects for survival to a normal, healthy reproductive age are less than those for singly born babies. An evolutionary tendency to overcome this deficiency would call for mothers to produce twins weighing in at 7.5 pounds each. This would be an enormous strain on the mother, since she would have to gain more weight during pregnancy. The only way to neutralize this liability would be for women to be much bigger, weighing more than 200 pounds. This would, however, introduce another liability: strains on the skeleton and musculature. Evolution would have to produce a complete redesign of the body. The gain in selective value produced by twinning would be far outweighed by these disadvantages. Modern civilization has not changed the fact that single births are optimum for human women.

34. What is the basic question on which the two scientists disagree?

    F. Is human evolution a continuing, ongoing process?

    G. Do human twins start life at a disadvantage?

    H. Does natural selection favor genes that produce twins?

    J. Is the tendency to produce twins hereditary?

35. To refute Scientist 2's argument, Scientist 1 might point out that:

    A. modern medical science has greatly improved the survival rate of infants with low birth weights.

    B. many twins result from the division of a single fertilized egg, and this is not genetically controlled.

    C. evolutionary change is extremely slow, and there is no evidence that the human species has changed much in the last 10,000 years.

    D. large women have twins as frequently as small women do.

36. The arguments of both Scientist 1 and Scientist 2 would be invalidated if new evidence indicated that:

    F. the rate of twin births has not changed in the past century.

G. genetics really makes very little difference in whether or not a woman produces twins.

H. women in hunter-gatherer societies have twins more often than women in civilization.

J. the genetic tendency to produce twins passes to women from their fathers, not their mothers.

37. What piece of statistical evidence would greatly strengthen Scientist 2's position?

A. Twins born at 5.5 pounds have a better survival rate than babies born singly at 5.5 pounds.

B. Twins born at 7 pounds have the same survival rate as babies born singly at 7 pounds.

C. Twins born to large women have a better survival rate than twins born to small women.

D. Twins born to small women have a better survival rate than twins born to large women.

38. Underlying the arguments of both scientists is the assumption that:

F. production of twins is a desirable prospect for the human species.

G. women who bear twins are healthier, on the average, than women who do not.

H. the genetic composition of the father is irrelevant to the probability of a woman's bearing twins.

J. natural selection acts on human beings in the same way as on other animals.

39. Which of the arguments of Scientist 1 was not refuted by Scientist 2?

A. Modern medicine has no effect on the rate at which twins are born.

B. In primitive conditions, natural selection will favor single births.

C. Survival rate is a basic biological factor that is not influenced by external conditions.

D. Large women are inherently capable of producing twins with large birth weights.

40. Scientist 2 claims that Scientist 1 has overlooked an important general principle of biological science. What is it?

    F. All biological factors interact with each other, and selective value depends on the optimal combination of values of many factors.

    G. Genetic factors influence all aspects of development, and must be considered in any long-term prediction.

    H. Genetic factors cannot be considered alone, but must be analyzed in terms of their interaction with external conditions.

    J. Evolution is the result of natural selection acting on the genetic composition of individuals.

Answer Key

1. D	8. J	15. D	22. J	29. A	36. G
2. F	9. B	16. G	23. A	30. G	37. C
3. D	10. G	17. D	24. G	31. B	38. J
4. J	11. C	18. G	25. C	32. J	39. B
5. D	12. G	19. B	26. H	33. C	40. F
6. F	13. D	20. F	27. D	34. H	
7. B	14. F	21. D	28. H	35. A	

Answer Explanations

1. D   Specific heat decreases as the atomic number rises. Note that the boiling points are all negative numbers, rising toward zero with increasing atomic number.

2. F   You might suspect that the gas with the largest atomic mass would have the greatest density, in proportion. The easiest way to check this is to obtain the ratio of the two variables for the smallest and largest values: for helium, 4.0/0.18 = 22.2; for radon, 222/9.91=22.4—close enough. G and J are inverse relationships; if one variable increases as the other decreases, they can never reach zero simultaneously. H is wrong because, as the values for atomic number increase to 86, the boiling point approaches zero.

3. D   The one with the highest boiling point would liquefy at the highest temperature, and radon's boiling point of −62°C is higher than any of the others.

4. J   The mass of a liter of gas is density, and it must be equal to the product of the number of molecules times the mass of a single molecule. If the number of molecules is constant, density must be proportional to atomic mass. None of the other choices makes any sense.

5. D   Look for a combination that seems to be an inverse ratio, and try it out. Again, the easiest way to check for a relationship of this sort is to use the smallest and largest values: for helium, 4.0 × 5.19 = 20.8; for radon, 222 × 0.093 = 20.6.

6. F   With two different strains in competition, one or the other might prove to be better adapted. G is wrong because crowding could be tested, without introducing a different variable, by simply using more eggs of either strain. H is wrong because there is no mating in the larval stage. J is wrong because the experimental design does not allow for the testing of any such transfer, which is most unlikely in any event.

7. B   If the effect of competition is to be established, it is important to know how well each strain survives when there is no competition. None of the other choices represents a variable in the experiment.

8. J The number of white-eyed adults that hatch is drastically less than the control number (Experiment 1) whenever one of the other strains is present. The number of surviving yellow-body flies is not affected either way by competition.

9. B Note that in Experiments 2 and 3 only about 60 larvae produced adults, even though there were 100 or 150 eggs. If there were no restriction on the food supply, it is possible that all the eggs could survive in the same numbers as in Experiment 1. A and C are necessary controls, but have nothing to do with competition. D is an arbitrary choice; a perfectly valid experiment could be done with more strains.

10. G Whenever other strains are present with the wild type, it is the others that suffer, while the wild type maintains its predominance. F is wrong because there is no reason to believe that the numbers of eggs laid in nature are like those in the bottle. H and J are wrong because competition does not completely eliminate the white-eyed and yellow-bodied forms.

11. C Do not confuse a culture bottle with nature. There is no evidence to support any of the other choices.

12. G All concentrations increased after the first 10 hours, so F is wrong. H is wrong because none of them increased steadily. J is wrong because the decrease for virulent bacteria in a nonimmune host is actually slower than the others at first.

13. D The graphs show clearly that, if the host is immunized to the bacteria, the concentration follows the same pattern as for nonvirulent bacteria. Choice A is wrong because the graph does not show death. B is wrong because the graph says nothing about how dangerous the bacteria are. C is surely wrong; the immune organism has converted the increase of concentration to a decrease.

14. F The graph shows that all concentrations, even for the virulent bacteria, decrease in the first 10 hours. G is wrong because even in the first 10 hours the concentration of virulent bacteria is greater if the host is not immune. H is wrong; the immune system has managed to reduce the concentration. J is wrong; no data for death are given.

15. D At all times, the concentration is less in the immune than in the nonimmune host.

16. G During the first 10 hours, there is an immune mechanism that is acting on all the bacteria; at 16 hours, the immune host has another mechanism. F and H are wrong because the concentration of virulent bacteria drops in the first 10 hours, even in the nonimmune host. Since there is no information about the way immunity develops, J is wrong.

17. D For best precision, you want the smallest scale that will incorporate the largest reading. The largest potential difference reading is 1 V, so a 1-volt scale will do very well. The largest current reading is 300 mA, or 0.3 A.

18. G The dimensions are being controlled to eliminate them from consideration, so H is wrong. The two experiments differ only in the substance of which the wire is made.

19. B The meter must be zeroed; that is, it must be adjusted to make sure that it reads zero when there is no current or potential difference.

20. F For all readings in the table, the ratio between potential difference and current is constant at 160 mA/V. The ratio for the 10-V setting, however, is only 110 mA/V. G is wrong because there is surely a usable rule below 1 V, and further investigation might turn up a usable rule at higher potentials. H is wrong; the large potential difference increased the current; it was just not as much as might have been expected. J is wrong because there is no evidence about the behavior of copper wire at higher potential differences.

21. D Checking the ratios at the smallest and largest values gives these results; copper wire, $0.20/60 = 0.0033$ and $1.00/300 = 0.0033$; aluminum wire, $0.20/40 = 0.0050$ and $1.0/200 = 0.0050$; transistor, $0.2/5 = 0.040$ and $1/190 = 0.0053$. The ratios are constant for each wire, but not for the transistor.

22. J Since transistors and wires have different but reliable properties, they can be used for different purposes. F is wrong because the ratio of potential difference to current (for small currents) is constant for each wire, but not for the transistor. G is wrong because no information is given about the circuits. H is wrong because Experiment 3 gives no information about the reliability of transistors.

23. A Adding male births (1063) and female births (1000) gives a total of 2063; males are 1063 of this total.

24. G Although the sex ratio went down, and then went up, it was always more than 0.5, which would indicate equal numbers of boys and girls. No information was given about total numbers.

25. C While parents are in their twenties, the sex ratio decreases by only about 1 or 2 parts per thousand, not enough to take into account.

26. H F is wrong because it is not an explanation; it fails to suggest a mechanism by which the result is brought about. G is wrong because the second graph indicates that older men produce a smaller fraction of boys, not a larger one. J is wrong; you are told that this effect has been noticed in many wars and many countries, so it is unlikely that this result is coincidental. By elimination, H is the only feasible answer of those offered.

27. D Because spouses are generally only a little different in age, there is no way that the graphs can distinguish the effect of the mother's age from that of the father.

28. H Copper has come out of solution in the form of copper metal. The loss of copper changes the color of the solution. Iron must have replaced copper in the solution, so iron is more active. This follows from the definition of a more active metal, given in the first paragraph of the passage.

29. A The blue color indicates the presence of copper in solution. B is wrong because we have no reason to believe that there is any such thing as the "true color" of the solution. C is wrong because we have no indication that the mercury coating is bluish. D is wrong because mercury cannot change into copper.

30. G   Since iron is more active than copper, copper cannot replace iron in the solution. F is wrong; in the blue solution, copper is dissolved. Nothing in the experiment points to either H or J.

31. B   Since iron is more active than copper (Experiment 1) and copper is more active than mercury (Experiment 4), it is reasonable to assume that iron is more active than mercury. Therefore, iron will replace mercury in solution, and the mercury will deposit on the steel wool.

32. J   We already know from the experiments that iron is more active than copper, and copper than mercury. Since metal X replaces copper and mercury from solution, it must be more active than either of them. It does not, however, replace iron.

33. C   The atomic structure of a metal atom is the same as it enters into any reaction. If atomic structure is what determines activity, then the relative activities of two metals do not depend on what the specific chemical reaction is. Choice A is wrong because a ranking with sulfates does not prove that the ranking would hold in other reactions. B and D prove only that there are different levels of activity in different reactions.

34. H   Both scientists agree that evolution continues and might involve changes in the frequency of genes producing twins, so F and J are wrong. They also agree that twins have lower survival rates, so G is wrong. The only point at issue is whether the result of selection will be a higher frequency of twinning.

35. A   Scientist 2 argues that twinning has a negative selective value because twins are born small, but gains in medical science might nullify this disadvantage. None of the other choices is germane.

36. G   Both Scientist 1 and Scientist 2 assume that the tendency to produce twins is hereditary; they disagree only on how this will change the evolutionary trend. F is wrong because both would agree that a century is too short a time to show any effect. H is wrong because neither scientist makes any such claim. J is wrong because it would make no difference in the survival value of the gene.

37. C   Scientist 2 claims that large, healthy twins could be produced only by larger women, and statistics to this effect would support his case. A and B are wrong because Scientist 2's argument is based on the birth weight of the babies, not on whether they are twins.

38. J   Both scientists base their arguments on natural selection of the most favorable combination of traits; they disagree on what that combination might be. F is wrong because neither scientist makes any value judgment. G is wrong because neither scientist makes any such claim. H is wrong because the arguments of neither scientist require any such assumption.

39. B   This claim is made by Scientist 1, and not addressed by Scientist 2. The others are wrong because Scientist 1 does not make any such claims.

40. F   This is the core of Scientist 2's rebuttal; Scientist 1 has not considered all the genetic interactions involved. G is wrong because both scientists agree that genetic factors are central to the issue. H is wrong because both scientists considered external conditions; they disagreed on which ones were important. J is wrong because they agreed on this point.

6

MODEL TESTS

The purpose of the Model Tests is to help you evaluate your progress in preparing for the actual ACT. Take each examination under simulated testing conditions and within the time limits stated at the beginning of each test. Try to apply the test-taking tactics recommended in this book. Detach the Answer Sheet and mark your answers on it.

After you finish each examination, check your answers against the Answer Keys and fill in the Analysis Charts. Rate your total scores by using the Performance Evaluation Chart on page 434. Read all of the Answer Explanations.

The Analysis Charts will indicate where you need further review. Go back to the "Preparing for..." sections to reinforce specific areas.

ANSWER SHEET—Model Test A

Directions: *Mark one answer only for each question. Make mark dark. Erase completely any mark made in error. (Additional or stray marks will be counted as mistakes.)*

Test 1: English

1 ⒶⒷⒸⒹ	**20** ⒻⒼⒽⒿ	**39** ⒶⒷⒸⒹ	**58** ⒻⒼⒽⒿ
2 ⒻⒼⒽⒿ	**21** ⒶⒷⒸⒹ	**40** ⒻⒼⒽⒿ	**59** ⒶⒷⒸⒹ
3 ⒶⒷⒸⒹ	**22** ⒻⒼⒽⒿ	**41** ⒶⒷⒸⒹ	**60** ⒻⒼⒽⒿ
4 ⒻⒼⒽⒿ	**23** ⒶⒷⒸⒹ	**42** ⒻⒼⒽⒿ	**61** ⒶⒷⒸⒹ
5 ⒶⒷⒸⒹ	**24** ⒻⒼⒽⒿ	**43** ⒶⒷⒸⒹ	**62** ⒻⒼⒽⒿ
6 ⒻⒼⒽⒿ	**25** ⒶⒷⒸⒹ	**44** ⒻⒼⒽⒿ	**63** ⒶⒷⒸⒹ
7 ⒶⒷⒸⒹ	**26** ⒻⒼⒽⒿ	**45** ⒶⒷⒸⒹ	**64** ⒻⒼⒽⒿ
8 ⒻⒼⒽⒿ	**27** ⒶⒷⒸⒹ	**46** ⒻⒼⒽⒿ	**65** ⒶⒷⒸⒹ
9 ⒶⒷⒸⒹ	**28** ⒻⒼⒽⒿ	**47** ⒶⒷⒸⒹ	**66** ⒻⒼⒽⒿ
10 ⒻⒼⒽⒿ	**29** ⒶⒷⒸⒹ	**48** ⒻⒼⒽⒿ	**67** ⒶⒷⒸⒹ
11 ⒶⒷⒸⒹ	**30** ⒻⒼⒽⒿ	**49** ⒶⒷⒸⒹ	**68** ⒻⒼⒽⒿ
12 ⒻⒼⒽⒿ	**31** ⒶⒷⒸⒹ	**50** ⒻⒼⒽⒿ	**69** ⒶⒷⒸⒹ
13 ⒶⒷⒸⒹ	**32** ⒻⒼⒽⒿ	**51** ⒶⒷⒸⒹ	**70** ⒻⒼⒽⒿ
14 ⒻⒼⒽⒿ	**33** ⒶⒷⒸⒹ	**52** ⒻⒼⒽⒿ	**71** ⒶⒷⒸⒹ
15 ⒶⒷⒸⒹ	**34** ⒻⒼⒽⒿ	**53** ⒶⒷⒸⒹ	**72** ⒻⒼⒽⒿ
16 ⒻⒼⒽⒿ	**35** ⒶⒷⒸⒹ	**54** ⒻⒼⒽⒿ	**73** ⒶⒷⒸⒹ
17 ⒶⒷⒸⒹ	**36** ⒻⒼⒽⒿ	**55** ⒶⒷⒸⒹ	**74** ⒻⒼⒽⒿ
18 ⒻⒼⒽⒿ	**37** ⒶⒷⒸⒹ	**56** ⒻⒼⒽⒿ	**75** ⒶⒷⒸⒹ
19 ⒶⒷⒸⒹ	**38** ⒻⒼⒽⒿ	**57** ⒶⒷⒸⒹ	

Test 2: Mathematics

1 ⒶⒷⒸⒹⒺ	16 ⒻⒼⒽⒿⓀ	31 ⒶⒷⒸⒹⒺ	46 ⒻⒼⒽⒿⓀ
2 ⒻⒼⒽⒿⓀ	17 ⒶⒷⒸⒹⒺ	32 ⒻⒼⒽⒿⓀ	47 ⒶⒷⒸⒹⒺ
3 ⒶⒷⒸⒹⒺ	18 ⒻⒼⒽⒿⓀ	33 ⒶⒷⒸⒹⒺ	48 ⒻⒼⒽⒿⓀ
4 ⒻⒼⒽⒿⓀ	19 ⒶⒷⒸⒹⒺ	34 ⒻⒼⒽⒿⓀ	49 ⒶⒷⒸⒹⒺ
5 ⒶⒷⒸⒹⒺ	20 ⒻⒼⒽⒿⓀ	35 ⒶⒷⒸⒹⒺ	50 ⒻⒼⒽⒿⓀ
6 ⒻⒼⒽⒿⓀ	21 ⒶⒷⒸⒹⒺ	36 ⒻⒼⒽⒿⓀ	51 ⒶⒷⒸⒹⒺ
7 ⒶⒷⒸⒹⒺ	22 ⒻⒼⒽⒿⓀ	37 ⒶⒷⒸⒹⒺ	52 ⒻⒼⒽⒿⓀ
8 ⒻⒼⒽⒿⓀ	23 ⒶⒷⒸⒹⒺ	38 ⒻⒼⒽⒿⓀ	53 ⒶⒷⒸⒹⒺ
9 ⒶⒷⒸⒹⒺ	24 ⒻⒼⒽⒿⓀ	39 ⒶⒷⒸⒹⒺ	54 ⒻⒼⒽⒿⓀ
10 ⒻⒼⒽⒿⓀ	25 ⒶⒷⒸⒹⒺ	40 ⒻⒼⒽⒿⓀ	55 ⒶⒷⒸⒹⒺ
11 ⒶⒷⒸⒹⒺ	26 ⒻⒼⒽⒿⓀ	41 ⒶⒷⒸⒹⒺ	56 ⒻⒼⒽⒿⓀ
12 ⒻⒼⒽⒿⓀ	27 ⒶⒷⒸⒹⒺ	42 ⒻⒼⒽⒿⓀ	57 ⒶⒷⒸⒹⒺ
13 ⒶⒷⒸⒹⒺ	28 ⒻⒼⒽⒿⓀ	43 ⒶⒷⒸⒹⒺ	58 ⒻⒼⒽⒿⓀ
14 ⒻⒼⒽⒿⓀ	29 ⒶⒷⒸⒹⒺ	44 ⒻⒼⒽⒿⓀ	59 ⒶⒷⒸⒹⒺ
15 ⒶⒷⒸⒹⒺ	30 ⒻⒼⒽⒿⓀ	45 ⒶⒷⒸⒹⒺ	60 ⒻⒼⒽⒿⓀ

Test 3: Reading

1 ⒶⒷⒸⒹ	11 ⒶⒷⒸⒹ	21 ⒶⒷⒸⒹ	31 ⒶⒷⒸⒹ
2 ⒻⒼⒽⒿ	12 ⒻⒼⒽⒿ	22 ⒻⒼⒽⒿ	32 ⒻⒼⒽⒿ
3 ⒶⒷⒸⒹ	13 ⒶⒷⒸⒹ	23 ⒶⒷⒸⒹ	33 ⒶⒷⒸⒹ
4 ⒻⒼⒽⒿ	14 ⒻⒼⒽⒿ	24 ⒻⒼⒽⒿ	34 ⒻⒼⒽⒿ
5 ⒶⒷⒸⒹ	15 ⒶⒷⒸⒹ	25 ⒶⒷⒸⒹ	35 ⒶⒷⒸⒹ
6 ⒻⒼⒽⒿ	16 ⒻⒼⒽⒿ	26 ⒻⒼⒽⒿ	36 ⒻⒼⒽⒿ
7 ⒶⒷⒸⒹ	17 ⒶⒷⒸⒹ	27 ⒶⒷⒸⒹ	37 ⒶⒷⒸⒹ
8 ⒻⒼⒽⒿ	18 ⒻⒼⒽⒿ	28 ⒻⒼⒽⒿ	38 ⒻⒼⒽⒿ
9 ⒶⒷⒸⒹ	19 ⒶⒷⒸⒹ	29 ⒶⒷⒸⒹ	39 ⒶⒷⒸⒹ
10 ⒻⒼⒽⒿ	20 ⒻⒼⒽⒿ	30 ⒻⒼⒽⒿ	40 ⒻⒼⒽⒿ

Test 4: Science Reasoning

1 Ⓐ Ⓑ Ⓒ Ⓓ	11 Ⓐ Ⓑ Ⓒ Ⓓ	21 Ⓐ Ⓑ Ⓒ Ⓓ	31 Ⓐ Ⓑ Ⓒ Ⓓ
2 Ⓕ Ⓖ Ⓗ Ⓙ	12 Ⓕ Ⓖ Ⓗ Ⓙ	22 Ⓕ Ⓖ Ⓗ Ⓙ	32 Ⓕ Ⓖ Ⓗ Ⓙ
3 Ⓐ Ⓑ Ⓒ Ⓓ	13 Ⓐ Ⓑ Ⓒ Ⓓ	23 Ⓐ Ⓑ Ⓒ Ⓓ	33 Ⓐ Ⓑ Ⓒ Ⓓ
4 Ⓕ Ⓖ Ⓗ Ⓙ	14 Ⓕ Ⓖ Ⓗ Ⓙ	24 Ⓕ Ⓖ Ⓗ Ⓙ	34 Ⓕ Ⓖ Ⓗ Ⓙ
5 Ⓐ Ⓑ Ⓒ Ⓓ	15 Ⓐ Ⓑ Ⓒ Ⓓ	25 Ⓐ Ⓑ Ⓒ Ⓓ	35 Ⓐ Ⓑ Ⓒ Ⓓ
6 Ⓕ Ⓖ Ⓗ Ⓙ	16 Ⓕ Ⓖ Ⓗ Ⓙ	26 Ⓕ Ⓖ Ⓗ Ⓙ	36 Ⓕ Ⓖ Ⓗ Ⓙ
7 Ⓐ Ⓑ Ⓒ Ⓓ	17 Ⓐ Ⓑ Ⓒ Ⓓ	27 Ⓐ Ⓑ Ⓒ Ⓓ	37 Ⓐ Ⓑ Ⓒ Ⓓ
8 Ⓕ Ⓖ Ⓗ Ⓙ	18 Ⓕ Ⓖ Ⓗ Ⓙ	28 Ⓕ Ⓖ Ⓗ Ⓙ	38 Ⓕ Ⓖ Ⓗ Ⓙ
9 Ⓐ Ⓑ Ⓒ Ⓓ	19 Ⓐ Ⓑ Ⓒ Ⓓ	29 Ⓐ Ⓑ Ⓒ Ⓓ	39 Ⓐ Ⓑ Ⓒ Ⓓ
10 Ⓕ Ⓖ Ⓗ Ⓙ	20 Ⓕ Ⓖ Ⓗ Ⓙ	30 Ⓕ Ⓖ Ⓗ Ⓙ	40 Ⓕ Ⓖ Ⓗ Ⓙ

Test 1: English   45 Minutes—75 Questions

Directions: The following test consists of 75 underlined words and phrases in context, or general questions about the passages. Most of the underlined sections contain errors and inappropriate expressions. You are asked to compare each with the four alternatives in the answer column. If you consider the original version best, choose letter A or F: NO CHANGE. For each question, blacken on the answer sheet the letter of the alternative you think best. Read each passage through before answering the questions based on it.

Passage 1

(1)

The knowledge, attitudes, and skill that children acquire concerning money come from a variety of sources. The most important is the family.

(2)

What a child learns at home is reinforced, weakened, or otherwise modified by the influence of his or her <u>friends adults</u> outside the home, and pressures in
1
the social world at large. ☐ 2 ☐

1. **A.** NO CHANGE
   B. friends—adults
   C. friends: adults
   D. friends, adults

2. Suppose that at this point in the passage the writer wanted to add more information about pressures in the social world of a child. Which of the following additions would be most relevant to the passage as a whole?
   F. A brief classification of the social strata that may be part of children's lives.
   G. A scientifically accurate definition of *social pressure*.
   H. A simple anecdote about the way a child was influenced by the spending behavior of his or her peers.
   J. A case history of a mentally disturbed teenager with a history of antisocial behavior.

(3)

There are several important principles involved with sound money management <u>and that</u> children
3
need to learn. The most important is to spend wisely in such a way as to get full enjoyment and satisfaction. Another is to save for future purchases. Still another is <u>understanding</u> credit and how to use
4
it well. Finally, children need to have experience in earning money for their own use. ☐ 5

3. A. NO CHANGE
B. and which
C. and whom
D. that

4. F. NO CHANGE
G. comprehending
H. to understand
J. earning

5. This paragraph is organized according to which of the following schemes?
A. A series of comparison/contrast sentences.
B. "Nested" classifications, with several subdivisions of each topic.
C. A general statement followed by specific examples.
D. A narrative, with one event after another.

(4)

In other words, <u>he needs</u> to learn that money is
6
valuable as a tool in reaching goals rather than as a goal in itself. The implication for parents is that they need to resist the temptation to regard money only as a restricting, rather than also as a facilitating, element in their lives. <u>Being as how</u> adults overempha-
7
size the importance of money, they should not be surprised when children also do so.

6. F. NO CHANGE
G. he or she needs
H. one needs
J. they need

7. A. NO CHANGE
B. If
C. Although
D. Thus,

(5)

These pressures are strong. Children themselves have become important consumers, having control over more money at earlier ages than ever before. A rise in family incomes, as well as an increase in the number of working adults, <u>have meant</u> that more
8
parents can give children more money for their own

8. F. NO CHANGE
G. has meant
H. will have meant
J. meant

use. Business is fully aware <u>of this</u>. Modern advertis-
9

ing regards children and teenagers as <u>awesome</u>
10

targets. <u>The cost of clothes is rising at a truly</u>
11

<u>alarming rate</u>. All of these factors emphasize the need
11

to teach children how to manage money.

9. A. NO CHANGE
B. that
C. that children are more mature
D. that cash is more available

10. F. NO CHANGE
G. massive
H. major
J. herculean

11. A. NO CHANGE
B. The cost of children's clothes has remained stable.
C. OMIT the underlined portion.
D. The cost of clothes is just one of the factors that have contributed to inflation.

(6)

On the other hand, <u>unless</u> adults in the company of
12

children can enjoy some of the many fine things in the world that require no expenditure of money and can consistently meet children's needs for affection and <u>companionship, they</u> are well on the way toward
13

teaching these children the proper place that material possessions <u>and worldly goods</u> should have in their
14

lives. 15

12. F. NO CHANGE
G. until
H. when
J. although

13. A. NO CHANGE
B. companionship they
C. companion-ship: they
D. companion-ship. They

14. F. NO CHANGE
G. OMIT the underlined portion.
H. and, thus, more worldly goods
J. and goods

15. Choose the sequence of paragraph numbers that makes the structure of the passage most logical.
A. NO CHANGE
B. 1, 2, 6, 4, 3, 5
C. 1, 2, 5, 3, 4, 6
D. 1, 5, 6, 3, 4, 2

Passage 2

(1)

Feet and shoes travel many miles. An average, healthy 7-year-old boy may take 30,000 steps every day, an accumulation that adds up to 10 miles per day and more than 300 miles a month. His mother, on a busy shopping day, may walk 10 miles. A police officer, in common with all of his or her fellow officers, walk about 15 miles on the beat.
16

16. F. NO CHANGE
G. walked
H. walks
J. was walking

(2)

The foot is a complicated structure of twenty-six small bones linked by many joints, attached to each other and to the leg bone by numerous ligaments, moved by muscles and tendons, nourished by blood vessels, controlled by nerves, and a covering of skin
17

protects it. In a newborn infant, some of the bones
17

17. A. NO CHANGE
B. and a covering of skin has protected it.
C. and being covered by a covering of skin.
D. and protected by a covering of skin.

are merely bone-shaped pieces of cartilage, a gristle-like substance. As a child grows, however, real bone
18

18. F. NO CHANGE
G. grows, however. Real
H. grows, however real
J. grows however, real

appears within, and gradually spreads throughout the cartilage form. The heel, the largest bone, is not completed until the age of about 20 years. **19**

19. Suppose that at this point in the passage the writer wanted to add more information about foot anatomy. Which of the following additions would be most relevant to the passage as a whole?
A. A discussion of common foot ailments and their treatment.

B. An account of foot operations on some well-known athletes.
C. More specific details about the muscles that control the feet, the bone tissue, the nerves and tendons.
D. A brief account of some famous myths involving the feet, such as the one about Achilles

(3)

During all this walking, feet carry the weight of the body, and provide means to propel a person when he
20
or she walks, climbs, and jumps. As a person steps out, the body weight travels down through the heel, along the outside of the foot to the ball, across the heads of the long bones to the first metatarsal, and to the big toe. The big toe launches the walking motion. One after the other, each foot in turn bears the total
21

weight of the body. If your feet ache, try massaging
22
them for 20 minutes. You will be amazed at the
22
results. 23
22

20. F. NO CHANGE
G. body. And provide
H. body and provide
J. body, and, provide

21. A. NO CHANGE
B. OMIT the underlined portion.
C. One after the other—
D. One after the other:

22. F. NO CHANGE
G. If your feet ache, massage them!
H. OMIT the underlined portion.
J. If your feet ache, try massaging them, and you will be amazed at the results.

23. Is the description of the physical functioning of the foot appropriate in the passage?
A. Yes, because the passage is actually about sports medicine.
B. Yes, because the passage is about the stresses on the foot and footwear that are brought about by walking.
C. No, there is no relevance to the rest of the passage.
D. No, because it is already well understood that the foot exerts pressure.

(4)

Because a 7-year-old boy weighs 55 pounds, he
<u>24</u>

puts more than 800 tons of weight on his shoes every day (55 pounds times 30,000 steps), or about 24 tons a month. But a boy does more than walk. He jumps, kicks, and <u>often has waded</u> through puddles.
25

His shoes lead a rough life. Estimates of the active life

of a pair of shoes <u>ranges</u> from 20 days to 7 or 9
26

months; the average is about 10 weeks. In fact, no

single component or characteristic <u>determine</u> the life
27

of a shoe. Fit is most important, and usually only the wearer can tell whether a shoe fits. Price alone certainly does not guarantee a good <u>fit!</u> | 29 | | 30 |
28

24. F. NO CHANGE
  G. If
  H. Being that
  J. Since

25. A. NO CHANGE
  B. wades
  C. waded
  D. will have waded

26. F. NO CHANGE
  G. would range
  H. range
  J. has ranged

27. A. NO CHANGE
  B. determines
  C. will determine
  D. is determining

28. F. NO CHANGE
  G. fit."
  H. fit?
  J. fit.

29. Are the statistics in the first sentence of the paragraph appropriate and meaningful?
  A. Yes, because the passage is about the stresses to the feet brought about by walking, jumping, and other physical activities.
  B. Yes, because the figures help us understand that everything has a physical consequence.
  C. No, because the passage is basically about the anatomy of feet.
  D. No, because the physical activity of a 7-year-old boy is irrelevant to the discussion.

30. Choose the sequence of paragraph numbers that makes the structure of the passage most logical.
  F. NO CHANGE
  G. 1, 2, 4, 3
  H. 1, 4, 2, 3
  J. 1, 3, 2, 4

Passage 3

(1)

A park in the old part of Philadelphia not only is preeminent among the sites associated with the signers of the Declaration of Independence, but also notably <u>commemorates</u> other major aspects of the
31

nation's founding and initial growth and many momentous national events. These include meetings of the First and Second Continental <u>Congresses,</u>
32

the Declaration was adopted and signed, which
33

marked the creation of the United States; and the labors of the Constitutional Convention of 1787, which perpetuated it. 34

31. A. NO CHANGE
  B. commemorate
  C. will commemorate
  D. has commemorated

32. F. NO CHANGE
  G. Congresses—
  H. Congresses;
  J. Congresses

33. A. NO CHANGE
  B. The Declaration was adopted and signed.
  C. the Declaration, adopted and signed,
  D. the adoption and signing of the Declaration,

34. Is the reference to the park a meaningful way to begin this passage?
  F. No, because the passage is not about recreational sites, but about the significance of Independence Hall.
  G. No, because everything it signifies is covered elsewhere in the passage.
  H. Yes, because the general reference to scenery is a good way to begin any discussion.
  J. Yes, because the park is the site of fundamental historical events described in the passage.

(2)

Independence Hall was originally the statehouse
35

for the province of Pennsylvania. In 1729 the provin-
35

35. Does the first sentence of the paragraph provide a
general basis for the specific supporting details which
follow?
   A. Yes, the sentence is a classic topic sentence followed by supporting details about the province of
   Pennsylvania.
   B. Yes, the sentence suggests a plan, and the rest of
   the paragraph spells out the plan.
   C. No, the sentence refers to a building this is mentioned again in the paragraph, but it does not
   adequately prepare the reader for the historical narrative that comprises the main part of the
   paragraph.
   D. No, the sentence does not relate to any supporting
   material.

cial assembly set aside funds for the building,
designed by lawyer Andrew Hamilton. Three years
later, construction began under the supervision and
36
overview of master carpenter Edmund Wooley. In
36
1736 the assembly moved into the statehouse, which
was not fully completed until 1756. Thomas Jefferson
37
was in France at the time. As American opposition to
37

British colonial policies mounted, Philadelphia
became a center of organized protest. To decide on a
unified course of action, in 1774 the First Continental
Congress met in newly finished Carpenters' Hall,
whose erection the Carpenters' Company of Philadelphia had begun four years earlier. In 1775 the
38

36. F. NO CHANGE
   G. supervision
   H. supervision as
   well as
   overview
   J. supervision,
   and overview,

37. A. NO CHANGE
   B. Thomas
   Jefferson had
   been in France
   at the time.
   C. OMIT the
   underlined
   portion.
   D. Thomas
   Jefferson
   would be in
   France at the
   time.

38. F. NO CHANGE
   G. began
   H. had began
   J. has begun

Second Continental Congress, taking over the east
room of the ground floor of the statehouse from the
Pennsylvania assembly, moved from protest to resistance; Congress had created an army and appointed
39

39. A. NO CHANGE
B. will have
created
C. has created
D. created

George Washington as commander in chief. Thus,
40

40. F. NO CHANGE
G. Finally,
H. Nevertheless,
J. In addition,

the final break with the Crown had not come; not until

a year later would independence have been declared.
41

41. A. NO CHANGE
B. be declared.
C. declare itself.
D. been declared.

42

42. This paragraph is organized according to which of the
following schemes?
F. A series of chronological references to Indepen-
dence Hall, each at important historical junctures.
G. A general statement about Independence Hall, fol-
lowed by specific information about the structure.
H. A series of statements comparing and contrasting
Independence Hall with other structures.
J. A series of arguments about the historical impor-
tance of Independence Hall, followed by answers.

(3)

On July 2, 1776, Congress passed Richard Henry
Lee's resolution of June 7 recommending independence. The delegates, then turning their attention to
43

Thomas Jefferson's draft of the Declaration, which
43

had been submitted on June 28. After modification, it
43

43. A. NO CHANGE
B. Then turning the delegates' attention to Thomas
Jefferson's draft of the Declaration, which had
been submitted on June 28.

C. The delegates then turned their attention to Thomas Jefferson's draft of the Declaration. Which had been submitted on June 28.
D. The delegates then turned their attention to Thomas Jefferson's draft of the Declaration, which had been submitted on June 28.

was adopted on July 4. Four days later, in Independence Square, the document was first read publicly, to the citizens of Philadelphia. In a formal ceremony on August 2, about fifty of the fifty-six signers affixed their signatures to the <u>Declaration, the</u> others appar-
                                                    44
ently did so later. [45]

44. F. NO CHANGE
G. Declaration the
H. Declaration —
the
J. Declaration;
the

45. Choose the sequence of paragraph numbers that makes the structure of the passage most logical
A. NO CHANGE
B. 2, 1, 3
C. 1, 3, 2
D. 2, 3, 1

Passage 4

(1)

The greatest problem with the abortion issue is that it is far more complex than it first appears. It is a moral issue, because it involves what both sides admit is a decision to begin or terminate a life; it is a political issue, because many laws encourage or discourage the practice of <u>abortion; finally,</u> <u>social</u>
                                    46   **47**
<u>concerns are addressed</u>, because all human beings
        47
are affected by the number of people born into the world.

46. F. NO CHANGE
G. abortion
finally,
H. abortion:
finally,
J. abortion,
finally,

47. A. NO CHANGE
B. social concerns
have been addressed,
C. it is of social
concern,
D. it is a social
issue,

(2)

One of the central issues of the 1980s is abortion. On one side of the question is the pro-lifers, a
48
minority who believe that abortion is the taking of a life and that the government must protect the rights of all its citizens, including the right of an unborn infant to live. On the other side are the pro-choice advocates, comprising a majority of Americans who
49
believe that abortion should be legal under certain circumstances, (particularly those involving the
50
health of the mother). Researchers and pollsters
50

48. F. NO CHANGE
   G. have been
   H. will be
   J. are

49. A. NO CHANGE
   B. Americans
      (who
   C. Americans,
      who
   D. Americans.
      Who

50. F. NO CHANGE
   G. circumstances, particularly those involving the
      health of the mother.
   H. circumstances (particularly those, involving the
      health of the mother).
   J. circumstances particularly those involving the
      health of the mother.

have been surprised at the strength of these convictions and at the extent to which most people have pondered their beliefs.

(3)

However, the majority group that believes in
51   **52**
some form of abortion is also willing to describe the medical process as when a life ends. A woman's
53

51. A. NO CHANGE
   B. Because
   C. For example,
   D. Although

52. F. NO CHANGE
   G. believe
   H. believed
   J. is believing

53. A. NO CHANGE
   B. where a
      life ends
   C. when you end
      a life.
   D. the end of
      a life.

decision to abort her pregnancy can be viewed, according to more than half of all the pro-choice people polled, as a choice between two evils and a conscious acceptance of guilt in the necessary termination of life. **54**

54. Suppose that at this point in the passage the writer wanted to add more information about the abortion issue. Which of the following additions would be most relevant to the passage as a whole?
   F. A brief summary of views on the issue held by significant religious and political leaders.
   G. A list of hospitals that perform abortions.
   H. An expose of unlicensed or substandard abortion clinics.
   J. A case history of an abortion.

(4)

The pro-lifer or anti-abortionist tends to be on the right side of the political spectrum, sometimes believing that social programs are inherently no good **55**

55. **A.** NO CHANGE
   B. ill advised
   C. bad news
   D. forbidden

and impeding human progress because they tend to **56** discourage initiative. Using the rule of common good, pro-lifers ask what decision made by a woman contemplating abortion would bring about the greatest number of positive consequences that are **57** beneficial for all concerned—one of those con- **57** cerned, of course, being the unborn fetus. A baby's **58**

56. **F.** NO CHANGE
   G. impeded
   H. impede
   J. impedes

57. **A.** NO CHANGE
   B. beneficial
   C. also beneficial
   D. OMIT the underlined portion.

fine features, such as eyelashes and fingernails, are
      58
fully developed by the age of ten weeks. |**59**| |**60**|
      58

58. F. NO CHANGE
   G. OMIT the underlined portion.
   H. A baby's fine features, for example, eyelashes and fingernails, are fully developed by the age of ten weeks.
   J. A baby's fine features, such as eyelashes and fingernails, being fully developed by the age of ten weeks.

59. For the most part, this passage is written according to which of the following strategies?
   A. Comparison/contrast
   B. Argument
   C. Description
   D. Narration

60. Choose the sequence of paragraph numbers that makes the structure of the passage most logical.
   F. NO CHANGE
   G. 1, 4, 3, 2
   H. 2, 3, 4, 1
   J. 2, 1, 3, 4

Passage 5

(1)

The California Constitution requires that the Governor submit a budget with an explanation to both houses of the Legislature before January 11 of each year. The explanation must contain a complete spending plan, as well as an itemized statement of all expenditures provided by law or proposed by the Governor, and the proposed budget must be com-
                                    61
pared with last year's. After the Governor has submit-
      61
ted the budget, an appropriation bill, known as the Budget Bill, which reflects the proposed budget, is introduced into each house of the Legislature and

61. A. NO CHANGE
   B. and it must be compared with last year's budget.
   C. together with a comparison of the proposed budget with last year's.
   D. and it should contain a comparison of last year's and this year's budget.

referred to the Assembly Ways and Means Committee and the Senate Finance Committee, respectively. The Constitution requires that the Legislature pass the Budget Bill by midnight, June 15. Until the Budget Bill <u>will have been enacted,</u> neither house can send to
62

the Governor any other appropriation bill, other than emergency measures. 63

62. F. NO CHANGE
G. has been enacted,
H. would have been enacted,
J. was enacted,

63. Which of the following statements is best supported by the details supplied in this paragraph?
A. The California Legislature and the Governor are in contention.
B. The California Constitution punishes lawmakers who violate its rules.
C. The California Constitution places a high priority on timely passage of the state budget.
D. The California budget process is hopelessly politicized.

(2)

<u>Being</u> a budget approaching 20 billion dollars, the
64

five months allowed by the Constitution for all the item disagreements, resolutions, lobbying by special interest groups, and "dealing" by the legislatures on behalf of their constituents is hardly enough time. Yet, if the budget is not passed, the state of California literally ceases to function. All state employees are asked to stay home. <u>Traffic on the freeways is mea-</u>
65
<u>surably reduced.</u> All state government offices and
65

64. F. NO CHANGE
G. Due to its being
H. Being as how it is
J. For

65. A. NO CHANGE
B. Traffic, because it is on the freeway, is measurably reduced.
C. OMIT the underlined portion.
D. Traffic is reduced, especially on the freeways.

agencies <u>close and even</u> the Legislature with its heavy
66
responsibilities has to operate with a skeletal staff.

66. F. NO CHANGE
G. close. And even
H. close: Even
J. close, and even

When an absolute halt in services and business is so
67

67. A. NO CHANGE
B. If
C. Because
D. Until

disruptive, and due to the very fact that no other
68
appropriation bill can be sent to the governor until the
budget is passed, both the Assembly and the Senate
usually stay in session continuously until the
69

68. F. NO CHANGE
G. unless
H. although
J. because

69. A. NO CHANGE
B. continually
C. interminably
D. repeatedly

impasse, whatever its genesis, is solved. It is not
surprising, under such conditions, that the Legislature and the Governor seem to find solutions rather
quickly to disputes and stalemates that have been
70
festering for months. |71|
70

70. F. NO CHANGE
G. have been
solved
H. have been
unresolved
J. have been
unknown

71. This passage was probably written for readers who:
A. are tax accountants seeking to learn more about
their vocation.
B. are taxpayers and voters interested in how a state
government works.
C. enjoy scientific and quantitative facts.
D. enjoy works of inspiration and solace.

(3)
The orderly operation of the Government of
California depends on the state budget, a document
controlling expenditures that are larger than those of
any American governmental jurisdiction with the
72
exception of the city of New York and the U.S.
Government. Each year, the process of creating

72. F. NO CHANGE
G. any other
American gov-
ernmental
jurisdiction
H. any, American
governmental
jurisdiction
J. any American,
governmental
jurisdiction

the many parts of the budget begins in January with
73

73. A. NO CHANGE
B. so many part of the budget
C. a budget
D. the workings of the budget

the Governor's message to the Legislature. 74
75

74. This paragraph emphasizes the importance of:
F. the Government of California.
G. the size of the budget.
H. the budget.
J. the Governor's message to the Legislature.

75. Choose the sequence of paragraph numbers that makes the structure of the essay most logical.
A. NO CHANGE
B. 3, 2, 1
C. 3, 1, 2
D. 2, 3, 1

Answers to English Test on page 318.

Test 2: Mathematics   **60 Minutes—60 Questions**

Directions: **After solving each problem, darken the appropriate space on the answer sheet. Do not spend too much time on any one problem. Make a note of the ones that seem difficult, and return to them when you finish the others. Assume that the word *line* means "straight line," that geometric figures are not necessarily drawn to scale, and that all geometric figures lie in a plane.**

1. Which of the following is a monomial?

   A. $\sqrt{2x}$ **B.** $\frac{2}{x}$ **C.** $\frac{x}{2}$ **D.** $x + 2$ **E.** 2^x

2. Lisa's salary was raised 8%. If she now receives $5.67 per hour, what was her hourly salary before her increase?

   F. $0.45   **G.** $5.22   **H.** $5.25   **J.** $5.30   **K.** $6.12

3. The expression $5 + 2 \cdot 3^2 = ?$

   A. 441   **B.** 121   **C.** 63   **D.** 41   **E.** 23

4. What is the complete factorization of the polynomial $81x^2 - 36y^2$?

   F. $(9x - 6y)(9x + 6y)$ **J.** $3(9x - 6y)(3x + 2y)$
   G. $9(3x - 2y)^2$ **K.** None of these
   H. $9(3x - 2y)(3x + 2y)$

5. Which of the following numbers is NOT irrational?

   A. π **D.** 7.313113111311113. . .
   B. $\sqrt{7}$ **E.** $\sqrt{7} - \sqrt{3}$
   C. $\sqrt{49}$

6. What is the simplified form of the algebraic fraction $\frac{(x - y)^2}{y^2 - x^2}$?

   F. 1   **G.** -1 **H.** $2xy$ **J.** $\frac{y - x}{y + x}$ **K.** $\frac{x - y}{x + y}$

7. Which of the following is a geometric sequence?

   A. 1, 3, 5, 7, . . .   **D.** 1, 4, 9, 16, . . .

   B. 1, 2, 4, 8, . . .   **E.** 1, 4, 13, 40, . . .

   C. 1, $\frac{1}{2}$, $\frac{1}{3}$, $\frac{1}{4}$, . . .

8. What is the solution set of the equation $4x - 2[3x - (x + 4)] = 5 - 2(x + 1)$?

   F. $\left\{\frac{-5}{2}\right\}$ **G.** $\left\{\frac{5}{3}\right\}$ **H.** $\left\{\frac{-11}{7}\right\}$ **J.** $\{-2\}$ **K.** ø

9. If $\overline{AB}$ is a diameter, $\overline{BC}$ is a tangent, and m $\angle ABD = 25°$, what is the measure of $\angle BCD$?

   A. 90°

   B. 65°

   C. $32\frac{1}{2}°$

   D. 25°

   E. $12\frac{1}{2}°$

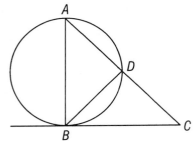

10. Which of the following numbers is smallest?

   F. 7.2%   **J.** (0.08)9

   G. $7.2(10^{-2})$ **K.** (0.08)(0.09)

   H. $\frac{72}{100}$

11. What is the value of the expression $xy^2(x - y)$ if $x = -3$ and $y = 2$?

   A. −180   **B.** −60   **C.** −12   **D.** 12   **E.** 60

12. If it takes 4 gallons of lemonade for a party of 20 children, how many gallons should one have on hand for a party of 30 children?

   F. 5   **G.** 6   **H.** 6.5   **J.** 7.5   **K.** 8

13. Which expression would be appropriate to complete the following equation in order for the equation to illustrate the associative property of addition: $3 + (-2 + 0) = ?$

A. 1

B. $3 + [0 + (-2)]$

C. $[3 + (-2)] + 0$

D. $3 + (-2)$

E. $(-2 + 0) + 3$

14. Which of the following is a pure imaginary number?

F. $\sqrt{-9}$

G. $-\sqrt{9}$

H. $5 + 2i$

J. -1

K. i^2

15. $7\frac{1}{4} - 2\frac{5}{6} = ?$

A. $4\frac{5}{12}$

B. $4\frac{1}{2}$

C. $5\frac{7}{12}$

D. $10\frac{1}{12}$

E. None of these

16. Stan can do a certain job in 4 hours. If Fred can do the same job in 5 hours, which of the following equations could be used to determine how long it would take them to do the job if they worked together?

F. $\frac{x}{4} + \frac{x}{5} = 1$

G. $4x + 5x = 1$

H. $\frac{x}{4} = \frac{x}{5}$

J. $\frac{4}{x} + \frac{5}{x} = 1$

K. None of these

17. Which of the following numbers is NOT composite?

A. 1 **B.** 28 **C.** 51 **D.** 93 **E.** 143

18. Which of the following is equivalent to $|x + 3| \geq 2$?

F. $x \geq -1$

G. $x \leq -5$

H. $x \geq -5$

J. $x \geq -1$ or $x \leq -5$

K. $-5 \leq x \leq -1$

19. What is the solution set of the equation
$$\frac{2x - 1}{3} + \frac{x + 2}{4} = \frac{1}{6}?$$
A. $\{0\}$ **B.** $\left\{\frac{1}{11}\right\}$ **C.** $\left\{\frac{-1}{11}\right\}$ **D.** $\left\{\frac{-3}{11}\right\}$ **E.** $\left\{\frac{4}{11}\right\}$

20. If $\overline{CE}$ is a tangent, $\overline{CD}$ is a radius and m $\angle ECB = 48°$, what is the measure of $\angle BAC$?

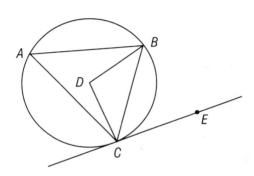

F. 24° **G.** 42° **H.** 48° **J.** 84° **K.** 96°

21. What is the degree of the expression $(3x^2 + 5x - 3)^3 + 5$?
A. 2 **B.** 3 **C.** 4 **D.** 5 **E.** 6

22. What is the simplified form of the expression $(2x - 3y)^2$?
F. $4x^2 + 9y^2$ **J.** $4x^2 - 12xy + 9y^2$
G. $4x^2 - 9y^2$ **K.** $4x^2 + 12xy + 9y^2$
H. $4x^2 - 6xy + 9y^2$

23. Which of the following ordered pairs corresponds to a point in quadrant IV?
A. $(2, 0)$ **D.** $(-1, -4)$
B. $(0, -4)$ **E.** $(2, -8)$
C. $(-2, 3)$

24. What base ten numeral corresponds to $110110_{(two)}$?

F. 27   **G.** 54   **H.** 63   **J.** 108   **K.** 55,055

25. What is the product of the roots of the equation $5x^2 - 8x + 7 = 0$?

A. $\frac{-7}{5}$ **B.** $\frac{7}{5}$ **C.** $\frac{8}{5}$ **D.** 7   **E.** 8

26. What is the value of $8^{-(2/3)}$?

F. 16   **G.** $\frac{-16}{3}$ **H.** 4   **J.** $\frac{1}{4}$ **K.** $\frac{-1}{4}$

27. The expression $3(10^5) + 2(10^3) + 4(10^2) + 7(10^1)$ is the expanded form for what number?

A. 3,247   **B.** 30,247   **C.** 32,470   **D.** 302,470   **E.** 324,700

28. What is the lowest common denominator of the fractions $\frac{2}{5a^2b^3}, \frac{7}{20ab^4}, \frac{8}{15a^3b^2}$?

F. $5ab^2$ **G.** $5a^3b^4$ **H.** $60ab^2$ **J.** $60a^3b^4$ **K.** $1500a^6b^9$

29. What is the average (mean) of the numbers 3, 4, 4, 5, 5, 5, 7, 8, 8, 9?

A. 5   **B.** 6   **C.** 5.8   **D.** 10   **E.** 58

30. Sue is paid $200 per week plus 7% of her total sales, t, for the week. Which of the following equations could she use to determine her salary, S, for a particular week?

F. $S = 0.07(200 + t)$ **J.** $S = 1.07(200 + t)$
G. $S = 0.07(200) + t$ **K.** $S = 200t^{0.07}$
H. $S = 200 + 0.07t$

31. What is the simplified form of the complex fraction $\dfrac{\frac{1}{x} - \frac{1}{3}}{\frac{1}{x^2} - \frac{1}{9}}$?

A. 3   **B.** $\frac{1}{x + 3}$ **C.** $\frac{3 - x}{3x}$ **D.** $\frac{3x}{3 + x}$ **E.** $\frac{9x - 3x^2}{9 - x^2}$

32. Which of the following are the coordinates of the vertex of the parabola whose equation is $y = -2(x + 6)^2 - 9$?

F. $(2, -9)$ **J.** $(6, -9)$
G. $(6, 9)$ **K.** $(-6, -9)$
H. $(-6, 9)$

33. What is the solution set of the equation $\dfrac{x^2 + 9}{x^2 - 9} - \dfrac{3}{x + 3} = \dfrac{-x}{3 - x}$?

A. ø   **B.** {0}   **C.** $\left\{\dfrac{1}{3}\right\}$ **D.** {2}   **E.** {3}

34. Which of the following is equal to $\dfrac{2.4(10^{-4})}{6(10^{-2})}$?

F. $0.4(10^{-6})$ **J.** $4(10^3)$
G. $4(10^{-1})$ **K.** $4(10^{-3})$
H. $4(10^{-2})$

35. What is the slope of the line that passes through the points with coordinates $(-5, 8)$ and $(-5, -3)$?

A. -11 **B.** 5   **C.** 0   **D.** $\dfrac{-1}{2}$ **E.** The line has no slope.

36. The Smith family has 100 gallons of heating fuel on January 1. During January the Smiths use 20% of their fuel, and in February they use 25% of the remaining fuel. How many gallons of fuel are left on March 1?

F. 40   **G.** 45   **H.** 50   **J.** 55   **K.** 60

37. If lines l, m, and n are parallel, $\overline{AE} \perp l$, $AC = 10$, $CD = 14$, and $AF = 6$, what is the length of $\overline{DG}$?

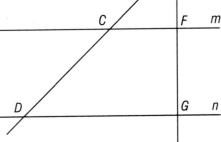

A. 11.2
B. 16
C. 19.2
D. $23\dfrac{1}{3}$
E. 24

38. Which of the following is always true of an acute angle?

    F. Its measure is greater than 90°.
    G. It is the supplement of another acute angle.
    H. It cannot be equal to its own complement.
    J. Every quadrilateral must have at least one.
    K. All of these statements are false.

39. A triangle is drawn with one side on line $\overline{AE}$. If m $\angle ABC = 140°$ and m $\angle CDE = 60°$, what is the measure of $\angle BCD$?

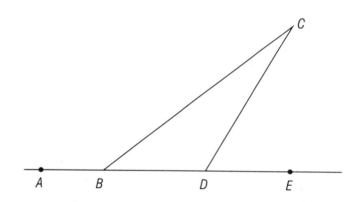

    A. 20° **B.** 30° **C.** 40° **D.** 45° **E.** 50°

40. A car radiator holds 12 liters. How much pure antifreeze, in liters, must be added to a mixture that is 4% antifreeze to make enough of a 20% mixture to fill the radiator?

    F. 0.48 **G.** 2 **H.** 2.4 **J.** 2.88 **K.** 3

41. In right triangle ABC, m $\angle C = 90°$, $AC = 2$, and $AB = 5$. What is the value of sin A?

    A. $\frac{2}{5}$ **D.** $\frac{\sqrt{21}}{5}$

    B. $\frac{5}{2}$
                    E. $\frac{5}{\sqrt{21}}$

    C. $\frac{\sqrt{21}}{2}$

42. Which equation corresponds to the graph?

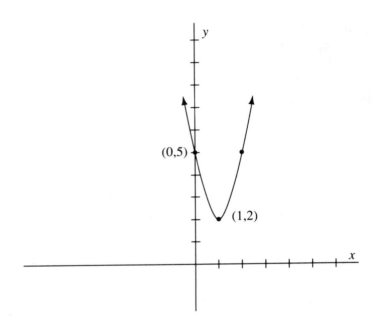

F. $y = 7(x - 1)^2 - 2$ **J.** $(x - 1)^2 + (y - 2)^2 = 1$
G. $y = 3(x - 1)^2 + 2$ **K.** None of these
H. $y = 7(x + 1)^2 - 2$

43. What is the standard form of the quotient of the complex numbers $\dfrac{3 - 2i}{2 + i}$?

A. $2 - i$ **D.** $3 + 2i$

B. $\dfrac{8 - 7i}{3}$ **E.** $4 - 2i$

C. $\dfrac{4}{5} - \dfrac{7}{5}i$

44. In how many ways can six different books be arranged on a shelf?

     F. 6   **G.** 30   **H.** 36   **J.** 64   **K.** 720

45. What is the value of $\log_2 \frac{1}{8}$?

    A. $\frac{1}{3}$ **B.** $\frac{-1}{3}$ **C.** $\frac{1}{4}$ **D.** -3 **E.** 3

46. The ratio of the areas of two similar triangles is 9 to 16. What is the ratio of the lengths of the corresponding altitudes of these triangles?

    F. 1 to 7   **G.** 3 to 4   **H.** 9 to 16   **J.** 4.5 to 8   **K.** 27 to 64

47. What is the smallest positive angle that is coterminal with $\frac{75\pi}{4}$ radians?

    A. $120°$ **D.** $\frac{3\pi}{4}$

    B. $\frac{\pi}{4}$ **E.** $\frac{11\pi}{4}$

    C. $\frac{-\pi}{4}$

48. If $AE = 6$, $AB = 1\frac{2}{3}$, $BC = 1\frac{1}{4}$, and $DE = 1\frac{1}{12}$, what is the length of $\overline{CD}$?

    F. $1\frac{1}{2}$ **G.** 2 **H.** $2\frac{2}{3}$ **J.** 4 **K.** $4\frac{11}{12}$

49. If the height, h, of a thrown object above the ground at any time, t, in seconds is given by the equation $h = -16t^2 + 64t$, in how many seconds will the object reach its maximum height?

    A. 8   **B.** 4   **C.** 3   **D.** 2   **E.** 1

50. What is equal to the product $\sqrt{54x^4y^5} \cdot \sqrt{2x^2y^4}$ of radicals in simplest radical form? (Assume that x and y are nonnegative.)

    F. $6x^3y^4 \sqrt{3y}$ **J.** $2y^3 \sqrt{27x^6}$

    G. $3x^3y^2 \sqrt{12y^5}$ **K.** None of these

    H. $6x^3 \sqrt{3y^9}$

51. Which of the following statements is always true regarding a parallelogram?

    A. The diagonals are perpendicular to each other.
    B. The sum of the angles is 180°.
    C. Opposite sides are both parallel and congruent.
    D. There cannot be a right angle in any parallelogram.
    E. Consecutive angles are complementary.

52. A square and a semicircular region have the same perimeter. If the length of the radius of the semicircular region is 8, what is the length of a side of the square?

    F. 8π **J.** $\frac{8}{\pi}$
    G. 8   **K.** $4 + 2\pi$
    H. 2π

53. Which of the following is a pair of vertical angles?

    A. ∠BAC, ∠CED   **D.** ∠ACB, ∠DCE
    B. ∠ACD, ∠ACB   **E.** ∠ACE, ∠BCD
    C. ∠CDE, ∠CED

54. Line $\overline{AD}$ is parallel to line $\overline{CE}$. If $AB = 4$, $BC = 9$, and $CE = 5$, what is the length of $\overline{AD}$?

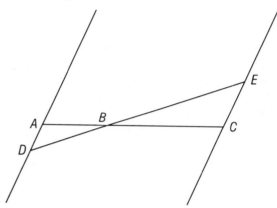

F. 1   **G.** 2   **H.** $2\frac{2}{9}$ **J.** $7\frac{1}{5}$ **K.** $11\frac{1}{4}$

55. A kite is flying at the end of a taut string that is 50 feet long. The string makes an angle of 25° with the horizontal, and the person flying the kite holds the string 5 feet off the ground. How high is the kite from the ground?

A. $5 + 50 \sin 25°$

B. $5 + 50 \cos 25°$

C. $5 + 50 \tan 25°$

D. $5 + \dfrac{50}{\sin 25°}$

E. $5 + \dfrac{\sin 25°}{50}$

56. Two chords, $\overline{AB}$ and $\overline{CD}$, intersect at E. If $AB = 8$, $CE = 2$, and $DE = 8$, what is the length of $\overline{AE}$?

F. 2
G. 3
H. 4
J. 5
K. 6

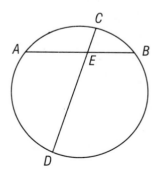

57. What is the maximum number of common tangents that can be drawn to any two circles?

A. 1   **B.** 2   **C.** 3   **D.** 4   **E.** 5

58. Which of the following statements is true about polygons?

F. All triangles are convex.
G. All rectangles are quadrilaterals.
H. The sum of the angles of a pentagon is 540°.
J. A square is a rhombus.
K. All these statements are true.

59. If $AB = BC$ and m $\angle ABC = 24°$, what is the measure of $\angle BDC$?

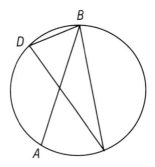

A. 24°   **B.** 48°   **C.** 72°   **D.** 78°   **E.** 90°

60. What is the period of the function
$y = -3 \sin (4x + \pi)$?

F. 3
G. 4
H. $\frac{\pi}{4}$

J. $\frac{\pi}{2}$
K. $\frac{\pi}{3}$

Answers to Mathematics Test on page 319.

Testing 3: Reading   35 Minutes—40 Questions

Directions: **This test consists of four passages, each followed by ten multiple-choice questions. Read each passage and then pick the best answer for each question. Fill in the spaces on your answer sheet that correspond to your choices. Refer to the passage as often as you wish while answering the questions.**

Passage 1

PROSE FICTION: This passage is an excerpt from *Germinal,* a novel written by Emile Zola. The novel takes place in a mining region of France where considerable conflict arises between the miners and their bosses.

Every night at about nine o'clock, when the bar would empty out, Etienne stayed on to talk to Souvarine. He would drink his beer in small sips, while the engineman would smoke one cigarette after another, his thin fingers
5   discolored by the tobacco. His veiled, mystic's eyes would dreamily follow the smoke; his unoccupied left hand would nervously move in the air. He usually ended up by putting a tame rabbit—a large female one, always swollen with pregnancy and allowed the freedom of the
10   house—on his lap. The rabbit, whom he had named Poland, had grown to love him, and she would come to sniff his trousers, sit up, and scratch with her paws until he would pick her up, like a child. Then, huddled against him her ears flat back, she would close her eyes while
15   he endlessly stroked the gray silk of her fur with an unconscious, caressing gesture, finding tranquillity in the soft and living warmth.

"You know, I've gotten a letter from Pluchart," Etienne said one evening.

20   There was no one else in the place but Rasseneur. The last customer had left, returning to the sleeping village.

"Well!" exclaimed the landlord, standing in front of his two roomers. "Pluchart! What's he up to?"

For two months Etienne had been carrying on a steady
25   correspondence with the Lille mechanic, whom he had decided to tell about his job at Montsou and who was now indoctrinating him, jumping at his chance to use Etienne to propagandize among the miners.

"What he's up to is that association, which is going
30   very well . . . It seems people from all over are joining up."

"And what do *you* think of their association?" Rasseneur asked Souvarine.

The latter, gently scratching Poland's head, blew out a
35   jet of smoke and murmured quietly:

"More foolishness."

But Etienne became excited. The initial illusions of his ignorance and his natural predisposition to rebelliousness both acted to throw him into the fight of labor
40   against capital. The association they were talking about was the Workers' International, the famous International that had just been set up in London. Wasn't that a wonderful effort, a campaign in which justice would finally be victorious? No more frontiers, but workers from all
45   over the world rising up and joining together to guarantee the workingman the bread he earns. And what a magnificently simple organization: at the bottom, the section, representing the commune; then the federation, grouping all the sections from the same province; then
50   the nation; and finally, above all of these, humanity itself, incarnated in a general council in which each nation was represented by a corresponding secretary. Within six months they would conquer the earth and lay down the law to the bosses if they fail to fall into line!

55   "Just foolishness!" repeated Souvarine. "Your Karl Marx is still at the stage of wanting to let natural laws operate. No politics and no conspiracies, isn't that right? Everything done in the open, and higher salaries the only

aim . . . Well, don't talk to me about your evolution!
60 Burn the cities, mow down the nations, wipe everything
out—and when there's nothing left of this rotten world,
maybe a better one will grow in its place."
     Etienne began to laugh. He did not always understand
what his friend was talking about, and this theory of
65 destruction seemed only a pose to him. Rasseneur,
more practical-minded, and with the common sense of a
well-established man, did not even bother to get angry.
He was interested only in precise information.
     "Then you're going to try to set up a section in
70 Montsou?"
     That was what Pluchart, who was secretary of the
Federation of the Nord, wanted, and he kept emphasiz-
ing the help the International would be able to give the
miners if they ever went on strike. Actually, Etienne did
75 think a strike was imminent: the business of the timber-
ing would end badly; it would take only one more unrea-
sonable demand on the part of the Company to bring all
the mines into a state of rebellion.
     "The trouble is the dues," said Rasseneur judiciously.
80 "Fifty centimes a year for the general fund and two
francs for the section doesn't seem like much, but I'll
bet lots of men will refuse to give it."
     "Especially," Etienne added, "since we would first
have to set up an emergency fund, which could be
85 turned into a strike fund if necessary . . . Still, now's the
time to think of these things. I'm ready, if the others
are."

Emile Zola, *Germinal*

1. The first paragraph of the passage portrays Souvarine as
someone who is:

A. tense.
B. intellectual.
C. arrogant.
D. soft-spoken.

2. Which of the following statements most accurately describes the relation of the characters in the passage?

   F. Etienne and Souvarine work together digging coal in the Montsou mine.

   G. Souvarine is Etienne's supervisor on the job.

   H. Rasseneur employs both Etienne and Souvarine.

   J. Etienne and Souvarine are Rasseneur's tenants.

3. Souvarine's attitude toward the Workers' International can best be described as:

   A. skeptical.

   B. supportive.

   C. indifferent.

   D. enthusiastic.

4. The letters that Pluchart, the Lille [a city in France] mechanic, sends to Etienne are meant to do all of the following EXCEPT:

   F. seek Etienne's help in the national union movement.

   G. educate Etienne about the international labor movement.

   H. stir up dissatisfaction among the miners.

   J. elicit information from Etienne about conditions at Montsou.

5. Etienne's enthusiasm for the Workers' International seems to stem mainly from his:

   A. Marxist background.

   B. natural tendency to be a troublemaker.

   C. long-time commitment to justice.

   D. quest for power.

6. Etienne laughs (line 63) because:

   F. he wants to annoy Souvarine.

   G. Souvarine has said something very funny.

   H. he thinks Souvarine himself is not being serious.

   J. he is showing that he is not afraid of Souvarine.

7. Rasseneur is doubtful that a strike will occur because:

    A. the mineowners will comply with the workers' demands.

    B. the workers are afraid to lose their jobs.

    C. the authorities at Montsou will forbid it.

    D. the workers won't pay the fee required to join the union.

8. For Etienne, Pluchart's most persuasive argument in favor of a strike is that:

    F. the Workers' International will give aid to the striking workers.

    G. it will allow the Workers' International to declare victory over the corrupt bosses.

    H. it will lead to better hours and working conditions.

    J. the strike is likely to end within half a year.

9. Rasseneur is probably inquisitive about Etienne's plans for a strike because:

    A. he supports the workers.

    B. if a strike occurs, his business will be affected.

    C. he is a former miner himself.

    D. he plans to report Etienne to the owners of the mine.

10. Which of the following most accurately describes where each character in the passage stands on issues of social and political change?

        I = most radical
        II = moderately radical
        III = least radical

    F. I - Souvarine; II - Etienne; III - Rasseneur

    G. I - Rasseneur; II - Etienne; III - Souvarine

    H. I - Souvarine; II - Rasseneur; III - Etienne

    J. I - Etienne; II - Souvarine; III - Rasseneur

Passage 2

HUMANITIES: This passage, from Gabriele Sterner's *Art Nouveau: An Art of Transition from Individual to Mass Society,* describes the unusual designs of the Spanish architect Antonio Gaudi.

Antonio Gaudi's strangely expressionistic architecture represented an attack against all previously known principles of construction. Straight lines were denied and hidden. The natural function of balances and supports was concealed from the beholder. Instead of
5 the old rules, imagination held sway; everything was permitted and nothing impossible. Just as Gallé reacted in a typically French way to the new style, Gaudi was honored almost as a saint; this can be explained by the situation that prevailed in Catalonia at the time. The Catalonian *Renaiça* demanded political
10 autonomy, since it was here alone in Spain that industrial progress was taking place. In addition, the province of Catalonia was the homeland of a prosperous middle class oriented toward international relations of all kinds. Gaudi's style affirmed this new patriotic independence, and his personality was a reflection
15 of the political sensibility of the region. Gaudi was also deeply religious in the sense of Spanish Catholicism; he was steeped in mystical ideas, which he sought to capture and express in his buildings. His world of forms included all types of animals and plants. Although abstract design was foreign to Gaudi, his art
20 was informed with social ideas and had a broad social basis. For example, he built housing projects under the auspices of the Societat Obrera Mataronese, a cooperative workers' association.

The most unique feature of Spanish art as opposed to that of northern countries is its Moorish influence. Since Arab art and
25 architecture are characterized by an absence of human representations, artists were forced to turn to ornamentation as the only permissible form of decoration and to perfect it. Europe and Africa unite with Spain, where incredible works have been produced over the course of centuries. The history of Spanish
30 art is filled with paradoxes. Spanish Gothic, for example, is true hybrid in which mystical and spiritualized forms stand in dialectical opposition to the dynamism of a purely decorative urge. One sees walls covered with a dense tangle of branches in

which pointed Gothic arches and the leaves of cruciferous plants
35 become lost. Although a kind of textile pattern emerges, it is one
in which the weave can neither be discerned nor unraveled. . . .
    This is the tradition in which Antonio Gaudi found himself.
His early works include palaces and villas; however, Gaudi's late
years were dedicated exclusively to the construction of the
40 otherworldly Sagrada Familia (Temple of the Poor), a church
that was built through collections and endowments alone.
Gaudi's bold solutions are combined with a great luxury of
forms and wealth of materials. A tremendous variety of costly
elements were incorporated into Gaudi's works. Architecture
45 was regarded as sculpture; façades were kneaded, as it were,
until the eye of the beholder could no longer identify the
individual elements. The ornamentation works its way from
inside out and from the ground floor to the spires. Gaudi's
preference for plantlike ornamentation was pushed to its
50 extreme. The churning dynamism of the entire structure
captivates the viewer even if the forms are so exalted as to leave
him breathless and confused.
    Gaudi's architecture is characterized by experiments with
colored segments. He often clothed apparently independent
55 architectural elements in colorful ceramic tiles which, in turn,
seem to produce the effect of independent added decoration.
The suggestion of straight lines is avoided. The tiles consist of
interlocking fragments; this arrangement has the effect of
exaggerating the artist's attack upon traditional architecture. On
60 the other hand, the asymmetrical tendency and amorphousness
of Gaudi's designs are concealed by some added labile element.
Everything is in motion. No other artist of the art nouveau
period matched this Catalonian individualist in eliciting highly
picturesque critical comparisons: "flamboyant extravagance,"
65 "architecture like the curved back of a salamanderlike saurian,"
"labyrinth," "dune formations," "dried foam on the beach,"
"hollow dream constructions," "elongated beehives," "gigantic
plant stalks," . . .

11. Based on information in the passage, Gaudi achieved recog-
    nition primarily for

    A. founding a school of Spanish architecture.

B. pioneering new architectural forms.

C. helping to solve social problems through his architecture.

D. designing churches.

12. A building designed by Gaudi would probably

F. have a symmetrical and balanced look.

G. be uniform in color.

H. have sharp angles and lots of glass.

J. look like a piece of clay sculpture.

13. According to the passage, Gaudi is part of which artistic movement?

A. Abstract expressionism

B. Neo-Moorish

C. Art Nouveau

D. Catalonian Spanish

14. Most often Gaudi decorated his buildings with

F. objects found in nature.

G. abstract designs.

H. bold murals depicting social problems.

J. textiles.

15. According to the passage, Gaudi designed all of the following types of structures EXCEPT

A. public libraries.

B. villas for wealthy patrons.

C. houses for working people.

D. places of worship.

16. A conclusion to be drawn from the discussion of Spanish Gothic architecture (lines 30–36) is that pure Gothic architecture

F. should not be altered or tampered with.

G. originated in Spain.

H. often includes representations of the human form.

J. conveys a sense of mysticism and spiritualism.

17. Gaudi owes some of his achievement as an architect to which of the following?

     I. He lived in Catalonia.
     II. He was a devout Catholic.
     III. Architectural critics such as Gallé supported his work.

  A. I only
  B. II only
  C. I and II
  D. I and III

18. Based on the contents of the passage, which of the following statements is probably NOT an accurate conclusion to draw about Gaudi's work?

  F. Most of Gaudi's buildings are different from each other.
  G. A Gaudi building costs more to build than an ordinary building.
  H. Gaudi's buildings are best suited for warm climates.
  J. Gaudi's buildings probably don't appeal to everyone.

19. According to the passage, the influence of Moorish art has been felt

  A. throughout the world.
  B. in Europe and Africa.
  C. primarily in Spain.
  D. primarily in prosperous countries

20. The statement that Gaudi's structures leave the viewer "breathless and confused" (line 52), suggests that

  F. some of Gaudi's work needs to be improved.
  G. Gaudi's work is surprising and exciting.
  H. few people understand Gaudi's architecture.
  J. viewing a Gaudi building is usually an unpleasant experience.

Passage 3

NATURAL SCIENCE: This passage is from *The Sea Around Us* by Rachel Carson. In this excerpt Carson tells of undersea life in the very deepest parts of the ocean.

In their world of darkness, it would seem likely that some of the animals might have become blind, as has happened to some cave fauna. So, indeed, many of them have, compensating for the lack of eyes with marvelously developed feelers and long, slender fins and processes with
5 which they grope their way, like so many blind men with canes, their whole knowledge of friends, enemies, or food coming to them through the sense of touch.

The last traces of plant life are left behind in the thin upper layer of water, for no plant can live below about 600 feet even in very clear
10 water, and few find enough sunlight for their food-manufacturing activities below 200 feet. Since no animal can make its own food, the creatures of the deeper waters live a strange, almost parasitic existence of utter dependence on the upper layers. These hungry carnivores prey fiercely and relentlessly upon each other, yet the whole
15 community is ultimately dependent upon the slow rain of descending food particles from above. The components of this neverending rain are the dead and dying plants and animals from the surface, or from one of the intermediate layers. For each of the horizontal zones or communities of the sea that lie, in tier after tier,
20 between the surface and the sea bottom, the food supply is different and in general poorer than for the layer above. There is a hint of the fierce and uncompromising competition for food in the saber-toothed jaws of some of the small, dragonlike fishes of the deeper waters, in the immense mouths and in the elastic and distensible bodies that
25 make it possible for a fish to swallow another several times its size, enjoying swift repletion after a long fast.

Pressure, darkness, and—we should have added only a few years ago—silence, are the conditions of life in the deep sea. But we know now that the conception of the sea as a silent place is wholly false.
30 Wide experience with hydrophones and other listening devices for the detection of submarines has proved that, around the shore lines of much of the world, there is the extraordinary uproar produced by fishes, shrimps, porpoises and probably other forms not yet identified. There has been little investigation as yet of sound in the deep,
35 offshore areas, but when the crew of the *Atlantis* lowered a hydrophone into deep water off Bermuda, they recorded strange mewing sounds, shrieks, and ghostly moans, the sources of which have not been traced. But fish of shallower zones have been captured and confined in aquaria, where their voices have been recorded for

40 comparison with sounds heard at sea, and in many cases satisfactory
identification can be made.

During the Second World War the hydrophone network set up by
the United States Navy to protect the entrance to Chesapeake Bay was
temporarily made useless when, in the spring of 1942, the speakers
45 at the surface began to give forth, every evening, a sound described
as being like 'a pneumatic drill tearing up pavement.' The extraneous
noises that came over the hydrophones completely masked the
sounds of the passage of ships. Eventually it was discovered that the
sounds were the voices of fish known as croakers, which in the spring
50 move into Chesapeake Bay from their offshore wintering grounds. As
soon as the noise had been identified and analyzed, it was possible to
screen it out with an electric filter, so that once more only the sounds
of ships came through the speakers.

21. According to the passage the layer of the ocean where food
for animal life is most plentiful is:

A. the bottom.
B. an area below 600 feet deep.
C. the area between 200 and 600 feet in depth.
D. the uppermost layers of water.

22. Based on information in the passage, which of the following
criteria is NOT likely to be used as a measure of underwater
depth?

F. Noise level recorded by undersea microphones
G. Pressure per square inch
H. Amount of light
J. Amount of plant life

23. The passage indicates that many underwater animals cannot
see because:

A. the lack of light has gradually eliminated their capacity to
see.
B. they use sound waves instead of light to navigate in the
darkness.
C. they have learned to survive without seeing their enemies
or their prey.
D. their sense of touch has eliminated their need to see.

24. According to the passage, which of the following is NOT a use for a hydrophone?

   F. To listen to the sound of undersea fauna
   G. To search for unknown species of fish and other creatures
   H. To monitor the passing of surface vessels
   J. To detect submerged submarines

25. Animals that live near the bottom of the sea are most likely to be carnivorous because:

   A. they have developed sharp teeth and strong jaws with which to kill their prey.
   B. plants that grow far below the surface are not edible.
   C. animals cannot make their own food, so they eat each other.
   D. most surface vegetation is eaten before it sinks to the bottom of the sea.

26. The passage indicates that fish living far under water sometimes do not eat for extended periods of time because:

   F. food is scarce at certain times of the year.
   G. fish in the deepest parts of the ocean digest their food very slowly.
   H. weaker fish must compete for food with stronger fish.
   J. one large meal satisfies most fish for a long time.

27. Which of the following statements about the state of oceanographic research does the passage most clearly support?

   A. Undersea research is still incomplete.
   B. Technology used in undersea studies is still in a very primitive stage of development.
   C. More undersea research is conducted near shore than in mid-ocean.
   D. Military researchers have made several momentous discoveries about undersea life.

28. The phrase "enjoying swift repletion," as used in line 26, probably means that the fish:

   F. are in a state of being sated, i.e., filled to capacity.
   G. seem to enjoy eating after a long fast.
   H. digest their prey very quickly.
   J. continue to hunt for food even after devouring their prey.

29. By using the phrase "saber-toothed" to characterize some of the fishes that live in the deepest waters, the author is suggesting that the fishes:

   A. are still at an early stage of evolution.

   B. appear frightening to behold.

   C. are ferocious food-gatherers.

   D. are soon likely to become extinct.

30. The author's main purpose in the passage is to:

   F. show that the United States coast was threatened by the enemy in World War II.

   G. explain some of the complexities of deepsea life.

   H. illustrate the main problems faced by undersea researchers.

   J. gain public support for oceanographic expeditions.

Passage 4

SOCIAL SCIENCE: This passage is from a U.S. Senate report entitled "The Constitutional Rights of Children." The passage discusses issues related to rights and responsibilities of both children and parents.

The classic liberal thinkers provided the principles for alleviating the repressed social conditions of the slave, the serf, the woman, for, in effect, assertion of individualism and equality of opportunity. But children were not to be included within these
5 principles. Sir Henry Maine was sure that "they do not possess the faculty of forming a judgment on their own interests; in other words . . . they are wanting in the first essential of an engagement by Contract." And John Locke was clear that the limited capacity of children necessarily excluded minors from participation in the
10 social contract. "Children . . . are not born in this state of equality, though they are born to it." Although Adam was "created" as a mature person, "capable from the first instant of his being to provide for his own support and preservation . . . and govern his actions according to the dictates of law and reason," children
15 lacked a "capacity of knowing that law." Parents were therefore under an obligation of nature to nourish and educate their children to help them attain a mature and rational capacity, "till [their]

understanding be fit to take the government of [their] will." "And thus we see how natural freedom and subjection to parents may
20 consist together and are both founded on the same principle."

There is of course no unalterable legal boundary between childhood and adulthood. In different societies and at different times, young people have been accepted into adult society at different ages and children have been variously viewed, and law
25 has differently regulated familial relations at different times. One writer has noted the changing from the early colonial days of this country to the present of the legal regulation of the assumption by the child of an adult economic role. Thus, from the early days till near the end of the 19th century, the economic needs of
30 communities and families in America necessitated early entry of children into the work force. At first, these children were closely restrained by law and custom, whether they lived at home or in an apprentice system in a master's home, and they worked not for their own account _but for the account of family or master.
35 Gradually, the law imposed upon parents some regard and consideration for the child's welfare, especially the obligation to prepare him for assumption of full adult responsibilities. But in the post-Civil War industrialization and the social dislocation accompanying it, social custom and supporting law shifted to a
40 greater requirement of retention of parental control over children for a longer period and to greater protection of family life. Three major institutional changes were legislatively implemented, the juvenile court system, the prohibition of child labor, and compulsory education, all looking toward "external support of the
45 family as the ideal way additionally to prepare children to face life . . . : bolster the family, leave even the delinquent child in the family—where possible, shield the child from adult roles and responsibilities, and formally educate him, and upward movement could be expected."
50 The result was an "extension of childhood," with the State "enjoining longer supervision, more protracted education, and the postponed assumption of adult economic roles." The writer notes some elements of reversal of the trend in the second half of this century in the context of the middle and late adolescent in
55 particular. The waning of parental immunity from a personal tort [*an injury or wrong done to someone*] action brought by an unemancipated child is one example, and another is the passage by

many States of medical emancipation laws by which minors are
enabled to receive medical treatment without parental consent. . . .
60   Concomitant with the increased emphasis upon family control
and responsibility, common law judges viewed parental rights "as
a key concept, not only for the specific purposes of domestic
relations law, but as a fundamental cultural assumption about the
family as a basic social, economic, and political unit. For this
65 reason, both English and American judges view the origins of
parental rights as being even more fundamental than property
rights." Parental power has been deemed primary, prevailing over
the claims of the State, other outsiders, and the children
themselves, unless there is some compelling justification for
70 interference. The primary compelling justification is the protection
of children from parental neglect, abuse, or abandonment; statutes
proscribing various forms of parental misconduct are found in
every State.

31. According to the passage, the principles of equality articulat-
ed by the classic liberal thinkers of the past applied mainly to:

    A. minority groups.
    B. women and slaves.
    C. children.
    D. all people of color.

32. In general, the laws governing parental responsibility for their
children in the early 19th century were:

    F. less strict than today's laws.
    G. more strict than present-day laws.
    H. of an altogether different nature.
    J. of about the same degree of strictness.

33. John Locke believed that minors should not share the bene-
fits of equality because young children:

    A. do not know right from wrong.
    B. cannot be trusted to distinguish truth from illusion.
    C. lack understanding of law and reason.
    D. are usually not competent witnesses.

34. Laws regarding children are sometimes difficult to interpret
because:

   F. they keep changing.
   G. previous court decisions do not serve as a reliable guide.
   H. there is no clearcut division between childhood and adult-
   hood.
   J. juveniles who commit serious crimes are increasingly
   being treated as adult offenders.

35. In making decisions about parent-child relationships judges
are often guided by the principle that:

   A. children and parents are equal in the eyes of the law.
   B. childhood is a special and sacred time of life.
   C. parents' ignorance of the law cannot be excused.
   D. the family unit is the basic unit of society.

36. The passage suggests that laws pertaining to children:

   F. change gradually.
   G. are easy to change when the need arises.
   H. change according to the periodic fluctuations in the econ-
   omy.
   J. are out-of-date and need to be changed.

37. The "extension of childhood" (line 50) has occurred for all of
the following reasons EXCEPT:

   A. children are not expected to go to work at an early age.
   B. children are required to stay in school until they are older.
   C. the courts are severe with parents who do not control
   their children.
   D. maturity is more difficult to achieve in an increasingly
   complex society.

38. According to the passage, the responsibilities of modern parents include:

   F. seeing to it that their children are properly clothed.
   G. providing adequate medical care for young children.
   H. preventing their minor children from harming others.
   J. arranging day care, when necessary.

39. Which of the following situations might cause a court to remove a minor child from the custody of his or her parents?

   A. The child refuses to go to school.

   B. The child is repeatedly left alone while the parents work .

   C. The child regularly runs away from home.

   D. The living conditions in the home are dirty and crowded.

40. Which of the following is the best interpretation of John Locke's statement that children "are not born in this state of equality, though they are born to it" (lines 10–11)?

   F. All children are created equal, but some are more equal than others.

   G. At birth children do not have the same rights as adults.

   H. The state must be responsible for controlling the rights of children until the children grow up.

   J. Children should not assume that the state will look after their rights.

Answers to Reading Test on page 320.

Test 4: Science Reasoning

35 Minutes—40 Questions

Directions: **This test consists of several distinct passages. Each passage is followed by a number of multiple-choice questions based on the passage. Study the passage, and then select the best answer to each question. You are allowed to reread the passage. Record your answer by blackening the appropriate space on the Answer Sheet.**

Passage 1

   The table below gives the amounts and sources of the various kinds of air pollutants produced in the United States during the year 1977, in millions of metric tons.

Source	Particulates	Oxides of sulfur	Oxides of nitrogen	Organic vapors	Carbon monoxide
Transportation	1.1	0.8	9.2	11.5	85.7
Electric utilities	3.4	17.6	7.1	0.1	0.3
Industries	6.6	7.4	5.7	11.4	8.9
Solid waste	0.4	0	0.1	0.7	2.6
Fires	0.7	0	0.1	4.5	4.9
Buildings	0.2	1.6	0.9	0.1	0.3

1. How much carbon monoxide was added to the air of the United States during an average month?

   A. 103 million metric tons
   B. 85.7 million metric tons
   C. 8.6 million metric tons
   D. 7.1 million metric tons

2. Acid rain is produced by the chemical combination of rain water with sulfur and nitrogen oxides in the air. Which of the following would be most effective in reducing the amount of acid rain?

   F. Insulation of buildings to reduce the amount of fuel used
   G. Cleaning of stack gases produced in manufacturing
   H. Better control of forest fires
   J. Cleaning of stack gases produced in electric power plants

3. Which of the following pollution control practices would NOT have an effect on the problem of acid rain?

   A. Improved antipollution devices in cars
   B. Reduction in the burning of tropical forests
   C. Use of low-sulfur coal in electric power plants
   D. Conversion of home heating from coal to nitrogen-free natural gas

4. Which of the following possible improvements in technology would reduce air pollution and, at the same time, improve the efficiency of the use of fuel?

   F. Filtering the particulates out of the waste gases produced by industrial processes

G. Recovering the sulfur from the smoke stacks of electric utilities for use in making sulfuric acid

H. Recovering the organic vapors from industrial processes for use in making commercial solvents

J. Returning the carbon monoxide produced by automobile engines into the cylinders to be burned as fuel

5. Which of the following technological innovations would probably NOT be a practical way to reduce air pollution?

A. Converting industries to reliance on electricity rather than on coal or oil-fired furnaces

B. A program to improve the insulation of buildings

C. Providing all new automobiles with afterburners to convert organic vapors to carbon dioxide and water

D. Light-rail transport systems that will greatly reduce the automobile traffic in cities

Passage 2

Experiments are done in a stream to determine how the size of particles eroded and deposited is affected by the velocity of the water.

Experiment 1

To study erosion, sediments composed of particles of various sizes are placed in the bottom of a stream at many different points. At each point, the velocity of the stream is measured. The minimum velocity needed to lift the particles off the stream bottom is determined for each size particle.

Material	Particle size (mm)	Minimum velocity (cm/s)
Clay	0.001	700
Silt	0.01	180
Fine sand	0.1	60
Coarse sand	1	90
Pebbles	10	210
Cobbles	100	600

Experiment 2

To study deposition, the sediments are dropped into the stream from the surface at various points in the stream. The minimum stream velocity that will prevent the particles from sinking to the bottom of the stream is measured for each size particle.

Material	Particle size (mm)	Minimum velocity (cm/s)
Clay	0.001	20
Silt	0.01	20
Fine sand	0.1	20
Coarse sand	1	30
Pebbles	10	100
Cobbles	100	300

6. A landslide dumps a mixture of particles of all sizes into a stream flowing at 40 cm/s. What kinds of material will be deposited in the stream bed?
   F. All sizes of particles
   G. Clay, silt, and sand
   H. None; all will wash away
   J. Pebbles and cobbles

7. A newly formed stream starts to flow at 30 cm/s over a land area where the soil contains particles of all sizes. After a number of years, what kinds of particles will remain in the stream bed?
   A. All kinds
   B. Clay, silt, and fine sand
   C. Coarse sand, pebbles, and cobbles
   D. Clay and cobbles only

8. At a construction site, a quantity of coarse sand finds its way into a stream flowing at 40 cm/s. What happens to it?

F. It falls to the bottom of the stream and stays there.

G. It is carried away by the stream and falls to the bottom if the stream speeds up to 90 cm/s.

H. It is carried away by the stream and falls to the bottom if the stream slows down to 25 cm/s.

J. It falls to the bottom of the stream and is then picked up and carried into quieter water.

9. A stream flows at 130 cm/s over soil containing a mixture of all kinds of particles. What kinds of particles will drop to the bottom at a point where the velocity has slowed down to 25 cm/s?

A. Pebbles and cobbles

B. Coarse and fine sand only

C. Coarse sand only

D. Clay, silt, pebbles, and cobbles

10. Which of the following hypotheses might be advanced to account for the fact that a very large stream velocity is required to lift clay off the bottom of the river?

F. Clay particles clump together to form lumps the size of cobbles.

G. Clay particles are much larger than sand grains.

H. Rivers always slow down when they flow over clay.

J. Clay particles have a high density, so they drop to the bottom very easily.

11. If similar experiments were done with other materials in other rivers, which of the following outcomes would always be found?

A. The velocity figures in Experiment 1 would always be larger than the corresponding values in Experiment 2.

B. The velocity figures would never be larger than 600 cm/s in either experiment.

C. The velocity figures would never be smaller then 20 cm/s in either experiment.

D. Medium-size particles are always picked up by the slowest part of the river and carried furthest.

Passage 3

The diagram below shows the changes in weather pattern as a thunderstorm passes by. The time scale goes from right to left.

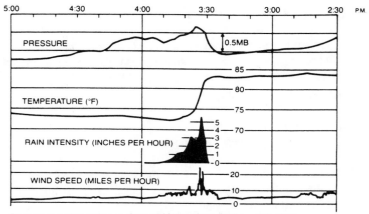

From Horace Robert Byers, *General Meteorology*, McGraw-Hill, 1959.

12. The rain was heaviest at:

    F. 3:00 P.M.
    G. 3:30 P.M.
    H. 4:00 P.M.
    J. 4:30 P.M.

13. How did the pressure vary?

    A. It increased substantially when the wind was strongest, and dropped off in the next hour.
    B. It built up slowly as the storm approached, and then dropped suddenly.
    C. It followed exactly the same pattern as the wind speed.
    D. It increased as the wind died down.

14. Which two variables were approximately inversely related?

    F. Rain intensity and wind speed
    G. Rain intensity and temperature
    H. Wind speed and pressure
    J. Pressure and temperature

15. What was the weather like while the pressure was nearing its maximum?

    A. The rain and wind were at their worst.
    B. It was warm, and the rain and wind were slowly building up.
    C. It had cooled off, and the rain was dying down.
    D. It was warm and windy, but the rain had not yet started.

16. About how much rain fell during the storm?

    F. 10 inches
    G. 5 inches
    H. 2 inches
    J. 1 inch

Passage 4

A chemist is investigating the effect of various kinds and amounts of solutes on the boiling point of a solution.

Experiment 1

Solutions are made of various amounts of glucose dissolved in 1 liter of water, and the boiling point of each solution is measured.

Glucose concentration (g/L)	Boiling point (° C)
0	100.0
100	100.3
200	100.6
300	100.9
400	101.2
500	101.5

Experiment 2

Solutions are made of various solutes (substances dissolved) in water, all with a concentration of 300 g/L. The boiling point of each solution is measured.

Substance	Molecular weight	Boiling point (° C)
Acetaldehyde	44	103.5
Glycerol	92	101.7
Glucose	180	100.9
Sucrose	342	100.5

Experiment 3

Solutions are made of various solutes dissolved in benzene (the solvent), which boils at 80.1° C. All concentrations are 300 g/L.

Solute	Molecular weight	Boiling point (° C)
Butyric acid	88	89.8
Triethylamine	101	88.6
Naphthalene	178	84.8
Cholesterol	387	82.3

17. If 200 g of glucose is dissolved in 500 mL of water, the boiling point of the solution will be:

A. 100.3° C. **C.** 101.2° C.
B. 100.6° C. **D.** 101.6° C.

18. Three hundred grams of a substance with a molecular weight of 65 is dissolved in 1 liter of water. The boiling point of the solution will be about:

F. 103.5° C. **H.** 101.7° C.
G. 102.4° C. **J.** 100.3° C.

19. For a given concentration and molecular weight of solute, how does the elevation of the boiling point depend on the kind of solvent?

   A. It is the same for all solvents.
   B. It is the same for water and for benzene.
   C. It is more for water than for benzene.
   D. It is more for benzene than for water.

20. The experiments indicate that the boiling point elevation is directly proportional to:

   F. the molecular weight of the solute.
   G. the number of molecules of solute per gram of solvent.
   H. the boiling point of the solvent used.
   J. a combination of solute concentration and molecular weight.

21. In Experiment 3, the solution of butyric acid in benzene boiled at a higher temperature than cholesterol in benzene. A possible explanation is:

   A. the molecules of cholesterol are larger, so they lower the boiling point of the benzene.
   B. the mass of cholesterol in solution was larger than the mass of butyric acid.
   C. cholesterol reacts chemically with benzene, but butyric acid does not.
   D. the butyric acid solution contains more molecules of solute than the cholesterol solution.

22. In trying to determine the nature of a newly discovered substance, a chemist might use experiments of this kind to discover its:

   F. chemical formula.
   G. concentration.
   H. molecular weight.
   J. boiling point.

Passage 5

The diagram below represents the forms of energy consumption in an old building, in the design for a new building, and in the actual new building after it was built.

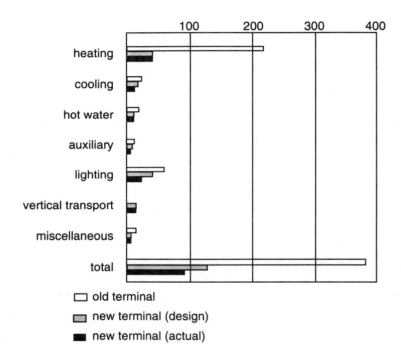

☐ old terminal
▨ new terminal (design)
■ new terminal (actual)

23. In attempting to improve the efficiency of energy use, the new design:

A. reduced the amount of energy used by about 15%.

B. was a great improvement but did not accomplish all that was expected of it.

C. was so good that the new building actually performed better than expected.

D. was unnecessary, since the new building was so much better than the old one.

24. What service was provided in the new building that was not available in the old one?

   F. Elevators
   G. Hot air heating
   H. Air conditioning
   J. Electronic energy control

25. The difference between the new design and the performance of the actual building seems to have been due mainly to miscalculation of the energy saving provided by:

   A. insulation.
   B. fluorescent lighting.
   C. air conditioning.
   D. improved boilers.

26. What approach to future problems of design of heating efficiency is suggested by these results?

   F. Since heating is the largest part of the energy cost even in the new building, this design did little to improve heating efficiency.
   G. Design emphasis should be placed on heating because this is where the major savings can be made.
   H. Better designs must be sought because this one did not produce a result better than the one achieved in the actual new building.
   J. Little additional research is needed because this design provided the maximum possible saving of heating fuel.

27. Which of the following questions had to be answered before a decision was made whether or not to use the new design in constructing the new building?

   A. Should the new building be equipped with air conditioning?
   B. Will the new design improve the efficiency of hot water heating?

C. Does the actual new building accurately reflect the gains suggested by the design?

D. Does the new design cost so much more to build that the fuel saving would not be worth the difference?

Passage 6

The purpose of this experiment is to study the rate at which the eyes of guppies become light-adapted.

Experiment 1

Three guppies are kept in daylight conditions at 24° C. They are fed 50 water fleas (*Daphnia*) once a day. The number of *Daphnia* captured in 5 minutes is counted. In six trials, the following results are obtained:

Number of *Daphnia* captured: 35   32   32   36   34   35

Experiment 2

The guppies are kept in the dark at 24° C for a full day. Then a light is turned on. After a measured time delay, 50 *Daphnia* are added to the tank, and the number captured in 5 minutes is counted. The experiment is repeated with various time delays.

Time delay (minutes)	Number captured in 5 minutes
2	0
4	18
6	24
8	33
10	33
12	32

Experiment 3

A similar experiment is done with the guppies, which have been kept at various temperatures. A uniform time delay of 8 minutes is used before the food is added.

Temperature (° C)	Number captured in 5 minutes
15	12
18	18
21	26
24	35
27	34
30	35
33	22
36	9

28. What assumption underlies the design of these experiments?

F. Guppies are most active when illumination is high.

G. The ability of guppies to find food depends on their ability to see it.

H. Temperature affects the ability of guppies to find food.

J. The eyes of guppies are just like the eyes of people.

29. What was the purpose of Experiment 1?

A. To establish a criterion as to when the guppies' eyes are light-adapted

B. To control any possible effect of temperature

C. To condition the guppies to respond to the presence of *Daphnia*

D. To keep the guppies in healthy condition

30. What was the purpose of the time delays in Experiment 2?

F. To see how long it would take for the guppies to find their food

G. To allow for differences between guppies in their feeding ability

H. To find out how long it takes for the eyes of the guppies to become completely light-adapted

J. To measure the time rate at which guppies find their food under standard conditions

31. What evidence is there that guppies depend solely on their eyesight to find food?

A. Experiment 3 shows that they cannot see well at low temperatures.

B. Experiment 2 shows that, in the first 2 minutes after being kept in the dark, they cannot find any.

C. Experiment 1 shows that they find food very efficiently in daylight.

D. Experiment 2 shows that the rate at which they find food diminishes as the food supply dwindles.

32. A time delay of 8 minutes was selected for Experiment 3 because this is the amount of time required for:

F. the guppies to consume most of the food.

G. the *Daphnia* to become adapted to the tank.

H. the guppies' eyes to become light-adapted at 24° C.

J. the water in the tank to reach a steady temperature.

33. Which hypothesis could NOT account for the results of Experiment 3?

A. Light adaptation is delayed at unusually high temperatures.

B. Guppies are damaged at very high temperatures, and are thus unable to feed well.

C. At high temperatures, *Daphnia* become immobile and more difficult to find.

D. The rate of adaptation to light increases uniformly with temperature.

Passage 7

Two scientists disagree about an important point in the theory of evolution.

Scientist 1

Darwin's theory of evolution by natural selection has a serious flaw. It cannot account for the origin of completely new organs. Consider, for example, the wings of insects. These originate in the embryo as outgrowths of the external skeleton of the thorax. How could such outgrowths have evolved? According to all we know about evolution, they must have started as tiny outgrowths that grew bigger generation by generation until they became functional wings. However, a small, incipient wing is useless; an insect cannot fly with 1% of a wing. Since those tiny wing buds would have no use, they could not contribute to the ability of the insects to survive, and thus could not contribute to the evolution of wings. It has been suggested that these small outgrowths were originally used as gliding surfaces, like the skin flaps of a flying squirrel. This does not solve the problem, however, for a good-sized surface would be needed for gliding; 1% of a surface is as useless for gliding as for flying. Somehow, such a surface must have gradually developed by some means other than natural selection. Natural selection could improve a gliding surface, and turn it into a functional, flapping wing, but it could not invent the surface in the first place. The insect wing is an example of preadaptation, the development of a new structure that subsequently evolves into something useful. Evolution gives us many such examples. Preadaptation surely exists, but it cannot be explained by the theory of natural selection. Explanation of the origin of new, useful structures is an unfinished task of biological science.

Scientist 2

The problem raised by Scientist 1 is not new. Darwin provided the answer a century ago, although at that time there was no real evidence. It all hinges on the meaning of the term *preadaptation*. It does not mean that a new feature arises and then develops for many evolutionary years while it has no function. What it does mean is that an existing structure, developed for one function, can acquire a totally different use. This is undoubtedly how insect wings evolved. Recent studies show that the wings of insects have an important function other than flight; they are temperature-regulating structures. Many insects control their body temperatures by sitting in the sun to warm up. In ancient, primitive insects, an expansion of the thorax exposed more surface. This expansion was promoted by selection, since it allowed for faster and more efficient warmup. Lateral projections provided additional surfaces for temperature regulation. When these projections grew big enough, they acquired a new function; they became useful as gliding surfaces. The ability to glide has developed many times, and it has sometimes evolved into real, controlled flight. Selection converted the clumsy gliding surfaces of ancient insects into the complex and effective insect wings of today. Preadaptation is simply a shift of function, and is perfectly incorporated into the theory of evolution by natural selection.

34. One of the scientists, but not the other, would agree that:
    F. natural selection results in improved functioning of insect wings.
    G. natural selection can explain the origin of the wings of insects.
    H. insects use their wings to help in temperature control.
    J. insect wings evolved from surfaces previously used for gliding.

35. What evidence does Scientist 2 advance to support her argument?
    A. Tests show that insects use their wings for temperature control.
    B. Darwin provided a competent explanation for preadaptation.
    C. In the development of an insect, the wings arise as outgrowths of the thoracic skeleton.
    D. Many insects use projections from the thorax for gliding.

36. According to Scientist 2, what principle has Scientist 1 overlooked in his argument?
    F. Natural selection can greatly improve the functioning of an organ.
    G. In the evolution of many different flying organisms, gliding always precedes real flying.
    H. New organs can arise even if they have no function at first.
    J. In the course of evolution, an organ can acquire a new function.

37. Which of the following discoveries would support the hypothesis of Scientist 2?

    A. Fossils of insects with primitive wings capable of gliding, but not of flying

    B. A living species of insect that can glide, but cannot fly

    C. A fossil insect with small lateral projections from the thorax

    D. A living insect in which juvenile stages have short wings used only for temperature regulation

38. How should the argument of Scientist 1 be evaluated in terms of its contribution to science?

    F. It is a foolish argument because the question was settled a long time ago.

    G. It is useful to raise the question because it challenges scientists to find evidence for shifts of function.

    H. It wastes valuable time because it has long been established that evolution results from natural selection.

    J. It challenges scientists to find an answer to a perplexing problem for which there is no satisfactory answer.

39. What would the two scientists expect to find in the fossil record?

    A. Scientist 1, but not Scientist 2, would expect to find that functional gliding surfaces appeared suddenly.

    B. Both scientists would expect to find gradual evolution of wings, starting with small projections.

    C. Scientist 2, but not Scientist 1, would expect to find gradual evolution, starting with small projections.

    D. Both scientists would expect to find that there are no fossil insects without some sort of gliding surface.

40. In a recent series of experiments, paper models of insects were exposed to sunlight, to aerodynamic tests in a wind tunnel, and to measurements of temperature. Size and wing length were varied to test the concept of:

    F. natural selection.   **H.** preadaptation.

    G. shift of function.   **J.** evolution.

Answers to Science Reasoning Test on page 320.

ANSWER KEYS AND ANALYSIS CHARTS
Test 1: English

1. D	20. H	39. D	58. G
2. H	21. B	40. H	59. A
3. D	22. H	41. B	60. H
4. H	23. B	42. F	61. C
5. C	24. G	43. D	62. G
6. J	25. B	44. J	63. C
7. B	26. H	45. A	64. J
8. G	27. B	46. F	65. C
9. D	28. J	47. D	66. J
10. H	29. A	48. J	67. C
11. C	30. J	49. C	68. J
12. H	31. A	50. G	69. A
13. A	32. H	51. C	70. H
14. G	33. D	52. F	71. B
15. C	34. J	53. D	72. G
16. H	35. C	54. F	73. C
17. D	36. G	55. B	74. H
18. F	37. C	56. H	75. C
19. C	38. F	57. D	

ANSWER ANALYSIS CHART			
Skills	Questions	Possible Score	Your Score
Usage/Mechanics			
Punctuation	1, 13, 18, 20, 28, 44, 46, 49, 50, 66	10	
Basic Grammar and Usage	6, 8, 9, 16, 26, 27, 31, 32, 39, 48, 52, 72	12	
Sentence Structure	3, 4, 12, 17, 24, 25, 33, 38, 40, 41, 43, 47, 51, 53, 56, 61, 62, 67	18	
Rhetorical Skills			
Strategy	2, 5, 19, 23, 29, 34, 42, 54, 59, 63, 71, 74	12	
Organization	11, 15, 22, 30, 35, 37, 45, 58, 60, 65, 75	11	
Style	7, 10, 14, 21, 36, 55, 57, 64, 68, 69, 70, 73	12	

Total: 75 _____

Percent Correct: _____

Test 2: Mathematics

1. **C**	16. **F**	31. **D**	46. **G**
2. **H**	17. **A**	32. **K**	47. **D**
3. **E**	18. **J**	33. **A**	48. **G**
4. **H**	19. **A**	34. **K**	49. **D**
5. **C**	20. **H**	35. **E**	50. **F**
6. **J**	21. **E**	36. **K**	51. **C**
7. **B**	22. **J**	37. **C**	52. **K**
8. **F**	23. **E**	38. **K**	53. **D**
9. **D**	24. **G**	39. **A**	54. **H**
10. **K**	25. **B**	40. **G**	55. **A**
11. **E**	26. **J**	41. **D**	56. **H**
12. **G**	27. **D**	42. **G**	57. **D**
13. **C**	28. **J**	43. **C**	58. **K**
14. **F**	29. **C**	44. **K**	59. **D**
15. **A**	30. **H**	45. **D**	60. **J**

ANSWER ANALYSIS CHART					
Content Area	**Skill Level**			**Possible Score**	**Your Score**
	Basic Skills	**Application**	**Analysis**		
Pre-Algebra Algebra	1, 5, 10, 13, 17, 23, 27, 29	2, 3, 6, 8, 11, 15, 19, 22, 28, 34, 36, 50	12, 16, 24, 30	24	
Intermediate Algebra Coordinate Geometry	7, 14, 21, 32, 42, 43, 45	4, 18, 25, 26, 31, 33, 35	40, 44, 49, 52	18	
Geometry	38, 48, 51, 53, 56, 57, 58	9, 20, 37, 39, 46, 54, 59		14	
Trigonometry	41, 60	47, 55		4	

Total: 60   _____

Percent Correct: _____

Test 3: Reading

1.	B	11.	B	21.	D	31.	B
2.	G	12.	J	22.	F	32.	F
3.	A	13.	C	23.	A	33.	C
4.	F	14.	F	24.	G	34.	H
5.	C	15.	A	25.	D	35.	D
6.	H	16.	J	26.	H	36.	F
7.	A	17.	C	27.	A	37.	D
8.	J	18.	H	28.	F	38.	H
9.	D	19.	B	29.	C	39.	B
10.	G	20.	G	30.	G	40.	G

ANSWER ANALYSIS CHART				
Passage Type	Referring	Reasoning	Possible Score	Your Score
Prose Fiction	2, 4, 6, 7	1, 3, 5, 8, 9, 10	10	
Humanities	13, 15, 19	11, 12, 14, 16, 17, 18, 20	10	
Social Sciences	31, 33, 38	32, 34, 35, 36, 37, 39, 40	10	
Natural Sciences	21, 23, 24, 26	22, 25, 27, 28, 29, 30	10	

Total: 40 _____

Percent Correct: _____

Test 4: Science Reasoning

1.	A	11.	A	21.	D	31.	B
2.	J	12.	G	22.	H	32.	H
3.	A	13.	A	23.	C	33.	D
4.	F	14.	J	24.	F	34.	G
5.	B	15.	A	25.	B	35.	A
6.	H	16.	J	26.	G	36.	J
7.	D	17.	C	27.	D	37.	D
8.	F	18.	G	28.	G	38.	G
9.	B	19.	D	29.	A	39.	B
10.	F	20.	G	30.	H	40.	G

ANSWER ANALYSIS CHART					
	Skill Level				
Kind of Question	Under-standing	Analysis	General-ization	Possible Score	Your Score
Data Representation	1, 12, 13, 23, 24	2, 3, 14, 15, 25	4, 5, 16, 26, 27	15	
Research Summaries	6, 17, 18, 28, 29, 30	7, 8, 9, 19 20, 31, 32	10, 11, 21, 22, 33	18	
Conflicting Viewpoints	34, 35	36, 37, 38	39, 40	7	

Total: 40   _____

Percent Correct: _____

See **"Evaluating Your Performance" on page 440.**

Answer Explanations   Test 1: English

1. (D)   Use a comma between the parts of a simple series.
2. (H)   It is important to maintain the established subject—the forces that influence the way a child handles money; the other options are all off the topic.
3. (D)   There is no need for *and* before the adjective clause *that children need to learn.* Choices B and C repeat the error. Choice C is wrong also because the pronoun *whom* is used to refer to a person, and the antecedent here is *principles.*
4. (H)   There is a parallel series of sentences in this paragraph, all employing the infinitive. For this reason, the infinitive *to understand* is correct.
5. (C)   The first sentence of the paragraph is a clear topic sentence that prepares the reader for the series of principles that forms the body of the paragraph.
6. (J)   The antecedent of the pronoun is the plural noun *children* at the end of the preceding paragraph.

7. (B) The phrase *being as how* is substandard English; the other words create an illogical statement.

8. (G) The subject of the sentence is the singular noun *rise.*

9. (D) The pronoun *this* is almost never adequate by itself; the sentence requires a more complete statement. The point made in the preceding sentences is that money is more available.

10. (H) *Major* is more in keeping with the tone of the passage. The other words do not mean the same as *major* and are less preferable in this context.

11. (C) The underlined statement is off the topic and so must be eliminated.

12. (H) The subordinating conjunction *when* forms a logical link with the rest of the sentence; the other options do not.

13. (A) An introductory adverbial clause, except a very short one, is set off from the main clause by a comma. A stronger mark of punctuation in this place, such as choice D, would create a sentence fragment.

14. (G) The phrase *material possessions* makes a clear point; *worldly goods* is redundant.

15. (C) Paragraph 2 ends with a mention about *pressures,* a train of thought that leads directly to paragraph 5, which begins with the statement *These pressures are strong.* In the same manner, the thought about managing money at the end of paragraph 5 is picked up in the first sentence in paragraph 3; the notion that children need experience in managing money is echoed in paragraph 4, and the emphasis on adults in paragraph 4 is continued in the first words of paragraph 6.

16. (H) A singular subject—in this case, *police officer*—followed by such a phrase as *in common with, accompanied by, in addition to,* or *together with,* takes a singular verb.

17. (D) To be parallel with the rest of the sentence, this part must begin with the participle *protected,* which modifies the noun *structure.*

18. (F) A parenthetical expression such as *however* is set off by commas.

19. (C) This choice is the only one that bears on anatomy.

20. (H) Compound verbs are not normally separated by a comma.

21. (B)   The words *One after the other* are redundant; the phrase *in turn* means the same.

22. (H)   This sentence has no bearing on the topic of the paragraph or passage and must be removed.

23. (B)   Because the entire passage deals with the great stress placed on the foot, this description of the physical process of using the foot is meaningful.

24. (G)   The word *if* is necessary at this point if the sentence is to be logical. Not all 7-year-old boys weigh 55 pounds.

25. (B)   A present-tense verb is necessary to agree with the other verbs in the sentence.

26. (H)   The subject of the verb is the plural noun *estimates;* the present tense is correct.

27. (B)   When parts of a compound subject are joined by *or* or *nor*, the verb agrees with the nearer part—in this case, *characteristic.* The simple present tense is correct.

28. (J)   The sentence is a simple declarative statement that requires a period.

29. (A)   The figures provided are quite impressive and clearly dramatize the point of the passage.

30. (J)   Paragraph 3 is a more general statement about the foot and should precede the very specific, detailed paragraphs 2 and 4. Note the clue in *During all this walking.*

31. (A)   The subject of the verb *commemorates* is the singular noun *park;* the present tense is correct (note *is* in the same sentence).

32. (H)   Items in a series are separated by semicolons if they contain commas within themselves. This sentence, when correctly constructed, includes a series of direct objects—*meetings, adoption,* and *labors*—the last two of which introduce clauses set off by commas.

33. (D)   To be parallel with the direct objects *meetings* and *labors,* this item must begin with a noun.

34. (J)   The park is the site of Independence Hall, around which most of the historical events described in the passage revolve.

35. (C)   The topic sentence of this paragraph is flawed; the general point it makes is not broad enough to embrace the historical events described. A better topic sentence would be this: *Independence Hall, originally the statehouse for the province of Pennsylvania, was the site of an important event in early American history.*

36. (G) The word *supervision* is adequate; *overview* is repetitious.

37. (C) Although Thomas Jefferson figures importantly in the events later described in the passage, where he was in 1736 has no bearing on this paragraph.

38. (F) The past perfect tense is required in this sentence because the action described took place *before* the past action that is the subject of the passage.

39. (D) All the actions in the sentence are in the simple past.

40. (H) The word *Nevertheless* provides the contrast that is needed in a sentence describing an unexpected consequence. The other connective words do not provide the contrast, and so make no sense in the context.

41. (B) In combination with the word *would, be declared* signals an event in the future; note "not until a year later."

42. (F) The paragraph, flawed because of a weak topic sentence, presents historical events that occurred in and near Independence Hall. Of the choices given, this is the only one that makes that point.

43. (D) This is the only correct, complete sentence. Choices A and B are sentence fragments. Choice C is a sentence plus a sentence fragment.

44. (J) A semicolon joins two main clauses; there is no conjunction. Anything weaker in this spot results in a run-on sentence.

45. (A) The paragraphs are correct as they stand. Since this passage is in chronological order, the sequence is self-explanatory.

46. (F) Items in a series are separated by semicolons if they contain commas.

47. (D) To be parallel with the other clauses in the sentence, this one must maintain the same pattern, *it is a . . . .*

48. (J) The subject of the verb is the plural noun *pro-lifers;* the present tense is needed.

49. (C) The comma is needed after *Americans* to set off the participial phrase *comprising a majority of Americans.* Otherwise, the sentence can be misread to mean that pro-choice advocates comprise a majority of all Americans who believe that abortion should be legal under certain circumstances, falsely implying that a minority of these Americans are not pro-choice.

50. (G)   This phrase is not a digression but rather is information essential to the point being made, and so should not be enclosed in parentheses.

51. (C)   This sentence needs to be introduced by a transition that signals the introduction of an example; the other transitions denote contrast *or cause,* and choices B and D result in sentence fragments.

52. (F)   The subject of the sentence is the singular noun *group;* the present tense is correct.

53. (D)   The word *process* is a noun; it must be described or restated as a noun, not as an adverbial clause.

54. (F)   The views of leaders would be useful in this passage about opinions. The information in the other options would be off the topic.

55. (B)   The adjective *ill advised* is clear and direct; the other options are colloquial or misleading.

56. (H)   The subject of the sentence is the plural noun *programs.* The passage is written in the present tense.

57. (D)   The clause *that are beneficial* merely repeats the meaning of the word *positive,* and so should be removed.

58. (G)   This sentence has nothing to do with the point of the passage.

59. (A)   For the most part, one view of the abortion issue is compared with the other in this passage.

60. (H)   Paragraph 2 clearly introduces the topic, and suggests the structure of the passage; paragraph 3 begins with an example of the quality of the thought mentioned at the end of paragraph 2; paragraph 4 presents the other view of the issue, and paragraph 1 sums up the complexity of the issue.

61. (C)   The sentence in which this question appears ends with a series of noun objects, in which *comparison of the proposed budget* should be included. Note that the correct choice is the only one that is not a clause.

62. (G)   The present perfect tense is required in this sentence because the action referred to extends, at least in its consequences, to the present.

63. (C) The entire passage emphasizes the point that no legislation is more important than the budget.

64. (J) Only the use of the preposition *For* creates a logical, correct sentence; the other choices are substandard English.

65. (C) The statement about traffic on the freeways has no bearing on the point of the passage.

66. (J) Use the comma before a coordinating conjunction linking main clauses.

67. (C) The logic that lies behind each of the options changes the meaning of the sentence dramatically. Only the use of *Because* results in a meaning consistent with the rest of the paragraph.

68. (J) The word *because* here creates an adverb clause that is parallel with the adverb clause that begins the sentence. Also, the other choices are either substandard English (F) or alter the meaning (G, H) of the sentence.

69. (A) *Continually* means "occurring in steady, rapid succession," while *continuously* means "occurring in uninterrupted duration," the latter meaning being preferable in this context.

70. (H) The idea of disputes and stalemates festering borders on a mixed metaphor. More sensible in this very businesslike passage is the use of the term *unresolved.* The other options make no sense in the sentence.

71. (B) The tone and message of the passage seem to be directed at constituents seeking to be informed.

72. (G) When the comparative (here, *larger*) is used for more than two, it is necessary to exclude from the group the object compared. In the original sentence the expenditures of the Government of California would be included in the group *those of any American governmental jurisdiction . . . U.S. Government.*

73. (C) The word *budget* is what is intended; additional words are distracting.

74. (H) The passage makes clear in several ways the importance of the state budget as an entity.

75. (C) Paragraph 3 is clearly the introductory paragraph for this passage. In addition, it refers to early January and the governor's message, two items mentioned also in the first sentence of paragraph 1. Paragraph 2 continues the chronological narrative, and even ends with a closing statement.

Answer Explanations   Test 2: Mathematics

1. (C) Only $\frac{x}{2}$ satisfies the definition of a monomial.

2. (H) Lisa now receives 108% of her previous salary, so $5.67 is 108% of what number? $A = 5.67$, $P = 108\%$, B is unknown. The percent proportion is

$$\frac{108}{100} = \frac{5.67}{B}$$

$$108B = 567$$
$$B = 5.25$$

3. (E) $5 + 2 \cdot 3^2 = 5 + 2 \cdot 9$ Exponents first.
$$= 5 + 18$$
$$= 23$$

4. (H) $81x^2 - 36y^2 = 9(9x^2 - 4y^2)$
$$= 9(3x - 2y)(3x + 2y)$$
Always do the greatest common factor first.

5. (C) $\sqrt{49} = 7$, which is rational.

6. (J) $\dfrac{(x - y)^2}{y^2 - x^2} = \dfrac{(x - y)(x - y)}{(y - x)(y + x)}$

$$= \frac{(-1)(x - y)}{y + x} \quad \text{Because } x - y \text{ and}$$
$$\qquad\qquad\qquad\quad y - x \text{ are opposites.}$$

$$= \frac{y - x}{y + x}$$

7. (B) Consecutive terms of a geometric sequence have a common ratio. Only in the sequence 1, 2, 4, 8, . . . is there a common ratio, 2.

8. (F)
$$4x - 2[3x - (x + 4)] = 5 - 2(x + 1)$$
$$4x - 2[3x - x - 4] = 5 - 2x - 2$$
$$4x - 6x + 2x + 8 = 5 - 2x - 2$$
$$8 = 3 - 2x$$
$$5 = -2x$$
$$x = \frac{-5}{2}$$

9. (D) Angle *ABC* is a right angle because a diameter is perpendicular to a tangent at the point of tangency. Angle *ADB* is also a right angle because it is inscribed in a semicircle. Therefore ∠ *DBC* is complementary to both ∠ *ABD* and ∠ *BCD*. Thus ∠ *ABD* and ∠ *BCD* are equal in measure.

10. (K)
$$7.2\% = 0.072$$
$$7.2(10^{-2}) = 0.072$$
$$\frac{72}{100} = 0.72$$
$$(0.08)9 = 0.72$$
$$(0.08)(0.09) = 0.0072$$

11. (E) $xy^2(x - y) = (-3)(2^2)(-3 - 2)$
$$= (-3)(4)(-5)$$
$$= 60$$

12. (G) This is a direct-variation-type problem. The proportion is
$$\frac{4}{x} = \frac{20}{30} \left(= \frac{2}{3} \right)$$
$$2x = 12$$
$$x = 6$$

13. (C) The associative property of addition allows regrouping of terms.

14. (F) A pure imaginary number is a complex number with the real part equal to 0. Only $\sqrt{-9} = 3i = 0 + 3i$ is this type.

15. (A)

$$7\tfrac{1}{4} \qquad 7\tfrac{3}{12} \qquad \text{The LCD is 12.}$$

$$-\,2\tfrac{5}{6} \qquad -\,2\tfrac{10}{12}$$

$$= \qquad 6\tfrac{15}{12} \qquad \text{Borrow } \tfrac{12}{12} \text{ from the 7.}$$

$$-\,2\tfrac{10}{12}$$

$$4\tfrac{5}{12}$$

16. (F) This is a work-type problem for which the formula $w = rt$ applies. Since Stan can do the job in 4 hours, his rate of work is $\tfrac{1}{4}$ of the job per hour. Fred's rate is then $\tfrac{1}{5}$ of the job per hour. Let $x =$ the number of hours it would take to do the job together.

	w	$=$	r	$\cdot$	t
Stan	$\tfrac{x}{4}$		$\tfrac{1}{4}$		x
Fred	$\tfrac{x}{5}$		$\tfrac{1}{5}$		x

The equation is $\tfrac{x}{4} + \tfrac{x}{5} = 1$ (one job completed).

17. (A) The definition of a composite number includes the phrase "greater than 1."

18. (J) A special rule about absolute value inequalities allows an immediate translation from $|x + 3| \geq 2$ to

$$x + 3 \geq 2 \text{ or } x + 3 \leq -2$$
$$x \geq -1 \text{ or } x \leq -5$$

19. (A) Multiply both sides by the LCD, which is 12.

$$12\left(\tfrac{2x - 1}{3} + \tfrac{x + 2}{4}\right) = 12\left(\tfrac{1}{6}\right)$$

$$4(2x - 1) + 3(x + 2) = 2$$
$$8x - 4 + 3x + 6 = 2$$
$$11x + 2 = 2$$
$$11x = 0$$
$$x = 0$$

20. (H) The measure of an angle formed by a chord and a tangent at the point of tangency is half of the intercepted arc. An inscribed angle is also measured by half of the intercepted arc. Therefore $\angle ECB = \angle BAC$.

21. (E) When completely simplified, the polynomial is
$$27x^6 + \text{(terms of lower degree)}$$
The degree of this polynomial is 6.

22. (J) Follow the rule for squaring a binomial:
$$(a + b)^2 = a^2 + 2ab + b^2$$
Here
$$(2x - 3y)^2 = 4x^2 - 12xy + 9y^2$$

23. (E) In quadrant IV, the first component of the ordered pairs is positive and the second is negative. Only $(2, -8)$ is of that type.

24. (G) $110110_{(two)} = 1(2^5) + 1(2^4) + 0(2^3) + 1(2^2) + 1(2^1)$
$$+ \ 0(2^0)$$
$$= 32 + 16 + 4 + 2 = 54_{(ten)}$$

25. (B) The sum of the roots of the quadratic equation $ax^2 + bx + c = 0$ is $\frac{-b}{a}$ and the product is $\frac{c}{a}$.

The product of the roots of
$5x^2 - 8x + 7 = 0$ is $\frac{7}{5}$.

26. (J) $8^{-(2/3)} = \dfrac{1}{8^{2/3}}$
$$= \frac{1}{\sqrt[3]{8^2}} = \frac{1}{\sqrt[3]{64}} = \frac{1}{4}$$

27. (D) The given expression is the expanded form of 302,470.

28. (J) First factor each denominator, then use each factor the greater number of times it occurs in any factorization.
$$5a^2b^3$$
$$20ab^4 = 2 \cdot 2 \cdot 5 \cdot ab^4$$
$$15a^3b^2 = 3 \cdot 5 \cdot a^3b^2$$
The LCD is $2 \cdot 2 \cdot 3 \cdot 5 \cdot a^3b^4 = 60a^3b^4$.

29. (C) The mean of n numbers is found by adding the numbers and dividing by n. The sum of the given numbers is 58, so the mean is 5.8.

30. (H) Sue is paid 7% only on her sales. Her salary is $S = 200 + 0.07t$.

31. (D) Multiply the numerator and denominator by the LCD, which is $9x^2$.

$$\frac{9x^2\left(\frac{1}{x} - \frac{1}{3}\right)}{9x^2\left(\frac{1}{x^2} - \frac{1}{9}\right)} = \frac{9x - 3x^2}{9 - x^2}$$

$$= \frac{3x(3 - x)}{(3 - x)(3 + x)}$$

$$= \frac{3x}{3 + x}$$

32. (K) The given equation is equivalent to $y + 9 = -2(x + 6)^2$. Compare this to the standard form of such an equation:

$$y - k = a(x - h)^2$$

which has its vertex at (h, k). The parabola's vertex is at $(-6, -9)$.

33. (A) Multiply both sides by the common denominator, $(x - 3)(x + 3)$. There are, therefore, restricted values 3 and -3.

$$(x - 3)(x + 3)\left(\frac{x^2 + 9}{x^2 - 9} - \frac{3}{x + 3}\right) = (x - 3)(x + 3)\left(\frac{-x}{3 - x}\right)$$

$$x^2 + 9 - 3(x - 3) = x(x + 3)$$

$$x^2 + 9 - 3x + 9 = x^2 + 3x$$

$$18 = 6x$$

$$x = 3$$

But since 3 is a restricted value, the solution set is empty.

34. (K) $\dfrac{2.4(10^{-4})}{6(10^{-2})} = 0.4(10^{-4-(-2)})$

$$= 0.4(10^{-2}) = [4(10^{-1})](10^{-2})$$

$$= 4(10^{-3})$$

35. (E) Substitute the given coordinates into the slope formula.

$$m = \frac{y_2 - y_1}{x_2 - x_1} = \frac{-3 - 8}{-5 - (-5)} = \frac{-11}{0}$$

which does not exist.

36. (K) During January the Smiths use 0.2(100) = 20 gallons and have 80 gallons left to begin February. In February they use 0.25(80) = 20 gallons, so they have 80 − 20 = 60 gallons left on March 1.

37. (C) Here is one possible approach:

Since $\overline{AE} \perp l$, it is perpendicular to each of the parallel lines. Then $\triangle ACF$ is a right triangle, and, by the Pythagorean theorem, $CF = 8$. Then $\triangle ACF$ is similar to $\triangle ADG$, giving the following proportion:

$$\frac{10}{8} = \frac{24}{DG}$$
$$10DG = 192$$
$$DG = 19.2$$

38. (K) All of these statements are false.

39. (A) Angles CBA and CDB are the supplements of the given angles. Their measures are 40° and 120°. Since the sum of the three angles of a triangle is 180°,

$$m \angle C = 180 - (40 + 120)$$
$$= 180 - 160 = 20°$$

40. (G) Imagine three containers in which the mixtures could be made.

$$\underset{4\%}{\boxed{12 - x}} + \underset{100\%}{\boxed{x}} = \underset{20\%}{\boxed{12}}$$

The equation reflects the fact that the amount of antifreeze does not change as a result of mixing the 4% and 100% solutions.

$$0.04(12 - x) + 1.00(x) = 0.2(12)$$
$$4(12 - x) + 100x = 20(12)$$
$$48 - 4x + 100x = 240$$
$$96x = 192$$
$$x = 2$$

41. (D) The length of side BC is $\sqrt{5^2 - 2^2} = \sqrt{21}$.

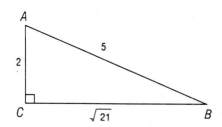

In a right triangle the sine function is

$$\frac{\text{length of opposite side}}{\text{length of hypotenuse}} = \frac{\sqrt{21}}{5}$$

42. (G) This is a parabola that opens upward and its vertex is $(1, 2)$. Therefore the equation in standard form is

$$y = a(x - 1)^2 + 2$$

Substitute the coordinates $(0, 5)$ into the equation to solve for a.

$$5 = a(0 - 1)^2 + 2$$
$$5 = a + 2$$
$$a = 3$$

The equation is $y = 3(x - 1)^2 + 2$.

43. (C) Multiply the numerator and denominator by the complex conjugate of the denominator.

$$\frac{(3 - 2i)(2 - i)}{(2 + i)(2 - i)} = \frac{6 - 3i - 4i + 2i^2}{4 - i^2}$$

$$= \frac{6 - 7i + 2(-1)}{4 - (-1)} \qquad (i^2 = -1)$$

$$= \frac{4 - 7i}{5}$$

$$= \frac{4}{5} - \frac{7}{5}i$$

44. (K) This is a problem of permutations because order is important.

$$_nP_r = \frac{n!}{(n-r)!}$$

$$_6P_6 = \frac{6!}{(6-6)!} = \frac{6!}{0!} = \frac{720}{1} = 720$$

45. (D) Let $x = \log_2 \frac{1}{8}$. Change the equation to its corresponding exponential form.

$$2^x = \frac{1}{8} = \frac{1}{2^3} = 2^{-3}$$

Therefore $x = -3$.

46. (G) The ratio of the corresponding linear measures of polygons is the ratio of the square roots of the areas. The ratio of the lengths of the corresponding altitudes is $\frac{\sqrt{9}}{\sqrt{16}} = \frac{3}{4}$.

47. (D) Coterminal angles are found by adding or subtracting multiples of 360° or 2π radians.

$$\frac{75\pi}{4} - \frac{9(8\pi)}{4} = \frac{75\pi}{4} - \frac{72\pi}{4}$$

$$= \frac{3\pi}{4}$$

48. (G) $CD = 6 - \left(1\frac{2}{3} + 1\frac{1}{4} + 1\frac{1}{12}\right)$

$$= 6 - 4 = 2$$

49. (D) The vertex of the graph of the equation would locate the time (t) and height (h) of the maximum height. Complete the square to put the equation in standard form.

$$h = -16(t^2 - 4t)$$
$$= -16(t^2 - 4t + 4) + 64$$
$$= -16(t - 2)^2 + 64$$

The vertex is at $(2, 64)$.

50. (F) $\sqrt{54x^4y^5} \cdot \sqrt{2x^2y^4} = \sqrt{108x^6y^9}$
$$= \sqrt{(36x^6y^8)(3y)}$$
$$= \sqrt{36x^6y^8} \cdot \sqrt{3y}$$
$$= 6x^3y^4 \sqrt{3y}$$

51. (C) Opposite sides of a parallelogram are both parallel and congruent.

52. (K) Let x be a side of the square. The perimeter of the square is $4x$, and the perimeter of the semicircular region is $2r + \pi r$.
$$4x = 16 + 8\pi$$
$$x = 4 + 2\pi$$

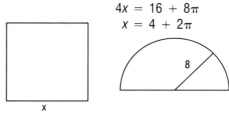

53. (D) Angles ACB and DCE are vertical angles.

54. (H) Triangles ABD and CBE are similar, and the corresponding sides have the same ratio.
$$\frac{4}{9} = \frac{x}{5}$$
$$9x = 20$$
$$x = \frac{20}{9} = 2\frac{2}{9}$$

55. (A) Since the sine is $\dfrac{\text{length of opposite side}}{\text{length of hypotenuse}}$, $\sin 25° = \dfrac{h}{50}$.

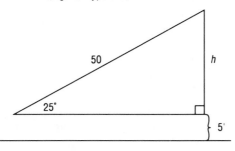

Then $h = 50 \sin 25°$. But the end of the string is 5 feet above the ground, so the total height is $5 + 50 \sin 25°$.

56. (H) Let $AE = x$; then $BE = 8 - x$. The product of the lengths of the segments of one chord equals the product of the lengths of the segments of the other.

$$x(8 - x) = 2 \cdot 8$$
$$8x - x^2 = 16$$
$$x^2 - 8x + 16 = 0$$
$$(x - 4)^2 = 0$$
$$x - 4 = 0$$
$$x = 4$$

57. (D) The maximum number of common tangents is 4.

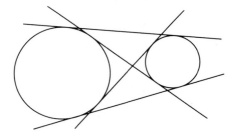

58. (K) All these statements are true.

59. (D) Equal chords intercept equal arcs in a circle. Therefore

$$\text{arc } BC = \tfrac{1}{2}(360 - 2 \cdot 24)° = \tfrac{1}{2}(312)° = 156°$$

Then

$$\angle BDC = \tfrac{1}{2}(156)° = 78°$$

60. (J) The period of the sine function

$$y = a \sin b(x - c) \text{ is } \frac{2\pi}{|b|} .$$

The given function can be written in the form

$$y = -3 \sin 4\left(x + \tfrac{\pi}{4}\right)$$

so the period is $\frac{2\pi}{4} = \frac{\pi}{2}$.

Answer Explanations   Test 3: Reading

1. (A)   Souvarine's actions portray his personality. He smokes one cigarette after another, his hand pokes the air nervously, and he "endlessly" strokes Poland, the rabbit. No evidence in the paragraph suggests that B, C, or D is correct.

2. (J)   Lines 22–23 indicate that both men are Rasseneur's tenants. Since Etienne is a miner and Souvarine an engineman, the other answers are incorrect.

3. (A)   Souvarine deems the international labor movement "just foolishness" (line 55). B and C are incorrect because Souvarine opposes the gradual change that the movement espouses. Souvarine's outburst against Karl Marx (lines 55–62) eliminates D as a correct choice.

4. (F)   Nothing in the passage alludes to a national labor movement. Pluchart's letters, however, are meant to get information about Montsou, inform Etienne about the movement, and breed discontent among the miners.

5. (B)   Line 38 says that Etienne has a "natural predisposition to rebelliousness." Choice A is not appropriate for Etienne; Souvarine's comments about Marx go right over his head. C is not a reasonable choice because the Workers' International's pursuit of justice is a new concept to him, and since he's not at all interested in personal power, D is not a good answer.

6. (H)   According to lines 63–65, Etienne thinks that Souvarine is just posing as a radical. With regard to choice F, nothing in the passage suggests that Etienne wants to annoy his friend. Nor (choice G) is Souvarine at all funny. While Etienne may not entirely understand Souvarine, he is not afraid of him either (choice J).

7. (D)   Rasseneur raises the issue of paying dues to support the strike in lines 79–82. In the passage, he never alludes to any of the issues raised by choices A, B, and C.

8. (F)   According to lines 72–74 and 83–85, Etienne believes that workers will be given both moral and economic support if they strike. Choices G and J occur to Etienne, but they are not his main reason for advocating a strike. H may be a consequence of a strike, but it is not mentioned in the passage.

9. (B)   Rasseneur is "practical-minded" and "well-established," someone interested in "precise information"—traits that suggest he would have more than a passing interest in the consequences of a strike at the mine. Nothing in the passage suggests that A, C, or D is correct.

10. (F)   Souvarine (lines 60–62) advocates violent revolution, Etienne prefers evolutionary change, and Rasseneur seems concerned about protecting the status quo.

11. (B)   The first paragraph of the passage describes Gaudi's revolutionary architectural forms. More specifically, his forms included "all types of animals and plants" (lines 18–19).

12. (J)   "Architecture was regarded as sculpture," according to lines 44–45. Some of the natural shapes that Gaudi used are suggested by lines 65–68.

13. (C)   Line 62 indicates that Gaudi was an artist of the art nouveau period.

14. (F)   Gaudi used animals and plants (lines 18–19), as well as "plantlike ornamentation" (line 49) in his designs for buildings.

15. (A)   Gaudi designed "palaces and villas" (line 38), "housing projects" (line 21), and "a church" (line 40). Libraries are not mentioned in the passage.

16. (J)   A characteristic of Gothic architecture is its use of "mystical and spiritualized forms" (line 31). Spanish architecture combines the pure Gothic and Moorish styles.

17. (C)   The passage says that Catalonia's political climate as well as its prosperous middle class contributed to Gaudi's growth as an architect. The fact that as a Catholic he was "steeped in mystical ideas" (lines 16–17) also influenced Gaudi.

18. (H)   Although architects cannot ignore the prevailing weather conditions at the site of their buildings, nothing in the passage suggests that climate influenced Gaudi's work.

19. (B)   Lines 23–24 refer to the Moorish influence on the architecture in Europe and Africa.

20. (G)   Spanish Gothic architecture draws its mysticism and spiritualism from the pure Gothic style (lines 30–31).

21. (D)   Lines 18–21 state that the food supply decreases as the water level deepens. Hence, the top layers contain the most food.

22. (F) Scientists used to believe that silence reigned in the deepest ocean waters. That theory no longer holds true, according to the second paragraph.

23. (A) Lines 1–2 state that many of the animals have gradually become blind because they exist in a world of complete darkness.

24. (G) Several uses of hydrophones are described in lines 30–41. Searching for unknown species is not mentioned.

25. (D) Lines 8–17 explain that plants cannot grow in the undersea darkness and that dead and dying plants are eaten before they reach the bottom layers of ocean.

26. (H) In the battle for food described in lines 21–26, the weaker fish often lose. Therefore, they must wait for long periods of time to eat.

27. (A) Only this answer is supported by the passage. Oceanographers seem to be making new discoveries all the time.

28. (F) Repletion means the state of being full or being gorged with food or drink.

29. (C) The ferocity of the creatures is being emphasized. The other choices may merely call to mind the extinct saber-toothed tiger.

30. (G) While each of the choices may be valid, most of the passage is devoted to a description of life far below the surface of the sea.

31. (B) Line 2 of the passage lists the people for whom principles for alleviating repression were created. Among those listed are women and slaves.

32. (F) According to the passage (lines 35–37), over time the laws imposed on parents gradually grew more severe.

33. (C) John Locke believed that children, unlike the fully-grown Adam, lacked the capacity to know "the dictates of law and reason" (line 14).

34. (H) Laws regarding children vary because there is no distinct line on which everyone can agree between the end of childhood and beginning of adulthood (lines 21–22).

35. (D) A fundamental assumption in western society is that the family is "the basic social, economic, and political unit" (lines 63–64).

36. (F) As described in the passage, the laws pertaining to chil-

dren have changed gradually rrom the early days until the present time.

37. (D) The passage says that children are not expected to assume the economic roles of adults. They are also required to stay in school for a longer period of time than before. Meanwhile, laws have given parents more responsibility to attend to their children's well-being. Changes in children's maturation are not mentioned in the passage.

38. (H) Based on modern laws, parents are held increasingly liable for personal torts (injuries or wrongs) done by their children to others.

39. (B) Based on the last paragraph of the passage, courts have the power to interfere in families when parents neglect their children.

40. (G) John Locke meant that, although a child may be born into a society that enjoys equality, the child is unable to assume equality until later in life.

Answer Explanations   Test 4: Science Reasoning

1. (C) This is simply a matter of reading the question carefully. Obtain the total carbon monoxide for the year by adding figures in the last column. To get the monthly average, divide by 12.

2. (J) The amount of sulfur and nitrogen oxides produced by electric power plants is far greater than that produced by all other sources combined. This is surely the best place to attack the problem.

3. (B) Because fires produce no oxides of sulfur, and very little of nitrogen, controlling forest fires would not do anything to reduce the amount of acid rain.

4. (J) While all four of the choices would help to reduce the amount of pollution in the air, and G and H would also produce useful byproducts, the question specifically asks for a method of improving fuel economy. Only burning of carbon monoxide as fuel meets this criterion.

5. (A)   Because electric power plants produce more pollutants than anything else, conversion of industries to electricity would not do any good. Improving insulation, B, would reduce the need to burn fuel in buildings; afterburners, C, would keep organic pollutants out of the air; light-rail transport, D, would cut down on the number of automobiles.

6. (J)   Experiment 2 shows that 40 cm/s is faster than the minimum velocity at which particles finer than pebbles will be carried with the current instead of dropping to the bottom.

7. (A)   Experiment 1 shows that a stream must flow at 60 cm/s to lift even the fine sand off the bottom.

8. (H)   Experiment 2 shows that coarse sand will not sink to the bottom until the speed of the stream is below 30 cm/s.

9. (C)   Experiment 1 shows that at a speed of 130 cm/s the stream will not pick up clay, silt, pebbles, or cobbles, but only fine and coarse sands. Experiment 2 shows that at 25 cm/s coarse sand will drop to the bottom but fine sand will not.

10. (F)   This would account for the fact that the very finest particles are not lifted off the bottom until the speed of the river is quite high. G is wrong because the table shows that clay particles are smaller than sand grains. There is no reason to think that H is true. J is wrong because all the evidence shows that it is the size of the particles that is the pertinent factor.

11. (A)   It is not possible for a river to be flowing too slowly to carry particles along, yet fast enough to lift them off the bottom. B and C are wrong because the experiments do not place limits on the behavior of other kinds of materials. D is wrong because there is nothing in the experiments to indicate how far the particles are carried.

12. (G)   The graph of rain intensity shows a sharp peak at 3:30 P.M.

13. (A)   The wind was strongest at 3:30 P.M. and the graph for pressure shows a sudden increase at that time (remember to read the graph from right to left). After 3:30, the pressure dropped gradually for the next hour. B is wrong because the time scale reads from right to left, as though the storm were moving from left to right past the observation point.

14. (J) At 3:30 P.M., when the pressure suddenly increased, the temperature suddenly dropped. This is an inverse relationship.

15. (A) The time involved was from about 3:25 to 3:35 P.M., and the rain and wind were at their worst at about 3:32, just in the middle of this period. B is wrong because the rain and wind did not build up gradually, but hit suddenly.

16. (J) The rain lasted nearly half an hour, and during that time, it averaged about 2 inches per hour. In half an hour, 1 inch fell.

17. (C) The concentration of 200 g of glucose in 500 mL of water is the same as 400 g/L; the table for Experiment 1 shows that at this concentration the boiling point is 101.2° C.

18. (G) Experiment 2 makes it clear that the boiling point elevation, at constant concentration, depends on the molecular weight of the solute. The new substance is made into a solution with the same concentration as the solutions in Experiment 2. The molecular weight of the new substance is about halfway between that of acetaldehyde and that of glycerol, so the boiling point would also be about halfway.

19. (D) Note that it is the *elevation* of the boiling point that is in question, not the actual boiling point. Naphthalene and glucose have very nearly the same molecular weight. Glucose raised the boiling point of water only 0.9° C from 100.0° C to 100.9° C, while naphthalene, at the same concentration, raised the boiling point of benzene 4.7° C, from 80.1° C to 84.8° C.

20. (G) This shows most clearly in Experiment 1, where each additional 100 g of glucose in the solution produces a rise of 0.3° C in the boiling point. F is wrong because the boiling point elevation is smaller, not larger, for larger molecules. H is wrong because the boiling point of benzene is lower than that of water, but benzene shows larger elevations. J is wrong because the data do not indicate any such direct proportionality.

21. (D) With its smaller molecular weight, a given mass of butyric acid has many more molecules than an equal mass of cholesterol. A is wrong because cholesterol does, in fact, raise the boiling point, although to a lesser degree than a substance with smaller molecules will. B is wrong because the experimental design specifies that 300 g was used in both cases. C is wrong because there is no reason to believe there was any chemical reaction; in fact, it is contraindicated because cholesterol follows the pattern of the relationship between molecular weight and boiling point elevation.

22. (H) Because there is a clear relationship between molecular weight and boiling point elevation, measuring this elevation would make it possible to calculate the molecular weight.

23. (C) The design predicted that the total energy use would drop to about 120 units, but it actually went to 95. It was the new design that made the new building more energy-efficient.

24. (F) The bar representing vertical transport (elevators) appears in the chart for new building, but not for the old one. Nothing in the chart says what kind of heating or what kind of energy control was used. Both buildings were cooled.

25. (B) The cost of lighting is nearly half as much in the actual building as in the design, while the costs of heating and cooling are about as planned.

26. (G) Savings in this area are already spectacular, but heating is still the greatest part of the energy budget; further research might produce even more savings.

27. (D) If the construction of the new design is very expensive, the builder might decide that it is cheaper, in the long run, to make a less efficient building. Air conditioning, A, is now a necessity, and the cost of hot water, B, is too small to make much difference. The new building clearly exceeds expectations from the design, C.

28. (G) This is a test of the time it takes for the eyes of the guppies to become light-adapted; using their ability to find food as a test assumes that they use their eyes to find it. F is wrong because no tests of rate of activity were made.

H is wrong because the basic experiment (Experiment 2) did not vary temperature. J is wrong because no comparison with people is made.

29. (A) The only way to know when the guppies are fully light-adapted is to find out how well they locate their food when their eyes are known to be light-adapted.

30. (H) This is the basic experiment; when the guppies can find more than 32 *Daphnia* in 5 minutes, their eyes are light-adapted.

31. (B) In the dark, all other senses function, but the guppies had to wait for their eyes to become light-adapted in order to find food. A is wrong because Experiment 3 shows only that low temperatures interfere somehow. C is wrong because all the senses of the guppies are functioning in daylight, and there is no evidence to indicate which one is used in finding food. D is wrong because, although the statement is true, it would probably hold no matter how the guppies find their food.

32. (H) Experiment 2 established a baseline from which temperature variations could be made. F is wrong because the pertinent question is light adaptation. G is wrong because the adaptation of the *Daphnia* is not dealt with anywhere. J is wrong because the tanks were kept steadily at the prescribed temperatures.

33. (D) The rate of adaptation increased up to a temperature of 24° C, but not above that level. Any of the other choices would be a plausible explanation of the results.

34. (G) Scientist 2 provides the explanation in terms of natural selection; Scientist 1 does not agree. F and J are wrong because both scientists incorporate these concepts into their theories. H is wrong because Scientist 1 has not committed himself on this issue.

35. (A) If wings are used for temperature control, it is conceivable that this was the original function of the protowings. B is wrong because a competent explanation is not experimental evidence. C and D are wrong because these points are not in contention.

36. (J) Scientist 2 uses this principle as her main argument, and Scientist 1 has not mentioned it at all. F and G are wrong because both scientists agree on these points. H is wrong because this is not a principle that Scientist 1 would accept.

37. (D)   This would confirm the priority of temperature control as a function of winglike projections. All of the other choices do not discriminate between the two theories.

38. (G)   Science advances by finding evidence that can be used to settle controversial questions. F is wrong because there is always room for difference of opinion, even in regard to long-established principles. H is wrong because Scientist 1 does not dispute the importance of natural selection; he claims only that it is an incomplete explanation. J is wrong because Scientist 2 has given a satisfactory answer, with evidence to back it up.

39. (B)   A and C are wrong, because the two scientists agree that wings evolved gradually from projections out of the thorax. D is wrong because neither theory precludes other kinds of insects.

40. (G)   The experiments must have been designed to test the effectiveness of various body and wing conformations in serving as temperature regulators and also as airfoils. F and J are wrong because the concept of evolution by natural selection is not in question. H is wrong because it is not the *concept* of preadaptation that is being tested, but its *mechanism.*

ANSWER SHEET—Model Test B

Directions: Mark one answer only for each question. Make mark dark. Erase completely any mark made in error. (Additional or stray marks will be counted as mistakes.)

Test 1: English

1 Ⓐ Ⓑ Ⓒ Ⓓ	**20** Ⓕ Ⓖ Ⓗ Ⓙ	**39** Ⓐ Ⓑ Ⓒ Ⓓ	**58** Ⓕ Ⓖ Ⓗ Ⓙ
2 Ⓕ Ⓖ Ⓗ Ⓙ	**21** Ⓐ Ⓑ Ⓒ Ⓓ	**40** Ⓕ Ⓖ Ⓗ Ⓙ	**59** Ⓐ Ⓑ Ⓒ Ⓓ
3 Ⓐ Ⓑ Ⓒ Ⓓ	**22** Ⓕ Ⓖ Ⓗ Ⓙ	**41** Ⓐ Ⓑ Ⓒ Ⓓ	**60** Ⓕ Ⓖ Ⓗ Ⓙ
4 Ⓕ Ⓖ Ⓗ Ⓙ	**23** Ⓐ Ⓑ Ⓒ Ⓓ	**42** Ⓕ Ⓖ Ⓗ Ⓙ	**61** Ⓐ Ⓑ Ⓒ Ⓓ
5 Ⓐ Ⓑ Ⓒ Ⓓ	**24** Ⓕ Ⓖ Ⓗ Ⓙ	**43** Ⓐ Ⓑ Ⓒ Ⓓ	**62** Ⓕ Ⓖ Ⓗ Ⓙ
6 Ⓕ Ⓖ Ⓗ Ⓙ	**25** Ⓐ Ⓑ Ⓒ Ⓓ	**44** Ⓕ Ⓖ Ⓗ Ⓙ	**63** Ⓐ Ⓑ Ⓒ Ⓓ
7 Ⓐ Ⓑ Ⓒ Ⓓ	**26** Ⓕ Ⓖ Ⓗ Ⓙ	**45** Ⓐ Ⓑ Ⓒ Ⓓ	**64** Ⓕ Ⓖ Ⓗ Ⓙ
8 Ⓕ Ⓖ Ⓗ Ⓙ	**27** Ⓐ Ⓑ Ⓒ Ⓓ	**46** Ⓕ Ⓖ Ⓗ Ⓙ	**65** Ⓐ Ⓑ Ⓒ Ⓓ
9 Ⓐ Ⓑ Ⓒ Ⓓ	**28** Ⓕ Ⓖ Ⓗ Ⓙ	**47** Ⓐ Ⓑ Ⓒ Ⓓ	**66** Ⓕ Ⓖ Ⓗ Ⓙ
10 Ⓕ Ⓖ Ⓗ Ⓙ	**29** Ⓐ Ⓑ Ⓒ Ⓓ	**48** Ⓕ Ⓖ Ⓗ Ⓙ	**67** Ⓐ Ⓑ Ⓒ Ⓓ
11 Ⓐ Ⓑ Ⓒ Ⓓ	**30** Ⓕ Ⓖ Ⓗ Ⓙ	**49** Ⓐ Ⓑ Ⓒ Ⓓ	**68** Ⓕ Ⓖ Ⓗ Ⓙ
12 Ⓕ Ⓖ Ⓗ Ⓙ	**31** Ⓐ Ⓑ Ⓒ Ⓓ	**50** Ⓕ Ⓖ Ⓗ Ⓙ	**69** Ⓐ Ⓑ Ⓒ Ⓓ
13 Ⓐ Ⓑ Ⓒ Ⓓ	**32** Ⓕ Ⓖ Ⓗ Ⓙ	**51** Ⓐ Ⓑ Ⓒ Ⓓ	**70** Ⓕ Ⓖ Ⓗ Ⓙ
14 Ⓕ Ⓖ Ⓗ Ⓙ	**33** Ⓐ Ⓑ Ⓒ Ⓓ	**52** Ⓕ Ⓖ Ⓗ Ⓙ	**71** Ⓐ Ⓑ Ⓒ Ⓓ
15 Ⓐ Ⓑ Ⓒ Ⓓ	**34** Ⓕ Ⓖ Ⓗ Ⓙ	**53** Ⓐ Ⓑ Ⓒ Ⓓ	**72** Ⓕ Ⓖ Ⓗ Ⓙ
16 Ⓕ Ⓖ Ⓗ Ⓙ	**35** Ⓐ Ⓑ Ⓒ Ⓓ	**54** Ⓕ Ⓖ Ⓗ Ⓙ	**73** Ⓐ Ⓑ Ⓒ Ⓓ
17 Ⓐ Ⓑ Ⓒ Ⓓ	**36** Ⓕ Ⓖ Ⓗ Ⓙ	**55** Ⓐ Ⓑ Ⓒ Ⓓ	**74** Ⓕ Ⓖ Ⓗ Ⓙ
18 Ⓕ Ⓖ Ⓗ Ⓙ	**37** Ⓐ Ⓑ Ⓒ Ⓓ	**56** Ⓕ Ⓖ Ⓗ Ⓙ	**75** Ⓐ Ⓑ Ⓒ Ⓓ
19 Ⓐ Ⓑ Ⓒ Ⓓ	**38** Ⓕ Ⓖ Ⓗ Ⓙ	**57** Ⓐ Ⓑ Ⓒ Ⓓ	

Test 2: Mathematics

1 ⒶⒷⒸⒹⒺ	16 ⒻⒼⒽⒿⓀ	31 ⒶⒷⒸⒹⒺ	46 ⒻⒼⒽⒿⓀ
2 ⒻⒼⒽⒿⓀ	17 ⒶⒷⒸⒹⒺ	32 ⒻⒼⒽⒿⓀ	47 ⒶⒷⒸⒹⒺ
3 ⒶⒷⒸⒹⒺ	18 ⒻⒼⒽⒿⓀ	33 ⒶⒷⒸⒹⒺ	48 ⒻⒼⒽⒿⓀ
4 ⒻⒼⒽⒿⓀ	19 ⒶⒷⒸⒹⒺ	34 ⒻⒼⒽⒿⓀ	49 ⒶⒷⒸⒹⒺ
5 ⒶⒷⒸⒹⒺ	20 ⒻⒼⒽⒿⓀ	35 ⒶⒷⒸⒹⒺ	50 ⒻⒼⒽⒿⓀ
6 ⒻⒼⒽⒿⓀ	21 ⒶⒷⒸⒹⒺ	36 ⒻⒼⒽⒿⓀ	51 ⒶⒷⒸⒹⒺ
7 ⒶⒷⒸⒹⒺ	22 ⒻⒼⒽⒿⓀ	37 ⒶⒷⒸⒹⒺ	52 ⒻⒼⒽⒿⓀ
8 ⒻⒼⒽⒿⓀ	23 ⒶⒷⒸⒹⒺ	38 ⒻⒼⒽⒿⓀ	53 ⒶⒷⒸⒹⒺ
9 ⒶⒷⒸⒹⒺ	24 ⒻⒼⒽⒿⓀ	39 ⒶⒷⒸⒹⒺ	54 ⒻⒼⒽⒿⓀ
10 ⒻⒼⒽⒿⓀ	25 ⒶⒷⒸⒹⒺ	40 ⒻⒼⒽⒿⓀ	55 ⒶⒷⒸⒹⒺ
11 ⒶⒷⒸⒹⒺ	26 ⒻⒼⒽⒿⓀ	41 ⒶⒷⒸⒹⒺ	56 ⒻⒼⒽⒿⓀ
12 ⒻⒼⒽⒿⓀ	27 ⒶⒷⒸⒹⒺ	42 ⒻⒼⒽⒿⓀ	57 ⒶⒷⒸⒹⒺ
13 ⒶⒷⒸⒹⒺ	28 ⒻⒼⒽⒿⓀ	43 ⒶⒷⒸⒹⒺ	58 ⒻⒼⒽⒿⓀ
14 ⒻⒼⒽⒿⓀ	29 ⒶⒷⒸⒹⒺ	44 ⒻⒼⒽⒿⓀ	59 ⒶⒷⒸⒹⒺ
15 ⒶⒷⒸⒹⒺ	30 ⒻⒼⒽⒿⓀ	45 ⒶⒷⒸⒹⒺ	60 ⒻⒼⒽⒿⓀ

Test 3: Reading

1 ⒶⒷⒸⒹ	11 ⒶⒷⒸⒹ	21 ⒶⒷⒸⒹ	31 ⒶⒷⒸⒹ
2 ⒻⒼⒽⒿ	12 ⒻⒼⒽⒿ	22 ⒻⒼⒽⒿ	32 ⒻⒼⒽⒿ
3 ⒶⒷⒸⒹ	13 ⒶⒷⒸⒹ	23 ⒶⒷⒸⒹ	33 ⒶⒷⒸⒹ
4 ⒻⒼⒽⒿ	14 ⒻⒼⒽⒿ	24 ⒻⒼⒽⒿ	34 ⒻⒼⒽⒿ
5 ⒶⒷⒸⒹ	15 ⒶⒷⒸⒹ	25 ⒶⒷⒸⒹ	35 ⒶⒷⒸⒹ
6 ⒻⒼⒽⒿ	16 ⒻⒼⒽⒿ	26 ⒻⒼⒽⒿ	36 ⒻⒼⒽⒿ
7 ⒶⒷⒸⒹ	17 ⒶⒷⒸⒹ	27 ⒶⒷⒸⒹ	37 ⒶⒷⒸⒹ
8 ⒻⒼⒽⒿ	18 ⒻⒼⒽⒿ	28 ⒻⒼⒽⒿ	38 ⒻⒼⒽⒿ
9 ⒶⒷⒸⒹ	19 ⒶⒷⒸⒹ	29 ⒶⒷⒸⒹ	39 ⒶⒷⒸⒹ
10 ⒻⒼⒽⒿ	20 ⒻⒼⒽⒿ	30 ⒻⒼⒽⒿ	40 ⒻⒼⒽⒿ

Test 4: Science Reasoning

1 Ⓐ Ⓑ Ⓒ Ⓓ	11 Ⓐ Ⓑ Ⓒ Ⓓ	21 Ⓐ Ⓑ Ⓒ Ⓓ	31 Ⓐ Ⓑ Ⓒ Ⓓ
2 Ⓕ Ⓖ Ⓗ Ⓙ	12 Ⓕ Ⓖ Ⓗ Ⓙ	22 Ⓕ Ⓖ Ⓗ Ⓙ	32 Ⓕ Ⓖ Ⓗ Ⓙ
3 Ⓐ Ⓑ Ⓒ Ⓓ	13 Ⓐ Ⓑ Ⓒ Ⓓ	23 Ⓐ Ⓑ Ⓒ Ⓓ	33 Ⓐ Ⓑ Ⓒ Ⓓ
4 Ⓕ Ⓖ Ⓗ Ⓙ	14 Ⓕ Ⓖ Ⓗ Ⓙ	24 Ⓕ Ⓖ Ⓗ Ⓙ	34 Ⓕ Ⓖ Ⓗ Ⓙ
5 Ⓐ Ⓑ Ⓒ Ⓓ	15 Ⓐ Ⓑ Ⓒ Ⓓ	25 Ⓐ Ⓑ Ⓒ Ⓓ	35 Ⓐ Ⓑ Ⓒ Ⓓ
6 Ⓕ Ⓖ Ⓗ Ⓙ	16 Ⓕ Ⓖ Ⓗ Ⓙ	26 Ⓕ Ⓖ Ⓗ Ⓙ	36 Ⓕ Ⓖ Ⓗ Ⓙ
7 Ⓐ Ⓑ Ⓒ Ⓓ	17 Ⓐ Ⓑ Ⓒ Ⓓ	27 Ⓐ Ⓑ Ⓒ Ⓓ	37 Ⓐ Ⓑ Ⓒ Ⓓ
8 Ⓕ Ⓖ Ⓗ Ⓙ	18 Ⓕ Ⓖ Ⓗ Ⓙ	28 Ⓕ Ⓖ Ⓗ Ⓙ	38 Ⓕ Ⓖ Ⓗ Ⓙ
9 Ⓐ Ⓑ Ⓒ Ⓓ	19 Ⓐ Ⓑ Ⓒ Ⓓ	29 Ⓐ Ⓑ Ⓒ Ⓓ	39 Ⓐ Ⓑ Ⓒ Ⓓ
10 Ⓕ Ⓖ Ⓗ Ⓙ	20 Ⓕ Ⓖ Ⓗ Ⓙ	30 Ⓕ Ⓖ Ⓗ Ⓙ	40 Ⓕ Ⓖ Ⓗ Ⓙ

Test 1: English   45 Minutes—75 Questions

Directions: **The following test consists of 75 underlined words and phrases in context, or general questions about the passages. Most of the underlined sections contain errors and inappropriate expressions. You are asked to compare each with the four alternatives in the answer column. If you consider the original version best, choose letter A or F: NO CHANGE. For each question, blacken on the answer sheet the letter of the alternative you think best. Read each passage through before answering the questions based on it.**

Passage 1

(1)

Abraham Lincoln has been quoted as advising a new lawyer, "Young man, it's more important to know what cases not to take than it is to know the law." New attorneys soon learn to recognize what cases will probably be unprofitable, or they quickly end up looking for new jobs <u>in the newspaper because of lack</u>
        1

<u>of funds.</u> 2
   1

1. A. NO CHANGE
   B. because of lack of funds.
   C. in the newspaper.
   D. OMIT the underlined portion.

2. Is the quotation from Abraham Lincoln an appropriate way to begin this passage?
   F. Yes, because quotations are always better than straight prose as attention-getters.
   G. No, because it misleads the reader, suggesting that Lincoln is the topic of the passage.
   H. No, because it is too short a quotation to add any meaning.
   J. Yes, because Abraham Lincoln is an authority figure, often quoted because of the truth and simplicity of his statements.

(2)

During the initial interview with the client, the lawyer discovers whether or not a case is meritorious. Examples of cases without merit include an argument with neighbors over a pesky dog or an

accident that results from the victim's own negligence, such as someone falling in a local supermarket because they were drunk. This questionable
3   4

3. A. NO CHANGE
  B. he or she was drunk.
  C. they had been drinking.
  D. they were considerably under the influence.

and dubious type of case can be easily seen as
4

lacking merit, because each of the elements of a tort (a civil wrongdoing) was not present, and thus no law

4. F. NO CHANGE
  G. OMIT the underlined portion.
  H. questionable
  J. dubious

was broken. We must all try to behave as adults as we
5

wend our way through this troubled interval.
5

5. A. NO CHANGE
  B. We must all try to be mature.
  C. We must all do our best.
  D. OMIT the underlined portion.

(3)

Finally, there is the type of case in which the prospective client has been represented in the matter by another attorney. Accepting such a case can be risky, although multiple lawyers are evidence of a
6

6. F. NO CHANGE
  G. when
  H. because
  J. similarly

worthless case an uncooperative client, or a client
7

7. A. NO CHANGE
  B. case. An
  C. case, an
  D. case: an

who does not pay his or her bill. Even if the reason for the client's changing attorneys is a good one—let's
8   9

say a personality clash between the client and the
9

8. F. NO CHANGE
  G. clients
  H. client
  J. clients'

prior attorney—it makes the new lawyer's task of reaching a fair settlement with the other party strategically difficult.

9. A. NO CHANGE
  B. one, let's say
  C. one (let's say
  D. one let's say

(4)

There are some cases that seem to have merit but are economically unfeasible for a new attorney to handle. Such cases are easy to spot once a full, <u>full,</u> **10** adequate enough disclosure of the facts has been **10** obtained from the client during the initial interview. One type of unprofitable case is the "hurt feelings" case stemming from an incident where the defendant has <u>been guilty of caddish behavior—but what young</u> **11** <u>man in springtime has been able to resist the pull of</u> **11** <u>the heart?—</u> but where the victim cannot prove he or **11** she has been specifically damaged, or where damages are nominal. For instance, in an action for slander, not only is it difficult to prove <u>slander but</u> **12** <u>also</u> the monetary damage to the victim resulting **12** from the slanderous action may be small or even nonexistent. In these kinds of cases, a prospective client may be so righteously angered as to say that he or she does not care about the money, that it is the principle that <u>matters, that may</u> be true for the **13** prospective client, but the attorney cannot pay his secretary's salary, his office rent, or his malpractice insurance <u>premium will not be reduced</u> with a client's **14** "principle." 15

10. F. NO CHANGE
  G. full, adequate disclosure
  H. full, adequate, complete disclosure
  J. full disclosure

11. A. NO CHANGE
  B. been guilty of caddish behavior—but sometimes that happens to young people—
  C. been guilty of wrongful behavior,
  D. OMIT the underlined portion.

12. F. NO CHANGE
  G. slander, but also
  H. slander. But also
  J. slander; but also

13. A. NO CHANGE
  B. matters that
  C. matters. That
  D. matters: that

14. F. NO CHANGE
  G. premium reduction
  H. premium reduced
  J. premium

15. Choose the sequence of paragraph numbers that makes the structure of the passage most logical.
  A. NO CHANGE
  B. 1, 4, 2, 3
  C. 1, 3, 2, 4
  D. 1, 2, 4, 3

Passage 2

(1)

Of all the many differences between people, there is one that goes more deeper than any other or than
16

all combined, and that is whether the person are
17

parents or not. Variations in cultural background,
17

religion, politics, or education do not come close to

parent versus nonparent differences. **18**

16. F. NO CHANGE
G. deeper
H. deep
J. deepest

17. A. NO CHANGE
B. is a parent or not.
C. is parents or not.
D. are a parent or not.

18. This passage was probably written for readers who:
F. are experts in child development.
G. are expecting a child.
H. are general readers.
J. are childless.

(2)

Conversely, few if any knickknacks remain whole in a home with small children, the only plants left are
19

those hanging, brown and wilted, from a very high

ceiling. Instead, toys strewn carelessly about the
20

various living areas. The somewhat disheveled
21

rooms usually look slightly askew, since little ones
21

delight in moving furniture around and are especially

19. A. NO CHANGE
B. children the only
C. children: the only
D. children. The

20. F. NO CHANGE
G. toys strew
H. toys were strewn
J. toys are strewn

21. A. NO CHANGE
B. disheveled rooms
C. rooms
D. somewhat, disheveled rooms

prone to do so <u>unless</u> a guest or two <u>are expected</u>.
22   23

Walls are usually smudged with the prints of tiny hands and feet (yes, feet—don't ask me how) and decorated with children's artwork, which also adorns the refrigerator, kitchen cabinets, message center, and any other available blank space. To a parent, there is no such thing as a sparkling clean mirror or window. <u>A handy way to clean windows and mirrors</u>
24

<u>is by using crushed newsprint.</u> Children simply can-
24

not keep from touching—with their hands, noses, mouths, whatever—clean mirrors and windows. It has something to do with marking one's territory, I believe. **25**

22. F. NO CHANGE
    G. after
    H. as
    J. when

23. A. NO CHANGE
    B. are expecting.
    C. is expected.
    D. will be
         expected.

24. F. NO CHANGE
    G. OMIT the
         underlined
         portion.
    H. Clean windows
         with newsprint.
    J. A handy way to
         clean windows is
         with newsprint.

25. Which of the phrases below demonstrate the intent of the writer to be whimsical and humorous?
    A. toys strewn carelessly
    B. marking one's territory
    C. sparkling clean mirror
    D. available blank space

(3)

The very way a house is decorated proclaims the owner's status. My childless friends have plants, expensive accessories, and elegant knickknacks placed strategically about their <u>finely-furnished</u>
26

homes. Framed prints hang on their spotlessly white walls, while their mirrors and windows sparkle. **27**

26. F. NO CHANGE
    G. finely furnished
    H. finely,
         furnished
    J. furnished

27. Examination of paragraphs 2 and 3 reveals that the author of this passage wants to emphasize:
    A. fine art in American homes.
    B. styles and decor in contemporary homes.
    C. the impact of children on a home.
    D. indoor plant styles in contemporary American
         homes.

(4)

Another distinguishing great difference between
28

people without children and people with them is their
attitude toward life. Before my daughter came along
five years ago, I was a competent legal secretary, a
faithful wife, and a person who enjoyed a quiet
lifestyle interspersed with an occasional party or
outing. I was well-adjusted but ill-prepared for cha-
29

otic living, and, I see now, quite naive. 30

28. F. NO CHANGE
G. OMIT this word
H. discriminating
J. differentiating

29. A. NO CHANGE
B. well adjusted
but ill-prepared
C. well adjusted
but ill prepared
D. well-adjusted
but ill prepared

30. Choose the sequence of paragraph numbers that
makes the structure of the passage most logical.
F. NO CHANGE
G. 1, 3, 2, 4
H. 1, 3, 4, 2
J. 1, 4, 2, 3

Passage 3

(1)

The very idea of a community among nations are
31

unique. From the city-states of ancient Greece to the
modern nations of our era, communities have to join
32

forces to defend their individual interests. Economic,
political, and military conditions have imposed their
own imperatives, requiring shifting alliances and
coalitions of expedience. But the contemporary community of nations—a free association based on
shared principles and an increasingly shared way of
life; emerged only with the evolution of the demo-
33

cratic idea. Just as a free people argue the issues and
choose their own government, so do free nations
34

31. A. NO CHANGE
B. had been
C. is
D. were

32. F. NO CHANGE
G. had
H. will have had
J. have had

33. A. NO CHANGE
B. life—emerged
C. life: emerged
D. life, emerged

34. F. NO CHANGE
G. its
H. his or her
J. our

choose their friends and allies. We are joined not just by common interests but also by ideals of freedom and justice that <u>transcends</u> the dictates of neces-
35
sity. 36

35. A. NO CHANGE
B. transcending
C. transcended
D. transcend

36. Is the reference to ancient Greece in the second sentence appropriate in this passage?
F. No, because there is no connection between two eras thousands of years apart.
G. Yes, because ancient Greece is a model for democratic societies.
H. No, because the United States does not have city-states.
J. Yes, because this is one of the earliest historical instances of communities joining forces for the common good.

(2)

Our community and our heritage <u>has</u> enemies.
37

Over the past two centuries, as separate entities or in concert, free peoples have defended themselves against marauders and tyrants, against militarists and imperialists, against Nazis and the Leninist totalitarians of our time. We have seen our heritage <u>shaking</u> to its roots. The graves of Normandy and the
38

death camps of the Third Reich <u>bears</u> permanent
39
witness to the vulnerability of all we cherish.

37. A. NO CHANGE
B. have
C. had
D. will have had

38. F. NO CHANGE
G. shaken
H. shook
J. shaked

39. A. NO CHANGE
B. bear
C. bore
D. borne

(3)

Today, we see other evidence of the determination of our adversaries. We see it in the Berlin Wall, standing <u>mute</u> as a symbol of the fear our civilization
40
and its values evoke in a totalitarian world. The Soviets, of course, have their values as well. They value a regime that imposes an unchallenged order in

40. F. NO CHANGE
G. in a mute way
H. mute and silent
J. mutely

their own sphere and foments instability and division
41

elsewhere. 42

41. A. NO CHANGE
B. its
C. there
D. they're

42. Is the reference to the Berlin Wall meaningful at this place in the passage?
F. No, because it virtually changes the subject.
G. No, because the Berlin Wall is an inanimate object, and the passage is about people.
H. Yes, because the Berlin Wall was created after World War II.
J. Yes, because it is a specific example of the determination mentioned in the first sentence of the paragraph.

(4)

This community has long been a minority of humanity. In our own time, however, we have seen
43

our numbers increase. In recent decades we have
43

43. How do you regard the supporting material that follows this statement?
A. It is ineffective; it does not support the initial statement at all.
B. It is effective because it lists countries that have made human rights a paramount concern.
C. It is ineffective because it does not list numbers or demonstrate with charts.
D. It is effective because it ends with a quotation from Lincoln.

been joined by like-minded nations around the Pacific Basin; by the struggling young democracies of Latin America; and, of course, by Israel, whose very existence is a constant reminder of the sacrifices and struggles that may be required if civilization is to be secured. Together, we stand for something that no other alliance in history has represented; the
44

advancement of the rights of the individual, and the conviction that governments founded on these rights

44. F. NO CHANGE
G. represented, the
H. represented: the
J. represented. The

are, in Lincoln's words, "the last best hope of men on earth." 45

45. Choose the sequence of paragraph numbers that makes the structure of the passage most logical.
A. NO CHANGE
B. 1, 4, 2, 3
C. 1, 3, 2, 4
D. 1, 4, 3, 2

Passage 4

(1)

My Ántonia depicts life on the Nebraska prairie during the early 1900s, mirroring Willa Cather's own experiences as a girl living on the "Great Divide," as that part of Nebraska had been called. The protago-
46

46. F. NO CHANGE
G. was called
H. is called
J. called

nist of the novel, Antonia Shimerda was modeled on
47

47. A. NO CHANGE
B. , Antonia Shimerda,
C. Antonia Shimerda
D. novel Antonia Shimerda,

Annie Sadilek, an actual living Bohemian girl hired by
48

48. F. NO CHANGE
G. actual, living
H. living
J. actual

one of Willa Cather's neighbors in the town of Red Cloud. 49

49. This paragraph serves as a summary of the novel being discussed in this passage. How might it be strengthened?
A. NO CHANGE
B. It should describe the Great Plains setting more fully.
C. It should give us the entire plot of the story, not part of it.
D. It should supply more details regarding the family background of the Shimerdas.

(2)

A close friend of Willa Cather, the author of *My Ántonia*, has written, "Willa forever preferred rural life, although she was never quite so inartistic as to announce that 'the country is preferable to the city'."
50

Certainly, *My Ántonia*, Willa Cather's third prairie novel, is a joyous song of praise for "the virtues of a settled agricultural existence" as opposed to life in the cities. Her belief that the ideal civilization is to be found in the country, albeit a country tempered with
51

such desirable urban qualities as cultural refinement

and order, is developed by the use of multi-level
52

contrasts and comparisons, both obvious and symbolic. **53**   **54**

---

50. F. NO CHANGE
G. city'".
H. city.'"
J. city."

51. A. NO CHANGE
B. nevertheless
C. and
D. yet

52. F. NO CHANGE
G. multi level
H. multilevel
J. many level

---

53. This paragraph begins with a quotation from a close friend of Willa Cather. Is the use of the quotation relevant to the passage?
A. No, it is irrelevant and has no bearing on the passage or paragraph.
B. No, it is misleading, dealing with Willa Cather's life, rather than the substance of the passage.
C. Yes, it is a valuable insight from a reliable source; in addition, it is relevant to the paragraph and passage.
D. Yes, it is a humorous touch that does no harm.

54. This passage was probably written for readers who:
F. are beginning readers in a youngsters' educational program.
G. are mature students of literature who are interested in critical analysis.
H. are middle-westerners who want to learn more about their heritage.
J. are authors themselves.

(3)

A richly creative novel, *My Ántonia* has been analyzed through a number of critical approaches. John H. Randall's criticism dealt with broad thematic

55

questions regarding Cather's arguments for certain values and ideas, such as the urban versus the bucolic life, using the mythic or archetypal school of criticism to explain many of the symbols employed by

56

the author to show her beliefs. James E. Miller explains the symbolism of the three different cycles used by Cather in the novel: the seasons of the year, the phases of Antonia's life, and, most important to this essay, the people move westward in cycles to

57

55. A. NO CHANGE
B. had dealt
C. deals
D. has been dealing

56. F. NO CHANGE
G. being employed
H. employing
J. employ

57. A. NO CHANGE
B. the people moved westward in cycles
C. the cycles in the movement of people westward
D. the people were frequently moving westward in cycles

America's frontiers. Wallace Stegner, a novelist in his own right, wrote an essay about *My Ántonia.* In

58

which he used archetypal criticism in relation to

58

Antonia's identification with the land, and the psychological approach to show how Cather's life and character were crucial to the novel's central theme of country versus city values. | 59 | | 60 |

58. F. NO CHANGE
G. *My Ántonia,* in which
H. *My Ántonia*; in which
J. *My Ántonia—* in which

59. This paragraph begins with the general statement: ". . . *My Ántonia* has been analyzed through a number of critical approaches." In what ways does the rest of the paragragh support or fail to support this statement?

A. It supplies the names of several critical approaches and defines them in detail.

B. It avoids the mention of critical approaches, but names three critics and discusses their ideas.

C. It names three critics, but says little about critical approaches.

D. It names three critics and their specific critical approaches to the novel, identifying the critical schools employed by two of them.

60. Choose the sequence of paragraph numbers that makes the structure of the passage most logical.

F. NO CHANGE
G. 2, 3, 1
H. 3, 2, 1
J. 3, 1, 2

Passage 5

(1)

It is impossible to adhere rigidly to a particular global vision without accepting the fact that, in practice, a certain number of contradictions and inconsistencies will always arise in the process of translating philosophy into <u>concrete and tangible</u> action. The fact
61

61. A. NO CHANGE
B. concrete, tangible, and material
C. concrete
D. concrete and palpable

that a nation possesses <u>a notion of its clear</u> inter-
62

national priorities, however, serves to minimize the chances that its policies will merely drift in the tide of global events or become deadlocked by their mutual incompatibility. ⃞63

62. F. NO CHANGE
G. a notion clear of its
H. a notion
J. a clear notion of its

63. The writer could most effectively strengthen the passage at this point by adding which of the following?

A. A list of countries that comprise the international population

B. A clearer introductory statement concerning what is meant by "translating philosophy into concrete action"

C. A list of "global events"

D. A list of "contradictions and inconsistencies"

(2)

By leading the more complex international decision
64
making structure of the 1990s, the United States will
have to recognize and accept that our major interna-

tional cronies will occasionally have priorities and
65

interests that differ from our own. This is inherently a
66
healthy sign of the pluralistic nature of modern

international politics, we need not be reluctant about
67
working for the advancement of our own interests,
but we should not despair when we sometimes fail to
achieve all that we desire. In practical terms, however, our prospects for success can be increased
though we are sensitive to the particular constraints
68
and policy goals that influence the actions of other

nations, states, and governments. ⬚ **70**
69

64. **F.** NO CHANGE
    G. Leading
    H. In order to lead
    J. Although
    leading

65. **A.** NO CHANGE
    B. partners
    C. buddies
    D. pals

66. **F.** NO CHANGE
    G. These priorities
    H. This priority
    J. This
    independence

67. **A.** NO CHANGE
    B. politics we
    C. politics. We
    D. politics yet we

68. **F.** NO CHANGE
    G. if
    H. but
    J. unless

69. **A.** NO CHANGE
    B. nations and
    governments.
    C. nations.
    D. nations, states,
    governments,
    provinces, and
    entities.

70. Readers are likely to regard the passage thus far as
    best described by which of the following terms?
    F. Conciliatory
    G. Hostile
    H. Apologetic
    J. Confessional

(3)

At the outset, we need to recognize that the solutions to the major foreign policy issues of the future will largely be determined on the basis of collective leadership. <u>The United States will no longer</u>
71
<u>be able simply to undertake unilateral action to</u>
71
<u>resolve specific international situations.</u> We have now
71
grown beyond the era in which the global power of the United States was absolute and <u>unchallenged, and</u> it
72
would be dangerous and futile to attempt a restoration of the postwar balance of forces. <u>The over-</u>
73
<u>whelming truth is that human beings have created</u>
73
<u>destructive weaponry they are no longer able to</u>
73
<u>control.</u> Instead we must move toward an apprecia-
73
tion of the central role that the United States will continue to play in reconciling competing international interests. |74| |75|

71. This sentence alone indicates that the intention of the author is to be:
A. descriptive.
B. persuasive.
C. poetic.
D. sentimental.

72. F. NO CHANGE
G. unchallenged and
H. unchallenged. And
J. unchallenged: and

73. A. NO CHANGE
B. Human beings have created destructive weaponry.
C. OMIT the underlined portion.
D. Human beings have created destructive weaponry they cannot control.

74. The word *instead* at the beginning of the last sentence serves as a transition between which of the following stances?
F. From unchallenged global power to peacemaker
G. From peacemaker to warrior
H. From unchallenged global power to warrior
J. From hostility to aggressiveness

75. Choose the sequence of paragraph numbers that makes the structure of the essay most logical.
A. NO CHANGE
B. 3, 1, 2
C. 3, 2, 1
D. 1, 3, 2

Answers to English Test on page 411.

Test 2: Mathematics   60 Minutes—60 Questions

Directions: After solving each problem, darken the appropriate space on the answer sheet. Do not spend too much time on any one problem. Make a note of the ones that seem difficult, and return to them when you finish the others. Assume that the word *line* means "straight line," that geometric figures are not necessarily drawn to scale, and that all geometric figures lie in a plane.

1. The following expression $\frac{a}{b} - \frac{c}{d} = $?

A. $\frac{a - b}{cd}$

D. $\frac{a - c}{bd}$

B. $\frac{a}{d} - \frac{c}{b}$

E. $\frac{a - d}{bc}$

C. $\frac{ad - bc}{bd}$

2. If $x \neq 0$, which of the following is equal to $\frac{2x^4 + x^3}{x^6}$?

F. $\frac{3}{x^3}$

J. $\frac{2x + 1}{x^3}$

G. $\frac{x + 1}{x^2}$

K. $\frac{2x + 1}{x}$

H. $2x^2 + x^3$

3. A certain city has 1,600 public telephones. Three-fourths of the phones have dials. If one-third of the dial phones are replaced by push-button phones, how many dial phones remain?

A. 800   **B.** 750   **C.** 700   **D.** 600   **E.** 400

4. If x and y are both positive integers, which of the following is NOT necessarily an integer?

F. $x + y$

J. x^y

G. $x - y$

K. $\frac{x}{y}$

H. $x y$

5. If a negative number is subtracted from a positive number, which of the following will always be the result?

A. Zero

B. A positive number

C. A negative number

D. A number having the sign of the number with the larger absolute value

E. A number having the sign of the number with the smaller absolute value

6. What is the solution set of the equation $\dfrac{5}{4x - 3} = 5$?

F. {7}   **G.** {4}   **H.** {2}   **J.** {1.5}   **K.** {1}

7. If t represents the tens digit of a two-digit number, and u represents the units digit, which of the following expressions represents the number?

A. $t + u$ **B.** $10t + u$ **C.** $10u + t$ **D.** $10(t + u)$ **E.** tu

8. What is the simplified form of the product of the two polynomials $(x - 1)(x^2 + x + 1)$?

F. $x^3 + 1$

G. $x^3 - 1$

H. $x^3 - x - 1$

J. $x^3 + x^2 + x$

K. $x^3 + 2x^2 + 2x + 1$

9. The number $3_{(five)}$ (written in base five) is equivalent to what symbol in base two?

A. 3   **B.** 11   **C.** 101   **D.** 100   **E.** 111

10. Which of the following numbers is unequal to the others?

F. 2.5%   **G.** $\dfrac{1}{40}$ **H.** $2.5(10^{-2})$ **J.** $\dfrac{75}{30}$ **K.** 0.025

11. If apples are 35 cents or 3 for $1.00, how much is saved on each apple by buying them 3 at a time?

A. 5 cents

B. $1.05

C. $\dfrac{3}{5}$ cents

D. $1\dfrac{2}{3}$ cents

E. $11\dfrac{2}{3}$ cents

12. If Joan can run 1 mile in a minutes, how much of a mile has she run after b minutes if she runs at a constant rate?

F. $\frac{a}{b}$ **G.** $\frac{b}{a}$ **H.** $\frac{1}{ab}$ **J.** ab **K.** $\frac{a+b}{a}$

13. Which of the following is NOT a real number?

A. $\sqrt[5]{0}$ **B.** 5^0 **C.** 0^5 **D.** $0 \cdot 5$ **E.** $\frac{5}{0}$

14. $3\frac{3}{5} \times 4\frac{1}{6} = ?$

F. 15   **G.** $7\frac{23}{30}$ **H.** $\frac{108}{125}$ **J.** $\frac{17}{30}$ **K.** $\frac{1}{15}$

15. Yvette has 5 more nickels than dimes. If the value of her money is $1.30, how many coins of each kind does she have?
A. 12 dimes and 7 nickels   **D.** 7 dimes and 12 nickels
B. 5 dimes and 16 nickels   **E.** 3 dimes and 20 nickels
C. 5 dimes and 10 nickels

16. What is the tenth term of the arithmetic sequence 3, 8, 13, . . .?
F. 18   **G.** 43   **H.** 48   **J.** 53   **K.** None of these

17. What is the solution set of the equation $0.2(100 - x) + 0.05x = 0.1(100)$?

A. $\left\{-33\frac{1}{3}\right\}$ **D.** $\left\{66\frac{2}{3}\right\}$

B. $\{10\}$ **E.** $\left\{95\frac{95}{399}\right\}$
C. $\{40\}$

18. Which of the following statements is false?
F. A regular triangle is equilateral.
G. A regular quadrilateral is a square.
H. An interior angle of a regular pentagon has a measure of 108°.
J. A regular polygon of seven sides does not exist.
K. All of these statements are true.

19. What is the simplest form of the radical $\sqrt[3]{54x^4y^6}$? (Assume that x and y are nonnegative.)

A. $3xy^2 \sqrt[3]{2x}$

B. $3x^2y^3 \sqrt[3]{6}$

C. $3y^3 \sqrt[3]{2x^4}$

D. $3x^2 \sqrt[3]{6y^6}$

E. $3xy^2 \sqrt[3]{6x}$

20. Which of the following is NOT an equation of a conic section?

F. $y = 5x^2 - 3x + 2$

G. $x^2 + y^2 - 5x + 2y - 7 = 0$

H. $2x^2 - 5y^2 = 7$

J. $y = x^3$

K. $\dfrac{(x + 2)^2}{25} + \dfrac{(y - 3)^2}{16} = 1$

21. What is the degree of $-5x^2y + 3xy^3 + 2xy + 6$?

A. 9   **B.** 5   **C.** 4   **D.** 3   **E.** 2

22. What is the solution set of the following system of equations?

$$2x - y = 5$$
$$x + y = 1$$

F. $\{(2,1)\}$ **G.** $\{2\}$ **H.** $\{(3, 1)\}$ **J.** $\{(4, -3)\}$ **K.** $\{(2, -1)\}$

23. A number from the set $\{1, 2, 3, \ldots, 20\}$ is chosen at random. What is the probability that the number is even and less than 10?

A. $\dfrac{1}{2}$ **B.** $\dfrac{9}{20}$ **C.** $\dfrac{1}{5}$ **D.** $\dfrac{9}{40}$ **E.** $\dfrac{1}{4}$

24. If $x \neq 0$ and $y \neq 0$, what is the simplified form of the complex fraction $\dfrac{x + y}{\dfrac{1}{x} + \dfrac{1}{y}}$?

F. $\dfrac{x + y}{xy}$

G. $\dfrac{xy}{x + y}$

H. $(x + y)^2$

J. $2 + \dfrac{x}{y} + \dfrac{y}{x}$

K. xy

25. If m ∠ *ABC* = 70°, then m ∠ *ADC* = ?

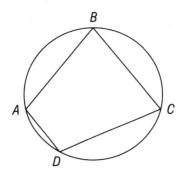

A. 35° **B.** 70° **C.** 90° **D.** 110° **E.** 140°

26. If $a > b$, then $|a - b| + |b - a|$ is equal to what expression?

F. 0 **G.** 2*a* **H.** 2*b* **J.** 2*a* + 2*b* **K.** 2*a* − 2*b*

27. What is the value of -3^{-2}?

A. 6 **B.** 9 **C.** −9 **D.** $\frac{-1}{9}$ **E.** $\frac{1}{9}$

28. What is the center of the ellipse with the equation $x^2 + 4y^2 - 4x + 24y + 36 = 0$?

F. (2, 1) **G.** (1, 2) **H.** (2, −3) **J.** (−2, 3) **K.** (1, 4)

29. Nick can do a certain job in 2 hours less time than it takes Bonnie to do the same job. If they can complete the job together in 7 hours, what equation could be used to determine how long it would take Bonnie to do the job alone?

A. $7(x - 2) = 7x$

B. $\dfrac{7}{x - 2} = \dfrac{7}{x}$

C. $7(x - 2) + 7x = 1$

D. $\dfrac{7}{x - 2} + \dfrac{7}{x} = 1$

E. None of these

30. Which of the following is the graph of a one-to-one function?

F.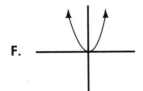

J.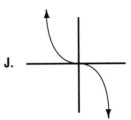

G.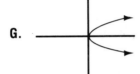

K.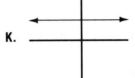

H.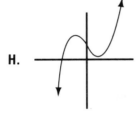

31. Which of the following numbers could NOT be the base of an exponential function?

    A. $\frac{1}{2}$ **B.** 1   **C.** 2   **D.** 3   **E.** $\sqrt{5}$

32. What is the simplified form of the expression $(5x - 3y^2)^2$?

    F. $25x^2 + 9y^4$ **J.** $25x^2 - 15xy^2 + 9y^4$

    G. $25x^2 - 9y^4$ **K.** $25x^2 - 30xy^2 + 9y^4$

    H. $25x^2 - 30xy + 9y^2$

33. What is the reciprocal of i?

    A. 1 **B.** -1 **C.** i **D.** $-i$ **E.** None of these

34. What is the simplified form of the expression $\dfrac{a^{-3}bc^2}{a^{-4}b^2c^{-3}}$? (Assume that the variables are not equal to zero. Write without negative exponents.)

F. $\dfrac{c^5}{a^7b}$

J. $\dfrac{c}{ab}$

G. $\dfrac{ac^5}{b}$

K. $\dfrac{a^7}{bc^5}$

H. $\dfrac{a^7c^5}{b}$

35. In right triangle ABC, $m \angle A = 30°$, $m \angle B = 60°$, and $AC = 6$. What is the length of $\overline{AB}$?

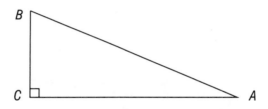

A. $3\sqrt{2}$ **B.** $6\sqrt{3}$ **C.** $4\sqrt{2}$ **D.** $3\sqrt{3}$ **E.** $4\sqrt{3}$

36. Which of the following is identically equal to sin $2A$?

F. $1 - \cos^2 2A$

J. $2 \sin A$

G. $2 \sin A \cos A$

K. None of these

H. $\dfrac{1}{\sec 2a}$

37. What is the solution set of $3x^2 - 4x - 6 = 0$?

A. $\left\{ \dfrac{-2}{3}, 3 \right\}$

D. $\left\{ \dfrac{4 + i\sqrt{66}}{6}, \dfrac{4 - i\sqrt{66}}{6} \right\}$

B. $\left\{ \dfrac{2 + 2\sqrt{22}}{3}, \dfrac{2 - 2\sqrt{22}}{3} \right\}$

E. $\left\{ \dfrac{2 + \sqrt{22}}{3}, \dfrac{2 - \sqrt{22}}{3} \right\}$

C. $\left\{ \dfrac{4 + \sqrt{22}}{3}, \dfrac{4 - \sqrt{22}}{3} \right\}$

38. What is the simplified form of the radical expression $3\sqrt{3} - \sqrt{48} + 3\sqrt{\frac{1}{3}}$?

F. 0
G. $\sqrt{3}$
H. $4\sqrt{3} - 2\sqrt{12}$

J. $3\sqrt{3} - 2\sqrt{12} + \sqrt{3}$
K. It is already in simplest form.

39. Which of the following equations does NOT define a function?

A. $y = x + 2$ **B.** $x = y + 2$ **C.** $y = 2^x$ **D.** $y = x^2$ **E.** $x = y^2$

40. If tangent $\overline{CD}$ is 6 cm long and $BC = 4$, what is the length of $\overline{AB}$?

F. $2\frac{2}{3}$
G. 3
H. 4
J. 5
K. 6

41. Diane averages 12 miles per hour riding her bike to work. Averaging 36 miles per hour on the way home by car takes her $\frac{1}{2}$ hour less time. What equation could be used to determine how far she travels to work?

A. $12x + 36x = 30$
B. $\frac{x}{12} = \frac{x}{36} - \frac{1}{2}$
C. $\frac{x}{12} + \frac{x}{36} = 30$

D. $\frac{x}{36} = \frac{x}{12} - \frac{1}{2}$
E. $\frac{36}{x} = \frac{12}{x} + \frac{1}{2}$

42. What are the coordinates of the midpoint of a segment with endpoints $A(3, 7)$ and $B(-5, -6)$?

F. $(0, 0)$
G. $\left(1, \frac{-1}{2}\right)$
H. $\left(-1, \frac{1}{2}\right)$

J. $(-2, 1)$
K. $(8, 13)$

43. What is the solution set of the radical equation $\sqrt{2x - 3} = -5$?

    A. $\{-1\}$ **B.** $\{4\}$ **C.** $\{7\}$ **D.** $\{14\}$ **E.** ø

44. Which of the following statements is false?

    F. Every whole number is an integer.
    G. Some rational numbers are natural numbers.
    H. The set of integers is a subset of the set of real numbers.
    J. $\sqrt{49}$ is a rational number.
    K. None of these statements is false.

45. If an equilateral triangle is inscribed in a circle of radius 8 cm, what is the perimeter of the triangle?

    A. $24\sqrt{3}$ **B.** $8\sqrt{3}$ **C.** $4\sqrt{3}$ **D.** 12 **E.** 24

46. What is the domain of the function
$f(x) = \dfrac{x + 3}{x^2 - 2x - 3}$?

    F. All real numbers
    G. $\{x \mid x$ is a real number and $x \neq -3\}$
    H. $\{x \mid x$ is a real number and $x \neq 3$ and $x \neq -1\}$
    J. $\{x \mid x$ is a real number and $x \neq 3, x \neq -1,$
        and $x \neq -3\}$
    K. $\{x \mid x \neq 0\}$

47. Circles A and B are tangent to each other. $\overline{CD}$ is a common tangent to the two circles. If the radius of circle A is 5 and the radius of circle B is 3, what is the length of $\overline{CD}$?

    A. 4
    B. 8
    C. $\sqrt{34}$
    D. $2\sqrt{15}$
    E. $2\sqrt{17}$

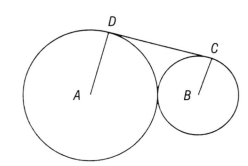

48. If $\overline{AD}$ is a diameter and m ∠ C = 125°, what is the measure of ∠ A?

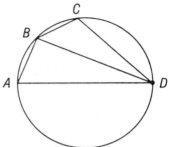

F. 35°   **G.** 55°   **H.** 62.5°   **J.** 90°   **K.** 125°

49. If AC = 8 and BD = 6, then what is the length of $\overline{BC}$?

A. 1
B. 5
C. $7\frac{1}{2}$

D. 15
E. There is not enough information.

50. If $A(-3, 4)$ lies on the terminal side of angle θ, what is the value of sec θ?

F. $\frac{-3}{5}$ **G.** $\frac{4}{5}$ **H.** $\frac{-5}{3}$ **J.** $\frac{-4}{3}$ **K.** $\frac{5}{4}$

51. What is the value of $\displaystyle\sum_{k=1}^{5} 2k^2$?

A. 2   **B.** 50   **C.** 52   **D.** 110   **E.** None of these

52. In which quadrant must θ lie if cos θ > 0 and cot θ < 0?

F. I   **G.** II   **H.** III   **J.** IV   **K.** No such angle exists.

53. Let A and B be any two sets. Which of the following statements is always true?

A. $(A \cup B) \subseteq A$
B. $(A \cap B) \subseteq B$
C. $(A \cup B) \subseteq (A \cap B)$

D. $B \subseteq (A \cap B)$
E. $(A \cup B) = (A \cap B)$

54. The length of the diagonal of a rectangular piece of wood is $\sqrt{145}$ feet. If one side is 1 foot longer than the other, what are the lengths of the sides?

F. 8 feet and -9 feet
J. 5 feet and 6 feet
G. 8 feet and 9 feet
K. 2 feet and 36 feet
H. 12 feet and 13 feet

55. What is the value of $\sin\left(\cos^{-1}\dfrac{2}{3}\right)$?

A. $\dfrac{2}{3}$ **B.** $\dfrac{\sqrt{5}}{3}$ **C.** $\dfrac{-\sqrt{5}}{3}$ **D.** $\dfrac{\pm\sqrt{5}}{3}$ **E.** $\dfrac{\sqrt{13}}{3}$

56. Jon scored 75, 84, and 80 on his first three tests. What score must he get on his fourth test so that his average will be at least 80?

F. 81
G. Greater than 81
H. Less than 81
J. Greater than or equal to 81
K. Less than or equal to 81

57. What is the measure of an exterior angle of a regular octagon?

A. 45° **B.** 60° **C.** 72° **D.** 120° **E.** 135°

58. If the lengths of the diagonals of a rhombus are 6 and 8 meters, what is the perimeter, in meters, of the rhombus?

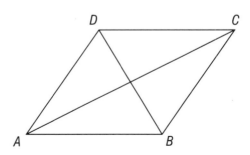

F. 5 **G.** 14 **H.** 20 **J.** 28 **K.** 40

59. Which of the following statements is true?

   A.   Complements of complementary angles are equal.

   B.   A line segment has only one bisector.

   C.   A line perpendicular to a segment also bisects the segment.

   D.   An isosceles triangle may also be scalene.

   E.   None of these statements is true.

60. In $\triangle ABC$, $\overline{AB} \perp \overline{BC}$ and $\overline{BD} \perp \overline{AC}$. If $BD = 4$ and $AC = 10$, what is the length of $\overline{AD}$ (the shorter portion of the hypotenuse)?

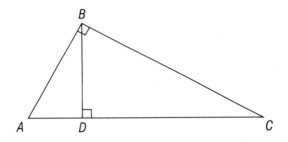

F. 2   **G.** 3   **H.** 4   **J.** 6   **K.** 8

Answers to Mathematics Test on page 412.

Test 3: Reading   35 Minutes—40 Questions

Directions: This test consists of four passages, each followed by ten multiple-choice questions. Read each passage and then pick the best answer for each question. Fill in the spaces on your answer sheet that correspond to your choices. Refer to the passage as often as you wish while answering the questions.

Passage 1

SOCIAL SCIENCE: This passage is from a governmental report on domestic violence titled "Characteristics of the Abusive Situation." It discusses several problems faced by abused and battered spouses.

Abusive husbands systematically isolate their wives from family and friends. Even women who seek legal, medical or emotional help view themselves as unable to succeed against their all-powerful husbands who, they fear, will "pay witnesses to lie in court," "kill my
5 family if I testify," "get custody of the children," and "refuse to give me a divorce." Physical and emotional abuse of women is an exercise of power and control in which the weight of society has been traditionally on the side of the oppressor. Thus, battered women who feel powerless to alter their circumstances are reacting realistically to
10 what they have experienced. They are trapped, and their descriptions of the responses of police, prosecutors and judges are not paranoid delusions.

Many victims have been beaten repeatedly and their attackers have not been apprehended and punished. Assault is a crime. Legally it
15 makes no difference if the victim and her attacker are strangers or are married to each other. Yet police officers often refuse to arrest husbands (or live-in companions) who beat their wives. Police, prosecutors, judges and society in general share the prejudice that women provoke men by constant nagging, overspending or question-
20 ing their virility. Verbal provocation, even assuming it exists, how-ever, is not justification for violence.

The absence of negative sanctions gives the abusive family mem-ber license to continue his threats and violence. The lack of societal

restraints on the husband's violence, the emphasis on defendant's
25 rights in the courts, the long court delays, the opportunity for
intimidation, the husband's promises of reform and the woman's fear
of economic privation contribute to the drop out rate of 50 percent by
battered-wife complainants in the criminal courts and in the Family
Court.

30   Civil actions for support, separation or divorce are also subject to
delays which make it virtually impossible to get emergency relief.
Judges frequently refuse to "throw a man out of his home," so it is the
woman and children who must leave. Crowded court calendars make
the legal process work in favor of the person who controls the family
35 income and assets. Getting temporary alimony or maintenance and
child support can take months, sometimes as long as a divorce itself.
Unless there is a refuge for battered women, the abused wife may be
forced to live with her husband during a divorce action.

   Equitable distribution of property may also be problematic for the
40 financially dependent spouse because the litigation to define, evaluate
and divide the property can continue for years and is very costly. The
ultimate irony is that, even when the battered wife gets an award for
alimony and child support, the amount of support is usually inadequate for her to maintain herself and the children. Moreover, often it is
45 not paid at all.

   Because the separated or divorced wife cannot rely on payment of
court-ordered support, many battered wives stay with their husbands. Professor Richard J. Gelles, a sociologist who studied battered wives, found that the wives who hold a job are better able to
50 obtain assistance and leave the abusive situation . . . Viewing the
difficult situation in which legal, economic and social realities place
the battered woman, one should ask: where does this woman get the
stamina to survive the attacks and the courage to leave? Part of the
work of the helping professionals is to convince the battered woman
55 that she must use the enormous strength she has for self-
preservation, not just for self-sacrifice.

   The legal system requires that an injured adult initiate and follow
through with the steps necessary to obtain protection, child custody,
financial support, divorce or money damages. Usually the injured

60 person bears the expense of engaging an attorney to represent her in
a civil case. The legal process is complex and confusing so that
referral to a sympathetic and competent lawyer is important. Other
helping professionals must understand the laws concerning family
violence if they are to provide effective support. Accompanying a
65 client to court helps develop a first-hand sense of the obstacles that
the client faces.

The victim of domestic violence is in the best position to decide if
legal action will be the most effective way to stop the violence or
psychological abuse. Her decision on this matter must be respected.
70 If just moving away (and getting a divorce if necessary) will work,
then there is no reason to get entangled in a complicated legal process
in which control is given to an unknown judge. But there are situations
in which police assistance and court protection are essential.

1. According to the passage, the main reason that abused women
often feel helpless is that:
  A. they don't know where to turn for help.
  B. society customarily takes the man's side.
  C. they can't afford to seek assistance.
  D. witnesses to incidents of abuse are hard to find.

2. One can infer that, in general, law enforcement officials think that
incidents of wife abuse:
  F. should be settled within the family, if possible.
  G. are less serious than conflicts between strangers.
  H. should be blamed equally on the husband and the wife.
  J. have often been provoked by the wife.

3. The clause "their descriptions . . . are not paranoid delusions. . ."
in lines 10–12 implies that battered women:
  A. often cannot separate fantasy from reality.
  B. tend to exaggerate incidents of abuse.
  C. feel maltreated by those from whom they seek help.
  D. frequently need psychological help.

4. The passage indicates that half the lawsuits brought against abusive husbands remain incomplete because of all the following reasons EXCEPT that the:

F. husband and wife are reconciled.

G. wife feels threatened by loss of financial support.

H. courts take too long to hear cases.

J. husband pledges to stop abusing his wife.

5. The passage suggests that, in an emergency, an abused wife should:

A. call a neighbor.

B. immediately report her husband to the police.

C. try to go to a shelter for battered women.

D. contact a social worker.

6. Which of the following statements most accurately summarizes the author's view on how to solve the problems of abused wives?

F. Change the legal system to give abused wives special consideration.

G. Help abused women overcome feelings of hopelessness.

H. Strictly enforce the laws governing alimony payments.

J. Educate society about the problems of abused wives.

7. A primary purpose of the passage is to:

A. argue for new laws to protect abused women.

B. convince readers that abusive behavior is never justified.

C. point out the injustices faced by abused women.

D. advise abused women of their rights.

8. The passage implies that the severest hardships of abused women pertain to:

F. fears of bodily harm.

G. lack of financial support.

H. psychological trauma.

J. the well-being of their children.

9. According to the passage, an abused wife may invoke all of the following legal remedies EXCEPT:

A. filing for an official separation from her husband.

B. maintaining custody of the children.

C. forcing the husband to continue financial support.

D. requiring the husband to pay her attorney's fees.

10. The passage suggests that, to stop domestic violence, an abused woman should turn to the courts only when:

F. there is no alternative.

G. she suffers psychological trauma.

H. her husband would be charged with criminal behavior.

J. she can get help from an understanding lawyer.

Passage 2

NATURAL SCIENCE: This passage is part of a research report from the National Institute of Health. It describes how scientists are analyzing human growth rates from birth to adulthood.

Scientists are discovering that children throughout the world tend to show remarkably similar capacities for growth. Nursing infants in developing nations follow much the same pattern of growth as that considered normal for infants in the United States. The likelihood is
5 that while each child proceeds to adulthood at his own pace, normal growth before puberty is dependent more on the life a child leads than upon the genes with which he is endowed.

The average, full-term male infant weighs 8 pounds and measures 20 inches. Some weight loss follows birth. Growth then becomes so
10 rapid that he will probably weigh 14 pounds and measure 25 inches by the age of 4 months.

After the 4th month, growth starts to slow down. Height now becomes more important than weight in evaluating the health of the growing child. When he celebrates his first birthday, the
15 average boy should have grown to the height of 30 inches.

By the time he is 2, the child's growth begins to reflect some genetic influence. The average healthy boy then measures about 35 inches and will have reached approximately half his adult height. On his third birthday, he is close to 38 inches. His growth
20 rate then starts to level off, and for the next 9 years, he will grow at the relatively constant rate of only 2-1/2 inches a year.

In marked contrast to the dramatic and rapid changes that occur during the pre- and early postnatal periods, growth during the later childhood years is slowly progressive, and
25 derangements may be subtle. Probably one of the simplest gauges of a child's health status is whether he is adding inches and pounds according to accepted timetables of normal growth. The first indication that something is amiss with a child's health may be the fall of his growth curve below the third percentile for
30 normal children. This youngster is probably suffering a period of depressed growth that should be investigated and its cause corrected.

Increase in height is due to progressive growth of bone. As noted earlier, development of the skeleton is quite incomplete at birth, and it
35 continues to undergo many changes throughout childhood. Most primary centers of ossification, for example, develop after birth; some do not make their appearance until adolescence. Epiphyses normally are not completely closed until the end of adolescence.

Many investigators discuss human growth in terms of two ages:
40 *chronological* age, timed from the date of birth, and *biological* age, a measure of the degree of physical maturity of the individual, determined by equating his degree of maturity with the average age at which that degree of maturity usually becomes manifest. X-rays of the bones are most often used to determine the biological
45 age of children. The greater the number of centers of ossification present on the X-ray, and the greater the degree of epiphyseal closure, the greater is the biological age of the child—regardless of his actual chronological age. Biological age, as measured by reference to X-rays of bones, is often referred to as *bone* age.

50 Bone X-rays have helped establish, for example, that skeletal maturation in a girl on the day of birth is one month ahead of that of her twin brother. The female, therefore, comes into life a biologically older, more highly developed organism. It will take the male close to 20 years to catch up.

55 Measures of height, weight, and bone age have served as the traditional bases of growth studies. Scientists now, however, are

seeking increasingly specialized techniques by which human growth may be analyzed. Enlargement of the human organism is basically the result of a myriad of chemical reactions, some of which can be
60 measured in a short period of time by new biochemical techniques. Researchers at General Clinical Research Centers and other facilities, therefore, are now investigating individual components of growth at the tissue, cellular, and even molecular levels.

At some General Clinical Research Centers, everything the
65 research subjects eat, drink, or eliminate is carefully measured for weight, chemical composition, and caloric value. In fact, the child who enters the bathroom without telling the nurse is interrupted by an alarm system; this prevents the loss of waste materials which must be carefully analyzed as part of precise metabolic studies.

11. According to the passage, how much does the average child grow during the first year of life?

A. Nearly a foot
B. About 6 inches
C. Almost 30 inches
D. Between 6 and 9 inches

12. Based on information in the passage, approximately how tall would a six-foot adult have been at age two?

F. 24 inches
G. 30 inches
H. 36 inches
J. 40 inches

13. According to the passage, the greatest amount of human growth takes place:

A. during the teenage years.
B. between the ages of 1 and 3.
C. just prior to and during puberty.
D. just before and just after birth.

14. According to the passage, growth studies of children reveal that girls:

    F. are more physically developed than boys of the same age.
    G. mature faster than boys.
    H. reach puberty at an earlier age than boys.
    J. are likely to be taller than boys during pre-adolescence.

15. According to the passage, *biological* age in comparison to *bone* age is:

    A. usually greater.
    B. usually less.
    C. always the same.
    D. sometimes more and sometimes less.

16. One can infer from the passage that growth in children before age 12 or 13 depends largely on:

    F. the pre-natal condition of the mother.
    G. traits inherited from both parents.
    H. diet and nutrition.
    J. breast feeding during the first months of life.

17. "Centers of ossification" (line 36 and line 45) are found in:

    A. brain cells.
    B. the central nervous system.
    C. the respiratory system.
    D. bones.

18. Based on information in the passage, one can infer that children suffering from abnormal growth can be helped:

    F. at almost any time until they reach adulthood.
    G. after they are 3 years old.
    H. only before puberty.
    J. only between 3 and 12 years old.

19. The passage indicates that genes influence a child's growth mostly:

    A. during the years before puberty.

B. after puberty.
C. after the age of 2
D. during the pre- and post-natal periods.

20. One can infer from the passage that analysts of human growth believe that:

F. traditional studies of height and weight yield limited data.
G. human growth may someday be genetically predetermined.
H. the meaning of "normal" growth keeps changing.
J. theoretically there is no limit to the size of human beings.

Passage 3

PROSE FICTION: This passage is from *The Awakening,* a novel by Kate Chopin. The passage describes the protagonist's feelings about her husband and her marriage.

It was eleven o'clock that night when Mr. Pontellier returned from Klein's hotel. He was in an excellent humor, in high spirits, and very talkative. His entrance awoke his wife, who was in bed and fast asleep when he came in. He talked to her while he
5   undressed, telling her anecdotes and bits of news and gossip that he had gathered during the day. From his trousers pockets he took a fistful of crumpled bank notes and a good deal of silver coin, which he piled on the bureau indiscriminately with keys, knife, handkerchief, and whatever else happened to be in his pockets. She
10   was overcome with sleep, and answered him with little half utterances.

He thought it very discouraging that his wife, who was the sole object of his existence, evinced so little interest in things that concerned him, and valued so little his conversation.
15   Mr. Pontellier had forgotten the bonbons and peanuts for the boys. Notwithstanding, he loved them very much, and went into the adjoining room where they slept to take a look at them and make sure that they were resting comfortably. The result of his investigation was far from satisfactory. He turned and shifted the
20   youngsters about in bed. One of them began to kick and talk about a basket full of crabs.

Mr. Pontellier returned to his wife the information that Raoul had a high fever and needed looking after. Then he lit a cigar and went and sat near the open door to smoke it.

25 Mrs. Pontellier was quite sure Raoul had no fever. He had gone to bed perfectly well, she said, and nothing had ailed him all day. Mr. Pontellier was too well acquainted with fever symptoms to be mistaken. He assured her the child was consuming at that moment in the next room.

30 He reproached his wife with her inattention, her habitual neglect of the children. If it was not a mother's place to look after children, whose on earth was it? He himself had his hands full with his brokerage business. He could not be in two places at once; making a living for his family on the street, and staying at home to

35 see that no harm befell them. He talked in a monotonous, insistent way.

Mrs. Pontellier sprang out of bed and went into the next room. She soon came back and sat on the edge of the bed, leaning her head down on the pillow. She said nothing, and refused to answer

40 her husband when he questioned her. When his cigar was smoked out he went to bed, and in half a minute he was fast asleep.

Mrs. Pontellier was by that time thoroughly awake. She began to cry a little, and wiped her eyes on the sleeve of her *peignoir*. Blowing out the candle, which her husband had left burning, she slipped her

45 bare feet into a pair of satin *mules* at the foot of the bed and went out on the porch, where she sat down in the wicker chair and began to rock gently to and fro.

It was then past midnight. The cottages were all dark. A single faint light gleamed out from the hallway of the house. There was no sound

50 abroad except the hooting of an old owl in the top of a water-oak, and the everlasting voice of the sea, that was not uplifted at that soft hour. It broke like a mournful lullaby upon the night.

The tears came so fast to Mrs. Pontellier's eyes that the damp sleeve of her. *peignoir* no longer served to dry them. She was holding

55 the back of her chair with one hand; her loose sleeve had slipped almost to the shoulder of her uplifted arm. Turning, she thrust her face, steaming and wet, into the bend of her arm, and she went on crying there, not caring any longer to dry her face, her eyes, her arms. She could not have told why she was crying. Such experiences as the foregoing

60 were not uncommon in her married life. They seemed never before

to have weighed much against the abundance of her husband's kindness and a uniform devotion which had come to be tacit and self-understood.

65 An indescribable oppression, which seemed to generate in some unfamiliar part of her consciousness, filled her whole being with a vague anguish. It was like a shadow, like a mist passing across her soul's summer day. It was strange and unfamiliar; it was a mood. She did not sit there inwardly upbraiding her husband, lamenting at Fate, which had directed her footsteps to the path which they had taken. She was

70 just having a good cry all to herself. The mosquitoes made merry over her, biting her firm, round arms and nipping at her bare insteps.

The little stinging, buzzing imps succeeded in dispelling a mood which might have held her there in the darkness half a night longer.

The following morning Mr. Pontellier was up in good time to take

75 the rockaway which was to convey him to the steamer at the wharf. He was returning to the city to his business, and they would not see him again at the Island till the coming Saturday. He had regained his composure, which seemed to have been somewhat impaired the night before. He was eager to be gone, as he looked forward to a lively week

80 in Carondelet Street.

Mr. Pontellier gave his wife half of the money which he had brought away from Klein's hotel the evening before. She liked money as well as most women, and accepted it with no little satisfaction.

"It will buy a handsome wedding present for Sister Janet!" she ex-

85 claimed, smoothing out the bills as she counted them one by one.

"Oh! we'll treat Sister Janet better than that, my dear," he laughed, as he prepared to kiss her good-by.

The boys were tumbling about, clinging to his legs, imploring that numerous things be brought back to them. Mr. Pontellier was a great

90 favorite, and ladies, men, children, even nurses, were always on hand to say good-by to him. His wife stood smiling and waving, the boys shouting, as he disappeared in the old rockaway down the sandy road.

A few days later a box arrived for Mrs. Pontellier from New Orleans. It was from her husband. It was filled with *friandises*, with luscious

95 and toothsome bits—the finest of fruits, *patés*, a rare bottle or two, delicious syrups, and bonbons in abundance.

Mrs. Pontellier was always very generous with the contents of such a box; she was quite used to receiving them when away from home. The *patés* and fruit were brought to the dining-room; the bonbons were

100 passed around. And the ladies, selecting with dainty and discriminating fingers and a little greedily, all declared that Mr. Pontellier was the best husband in the world. Mrs. Pontellier was forced to admit that she knew of none better.

21. Upon arriving home from Klein's hotel, Mr. Pontellier lost his good mood because:
    A. one of his children was sick.
    B. Mrs. Pontellier was asleep.
    C. he had forgotten to bring presents to his sons.
    D. his wife seemed indifferent to him.

22. Mrs. Pontellier goes back to bed when:
    F. she feels better after having had a good cry.
    G. she can no longer stand being stung by the mosquitoes.
    H. the dark night sky begins to lighten.
    J. she is certain that Mr. Pontellier is asleep.

23. Which activity does Mr. Pontellier appear to enjoy the most?
    A. Smoking a cigar before going to bed.
    B. Sending presents to his wife and family
    C. Going to work in New Orleans
    D. Playing games with his children

24. Mr. Pontellier scolds his wife for:
    F. not appreciating how hard he works in his business.
    G. paying too little attention to the children.
    H. expecting him to look after the children.
    J. failing to respond to his questions.

25. After her husband is asleep, Mrs. Pontellier weeps for all of the following reasons EXCEPT that she:
    A. is worried about her son's health.
    B. thinks that Mr. Pontellier does not appreciate her.
    C. has been unjustly criticized by her husband.
    D. feels lonely.

26. Mr. Pontellier sends his wife a package of food (lines 93-96) to:

    F. show that he loves her very much.

    G. assure that his loved ones will be well-fed.

    H. prove that he's a good husband and provider.

    J. make up for criticizing her.

27. That Mr. Pontellier forgot to bring presents for the boys (line 15) suggests that:

    A. he is a careless person.

    B. his mind is occupied with other matters.

    C. he had had no time to go shopping.

    D. he doesn't love his sons as much as he claims.

28. What explains the main problem in Mr. and Mrs. Pontellier's marriage?

    F. He loves her more than she loves him.

    G. They have too few interests in common.

    H. His job keeps him away from his family too much.

    J. She feels trapped by her role as wife and mother.

29. Mr. and Mrs. Pontellier's discussion of a wedding present for Sister Janet (lines 84–87) implies that:

    A. Mrs. Pontellier is stingy.

    B. Mr. Pontellier would not use money won at gambling to buy a wedding gift.

    C. Mr. Pontellier has a higher regard for Sister Janet than for his wife.

    D. the crumpled bills are not good enough for his sister.

30. Why does Mrs. Pontellier concur with her friends' opinion of Mr. Pontellier (lines 102–103)?

    F. She doesn't want to criticize him behind his back.

    G. She doesn't want to contradict her friends.

    H. She thinks they wouldn't understand why she is discontent.

    J. He gives her money.

Passage 4

HUMANITIES: This passage is adapted from "Wanted: A World Language," by Mario Pei. In this selection, Pei explains the difficulties of developing a single international language.

In the 17th century, French philosopher René Descartes came forth with a revolutionary idea. He proposed the creation of a language that could be used internationally by all sorts of people, peasants as well as
5   scholars.

But Descartes made the mistake of concentrating on the logical aspects of such a language, the progression of ideas from the general to the specific. This logical structure exists in no living language, not even in the
10   great classical tongues of antiquity, which are replete with illogical exceptions and arbitrary features.

While Descartes offered no sample of his ideal constructed language, several of his contemporaries immediately came to the fore with offerings. Some of their
15   suggestions were quite ingenious, but all embodied the principle of logical progression at the expense of familiarity and ease. For example, Bishop John Wilkins' *Essay* of 1668 presents a language in which *Z* indicates animals in general, *Za* indicates fish, and successive conso-
20   nants and vowels further restrict the concept to particular classes of fish.

But alongside these attempts at constructed languages which had no connection with any existing language, there was also a startlingly modern proposal, one made
25   by the Bohemian scholar Comenius. He suggested the use of existing languages, not on a universal, but on a zonal basis (he actually proposed English and French for use in Western Europe, Russian as a common tongue for Eastern Europe). This type of solution, still widely
30   advocated today, is in the nature of a temporary makeshift, because it does not supply us with one universal language, but merely makes the existing linguistic confusion a little easier to bear.

Since the days of Descartes, Wilkins, and Comenius,
35 at least a thousand proposals of one description or
another have been advanced. These include several distinct types:
1)The selection and use of an existing language,
ancient or modern, such as Latin, French, or English.
40 2)The combination of two or more existing languages,
either in zonal distribution, as advocated by Comenius
and, much later, by Stalin; or existing side by side, like
the Greek and Latin of antiquity. (The French *Monde
Bilingue* organization, for instance, advocates that all
45 English speakers learn French, all French speakers learn
English, and all speakers of other tongues learn one or
the other. This does not solve the problem of communi-
cating when a Czech who has learned French meets a
Japanese who has learned English.)
50 3) The choice of a modified national language, such as
Basic English, which works with reduced vocabulary
made to serve all purposes by a process of substitution
and paraphrase (*bush*, for instance, is replaced by *small
tree; selfish* is replaced by *without thought of others*); or
55 works with the modification applied not to the vocabulary, but to the system of spelling or the grammatical
structure (*thru, filozofi*, would be samples of spelling;
goed, dood, oxes, mouses instead of the irregular *went,
did, oxen, mice* would be examples of grammar).
60 4) Blends of two or more existing languages, with
words and constructions arbitrarily taken from one or
another of the constituent languages.
5) Fully constructed languages showing no connection
with any known languages (like the American Ro and
65 Suma).
6) Constructed languages in which existing languages
are freely utilized to supply, or at least to suggest, both
vocabulary and grammatical structure, but with concern
for component elements familiar to the greatest possible
70 number of people with different language backgrounds
(Volapuk, Esperanto, Ido, Interlingua).
While many of these projects are impractical and pre-

sent discouraging features, there are at least as many, of all types outlined above, that could easily become opera-
75   tional. It is therefore not the lack of suitable schemes that has prevented, up to the time of writing, the adoption of a language for universal use. . .

    The crux of the problem lies not in the principle, but in its application. *Which* language shall be adopted for
80   international use? There are in existence some 3,000 natural languages, including the better-known classical ones, such as Latin and Greek; plus at least 1,000 fully constructed languages, or modified national tongues, that have been presented since the days of Descartes.

Mario Pei, "Wanted: A World Language"

31. For a language to be designated "constructed," it must:

  A. be different from any existing language.
  B. have no connection whatever to any known language.
  C. sound familiar to the greatest number of people, regardless of their native tongues.
  D. combine elements from at least three existing languages.

32. Which of the following ideas is clearly indicated by the passage?

  F. Speakers of French are unwilling to replace their own tongue with a universal language.
  G. Josef Stalin advocated a language plan that no one had thought of before.
  H. Ancient Latin and Greek are the foundation of most modern languages.
  J. Natural languages are far more common than constructed languages.

33. The author's principal argument is that:

  A. the world has too many languages.

B. an international language will contribute to the formation of international government.

C. a single international language will be beneficial to mankind.

D. a universal language will simplify communications among Eastern and Western European nations.

34. The passage implies that the language proposed by Bishop John Wilkins is a:

F. blend of two or more existing languages.

G. type of zonal language.

H. modified national language.

J. constructed language

35. The author of the passage believes that adoption of a universal language:

A. is not as difficult as it may seem.

B. will probably never happen.

C. will occur when the right language is invented.

D. will take place when linguists agree on which language to use.

36. The passage implies that Descartes' proposal for an international tongue failed because it:

F. was illogical.

G. contained too many exceptions to the rules of language.

H. contradicted a basic principle of language usage.

J. was too much like old Latin and Greek.

37. By calling Comenius' scheme for an international language "startlingly modern" (line 24), the author means that:

A. Comenius devised a plan that could work in today's world.

B. Comenius' proposal had never been thought of before.

C. Comenius' ideas parallel the ideas of many 20th-century linguists.

D. Comenius' language was simple and easy to learn.

38. Which of the following is the most valid generalization about the language types proposed for international use (lines 34–71)?

    F. They are simpler to use than most present-day languages.
    G. They are based on universal rules of grammar.
    H. They are rooted in existing languages.
    J. They appeal equally to all nationalities.

39. According to the passage, many proposals for an international language originated during the 17th century because:

    A. Descartes' proposal was incomplete.
    B. it was an enlightened time.
    C. it was a revolutionary era.
    D. international travel began to flourish.

40. The passage implies that, in order to be functional, a constructed language:

    F. must borrow from the widely spoken languages of the world.
    G. may not be based solely on logical principles.
    H. may use the grammar of English or of any other popular language.
    J. must be translatable into several thousand natural languages.

Answers to Reading Test on page 413.

Test 4: Science Reasoning

35 Minutes—40 Questions

Directions: This test consists of several distinct passages. Each passage is followed by a number of multiple-choice questions based on the passage. Study the passage, and then select the best answer to each question. You are allowed to reread the passage. Record your answer by blackening the appropriate space on the Answer Sheet.

Passage 1

The graph below shows the rate of carbon dioxide uptake in the leaves of a soybean plant, at various concentrations of oxygen and carbon dioxide in the air (ppm = parts per million; μg = microgram). Plants use carbon dioxide in photosynthesis, but they also use oxygen and make carbon dioxide in respiration.

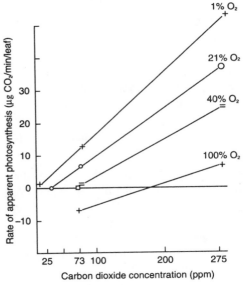

From *Photosynthesis* by Devlin and Barker, Van Nostrand Reinhold Co., New York, 1971.

1. In a normal atmosphere, 21% oxygen and 250 ppm carbon dioxide, how much CO_2 does a leaf take up in an hour?

   A. 37 μg
   B. 1200 μg
   C. 2200 μg
   D. 5250 μg

2. The rate of uptake of carbon dioxide increases as:

   F. carbon dioxide concentration increases and oxygen concentration decreases.
   G. oxygen concentration increases and carbon dioxide concentration decreases.
   H. both oxygen and carbon dioxide concentrations increase.
   J. both oxygen and carbon dioxide concentrations decrease.

3. It is reasonable to conclude that:

   A. the leaves need a certain minimum level of oxygen concentration in order to take up carbon dioxide.
   B. high concentrations of carbon dioxide have a tendency to inhibit photosynthesis.
   C. If the CO_2 concentration is high enough, uptake with 40% oxygen in the air would exceed 50 μg/min/leaf.
   D. leaves will take up carbon dioxide only if there is a certain minimum concentration of CO_2 in the air.

4. Which of the following is NOT a reasonable supposition from the data?

   F. The leaf produces more carbon dioxide than it uses in photosynthesis only if the oxygen concentration is 100%.
   G. High levels of oxygen in the air inhibit photosynthesis.
   H. Respiration, producing carbon dioxide, is much greater at higher levels of oxygen concentration.
   J. The rate of photosynthesis is greater at higher levels of CO_2 concentration.

5. Measurements have shown that, due to the growth of industry, the concentration of CO_2 in the atmosphere has increased in the past century. How do forests influence this situation?

   A. They mitigate the problem by increasing their uptake of CO_2.
   B. They aggravate the problem by increasing their use of oxygen.
   C. They aggravate the problem by increasing their growth rate.
   D. They have no effect because respiration rate increases as fast as photosynthesis.

Passage 2

A biologist is investigating the activity of an enzyme extracted from a fish by timing its action on a standard piece of bean curd. The data represent the number of minutes the enzyme takes to digest the sample completely at various values of temperature and pH.

Temperature (°C)	pH						
	2	3	4	5	6	7	8
5	*	*	*	*	*	*	*
10	*	*	*	*	98	*	*
15	96	75	62	50	45	80	144
20	*	49	33	27	26	61	97
25	*	*	39	30	31	75	*
30	*	*	*	87	72	*	*
35	*	*	*	95	*	*	*
40	*	*	*	*	*	*	*

*No reaction occurred.

6. The enzyme is most active at:
   F. pH 8 and 15° C.
   G. pH 5 and 35° C.
   H. pH 5 and 15° C.
   J. pH 6 and 20° C.

7. In nature, this fish most probably lives in:
   A. highly acid water.
   B. very cold water.
   C. highly alkaline water.
   D. warm water.

8. In comparison with its activity at 20° C, how does the enzyme function at 15° C?
   F. More rapidly and at lower values of pH
   G. More slowly and over a wider range of pH values
   H. More nearly completely and at lower values of pH
   J. Less nearly completely and at a wider range of pH values

9. Which of the following hypotheses is suggested by the data?
   A. The enzyme is most stable at pH 7.
   B. Enzyme activity increases indefinitely with temperature.
   C. The enzyme is destroyed at temperatures higher than 35° C.
   D. The enzyme is destroyed at a pH lower than 2.

10. To find the absolute limits of the range of conditions under which the enzyme functions, under what additional conditions should experiments be performed?
    F. pH 3 and 25° C
    G. pH 1 and pH 9 at all temperatures
    H. pH 1 and pH 9 at 15° C
    J. pH 5 over a full range of temperatures

Passage 3

Experiments are done to study some of the factors that determine the rate of a reaction. When sulfuric acid acts on potassium iodate, elemental iodine is released. Elemental iodine signals its presence by turning starch blue.

Experiment 1

A test solution is made of sulfuric acid and soluble starch in water. If potassium iodate is added, iodine accumulates at some definite rate. When the iodine reaches a certain concentration, the solution suddenly turns blue. Various concentrations of potassium iodate solution are used, and the time required for the mixture to turn blue is measured.

Potassium iodate concentration (%)	Time (seconds)
10	18
9	20
8	22
7	24
6	26
5	29
4	32

Experiment 2

To determine the effect of temperature on reaction rate, a 5% solution of potassium iodate is added to the test solution at various temperatures.

Temperature (° C)	Time (seconds)
5	36
15	31
25	27
35	24
45	22

11. Starch was added to the solution because:
    A. it speeds the reaction that produces iodine.
    B. it provides a test for the presence of elemental iodine.
    C. it slows down the reaction so that the time becomes easily measurable.
    D. it prevents the sulfuric acid from destroying the potassium iodate.

12. Experiment 1 shows that:
  F. elemental iodine turns starch blue.
  G. at higher iodate concentration, iodine is liberated more quickly.
  H. the rate of the reaction depends on the concentration of sulfuric acid used.
  J. the release of elemental iodine occurs suddenly.

13. Experiment 2 is an example of a general rule that:
  A. higher concentrations speed reactions.
  B. higher concentrations slow down reactions.
  C. higher temperatures speed reactions.
  D. higher temperatures slow down reactions.

14. Experiment 1 was done at a temperature of about:
  F. 10° C
  G. 20° C
  H. 30° C
  J. 40° C

15. By studying the results of this experiment, what can be concluded as to the time the reaction would take at a temperature of −15° C?
  A. It would take about 48 seconds.
  B. It would take longer than 36 seconds, but it is impossible to predict how long.
  C. It is not possible to make any prediction because the results of the experiment are too scattered.
  D. It might take a long time, or the whole thing might freeze and stop the reaction.

16. About how long would it take for the starch to turn blue if a 10% solution of potassium iodate was used at 45° C?
  F. 15 seconds
  G. 18 seconds
  H. 22 seconds
  J. 29 seconds

Passage 4

The graphs below represent the percentages of fat and of water in the human body, by age and sex.

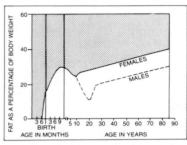
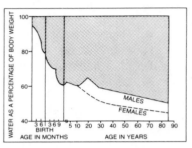

Illustration by Bob Conrad from "Fatness and Fertility," by Rose E. Frisch. Copyright © March 1988 by *Scientific American, Inc*. All rights reserved.

17. During the adolescent years, the most notable change is:
- **A.** a decrease in fat percentage for boys.
- **B.** an increase in fat percentage for girls.
- **C.** a decrease in water percentage for boys.
- **D.** an increase in water percentage for girls.

18. The percent of fat in the body increases most rapidly during:
- **F.** middle age.
- **H.** babyhood.
- **G.** adolescence.
- **J.** the prenatal period.

19. At age 60, the amount of water in the body of a 150-pound man is:
- **A.** the same as that in a 150-pound woman.
- **B.** twice as much as that in a 150-pound woman.
- **C.** about the same as that in a 140-pound woman.
- **D.** about the same as that in a 160-pound woman.

20. The percentage of body weight made up of both water and fat is:
- **F.** greater for females after adolescence.
- **G.** greater for males after adolescence.
- **H.** approximately the same for both sexes after adolescence only.
- **J.** approximately the same for both sexes at all ages after birth.

21. What hypothesis about the role of sex hormones might be advanced from the graphs?

    A. Both male and female sex hormones cause an increase in the percent of fat in the body.

    B. Male hormones cause a reduction in the percent of fat and in increase in the percent of water.

    C. Female hormones have a much greater influence than male hormones on the percent of water.

    D. Male hormones cause the growth of male secondary sex characteristics.

Passage 5

Seeds are tested for their ability to produce substances that kill microorganisms. Each seed is placed on a culture of the microorganism. Seeds are classified on a scale of 0 (no effect) to 5 (strong effect), according to the amount of microorganism-free space that develops around the seed.

Experiment 1

Seeds of two members of the Lily family are tested against four different microorganisms:

Microorganism	Lily Family	
	Garlic	Daylily
Staphylococcus	4	0
Escherichia	5	4
Bread mold	2	2
Penicillium mold	3	0

Experiment 2

The same experiment is repeated using seeds of two members of the Composite family:

Microorganism	Composite Family	
	Dandelion	Thistle
Staphylococcus	5	5
Escherichia	4	5
Bread mold	4	3
Penicillium mold	2	2

Experiment 3

The experiment is then done with two members of the Legume family:

Microorganism	Legume Family	
	Soybean	Alfalfa
Staphylococcus	0	0
Escherichia	4	2
Bread mold	2	3
Penicillium mold	3	4

22. Which of the microorganisms is most susceptible to attacks by the chemicals produced by seeds?
    F. *Staphylococcus*
    G. *Escherichia*
    H. Bread mold
    J. *Penicillium* mold

23. Of the following, which kind of seed is more effective against molds than against bacteria?
    A. Alfalfa
    C. Thistle
    B. Daylily
    D. Garlic

24. To find an antibiotic that will protect oranges against *Penicillium* mold, a scientist would concentrate on:
    F. seeds of the thistle and its close relatives.
    G. a variety of members of the Composite family.
    H. members of the Legume family.
    J. seeds of the daylily and its relatives.

25. What conclusion can be reached about bread mold?
    A. It can survive by attacking seeds.
    B. It is highly resistant to chemical poisoning.
    C. It cannot be destroyed by seeds of the Composite family.
    D. It is moderately susceptible to attack by many kinds of seeds.

26. What hint might a scientist trying to find an antibiotic to control *Staphylococcus* infections get from these experiments?

   F. Looking for seeds that produce such an antibiotic would be a waste of effort.

   G. It would be inadvisable to concentrate on seeds of the Legume family.

   H. It would be wise to concentrate on *Penicillium* mold and its close relatives.

   J. The scientist should not waste time trying the bread mold and its close relatives.

27. Which of the following ecological hypotheses is supported by the evidence of these experiments?

   A. Molds are better able to survive than bacteria wherever the two kinds of microorganisms compete.

   B. The Legume family produces valuable fodder crops because its seeds have a high survival rate.

   C. The bacteria *Escherichia* and *Staphylococcus* may be highly damaging to leguminous crops.

   D. The Composite family has so many successful sturdy weeds because its seeds destroy microorganisms.

Passage 6

Experiments are done to test the optical properties of lenses immersed in media having different indices of refraction.

Experiment 1

A lens made of flint glass, index of refraction 1.720, is tested. A beam of parallel light rays is sent into the lens, and the distance from the lens to the point of convergence of the beam is measured. This is the focal length of the lens. This focal length is measured with the lens immersed in media of various indices of refraction.

Medium	Index of refraction	Focal length (cm)
Air	1.00	8
Folinol	1.24	13
Water	1.33	20
11% Sugar solution	1.50	39
Carbon disulfide	1.62	95
Methylene iodide	1.74	*

Experiment 2

Another lens is tested. It is made of the same kind of glass as in Experiment 1, but this lens is thicker, more strongly curved.

Medium	Index of refraction	Focal length (cm)
Air	1.00	5
Folinol	1.24	8
Water	1.33	12
11% Sugar solution	1.50	24
Carbon disulfide	1.62	60
Methylene iodide	1.74	*

Experiment 3

A lens made of a new plastic is then tested. This lens is identical in size and shape to the glass lens in Experiment 2.

Medium	Index of refraction	Focal length (cm)
Air	1.00	13
Folinol	1.24	34
Water	1.33	360
11% Sugar solution	1.50	*
Carbon disulfide	1.62	*
Methylene iodide	1.74	*

*Rays do not converge at all.

28. The index of refraction column is the same in all three experiments because:

F. all three lenses have the same basic properties.

G. the same liquids are used in all three experiments.

H. the temperatures at which the experiments are performed are carefully controlled.

J. the color of the light source is not allowed to change from one experiment to another.

29. As the index of refraction of the medium increases, what happens to the rays of light emerging from the lens?

A. They converge more strongly in all cases.

B. They converge more strongly on leaving the glass lenses, but not the plastic lens.

C. They converge less strongly in all cases.

D. They converge less strongly on leaving the plastic lens, but not the glass lens.

30. Making a lens thicker and more strongly curved:

F. shortens the focal length.

G. increases the focal length.

H. increases the index of refraction.

J. decreases the index of refraction.

31. In Experiment 3, why do the rays not come to a focus at all when they pass through the lens into certain materials?

A. The index of refraction of each of those materials is greater than that of the lens.

B. The curvature of the lens is not great enough.

C. Chemical reactions turn some of those materials opaque.

D. In some materials, the light rays are unable to bend as they pass out of the lens.

32. Measurements of the kind made in these experiments would NOT be useful in efforts to find:

F. the index of refraction of a liquid.

G. the way a prism in a fluid would bend light rays.

H. the concentration of a sugar solution.

J. the chemical composition of an unknown liquid.

33. The index of refraction of the plastic lens in Experiment 3 must be:

A. less than 1.33.
B. between 1.33 and 1.50.
C. more than 1.33.
D. more than 1.50.

Passage 7

Is it important to keep the blood cholesterol level low and to lower it if it is too high? Two scientists express opposing opinions.

Scientist 1

Cholesterol is a substance, made in the liver, that is necessary for the normal chemical functioning of the body. It also enters the body in certain foods. Cholesterol circulates in the blood; when there is too much of it, it is deposited, with other fatty materials, inside the arteries of the heart. The resulting blockage of the blood flow is the leading cause of death in the United States.

It is now generally understood that high levels of cholesterol in the blood lead to heart trouble. The famous Framingham study, which followed the medical history of thousands of men for a period of many years, showed that men with cholesterol levels higher than 250 suffered fatal heart attacks at twice the rate of those at the 200 level. This has led to a massive program of public education, alerting physicians and the general public to the danger of high cholesterol levels in the blood. Now, when cholesterol level is above 200, the doctor will recommend a change in the diet, reducing the use of foods containing cholesterol and the saturated fats that promote the formation of cholesterol in the body. If dieting is unsuccessful, medication that reduces the cholesterol level is prescribed. Public awareness, along with changes in diet and medication where necessary, can make a significant contribution to the fight against death from heart disease.

Scientist 2

The evidence is now firm that lucky people with naturally low levels of cholesterol in their blood are less subject to heart attack than others. People with natural levels of 300 and over do indeed tend to die young of heart disease.

It does not follow that the twenty-five million Americans with cholesterol levels around 250 should take draconian measures to reduce this figure to 200. The body strongly resists the effort to reduce cholesterol level; the liver tries to maintain a constant level no matter what you do. The cholesterol-lowering diet rarely works, since it is severely restricted and must be adhered to rigorously. Patients are then put on medication that they must take for life, putting up with some rather unpleasant side effects.

Billions of research dollars have been spent in studying hundreds of thousands of men and women, but the research has never produced convincing evidence that all this effort pays off. In contrast, other studies have clearly shown that liability to heart attack is reduced by exercise and weight control, and increased by smoking. The drastic cholesterol-reducing regime can result in a somewhat lower rate of cardiac disease, although even this has not been shown consistently. From the start, all these studies show that medicating to lower the cholesterol level increases the death rate from stroke, colon and liver cancer, alcoholism, and clinical depression leading to suicide. The massive anti-cholesterol campaign turns healthy people into lifelong drug-takers, changing nothing but the profits of the drug companies and what it says on death certificates.

34. The two scientists agree that:

    F. high cholesterol levels tend to increase the danger of heart attack.

    G. efforts should be made to lower cholesterol levels down to about 200.

    H. it is a good idea to look for foods with reduced cholesterol, such as specially produced eggs.

    J. scientific research has produced clear guidelines as to how to deal with the cholesterol problem.

35. The chief piece of evidence given by Scientist 1 is a study showing that:

    A. certain drugs can reduce the level of cholesterol in the body.

    B. cholesterol in the blood produces deposits in the arteries of the heart.

    C. medically lowering the cholesterol level in the blood reduces the risk of heart attack.

    D. men with higher levels of blood cholesterol are more subject to heart disease.

36. Scientist 2 claims that Scientist 1's error is:

    F. misinterpretation of the Framingham study.

    G. ignorance of the metabolic functions of cholesterol.

    H. looking at the causes of death too narrowly.

    J. failure to study enough cases to reach a valid conclusion.

37. Neither scientist would dispute the statement that cholesterol is:

    A. a substance vitally necessary for the body's functions.

    B. a dangerous material that should be reduced in the blood.

    C. a substance that should be carefully monitored in the diet.

    D. a blood chemical that should be tested for at every physical examination.

38. What would Scientist 2 logically recommend concerning the current public information campaign alerting people to the dangers of high cholesterol level?

    F. It should be intensified so that it will produce maximum effect.

    G. It should be reevaluated in view of new information.

    H. It should be modified to emphasize the importance of good diet.

    J. It should attempt to concentrate on people with known heart problems.

39. For persons who wish to reduce their susceptibility to heart attack, which of the following recommendations would NOT be agreed to by both scientists?

A. Select foods with low cholesterol content.
B. Stop smoking.
C. Take off weight by controlling your diet.
D. Do a moderate amount of exercise.

40. In general, what is Scientist 2's attitude concerning the widespread high cholesterol levels in the blood of Americans?

F. It is not a health concern at all, so there should be no action in the public health domain.
G. Efforts should be made to have everyone tested for cholesterol level.
H. High cholesterol levels do in fact present a danger of heart disease, but no one has a good answer to the problem.
J. Further studies are needed to determine the cholesterol levels in the blood of the American population.

Answers to Science Reasoning Test on page 413.

ANSWER KEYS AND ANALYSIS CHARTS

Test 1: English

1.	B	20.	J	39.	B	58.	G
2.	J	21.	C	40.	J	59.	D
3.	B	22.	J	41.	B	60.	G
4.	G	23.	A	42.	J	61.	C
5.	D	24.	G	43.	B	62.	J
6.	H	25.	B	44.	H	63.	B
7.	C	26.	G	45.	B	64.	H
8.	F	27.	C	46.	H	65.	B
9.	A	28.	G	47.	B	66.	J
10.	J	29.	C	48.	J	67.	C
11.	C	30.	G	49.	C	68.	G
12.	G	31.	C	50.	H	69.	C
13.	C	32.	J	51.	A	70.	F
14.	J	33.	B	52.	H	71.	B
15.	D	34.	F	53.	C	72.	F
16.	G	35.	D	54.	G	73.	C
17.	B	36.	J	55.	C	74.	F
18.	H	37.	B	56.	F	75.	D
19.	D	38.	G	57.	C		

ANSWER ANALYSIS CHART			
Skills	**Questions**	**Possible Score**	**Your Score**
Usage/Mechanics			
Punctuation	7, 9, 12, 26, 29, 33, 44, 47, 50, 72	10	
Basic Grammar and Usage	3, 8, 23, 31, 34, 35, 37, 38, 39, 40, 41, 66	12	
Sentence Structure	6, 13, 14, 16, 17, 19, 20, 22, 32, 46, 55, 56, 57, 58, 62, 64, 67, 68	18	
Rhetorical Skills			
Strategy	2, 18, 25, 27, 36, 42, 43, 49, 53, 54, 70, 71	12	
Organization	5, 15, 24, 30, 45, 59, 60, 63, 73, 74, 75	11	
Style	1, 4, 10, 11, 21, 28, 48, 51, 52, 61, 65, 69	12	

Total: 75   _____

Percent Correct: _____

Test 2: Mathematics

1.	**C**	16.	**H**	31.	**B**	46.	**H**
2.	**J**	17.	**D**	32.	**K**	47.	**D**
3.	**A**	18.	**J**	33.	**D**	48.	**G**
4.	**K**	19.	**A**	34.	**G**	49.	**E**
5.	**B**	20.	**J**	35.	**E**	50.	**H**
6.	**K**	21.	**C**	36.	**G**	51.	**D**
7.	**B**	22.	**K**	37.	**E**	52.	**J**
8.	**G**	23.	**C**	38.	**F**	53.	**B**
9.	**B**	24.	**K**	39.	**E**	54.	**G**
10.	**J**	25.	**D**	40.	**J**	55.	**B**
11.	**D**	26.	**K**	41.	**D**	56.	**J**
12.	**G**	27.	**D**	42.	**H**	57.	**A**
13.	**E**	28.	**H**	43.	**E**	58.	**H**
14.	**F**	29.	**D**	44.	**K**	59.	**E**
15.	**D**	30.	**J**	45.	**A**	60.	**F**

ANSWER ANALYSIS CHART					
Content Area	**Skill Level**			**Possible Score**	**Your Score**
	Basic Skills	**Application**	**Analysis**		
Pre-Algebra Algebra	1, 4, 5, 9, 10, 14, 21, 44	2, 6, 7, 17, 22, 24, 27, 32, 34, 37, 38, 43	3, 11, 12, 15	24	
Intermediate Algebra Coordinate Geometry	13, 20, 30, 31, 39, 46, 53	8, 16, 19, 23, 26, 28, 33	29, 41, 54, 56	18	
Geometry	18, 35, 42, 49, 51, 57, 59	25, 40, 45, 47, 48, 58, 60		14	
Trigonometry	36, 50	52, 55		4	

Total: 60 _____

Percent Correct: _____

Test 3: Reading

1.	B	11.	A	21.	D	31.	A
2.	J	12.	H	22.	G	32.	J
3.	C	13.	D	23.	C	33.	C
4.	F	14.	F	24.	G	34.	J
5.	C	15.	C	25.	A	35.	D
6.	G	16.	H	26.	H	36.	H
7.	C	17.	D	27.	B	37.	C
8.	G	18.	F	28.	J	38.	H
9.	D	19.	B	29.	C	39.	A
10.	F	20.	F	30.	H	40.	G

ANSWER ANALYSIS CHART

Passage Type	Referring	Reasoning	Possible Score	Your Score
Prose Fiction	21, 22, 24 25	23, 26, 27, 28 29, 30	10	
Humanities	32, 35, 39	31, 33, 34, 36, 37, 38, 40	10	
Social Sciences	1, 4, 9	2, 3, 5, 6, 7, 8, 10	10	
Natural Sciences	12, 14, 15, 19	11, 13, 16, 17, 18, 20	10	

Total: 40 _____

Percent Correct: _____

Test 4: Science Reasoning

1.	C	11.	B	21.	B	31.	A
2.	F	12.	G	22.	G	32.	J
3.	D	13.	C	23.	A	33.	B
4.	F	14.	G	24.	H	34.	F
5.	A	15.	D	25.	D	35.	D
6.	J	16.	F	26.	G	36.	H
7.	D	17.	A	27.	D	37.	A
8.	G	18.	J	28.	G	38.	G
9.	C	19.	D	29.	C	39.	A
10.	H	20.	J	30.	F	40.	H

ANSWER ANALYSIS CHART					
Kind of Question	**Skill Level**			**Possible Score**	**Your Score**
	Under-standing	**Analysis**	**General-ization**		
Data Representation	1, 6, 17, 18, 19	2, 3, 7, 8, 20	4, 5, 9, 10 21	15	
Research Summaries	11, 12, 14, 22, 23, 28, 29	13, 24, 25 30, 31	15, 16, 26, 27, 32, 33	18	
Conflicting Viewpoints	34, 35, 36	37, 38	39, 40	7	

Total: 40   _____

Percent Correct: _____

See **"Evaluating Your Performance"** on page 440.

Answer Explanations   Test 1: English

1. **(D)** All meanings carried by the underlined portion are implicit in the words preceding it. The entire portion is redundant.

2. **(J)** The quotation is pertinent, short, and authoritative. As such, it is a sound way to begin the passage.

3. **(B)** The antecedent of the pronoun in question is the singular *someone.*

4. **(G)** The phrase *lacking merit* at the end of the clause is adequate characterization of the type of case under discussion.

5. **(D)** As idealistic as the thought is, it is off the topic and has no place in this passage.

6. **(H)** The logic of this sentence requires that a transitional word indicating *cause* be employed in this spot.

7. **(C)** Three or more items in a series must be set off by commas.

8. **(F)** The phrase *changing attorneys* is a gerund phrase, that is, a *noun* phrase. Since it is an activity of the noun *client,* that noun requires the possessive apostrophe and final *s.*

9. (A) Dashes are appropriate marks to set off a parenthetical phrase, especially if one intends to emphasize the phrase.

10. (J) All other options are wordy or redundant.

11. (C) Colloquial and whimsical language is not in keeping with the matter-of-fact tone of the passage.

12. (G) Coordinate clauses must be separated by a comma.

13. (C) A new sentence begins at this point.

14. (J) At this spot a third noun—namely, *premium*—should parallel the objects *salary* and *rent*.

15. (D) Paragraph 3 begins with a clear signal that it should follow paragraph 4 rather than precede it, specifically the word *Finally.*

16. (G) The adverb *more* and the comparative adverb ending *-er* are equivalent, and cannot be used together. The result is a double comparison.

17. (B) The subject of this clause is the singular *person.*

18. (H) There is no suggestion or clue to suggest that the passage is intended for any one group.

19. (D) As it stands, the text contains a comma splice at this point; of the options, only the period break is correct.

20. (J) The present-tense, passive-voice verb is appropriate because the focus is on the toys, and the passage is written in the present tense. As it stands, this is a sentence fragment.

21. (C) The fact that the sentence later mentions that the rooms are "slightly askew" is reason enough to avoid the modifiers of the word *rooms.*

22. (J) The logic of this sentence requires that a conjunction indicating time be used at this transition; *when* is the only choice that makes sense.

23. (A) The verb agrees with the nearer subject (two) and is in the present tense.

24. (G) As interesting as the information may be, this sentence is wholly off the topic, and must be removed.

25. (B) The notion of children marking their territory with smudges and smears is humorous and whimsical. The other options do not suggest humor.

26. (G) A compound adjective preceding the noun it modifies is hyphenated, but the two words before *homes* do not comprise a compound adjective; one, *finely,* is an adverb modifying the adjective *furnished.*

27. (C)   The enormous difference in the size of these paragraphs, as well as the amount of data they contain, shows the writer's bias.

28. (G)   The noun *difference* clearly indicates that two kinds of people are being compared; *distinguishing* is not needed.

29. (C)   A compound adjective that *precedes* the noun is hyphenated; one that *follows* the noun usually is not.

30. (G)   The word *Conversely* is a clue that paragraph 2 must occur after paragraph 3; the words *another great difference* at the outset of paragraph 4 place it after paragraph 2.

31. (C)   The subject of the sentence is the singular noun *idea.* The prepositional phrase *of a community among nations* is a modifier of that noun. When the entire passage is read, it becomes apparent that the present tense is correct.

32. (J)   The only tense that conveys past action over a span of time to the present is the present perfect tense of the verb, that is, *have had.*

33. (B)   The parenthetical phrase *a free association based on shared principles and an increasingly shared way of life* has been set off by dashes rather than by brackets, an option generally chosen by writers to emphasize a phrase. There must be a dash at the end as well as the beginning of the phrase.

34. (F)   When a collective noun such as *people* clearly refers to individual members of a group, it takes a plural pronoun. Here the plural verbs *argue* and *choose* indicate reference to individuals.

35. (D)   The subject of the verb is the plural noun *ideals.* The prepositional phrase *of freedom* is a modifier of that noun.

36. (J)   The writer is attempting to establish a precedent for nations to join forces; reference to the cooperation of Greek city-states is logical and meaningful.

37. (B)   When a sentence has two or more subjects joined by *and,* the verb almost always is in the plural form. The present tense is correct.

38. (G)   Here the past participle of the verb *to shake* acts as an adjective modifying the noun *heritage.*

39. (B) The subjects of this verb are the plural nouns *graves* and *camps*, not the noun *Reich*, which is part of a prepositional phrase modifying the noun *camps*.

40. (J) An adverb is needed to modify the participle *standing*. Choice G is wordy; *mute* and *silent* (H) mean the same thing.

41. (B) The antecedent of the pronoun is the singular noun *regime*, not the pronoun *they*.

42. (J) The Berlin Wall is a very direct example of the evidence mentioned in the paragraph's first sentence, and the reference is therefore meaningful.

43. (B) The statement is followed by a list that supports the assertion that the number of "like-minded nations" is increasing.

44. (H) A colon is often used to introduce an appositive more dramatically or emphatically at the end of a sentence. A comma would be ineffective here.

45. (B) The first paragraph introduces the notion of "a community among nations." Perusal of the passage quickly reveals that paragraph 4 begins with the words *This community* and belongs in position 2. Paragraphs 2 and 3 follow with appropriate clues at the beginning of each ("our community" and "other evidence") which point to the preceding paragraph.

46. (H) This verb must be in the present tense to express what is still true.

47. (B) The name *Antonia Shimerda* is in apposition with *protagonist* and is properly set off with two commas.

48. (J) The adjective *actual* is the only choice that indicates what is intended, that the girl was a genuine Bohemian girl. The other choices are either redundant or misleading.

49. (C) This "summary" is inconclusive; it should include more information about the story.

50. (H) Commas and periods are *always* placed *inside* quotation marks, even when there are single and double quotation marks because the sentence contains a quote within a quote.

51. (A) The word *albeit* means literally "although it be," a meaning that is required for the sense of the clause to remain intact, and which is not repeated in the other options.

52. (H) The prefix *multi* is most often incorporated with another word as a unit.

53. (C) Since the paragraph deals with Cather's preference in the novel to the country over the city, and since the entire passage is about the novel *My Antonia,* the quotation is clearly meaningful.

54. (G) This passage represents a relatively concentrated discussion of other critical works, and is likely to interest only readers who are knowledgeable about and interested in critical essays.

55. (C) The passage is written in the present tense, and employs the historical present whenever necessary.

56. (F) *Employed* in this sentence is a participle modifying the noun *symbols.*

57. (C) To be parallel with the phrases naming the first two cycles, this one must begin with the noun *cycle,* rather than a clause describing it.

58. (G) Only the comma, introducing a nonrestrictive clause, is correct. Choice F results in a sentence fragment beginning with *In which*, and neither the semicolon (H) or the dash (J) is appropriate.

59. (D) The body of the paragraph does a comprehensive job of developing the beginning generalization.

60. (G) Paragraph 2 begins with broad, general statements about the novel, and spells out what the passage will be about. Accordingly, it is the introductory paragraph, and is logically followed by paragraph 3, which develops the critical analysis begun at the end of paragraph 2. The summary paragraph logically follows.

61. (C) The word *concrete* is clear; added words with the same meaning are unproductive and uneconomical.

62. (J) The adjective *clear* is meant to modify the noun *notion* and so must be placed before it. When *clear* is placed in other positions, it modifies other nouns and creates confusion.

63. (B) The introductory paragraph of this passage might well have spelled out the meaning of *translating philosophy into concrete action,* rather than leaving the expression in its somewhat unclear form.

64. (H) In its original form, this sentence creates an error in *predication,* that is, an error in which the beginning of the sentence is not consistent with the end.

65. (B) The other choices are colloquial and inconsistent with the rather formal and businesslike tone of the passage.

66. (J) The pronoun *this* almost never is adequate by itself; it must be followed by a noun for clarity of meaning.

67. (C) Any mark of punctuation weaker than a period or semi-colon creates a run-on sentence. Two completely independent clauses are joined here.

68. (G) The logic of the sentence requires a conjunction signaling *condition,* such as *if,* in this spot. Conjunctions signaling other logical shifts, like *contrast* (F or H) or *restriction* (J) render the sentence meaningless.

69. (C) There is no point in repeating the meaning of a word redundantly. The word *nation* is clear; neither its meaning nor the meaning of the sentence is enriched or clarified by the additions of synonyms.

70. (F) The passage is clearly an attempt to demonstrate a peaceful foreign policy to the world.

71. (B) The attempt in this sentence and throughout the passage is to persuade more conservative Americans that we cannot be what we were after World War II.

72. (F) Coordinate clauses, that is, independent clauses joined together by a coordinating conjunction (*and, but, for, or, yet*), are separated by a comma.

73. (C) As truthful as the statement may be, and as related to world politics, it has nothing to do with the point of the passage and must be removed.

74. (F) The passage progresses from the statement that *We have now grown beyond the era* (of unchallenged power) to the recognition that *we must move toward appreciation* (of our role as conciliators).

75. (D) The clue at the beginning of paragraph 3, *At the outset,* indicates the placement of the paragraph just after the introduction. The beginning of paragraph 2 is meaningful only if one has read paragraph 3.

Answer Explanations   Test 2: Mathematics

1. (C) $\dfrac{a}{b} - \dfrac{c}{d} = \dfrac{ad}{bd} - \dfrac{bc}{bd}$

$\qquad\qquad = \dfrac{ad - bc}{bd}$

2. (J) First factor the numerator.

$\qquad \dfrac{2x^4 + x^3}{x^6} = \dfrac{x^3(2x + 1)}{x^6}$ Cancel x^3.

$\qquad\qquad\qquad = \dfrac{2x + 1}{x^3}$

3. (A) $\qquad \dfrac{3}{4}(1600) = 1200$ phones have dials.

$\qquad \dfrac{1}{3}(1200) = 400$ dial phones are replaced by push-button phones.

$\qquad 1200 - 400 = 800$ dial phones remain.

4. (K) $\dfrac{x}{y}$ is not necessarily an integer.

5. (B) For example: $5 - (-7) = 12$, which is positive.

6. (K) Multiply both sides by $4x - 3$.
$\quad$($\dfrac{3}{4}$ is a restricted value.)

$\qquad\qquad \dfrac{4}{4x - 3}(4x - 3) = 5(4x - 3)$

$\qquad\qquad\qquad\qquad 5 = 5(4x - 3) = 20x - 15$

$\qquad\qquad\qquad\quad 20 = 20x$

$\qquad\qquad\qquad\quad\ x = 1$

7. (B) Ten times the tens digit plus the units digit: $10t + u$.

8. (G) Multiply each term of the first polynomial times each term of the second polynomial.
$(x - 1)(x^2 + x + 1)$
$= x^3 + x^2 + x - x^2 - x - 1$
$= x^3 - 1$

9. (B) Divide 3 by 2. The quotient is 1 and the remainder is 1. The base two numeral is $11_{(two)} = 1(2) + 1$.

10. (J)

$$2.5\% = 0.025$$
$$\frac{1}{40} = 0.025$$
$$2.5(10^{-2}) = 0.025$$
$$\frac{75}{30} = 2.5$$

11. (D) Each apple costs $\frac{100}{3} = 33\frac{1}{3}$ in the 3 for \$1.00 deal. The difference between 35 cents and $33\frac{1}{3}$ is $1\frac{2}{3}$ cents.

12. (G) In 1 minute Joan can run $\frac{1}{a}$ part of a mile. After b minutes, she has run $b\frac{1}{a} = \frac{b}{a}$.

13. (E) Division by 0 is never allowed.

14. (F) $3\frac{3}{5} \cdot 4\frac{1}{6} = \frac{18}{5} \cdot \frac{25}{6}$

$$= \frac{3}{1} \cdot \frac{5}{1} \quad \text{Cancel.}$$
$$= 15$$

15. (D) Write two equations with two variables, n and d.

$$n = d + 5$$
$$5n + 10d = 130 \quad \text{Then substitute for } n.$$
$$5(d + 5) + 10d = 130$$
$$5d + 25 + 10d = 130$$
$$15d + 25 = 130$$
$$15d = 105$$
$$d = 7$$

Then $n = 12$.

16. (H) In an arithmetic sequence, the nth term is given by

$$a_n = a_1 + (n - 1)d$$

in which a_1 is the first term, n is the number of the term, and d is the common difference between terms. In the given sequence the tenth term is sought and the common difference is 5.

$$a_{10} = 3 + (10 - 1)5 = 3 + 45 = 48$$

17. (D) First multiply by 100 to get rid of the decimals.

$$
\begin{aligned}
100[0.2(100 - x) + 0.05x] &= 100[0.1(100)] \\
20(100 - x) + 5x &= 10(100) \\
2000 - 20x + 5x &= 1000 \\
-15x &= -1000 \\
x &= 66\tfrac{2}{3}
\end{aligned}
$$

18. (J) There certainly is a regular polygon of seven sides.

19. (A) $\sqrt[3]{54x^4y^6} = \sqrt[3]{27x^3y^6 \cdot 2x}$ Separate the radicand into cube and noncube parts.

$$= 3xy^2\sqrt[3]{2x}$$

20. (J) Conic sections are second-degree (or less) curves only. The equation $y = x^3$ is not of degree 2.

21. (C) The degree of a polynomial is the greatest of the degrees of its terms. The degrees of the terms of the given polynomial are 3, 4, 2, and 0. The greatest degree is 4.

22. (K) Add.

$$
\begin{aligned}
2x - y &= 5 \\
x + y &= 1 \\
\hline
3x &= 6 \\
x &= 2
\end{aligned}
$$

Substitute $x = 2$ into either equation (say the second one).

$$
\begin{aligned}
2 + y &= 1 \\
y &= -1
\end{aligned}
$$

23. (C) The numbers 2, 4, 6, and 8 satisfy the conditions of being even and less than 10. $P(A) = \frac{4}{20} = \frac{1}{5}$.

24. (K) Multiply the numerator and denominator by the LCD, which is xy.

$$\frac{xy(x + y)}{xy\left(\dfrac{1}{x} + \dfrac{1}{y}\right)} = \frac{xy(x + y)}{y + x}$$

$$= xy$$

25. (D) Inscribed angle ABC intercepts an arc that is twice the measure of the angle, so arc ADC measures 140° and the measure of arc ABC is $(360 - 140)° = 220°$. The measure of inscribed angle ADC is half the measure of its intercepted arc: 110°. (Opposite angles of an inscribed quadrilateral are supplementary.)

26. (K) Since $a > b$, then $a - b > 0$ and $b - a < 0$. The absolute value of a positive number is equal to that number, but the absolute value of a negative number is the opposite of the number.

$|a - b| = a - b$ and $|b - a|$
$= -(b - a) = a - b$.
$|a - b| + |b - a| = (a - b) + (a - b) = 2a - 2b$.

27. (D) The expression -3^{-2} is properly read as "the opposite of 3 to the -2 power." Follow the rules for the order of operations:

$$-3^{-2} = -(3^{-2}) = -\left(\frac{1}{3^2}\right) = -\left(\frac{1}{9}\right)$$

28. (H) To put this equation into standard form, complete the square in both variables.

$$(x^2 - 4x \quad\quad) + 4(y^2 + 6y \quad\quad) = -36$$
$$(x^2 - 4x + 4) + 4(y^2 + 6y + 9) = -36 + 4 + 36$$
$$(x - 2)^2 + 4(y + 3)^2 = 4$$
$$\frac{(x - 2)^2}{4} + \frac{(y + 3)^2}{1} = 1$$

The center is $(2, -3)$.

29. (D) This is a work-type word problem, for which the formula $w = rt$ applies. Let Bonnie's time to complete the job be x

hours, then Nick's time is $x - 2$ hours. Her rate of work is $\frac{1}{x}$ part of the job per hour. His rate is $\frac{1}{x-2}$.

	w	$=$	r	t
Nick	$\frac{7}{x-2}$		$\frac{1}{x-2}$	7
Bonnie	$\frac{7}{x}$		$\frac{1}{x}$	7

The sum of the work column is equal to 1 (one completed job). The equation is

$$\frac{7}{x-2} + \frac{7}{x} = 1.$$

30. (J) A function is one-to-one if all of the ordered pairs in the function not only have different first components but also have different second components. This means that the graph must pass both the vertical line test and the horizontal line test. If a vertical line crosses the graph once at most, then it is a function. If a horizontal line crosses the graph once at most, then the function is one-to-one (and thus it has an inverse). Only J satisfies both tests.

31. (B) An exponential function is any function of the type:
$$f(x) = a^x, \text{ for } a > 0, a \neq 1.$$

32. (K) $(5x - 3y^2)^2 = 25x^2 - 30xy^2 + 9y^4$.

33. (D) The reciprocal of i is $\frac{1}{i}$. Multiply both numerator and denominator by the conjugate of the denominator $-i$: $\frac{-i(1)}{-i(i)}$.

$$\frac{-i}{1} = -i$$

34. (G) $\dfrac{a^{-3}bc^2}{a^{-4}b^2c^{-3}} = a^{-3-(-4)}b^{1-2}c^{2-(-3)}$
$$= a^1 b^{-1} c^5$$
$$= \frac{ac^5}{b}$$

35. (E) The length of the longer leg of a 30-60-90 triangle is equal to $\sqrt{3}$ times the length of the shorter leg, and the length of the hypotenuse is twice the length of the shorter leg. The length of the longer leg is given, so to find the length of the shorter leg divide by $\sqrt{3}$.

$$BC = \frac{6}{\sqrt{3}} = 2\sqrt{3}$$

Therefore $AB = 2(2\sqrt{3}) = 4\sqrt{3}$

36. (G) The identity is $\sin 2A = 2 \sin A \cos A$.

37. (E) Use the quadratic formula:

$$x = \frac{-b \pm \sqrt{b^2 - 4ac}}{2a}$$

Here

$$x = \frac{4 \pm \sqrt{16 - (-72)}}{6}$$

$$= \frac{4 \pm \sqrt{88}}{6} = \frac{4 \pm 2\sqrt{22}}{6} = \frac{2 \pm \sqrt{22}}{3}$$

38. (F) $3\sqrt{3} - \sqrt{48} + 3\sqrt{\frac{1}{3}} = 3\sqrt{3} - 4\sqrt{3} + \sqrt{3}$

$$= 0$$

39. (E) The two ordered pairs (4, 2) and (4, −2) both satisfy the equation $x = y^2$, and so it does not define a function.

40. (J) The length of a tangent is the mean proportional between the length of a secant from a common external point and the length of the secant's external segment.

$$\frac{x + 4}{6} = \frac{6}{4}$$

$$\begin{aligned} 4x + 16 &= 36 \\ 4x &= 20 \\ x &= 5 \end{aligned}$$

41. (D) This is a uniform motion-type word problem, for which the formula $d = rt$ applies.

D	=	r	t
Bike	x	12	$\dfrac{x}{12}$
Car	x	36	$\dfrac{x}{36}$

The time for the car trip is $\frac{1}{2}$ hour less than the time for the bike trip. The equation is:

$$\frac{x}{36} = \frac{x}{12} - \frac{1}{2}$$

42. (H) The midpoint formula is $\left(\dfrac{x_1 + x_2}{2}, \dfrac{y_1 + y_2}{2}\right)$

Here

$$\left(\frac{3 + (-5)}{2}, \frac{7 + (-6)}{2}\right) = \left(-1, \frac{1}{2}\right)$$

43. (E) A square root radical by definition is positive. The solution set is empty.

44. (K) All these statements are true.

45. (A) The diagram shows a 30-60-90 triangle with the hypotenuse equal in length to the radius of the circle, the length of the shorter leg half the length of the hypotenuse, and the length of the longer leg $\sqrt{3}$ times the length of the shorter leg. The perimeter of the triangle is equal to 6 times the length of the longer leg of the triangle.

$6(4\sqrt{3}) = 24\sqrt{3}$

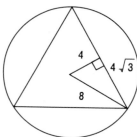

46. (H) The domain contains all real numbers except those for which the denominator is zero. Set the denominator equal to zero and solve.

$$x^2 - 2x - 3 = 0$$
$$(x - 3)(x + 1) = 0$$
$$x - 3 = 0 \qquad x + 1 = 0$$
$$x = 3 \qquad x = -1$$

47. (D) Draw the line of centers and a line parallel to $\overline{CD}$ through B $(\overline{BE} \parallel \overline{CD})$. The length of $\overline{AB}$ is the sum of the lengths of the radii of the circles. A radius of a circle is perpendicular to a tangent at the point of tangency. Therefore $BCDE$ is a rectangle.

$BC = 3$, so $DE = 3$.
$AD = 5$, so $AE = 2$.

Apply the Pythagorean Theorem to right triangle ABE.

$$(BE)^2 + 2^2 = 8^2$$
$$(BE)^2 + 4 = 64$$
$$(BE)^2 = 60$$
$$BE = \sqrt{60} = 2\sqrt{15}$$

And $BE = CD = 2\sqrt{15}$.

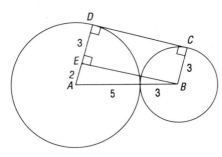

48. (G) The measure of inscribed angle C is half the measure of its intercepted arc BAD.

$$m \angle C = \tfrac{1}{2}(180 + m \text{ arc } AB)$$
$$125 = \tfrac{1}{2}(180 + m \text{ arc } AB)$$
$$250 = 180 + m \text{ arc } AB$$
$$m \text{ arc } AB = 70$$

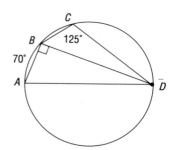

Therefore arc $BCD = 180 - 70 = 110$. The measure of inscribed angle A is half the measure of its intercepted arc.

$$m \angle A = \tfrac{1}{2}(110) = 55.$$

49. (E) There is not enough information to answer this question uniquely.

50. (H) The distance from the origin to A is $r = \sqrt{(-3)^2 + 4^2} = 5$.

The definition of $\sec \theta$ is $\frac{r}{x}$, so $\sec \theta = \frac{5}{-3}$

51. (D) $\displaystyle\sum_{k=1}^{5} 2k^2 = 2 \cdot 1^2 + 2 \cdot 2^2 + 2 \cdot 3^2$
$+ 2 \cdot 4^2 + 2 \cdot 5^2$
$= 2 + 8 + 18 + 32 + 50 = 110$

52. (J) Cosine is positive in quadrants I and IV; cotangent is negative in quadrants II and IV. There is an angle in quadrant IV that satisfies the given conditions.

53. (B) A Venn diagram will help clarify these statements. The statement in B, $(A \cap B) \subseteq B$, is true. Every element in the intersection of sets A and B is contained in B.

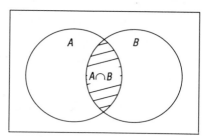

54. (G) Let one side be x; then the other side is $x + 1$. Use the Pythagorean Theorem:

$$x^2 + (x + 1)^2 = (\sqrt{145})^2$$
$$x^2 + x^2 + 2x + 1 = 145$$
$$2x^2 + 2x - 144 = 0$$
$$x^2 + x - 72 = 0$$
$$(x + 9)(x - 8) = 0$$

$x + 9 = 0$	$x - 8 = 0$
$x = -9$ (extraneous)	$0 - x = 0$

Then $x + 1 = 8 + 1 = 9$.

$x + 1$

55. (B) Think of $\cos^{-1} \frac{2}{3}$ as an angle, θ. Then the question asks for $\sin \theta$, where θ is the angle whose cosine is $\frac{2}{3}$. This angle is in quadrant I.

$$\sin \theta = +\sqrt{1 - \cos^2 \theta}$$

$$= \sqrt{1 - \left(\frac{2}{3}\right)^2} = \sqrt{1 - \frac{4}{9}}$$

$$= \sqrt{\frac{5}{9}} = \frac{\sqrt{5}}{3}$$

56. (J) Let x be the score on the fourth test. Then

$$\frac{75 + 84 + 80 + x}{4} \geq 80$$
$$239 + x \geq 320$$
$$x \geq 81$$

57. (A) The sum of the exterior angles of any polygon is 360°. In a regular polygon the angles have the same measure, so one exterior angle of a regular octagon is $\frac{360°}{8} = 45°$.

58. (H) The diagonals of a rhombus are perpendicular bisectors of each other. Therefore in right triangle ABE, $AE = 4$ and $BE = 3$. Use the Pythagorean Theorem.
$$(AB)^2 = 4^2 + 3^2 = 16 + 9 = 25$$
$$AB = 5$$
The perimeter of the rhombus is $4(5) = 20$.

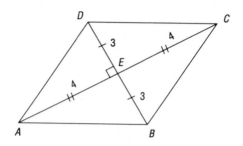

59. (E) All these statements are false.

60. (F) The length of the altitude of a right triangle is the mean proportional between the lengths of the two segments of the hypotenuse.

$$\frac{x}{4} = \frac{4}{10 - x}$$
$$x(10 - x) = 16$$
$$10x - x^2 = 16$$
$$0 = x^2 - 10x + 16$$
$$(x - 8)(x - 2) = 0$$

$x - 8 = 0$ $x - 2 = 0$
$x = 8$ (extraneous) $x = 2$

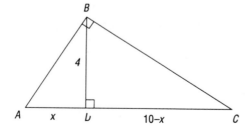

Answer Explanations   Test 3: Reading

1. (B) Lines 7–8 state that the "weight of society has been traditionally on the side of the oppressor."

2. (J) Lines 17–20 suggest that police and others believe that abused women often provoke violent behavior in men.

3. (C) The clause implies that police, prosecutors, and judges sometimes contribute to the victim's feelings of helplessness.

4. (F) Reconciliation is not mentioned among the reasons listed in the third paragraph.

5. (C) Line 37 suggests that, if possible, the wife should seek refuge in a shelter for battered women.

6. (G) Lines 53–56 state that battered women need help to use the enormous strength they have for self-preservation.

7. (C) Most of the passage deals with the problems confronting abused women.

8. (G) The passage emphasizes financial hardships faced by abused women.

9. (D) This is not indicated by the passage.

10. (F) Lines 71–72 imply that the court should be used only as a last resort.

11. (A) A newborn averages 20 inches, a one-year old, 30 inches. Therefore, a child grows almost a foot during the first year of life.

12. (H) At age two children reach approximately half their adult height. A six-foot adult, therefore, was about 36 inches tall at age two.

13. (D) Lines 9–11 indicate the rapidity at which young children grow. Growth begins to slow down after the fourth month of life.

14. (F) Lines 50–53 discuss the fact that females are biologically older than males.

15. (C) Lines 48–49 state that *biological* age is merely another term for *bone* age.

16. (H) The first paragraph says that "normal growth before puberty is dependent . . . on the life a child leads," which includes diet and nutrition.

17. (D) The passage implies that centers of ossification are the rigid segments of bone which grow in size and number as a person matures.

18. (F) A child's depressed growth can be investigated and corrected at any time, according to lines 30–32.

19. (B) Normal growth prior to puberty depends on the life a child leads; after puberty, genetic influence is greater, according to lines 4–7.

20. (F) The fact that sophisticated techniques for studying human growth are presently being used at various research centers suggests that traditional studies have not yielded as much data as scientists had hoped.

21. (D) This answer is correct because Mr. Pontellier finds it discouraging that his wife seems so uninterested in what he tells her (lines 12–14). Choice A may be true, but Mr. Pontellier is already in a bad mood when he discovers Raoul's fever. B is wrong because he wakes her without a second thought. C does not seem to disturb him.

22. (G) This answer is indicated by lines 72–73. She would have stayed longer if the mosquitoes had not been biting. F is incorrect because Mrs. Pontellier does not feel better. H and J are not mentioned in the passage.

23. (C) Lines 79–80 suggest Mr. Pontellier's enthusiasm for work in the city. A is wrong. Mr. Pontellier smokes, but the passage says nothing about his enjoying it. B and D are what Mr. Pontellier does out of duty, not enjoyment.

24. (G) Mr. Pontellier reproaches his wife (lines 30–32) for neglecting the children. F is something Mr. Pontellier may think, but he doesn't say so to his wife. H is something that Mr. Pontellier says sarcastically; he knows it's not true. J is not a topic about which Mr. Pontellier scolds.

25. (A) A is correct because Mrs. Pontellier knows that her son is not sick (lines 25–26). B, C, and D are all implied by Mrs. P's thoughts as she weeps on the porch in the middle of the night.

26. (H) H is correct. Sending a box of exotic food is what he thinks a husband ought to do. It's not a gesture of affection, support, or remorse, as suggested by F, G, or J.

27. (B) B is the best answer. Descriptions of Mr. Pontellier throughout the passage suggest that he is a busy man and has more important things to worry about. A is wrong because he is not at all careless—thoughtless perhaps, but not careless. C is not mentioned. D is not suggested. He loves his sons as much as he is expected to.

28. (J) J suggests the cause of Mrs. Pontellier's plight throughout the passage—that she is discontent with the role society has given her. F, G, and H may all be true, but they are not the main cause of Mrs. Pontellier's dissatisfaction.

29. (C) Mr. Pontellier recognizes that he gave his wife a paltry sum of money, certainly not enough to buy Sister Janet a gift. A is not suggested, nor are B and D.

30. (H) This choice best sums up Mrs. Pontellier's feelings. It's difficult to explain discontent with a husband who on the surface does whatever all he is supposed to do. F, G, and J are all true but do not explain why Mrs. Pontellier agrees with her friends.

31. (A) Items 5 and 6 (lines 63–69) imply that a constructed language is derived from several existing languages or is built from scratch. Either way, it must differ from any existing language.

32. (J) Lines 80–83 say that some 3,000 natural languages and at least 1,000 constructed languages exist.

33. (C) The premise implied throughout the passage is that mankind will be better off with a universal language. Choices A and B are too specific. Choice D refers to Comenius's proposal, which did *not* call for a universal language.

34. (J) Because the words of Wilkins' language (lines 17–21) were newly coined, the language is considered a constructed language.

35. (D) Lines 72–77 argue that there are plenty of languages to choose from for a universal tongue, but an agreement about which to use remains a major stumbling block.

36. (H) Lines 6–11 explain that Descartes' logical scheme failed to reflect the way actual languages are constructed.

37. (C) Lines 29–30 say that the type of solution proposed by Comenius is "still widely advocated today."

38. (H) Of the six types of languages listed between lines 38 and 72, four are based on existing languages.

39. (A) Lines 12–14 state that Descartes' contemporaries offered proposals because Descartes failed to offer an example of his scheme for them to consider.

40. (G) Lines 14–17 make the point that languages built solely on logic won't work because they lack the familiarity and ease of natural languages.

Answer Explanations   Test 4: Science Reasoning

1. (C) On the graph marked 21% oxygen, the point at about 250 ppm CO_2 corresponds to about 37 μg CO_2 per minute. Multiplying by 60 gives the amount taken up in an hour.

2. (F) All of the graphs show rising values toward the right, where the CO_2 concentration is rising. Comparing the graphs with each other shows that the highest values of uptake occur with the upper graphs, where O_2 concentration is smallest.

3. (D) All four graphs reach zero uptake at some minimum value of CO_2 concentration. A is wrong because there is no evidence dealing with a complete absence of oxygen. B is wrong because all graphs show that the rate increases as CO_2 concentration goes up. C is wrong because there is no reason to believe that the graph for 40% oxygen keeps going up indefinitely.

4. (F) The excess of production over uptake of CO_2 is shown by only one data point, but there is no reason to doubt that it would occur if readings were taken at 40% O_2, 25 ppm CO_2. And how about 99% O_2? G is wrong because the data show that CO_2 uptake goes down when O_2 rises. H is wrong because it is possible that at high O_2 level, CO_2 is depleted in the air. And one graph shows that uptake of CO_2 increases when the concentration is high.

5. (A) The data in the graph show that at any oxygen concentration, plants will take up more CO_2 as the amount in the air rises. If they grow more, they take up still more.

6. (J) Greatest activity means the shortest time for complete digestion, and the 26 minutes at pH6 and 20°C is the shortest time of all.

7. (D) The enzyme is probably most active at the temperature in which the fish thrives, which is a warm 20°C. The optimum pH is neither very strongly acid nor strongly basic; this is probably irrelevant anyway, since internal pH is controlled by sections.

8. (G) At 15°C, times are longer, but the enzyme works all the way down to pH 2. H and J are wrong because the data say nothing about the completeness of the reaction.

9. (C) At any pH, there is no sign of enzyme activity above 35°C. A is wrong because there is not enough information to determine the stability of the enzyme. B is wrong because activity ceases at very high temperatures. D is wrong because we do not know whether there is any activity below pH 2.

10. (H) The range of pH values is greatest at 15°C, and might extend above or below those values on the chart. F is wrong because these conditions have already been tried. G is wrong because there is no need to repeat trials already made. J is wrong because the range of temperatures for pH 5 is already known.

11. (B) The passage informs us that starch turns blue in the presence of elemental iodine, and the gist of the experiments is the determination of the liberation of iodine from the iodate.

12. (G) Looking down the data columns, you can see that, as the concentration of iodate gets smaller, the time delay increases. F is wrong because this is part of the design of the experiment, not a hypothesis to be tested. H is wrong because the concentration of sulfuric acid is kept constant throughout. J is wrong because the passage says that the concentration of iodine increases gradually until it gets strong enough to turn the starch blue.

13. (C) Experiment 2 shows that, as the temperature increases, the time for the reaction decreases. A and B are wrong because the iodate concentration was not changed in Experiment 2.

14. (G) The iodate concentration in Experiment 2 was 5%. In Experiment 1 the time delay at 5% concentration was 29 seconds. Experiment 2 shows that this delay, with 5% iodate, occurs at a temperature between 15° C and 25° C.

15. (D) The temperature given is well below the freezing point of water, and if the whole setup freezes, the whole reaction might stop. All the other answers neglect this probability.

16. (F) Experiment 2 shows that the time for a 5% solution at 45°C is 22 seconds, and we would have to expect that it would be less for a 10% solution. The time would also have to be less than 18 seconds, because that was the time (Experiment 1) for a 10% solution at 20°C.

17. (A) The graph for fat content in males (dashed line) shows a strong dip in the years 10 through 20.

18. (J) The rate of increase is represented by the steepness of the graph. The graph for fat content rises very sharply in the last 3 months before birth.

19. (D) The water content of a man is about 7% more than that of a woman of equal weight, so a woman would have to be approximately 7% heavier than a man to have the same amount of water. B is wrong because the graph does not have a zero for water content, and the value for a man only looks like (but is not actually) twice as much as for a woman.

20. (J) The graphs show that after birth, whenever the fat content is low, the water content is high, and the rule also applies to the sex difference. Thus, the sum of water and fat percentages differs very little at any age.

21. (B) In adolescence, when sex hormone activity is beginning very strongly, the fat content of boys drops and the water content increases. A is wrong because this sex-hormone effect is not seen in girls. C is wrong because at adolescence there is a marked change in the water content of boys, but only a gradual drop in girls.

22. (G) The ratings for attack against *Escherichia* are greater in four of the six trials than for any of the other microorganisms.

23. (A) Ratings for alfalfa seeds against molds are 4 and 3, but only 2 and 0 against bacteria. None of the others shows this kind of difference.

24. (H)   The strongest attack on *Penicillium* was made by seeds of the legumes, soybean and alfalfa.

25. (D)   All six seeds attacked the bread mold, at the 2 level or higher. A is wrong because the experiment does not address this question. B is wrong because all 6 of the test seeds had some effect on the bread mold. C is wrong because both the dandelion and the thistle seeds had some effect.

26. (G)   Neither of the legumes had any effect on *Staphylococcus,* so this family is not the place to look. F is wrong because some of the other seeds do attack *Staphylococcus.* H and J are wrong because this experiment gives no information about one microorganism attacking another.

27. (D)   The dandelion and the thistle seeds attacked all microorganisms, mostly at high levels. A is wrong because the experiment gives no information about microorganisms competing with each other. B is wrong because the two legumes do not show a significantly higher ability to attack than any others. C is wrong because the experiment does not deal with the question of damage to crops.

28. (G)   The index of refraction is a property of the liquid used. F is wrong because the index of refraction of the liquid has nothing to do with the lens. H and J are wrong because the experimental design says nothing about temperature or color of light.

29. (C)   All three data tables show an increase in focal length as the index of refraction of the medium increases. This means that the rays converge further from the lens.

30. (F)   Comparing the results of Experiments 1 and 2 shows that the focal length of the thicker lens was always less than that of the thinner one, given the same medium.

31. (A)   As the index of refraction of the medium increases in Experiments 1 and 2, the rays converge ever further from the lens; when the index of refraction is more than 1.720, they do not converge at all. B is wrong because in other media the rays do converge. C is wrong because there is no evidence for any chemical reactions. D is wrong because there is no reason to believe the rays do not bend; they bend the wrong way.

32. (J) There is no reason to believe that knowledge of index of refraction would lead to knowledge of chemical composition. F is wrong because there is a clear correlation between focal length of the lens and the index of refraction of the liquid. G is wrong because knowledge of the behavior of light passing through a lens can be used in determining how it would act in passing through a prism. H is wrong because index of refraction could depend on the concentration of a sugar solution; in fact, it is so used.

33. (B) The experiment shows that the rays will converge only if the index of refraction of the lens is greater than that of the medium. Thus, the index of refraction of the lens must be greater than 1.33. If it were greater than 1.50, however, there would be convergence when the lens is in the 11% sugar solution, so it must be between 1.33 and 1.50.

34. (F) This is the main contention of Scientist 1. Scientist 2 agrees that very high levels are dangerous to the heart, but that attempts to reduce the level in most cases accomplish nothing.

35. (D) There is no dispute that the Framingham study showed that men with naturally low cholesterol levels are less subject to heart attack. The other choices are wrong because Scientist 1 did not cite studies.

36. (H) Scientist 2 complains that his colleague considered death from heart disease without taking into account other causes of death. There is no claim that Scientist 1 was incompetent in his interpretation of the Framingham study or in any other process.

37. (A) Scientist 1 claims that cholesterol has many functions in the body; Scientist 2 does not dissent. Scientist 2 questions the usefulness of testing for cholesterol and making efforts to reduce it artificially.

38. (G) Scientist 2 believes that this campaign is based on unproven and even misleading information. This scientist has no faith in the efficacy of dietary control; neither scientist had anything to say about selecting individuals with known heart problems.

39. (A) Neither scientist expresses any doubts about the effectiveness of weight control, excerise, and stopping smoking, but Scientist 2 does not believe that a low cholesterol diet is of any value.

40. (H) Scientist 2 concedes that naturally high cholesterol levels do indeed produce increased liability to heart disease, and that American levels are known to be high, but feels that in the present state of knowledge, no techniques are known that will deal with the problem.

EVALUATING YOUR PERFORMANCE

After taking the Model Tests, evaluate your performance by following these steps:

1. Check your answers using the answer key provided after each examination.
2. Turn to the Analysis Chart and cross out each wrong answer with an **X**. Count the number of correct answers in each horizontal row, and write the total in the column headed "Your Score." The sum of your correct answers is your total score on this examination. To find your Percentage Correct, divide "Your Score" by "Possible Score." The completed chart enables you to analyze the results and determine your specific strengths and weaknesses.
3. Evaluate your performance using the chart below. The ratings shown are based on analysis of student performance on past ACT's and on expectations for student performance on the examinations in this book. (The figures do not represent official ACT values, which are standardized for individual examinations.) Examine the rating you earned for each of the four tests. To boost your score in any area, study the appropriate sections of Chapters 2–5. Also, identify the types of questions you answered incorrectly. If you find that you consistently missed certain types, review the relevant sections of those chapters.
4. Read the answer explanations for the test you took. Don't skip over explanations for questions you got right because these explanations often contain helpful insights into shorter or different methods of answering questions. For each question you got wrong, be sure you understand why you made an error. That will help you to avoid making a similar mistake in the future.

Performance Evaluation Chart

Rating	English	Mathema-tics	Reading	Science Reasoning
Excellent	66–75	54–60	35–40	36–40
Very good	54–65	44–53	29–34	29–35
Above average	45–53	30–43	24–28	20–28
Below average	36–44	21–29	19–23	14–19
Weak	25–35	14–20	14–18	9–13
Poor	0–24	0–13	0–13	0–8